BLIND SPOT

AMERICA

and the

PALESTINIANS,

BLIND SPOT

from

BALFOUR

to

TRUMP

Khaled Elgindy

BROOKINGS INSTITUTION PRESS
Washington, D.C.

Copyright © 2019
THE BROOKINGS INSTITUTION
1775 Massachusetts Avenue, N.W., Washington, D.C. 20036
www.brookings.edu

The Brookings Institution is a private nonprofit organization devoted to research, education, and publication on important issues of domestic and foreign policy. Its principal purpose is to bring the highest quality independent research and analysis to bear on current and emerging policy problems. Interpretations or conclusions in Brookings publications should be understood to be solely those of the authors.

Library of Congress Cataloging-in-Publication Data

Names: Elgindy, Khaled.
Title: Blind spot : America and the Palestinians from Balfour to
    Trump / Khaled Elgindy.
Description: Washington, DC : Brookings Institution Press, 2019. |
    Includes bibliographical references and index.
Identifiers: LCCN 2019001459 (print) | LCCN 2019002843 (ebook)
    | ISBN 9780815731566 (ebook) | ISBN 9780815731559
    (hardcover : alk. paper)
Subjects: LCSH: Arab-Israeli conflict. | Palestinian Arabs—Politics
    and government. | Israel—Politics and government. | United
    States—Foreign relations—Middle East. | Middle East—Foreign
    relations—United States. | United States—Foreign relations—
    Israel. | Israel—Foreign relations—United States.
Classification: LCC DS119.6 (ebook) | LCC DS119.6 .E418 2019
    (print) | DDC 956.04—dc23
LC record available at https://lccn.loc.gov/2019001459

9 8 7 6 5 4 3 2 1

Typeset in Janson and Gira
Composition by Westchester Publishing Services

For Amr, who taught me to question
and challenge everything, including myself

Contents

4
Abnormal Normalization 105

List of Maps

Preface and Acknowledgments

In July 2007, President George W. Bush declared that the United States would convene an international conference to relaunch long-stalled Israeli-Palestinian peace negotiations. The announcement came as welcome news to Mahmoud Abbas, the affable if uncharismatic Palestinian leader. As one of the architects of the 1993 Oslo Declaration of Principles on Interim Self-Government Arrangements, or Oslo Accords, the secret agreement reached between Israel and the Palestine Liberation Organization (PLO) that launched the current peace process, and the PLO's most ardent champion of negotiations, Abbas had been calling for the resumption of peace talks since he came to power in January 2005 following the death of Yasser Arafat, the longtime Palestinian leader. Like Arafat, Abbas headed both the PLO, the umbrella organization that represented Palestinians worldwide, and the Palestinian Authority (PA), the administrative body created by the Oslo Accords that governed Palestinians in the occupied territories. The PLO was the international political address of the Palestinian people, including some 5 million refugees displaced during Israel's creation in 1948, while the PA represented the seedling of a future Palestinian state in the West Bank and Gaza Strip.

The proposed peace conference, which was eventually held in Annapolis, Maryland in November 2007, would be the first direct talks between the two sides since the eruption of the Palestinian uprising, known as the Al-Aqsa Intifada, some seven years earlier. The horrific violence, marked by waves of deadly suicide bombings by Palestinian militants and disproportionate and often indiscriminate attacks by the Israeli army, had claimed the lives of some 3,200 Palestinians and nearly 1,000 Israelis and left the bulk of the PA's security and governing institutions in shambles.

Bush's announcement was a clarifying moment for me as well. At the time I was serving as an adviser to the Palestinian leadership in Ramallah, the PA's de facto capital in the West Bank. As a member of a European-funded team of experts tasked with providing technical support to Palestinian negotiators, I had spent the previous three years preparing for precisely this moment. And yet most of us instinctively understood that the negotiations stood virtually no chance of producing a conflict-ending agreement between Israel and the Palestinians. Only a few weeks earlier, the Palestinian Islamist faction, Hamas, had routed and expelled the PA's security forces from the Gaza Strip, home to roughly 40 percent of the Palestinians in the occupied territories. In January 2006, Hamas had defeated Abbas's Fatah party for control of the PA's parliament, the Palestinian Legislative Council, ending nearly four decades of Fatah dominance of Palestinian politics. The internal schism between the Fatah-dominated PA in the West Bank and the Hamas-ruled Gaza Strip, which continues to this day, marked one of the lowest points in the history of the Palestinian national movement.

A few days after Bush's announcement, our team was summoned to the office of Saeb Erekat, the chief Palestinian negotiator and a close aide to Mahmoud Abbas, for a briefing on the proposed conference. At the conclusion of the briefing, I raised the question I knew was on everyone's mind. "With all due respect," I began, "does Abu Mazen"—Abbas's traditional Arabic moniker—"even have a mandate to negotiate?" Visibly annoyed, Erekat replied in the affirmative, assuring us that Hamas's "coup," as the leadership called it, had no bearing on the legitimacy of

Abbas, who after all was still the elected president of the PA and chairman of the PLO's Executive Committee.

That Abbas and his Fatah party had just lost a civil war and a major election was even less of a problem for U.S. officials—to the contrary. The Bush administration had led the 2006 campaign to cut off the PA's international funding following the election of Hamas, a group that had carried out numerous attacks on Israeli civilians and was officially designated a "foreign terrorist organization," and had previously insisted on Arafat's replacement before peace talks could resume. While most ordinary Palestinians viewed the West Bank–Gaza split as a setback to the national project, the Bush administration saw it as an opportunity to advance the peace process without the negative influences of Hamas, now ostensibly contained in Gaza by an international boycott and an Israeli blockade.

Events took a very different turn, however. After a highly elaborate yearlong negotiation process, the Annapolis talks collapsed when fighting broke out between Israel and Hamas in late December 2008. It was the first of several deadly Gaza wars in the decade that followed. In the meantime, Gaza's continued isolation and the ongoing Palestinian division would remain an albatross around Abbas's neck for the duration of his tenure, paralyzing internal Palestinian politics and repeatedly foiling peace negotiations.

The fact that U.S. officials saw a weak and increasingly dysfunctional Palestinian leadership as an asset to the peace process rather than a liability was striking in and of itself. More important, it was indicative of a systemic blind spot in America's stewardship of the peace process in two critical areas of diplomacy: power and politics. Since the 1990s, American peacemaking in the Middle East has operated according to two interrelated and equally flawed assumptions: first, that a credible peace settlement could be achieved without addressing the vast imbalance of power between Israel and the Palestinians, and second, that it would be possible to ignore or bend internal Palestinian politics to the perceived needs of the peace process. The size of the blind spot has varied from one U.S. administration to another but has always been present.

This book explores the dynamics of U.S. policy with respect to the Palestinians, how it has evolved over the decades, and how these matters have affected the United States' role as the sole mediator between Israelis and Palestinians. There is no shortage of writing on the Arab-Israeli conflict and the role of the United States in it. The critical corpus includes works that have as their primary focus the nature of U.S. diplomacy in the Middle East. Among them are William B. Quandt's *Peace Process: American Diplomacy and the Arab-American Conflict since 1967* (Brookings, 2005), Daniel C. Kurtzer, Scott B. Lasensky, William Quandt, Steven Spiegel and Shibley Telhami, *The Peace Puzzle: America's Quest for Arab-Israeli Peace, 1989–2011* (Cornell University Press, 2013), and Nathan Thrall, *The Only Language They Understand: Forcing Compromise in Israel and Palestine* (Henry Holt, 2017). The literature also includes numerous firsthand accounts by a wide range of former U.S. officials, such as Martin Indyk, *Innocent Abroad: An Intimate Account of American Peace Diplomacy in the Middle East* (Simon and Schuster, 2009), Aaron David Miller, *The Much Too Promised Land: America's Elusive Search for Arab-Israeli Peace* (Random House, 2008), Dennis Ross, *Doomed to Succeed: The U.S.-Israel Relationship from Truman to Obama* (Farrar, Straus and Giroux, 2015), Elliott Abrams, *Tested by Zion: The Bush Administration and the Israeli-Palestinian Conflict* (Cambridge University Press, 2013), Robert Malley and Hussein Agha, "Camp David: The Tragedy of Errors" (*New York Review of Books*, August 9, 2001), as well as various Israeli and Palestinian perspectives, such as Shlomo Ben-Ami, *Scars of War, Wounds of Peace: The Israeli-Arab Tragedy* (Oxford University Press, 2006), and Ahmed Qurie, *Beyond Oslo, the Struggle for Palestine: Inside the Middle East Peace Process from Rabin's Death to Camp David* (I. B. Taurus, 2008).

Some of these authors, such as Ross and Abrams, have taken a generally positive view of the U.S. and Israeli roles in the peace process while placing the lion's share of the blame for past failures on the Palestinians. Others, such as Miller, have taken a slightly more self-critical view of the U.S. role while insisting that the United States generally did its best and was ultimately hampered by leaders on both sides. A handful of mainly Washington outsiders explicitly blame the repeated failures of the peace process on the United States and what they regard as its blatant bias in favor of Israel and the undue influence of the pro-Israel lobby. These include John J. Mearsheimer and Stephen M. Walt, *The Israel Lobby and U.S. Foreign Policy* (Farrar, Straus and Giroux, 2007), and Rashid Khalidi, *Brokers of Deceit: How the US Has Undermined Peace in the Middle East* (Beacon Press, 2013).

Of this large number, only a few authors have dealt directly with the power dynamics among the three parties or the role of internal Palestinian politics in the conflict. This book attempts to move this effort forward by examining the interplay between the peace process and internal Palestinian politics. Although often undervalued by policymakers in Washington, internal Palestinian political dynamics have had a direct bearing on matters of war and peace. Contrary to the views of many U.S. policymakers, the experiences of the last half century have shown that a weak, dependent, or fragmented Palestinian political leadership is not an asset to the peace process but a major liability—not only because a credible and durable peace deal will require leaders with a modicum of political legitimacy but also because periods of Palestinian political fragmentation and dysfunction historically have often been accompanied by an increase in violence and terror. Moreover, while the problems within Palestinian politics are mostly self-inflicted and have long been in the making, the peculiar power dynamics of the peace process have helped to reinforce and even normalize them. In making this case, the book also challenges much of the conventional thinking about the Middle East peace process and America's involvement in it, particularly with regard to the effectiveness of U.S. mediation.

ACKNOWLEDGMENTS

This book could not have come about without the active support and encouragement of so many of my colleagues, friends, and family.

I have been fortunate to have worked with an enormously talented and dedicated group of individuals at the Brookings Institution, particularly my friends and colleagues at the Center for Middle East

Policy. Special thanks go to Martin Indyk, Tamara Wittes, and Daniel Byman for their advice, mentorship, and encouragement over the years. I owe a special debt of gratitude to Samer Khoury and Ramez Sousou for their generous support of my work at the center, without which this book would not have been possible.

Several of my Brookings colleagues offered invaluable guidance and feedback on the manuscript, particularly Michael O'Hanlon, Daniel Byman, and Suzanne Maloney. I am also immensely grateful to William Quandt, Daniel Kurtzer, and Shibley Telhami, three giants in the field, for sharing their profound knowledge of the subject matter and for their guidance and invaluable feedback on the manuscript at various stages of its development. Lisa Goldman, Nathan Brown, Margaret DeReus, and Daniel Levy also provided essential insights and suggestions on various aspects of the manuscript. I am also indebted to the brilliant Walid Khalidi of the Institute for Palestine Studies, who, in addition to giving me access to his encyclopedic knowledge of many of the events described in the book, was among the first to recognize the value of the project.

I was privileged to have had the support of so many truly exceptional research assistants. Emma Borden played a crucial role in serving as a sounding board, reviewing drafts, tracking down missing information and sources, and keeping me focused. I am equally grateful to Israa Saber, Lauren Mellinger, and Jomana Qaddour for their resourcefulness, efficiency, and attention to detail in support of this work as well as to Kristen BelleIsle for her help in editing drafts. Several outside researchers and scholars also provided me with crucial background and other materials, including Lara Friedman, Maia Tabet, Tareq Baconi, and Noura Erakat. The project also benefited from the assistance of several talented interns, including Faisal Kattan, Adham Sahloul, Yousuf Abdelfatah, Sahira Akram, and Liam Foskett.

Warm thanks go to William Finan at Brookings Institution Press, who helped shepherd this project along almost from its inception, along with his highly skilled team of editors and others involved in the production of this book: at Brookings, Marjorie Pannell and Elliott Beard, and at Westchester Publishing Services, Angela Piliouras and Katherine Scott.

Of course, none of this would have been possible without the loving support, encouragement, and, above all, patience of my wife, Nabila Assaf, and our two children, Maryam and Amin, who were instrumental in helping me maintain my sanity throughout this project even as it no doubt took a toll on theirs.

United Nations, Department of Public Information, Cartographic Section Map, No. 4013, July 1997

TERRITORIES OCCUPIED
BY ISRAEL
SINCE JUNE 1967

35°
36°

LEBANON
Quneitra
Nahariyya
GOLAN
Nawa
Haifa
Tiberias
33°
Nazareth
SYRIAN ARAB
REPUBLIC

MEDITERRANEAN
SEA
Netanya
Jenin
Tulkarm
Nablus
Qalqilya
Tel Aviv
WEST BANK
Jordan
Ramla
Jericho
Amman
Jerusalem
32°
32°
Bethlehem
Gaza
Hebron
Dead
Sea
GAZA
Rafah
JORDAN
Bersheeba

ISRAEL
31°
31°

EGYPT

SINAI

Armistice Demarcation
Line, 1949

Boundary of Former
Palestine Mandate

International Boundary

30°
30°

The designations employed and the
presentation of material on this map do
not imply the expression of any opinion
whatsoever on the part of the Secretariat of
the United Nations concerning the legal status
of any country, territory, city or area or of its
authorities or concerning the delimitation of its
frontiers or boundaries.

0   10   20   30   40 km
0   10   20   30 mi

34°
Elat
36°

United Nations, Department of Public Information, Cartographic Section, Map
No. 3243 Rev. 4 August 1997

BLIND SPOT

Introduction: Power and Politics

Even before Israel captured the West Bank and Gaza Strip following the 1967 Arab-Israeli war, the now century-old conflict between Arabs and Jews in the Holy Land had already undergone a number of transformations. During the period of British rule over Palestine, from 1917 to 1948, the conflict centered on a struggle between Zionist Jews who sought to transform the country into a Jewish national home through immigration and colonization and an Arab majority that demanded that Palestine be given its independence, just as neighboring Arab states had. After the creation of Israel, during which some two-thirds of Palestine's Arab population fled or were expelled from their homes, the conflict was transformed from a communal struggle between two competing national groups into a war between the nascent Jewish state and neighboring Arab states, while the Palestinian refugee crisis was treated as a humanitarian problem rather than a political one.

With the emergence of an autonomous Palestinian national movement following Israel's conquest of the West Bank, East Jerusalem, and the Gaza Strip in 1967, American and Israeli officials could no longer ignore the political dimension of the Palestinian question, though U.S. and Israeli policymakers continued to marginalize the Palestine Liberation Organization (PLO), the umbrella organization representing Palestinians worldwide, and keep it out of the peace process. The Palestinian uprising, or Intifada, against Israeli military rule between 1987 and 1992 forced Israeli and American leaders to come to terms with Palestinian nationalism and ultimately with the PLO itself. With the signing of the Oslo Declaration of Principles on Interim Self-Government Arrangements, better known as the Oslo Accord, in 1993, Israel and the PLO agreed to resolve their conflict peacefully while laying the groundwork for Palestinian self-rule in the occupied territories and the creation of the Palestinian Authority (PA), an administrative body to govern Palestinians in the occupied territories.

Since that time, the United States has served as the chief sponsor and sole mediator in the peace process between Israelis and Palestinians. This has been both a blessing and a curse. On the one hand, as a superpower and Israel's closest ally in the region, the United States is the only global actor trusted enough by Israel's leaders to guarantee Israel's security. On the other hand, it also means that the peace process has been infused with the idiosyncrasies of American politics, including Washington's sacred "special relationship" with Israel and the inordinate influence of the pro-Israel lobby. Put differently, American peacemaking in the Middle East has assumed that peace could be achieved without addressing the negative consequences of Israel's occupation, on the one hand, or the realities of internal Palestinian politics on the other. This blindness to the unequal power dynamics between the Palestinians and Israel and to the internal politics of both sides has critically hampered the ability of the United States to serve as an effective peace broker.

THE BLIND SPOT

The breakdown of the Annapolis peace talks in December 2008 after an arduous yearlong effort, conducted under the oversight of the George W. Bush administration, foregrounded a basic fault in America's stewardship of the Israeli-Palestinian peace process. On the surface, the negotiations were highly substantive, and many observers believed the two sides came very close to clinching a deal.[1] Israel's prime minister, Ehud Olmert, had made a far-reaching proposal that included a sovereign Palestinian state based on the 1967 borders, with some adjustments for the annexation of Israeli settlements close to the border, in return for a land swap of an almost equal amount of Israeli territory, and a Palestinian capital in Jerusalem, with an international body to oversee the highly contested Al-Aqsa Mosque/Temple Mount compound. Mahmoud Abbas, the Palestinian leader, also took the process seriously and made a proposal of his own that would have allowed Israel to annex most Israeli settlements in the West Bank and East Jerusalem and hence for a majority of Israeli settlers to remain where they were. On substance, at least, the gaps between the two sides would not have been impossible to bridge, particularly in light of U.S. Secretary of State Condoleezza Rice's commitment to and level of involvement in the process.

But substance was not the only—or even the most critical—factor in the process. As most politicians and diplomats understand, the success of a negotiation process depends as much on the dynamics and conditions outside the negotiating room as on what gets discussed inside, including the power dynamics between the parties and the internal politics of each of them. Although no outside actor could completely level the playing field, U.S. mediation between Israel and the Palestinians has generally been in the opposite direction: the United States has consistently put its thumb on the scale in Israel's favor while simultaneously discounting the importance of internal Palestinian political realities.

Since the start of the Oslo peace process in the early 1990s, successive U.S. administrations have largely avoided applying pressure on Israel to advance the goals of the peace process and have actively worked in the United Nations and other international forums to prevent such pressure being put on Israel. This preference stemmed from the theory, long espoused by the pro-Israel community, that Israeli leaders would be more willing to "take risks for peace" if they felt secure politically and militarily. Most presidents have adhered to this logic, whether out of genuine conviction or simply to avoid running afoul of the powerful pro-Israel lobby and its supporters on Capitol Hill. As part of the perennial quest to reassure Israel's leaders, U.S. presidents from both political parties have often been prepared to deviate from the established ground rules of the peace process and even from official U.S. policy on several core issues of the conflict, such as withdrawal of settlements, control of Jerusalem, and the return of Palestinian refugees.

While Israel's special relationship with the United States remained immune to the ups and downs of the peace process, the opposite held true of the Palestinians. The signing of the Oslo Accord in 1993 allowed American officials to deal directly with the Palestinian leaders for the first time and eventually to come to terms with the idea of Palestinian statehood as well. However, both these realities remained highly restricted, conditional, and ultimately reversible. It wasn't simply that American officials had a tin ear for Palestinian domestic politics. Because of Washington's tendency to view the peace process through the lens of its special relationship with Israel and American domestic politics, the Oslo peace process became a vehicle not just for resolving the conflict, but for transforming certain aspects of Palestinian politics in order to turn the Palestinians into a suitable partner. Unlike its relationship to Israeli politics, the Oslo peace process was not agnostic toward Palestinian internal politics. As the center of gravity of Palestinian politics shifted from the diaspora to the West Bank and Gaza and as the PA effectively replaced the PLO as the de facto address of the Palestinian national movement, the Oslo process fundamentally reorganized and redefined Palestinian politics and governing institutions, including their main sources of legitimacy. Moreover, the highly intrusive nature of the peace process meant, among other things, that the United States as the chief mediator, along with donor countries and even the Israelis, had a direct say—and often an effective veto—over key aspects of Palestinian political life. As a result, the PA, which remained heavily dependent on foreign aid and Israeli goodwill for its survival, was subject to an ever-widening assortment of conditions and restrictions regarding its security performance, internal governance, and even diplomatic activities, many of which were enshrined in U.S. law. Indeed, the peace process often became a platform for reforming, and occasionally even re-engineering, Palestinian politics and governing institutions to align with American or Israeli preferences.

This was not an entirely one-sided arrangement. As part of the bargain struck during Oslo, the Palestinian leadership, under both Yasser Arafat and Mahmoud Abbas, agreed to give up a degree of control over their internal politics and decision making in the hope that the United States ultimately would "deliver" Israel. Among other things, this meant the legitimacy of Palestinian leaders would now be intimately bound up with the success or failure of the peace process: when one foundered, the other necessarily suffered as well. However, American "deliverance" of Israel rarely came. Although there were times when Washington was prepared to use its leverage with Israel or to boost Palestinian leaders to advance the peace process—most notably at the height of the Oslo process in the late 1990s—these have been the exception rather than the rule. To be clear: In attempting to explain why the United States is hampered, perhaps hopelessly, in its mediation effort in this conflict, I do not mean to imply that Palestinians and Israelis do not share the blame for failure; they do. My goal here is to focus specifically on the role of the United States as the sole mediator in the conflict, and the reasons it has not been as effective as it might have been—even given the obstacles that the parties themselves may have placed along the way.

In the end, Washington's unique approach to peacemaking did not—and most likely could not—succeed. Indeed, by focusing on reassuring Israel and reforming the Palestinians rather than on changing the dynamics that sustained the conflict, most notably Israel's ongoing military occupation, the U.S.-led peace process effectively reversed the standard model of mediation: it alleviated pressure on the stronger party and increased pressure on the weaker party. The absence of American pressure or international accountability helped defray the costs of Israel's occupation while allowing Israeli leaders to avoid the difficult and politically unpopular decisions that a two-state solution required, such as the removal of Jewish settlements, transferring territory to Palestinian

sovereignty, and dividing Jerusalem to provide a capital for a Palestinian state. At the same time, Washington's heavy reliance on sticks in its
dealings with Palestinian leaders, although it succeeded in making them
more pliant, left them too weak to serve as effective peace partners.
The debilitating split between Hamas and Fatah, while largely home-
grown, was to a great extent nurtured and held in place by the peace
process. Moreover, Palestinian compliance with the ever-evolving demands of the peace process rarely yielded tangible political rewards; in
the end, neither the success of Prime Minister Salam Fayyad's famed
state-building project, affectionately known as "Fayyadism," nor the
PA's continued security coordination with Israel was enough to generate
movement toward Palestinian statehood or even to inoculate the PA
from congressional sanctions.

The fact that the Palestinians were up against a vastly more powerful
adversary as well as formidable political forces in the United States did
not, of course, negate their own agency. Whether it was President
Abbas's overreliance on the Americans to "deliver" Israel or the use of
indiscriminate violence by Hamas and other groups, the choices made—
or not made—by Palestinian political actors had real and often tragic
consequences in both human and political terms. Yet, even though
Americans, Israelis, and Palestinians all had equal agency, they did not
have the same ability to shape events or impose outcomes. Israel, pos-
sessing the most powerful military in the region and being the occupying power, could, and frequently did, use its power to impose its own
preferences or preempt outcomes through settlements, brute military
force, and other coercive measures. This unchecked power imbalance
was also why the principle of "constructive ambiguity," a mainstay of
Henry Kissinger's shuttle diplomacy in the 1970s and a pillar of the
Oslo process, ultimately did more harm than good, since any ambiguity
would naturally be interpreted through the lens of the more powerful
side. The same held true for spoilers, who existed on all three sides.
Palestinian rejectionists had the ability to violently disrupt the political
process, but anti-Oslo forces in Israel and the United States had the
added advantage of being able to shape the nature and direction of the
peace process itself.

These basic dynamics of power and politics set the Israeli-Palestinian peace process apart from other American-led mediation efforts. As prominent peace process scholar William Quandt explains, "The United States is structurally at a disadvantage in trying to develop and sustain policies for regions like the Middle East."[2] These structural limitations are more pronounced in the case of Israel's conflict with the Palestinians, where domestic U.S. politics were so skewed in one direction and the power disparities were so vast, not only between the parties themselves but also between the mediator and the weakest party. The 1981 sale of airborne warning and control system (AWACS) aircraft to Saudi Arabia and the 2015 Iran nuclear deal are two cases where American administrations successfully defied the Israel lobby and overcame congressional opposition when they deemed broader U.S. interests to be at stake. There are no comparable incentives in the case of the Palestinians, who have few strategic assets to offer the United States and whose cause still engenders considerable hostility on Capitol Hill.

The unique power dynamics of the Israeli-Palestinian peace process may also help explain why the United States could be an effective broker in other conflicts, such as between Egypt and Israel in the 1970s or in Northern Ireland in the 1990s, where the power disparities were much less severe and the domestic politics far less constraining. In contrast to the Palestinians, Egypt was a sovereign state and the largest Arab military force in the region, which the United States had been working to pry away from the Soviet Union's sphere of influence. While the Sinai Peninsula also contained important religious sites for Jews as well as a few thousand Israeli settlers, these paled in comparison to the centrality of Jerusalem to Jewish identity or the half million settlers living in the biblical lands of "Judea and Samaria." The Palestinian case was perhaps more analogous to the conflict in Northern Ireland, in which the British were viewed by the Irish republican movement as foreign occupiers and yet also had deep historical ties with the United States. In the Irish case, however, the domestic political dynamics were reversed. The Irish republican cause enjoyed the support of large segments of the American public, including numerous members of Congress, which to a great extent helped to offset the influence of the

U.S.-U.K. special relationship. In any event, neither of these cases involved anything like the level of intrusiveness in Palestinian internal affairs that characterized the Oslo process.

THE PAST AS PROLOGUE

Washington's blind spot in the Middle East was not only wide but deep. Its origins could be traced to the Balfour Declaration, Britain's 1917 pledge to establish a Jewish "national home" in Palestine, despite strong opposition from the country's Arab majority. In looking at the century since Balfour, my intention is not to rehash the history of the conflict between Arabs and Jews in the Holy Land nor to relitigate the claims of one side or the other but to highlight key patterns, parallels, and precedents that help explain the United States' current approach to the peace process in general and toward the Palestinians in particular. Many of the familiar features of American policy in the Middle East, including an influential Zionist lobby and a strongly sympathetic Congress, as well as a deeply ambivalent executive branch, were already evident in the 1920s. It was also during the period of British control of Palestine, from 1918 to 1948, that current American political attitudes toward Palestinians first began to take shape. As early as the 1920s, well before the advent of the PLO charter or Hamas terrorism, American politicians were already dismissing Palestinian opposition to the Zionist project as either artificially generated or the product of an irrational hatred of Jews, rather than a manifestation of Palestinians' own political aspirations. Long before the terms "quality of life," "economic peace," or "Fayyadism" entered the U.S. political lexicon, the notions that Palestinians could be enticed with economic incentives over political ones or that they would first need to demonstrate their fitness to govern themselves were already being discussed in Washington. The experiences of the British Mandate itself, in which a superpower sought to mediate between two groups with competing national claims while heavily favoring one of them, foreshadowed many of the problems that would later hamper American peace efforts.

Another recurring theme in American policy during the last century is ambivalence, reflecting the perennial tension between the desire to safeguard U.S. national interests, on one hand, and the demands of American domestic political and ideological considerations on the other. Whether it was the Balfour Declaration, the United Nations partition plan of 1947, UN Security Council Resolution 242 in 1967, or the 2003 Roadmap for Peace, official U.S. policy seldom aligned with the actual policies pursued by the White House and Congress. But rarely was the gap between official and unofficial U.S. policy more pronounced than in the period immediately following Israel's creation in 1948. Much like today, American diplomacy was grounded in two UN resolutions. Long before Security Council Resolutions 242 (1967) and 338 (1973) became pillars of the Middle East peace process, U.S. and international policies were guided by two other UN resolutions: General Assembly Resolutions 181 (1947) and 194 (1948), which together defined the core issues of the conflict—including Israel's borders, the status of Jerusalem, and the fate of Palestinian refugees displaced during Israel's creation. At first, Washington decried Israel's refusal to address the issue that was widely seen as the source of the conflict and the key to a political resolution: Palestinian refugees. As time wore on, however, American policymakers gradually acquiesced to Israeli-imposed realities on the ground while deferring a political resolution of the refugee problem and focusing instead on economic and humanitarian "solutions." Deferral gradually gave way to denial, even as the refugee issue remained a source of instability and violence. Within less than a generation, on the eve of the 1967 Arab-Israeli war, both the political significance of the Palestinian refugee problem and the roots of the conflict were all but forgotten in Washington, to the extent that even the president of the United States, Lyndon Johnson, denied their centrality.

A similar process of attrition in U.S. policy has been under way since 1967, albeit at a much slower pace. The rise of an autonomous Palestinian national movement following the 1967 war led to a rediscovery of the "Palestinian question" in Washington as well as renewed efforts to keep the Palestinians out of the diplomatic process. Although terrorism

was immensely damaging to the Palestinian cause and was highly problematic for U.S. officials, it was not the primary motivation behind the
PLO's exclusion from the peace process throughout the 1970s and
1980s. Despite the PLO's involvement in a number of terrorist operations in the early 1970s, Secretary of State Henry Kissinger's September
1975 pledge to Israel that the United States would have no dealings with
the PLO until it recognized Israel's right to exist and accepted Security
Council Resolutions 242 and 338 made no mention of terrorism. The
pledge, signed shortly after the UN General Assembly recognized the
PLO as the representative of the Palestinian people, reflected Kissinger's belief that excluding and weakening the PLO would ultimately
benefit the peace process.

It was not until a decade later, in August 1985, that Congress formally codified Kissinger's pledge into law and added the third condition, a requirement that the PLO "renounce the use of terrorism." The
violence and instability of the 1980s also provided an opportunity to test
Kissinger's hypothesis regarding a weak Palestinian leadership, which
remains equally relevant today. Instead of facilitating peace, internal
PLO weakness and division following Israel's 1982 Lebanon war were
accompanied by a wave of terror attacks by radical and rogue Palestinian elements hostile to both Arafat and the peace process.

A FLAWED PEACE PROCESS

The popular uprising by Palestinians in the West Bank and Gaza against
Israel's occupation in the late 1980s, known as the First Intifada, forced
U.S. officials into an uneasy accommodation with Palestinian leaders
and ultimately led to their inclusion in the peace process. Yet neither
the short-lived U.S.-PLO dialogue of 1998–90 nor the signing of the
Oslo Declaration of Principles in 1993 was enough to alter Washington's
ambivalence toward the Palestinians and the Israel-Palestine conflict, which continued throughout the U.S. stewardship of the peace
process. The competing priorities within the foreign policy and
intelligence establishments, pressures from Congress, a formidable
pro-Israel lobby, and the sitting president's personal views all pulled

American policy in different directions. In an effort to bridge these divergent forces, presidents often ended up straddling two opposing positions or splitting the difference between them. Contradictions with the goals of the peace process or within U.S. policy were easily rationalized or simply ignored, since most of the immediate costs would be borne by the Palestinians. The fact that UN Security Council Resolution 242 remained an official pillar of U.S. policy did not prevent various administrations from repeatedly poking holes in it to accommodate Israeli demands. American policymakers routinely decried Israeli settlement construction in the occupied territories as an obstacle to peace but devised various loopholes and exemptions for "natural growth," for settlements in East Jerusalem, and for the large settlement blocs in the West Bank.

These outcomes were less a function of malice or ignorance than of simple political arithmetic. As the two most powerful actors, which were bound by a "special relationship," the United States and Israel had both the incentive and the means to shift as many of the risks and political costs onto the Palestinians as possible—especially when things went wrong. The higher the stakes and the potential political costs, the more likely U.S. and Israeli leaders were to deflect those costs onto the Palestinians. It was perhaps inevitable that the Palestinians, as the weakest link in the political chain, would bear the brunt of the chronic failures of the peace process, but the results have been no less damaging to all sides.

The administrations of Bill Clinton and George W. Bush in many ways represented both the best and the worst of what American mediation had to offer. Both presidents broke important new ground toward the goal of a two-state solution and in advancing American-Palestinian relations. Yet both simultaneously pursued policies that helped weaken Palestinian leaders, embolden Israeli hardliners, consolidate Israeli facts on the ground, and erode the basic principles undergirding the peace process. No other president has come closer to brokering an Israeli-Palestinian peace deal than Bill Clinton. But he was also the first to break with decades of U.S. policy and UN precedent on issues such as settlements, the status of Jerusalem, and the status and plight of refugees.

Clinton's most significant contribution, however, came in the final months of his presidency following the failure of the Camp David Summit and the outbreak of the Second Intifada (also known as the Al-Aqsa Intifada). Although both sides had contributed to the failure of negotiations before and after the summit as well as to the escalating violence, Clinton's decision to lay the blame solely on Arafat and the Palestinians would have far-reaching consequences. In addition to narrowing the political space for an agreement during Clinton's remaining time in office, the decision helped cement Israel's narrative that it had "no partner" for peace, which helped to fuel violence in the months and years that followed.

The view that Arafat's intransigence and Palestinian militancy were the primary drivers of the conflict, rather than Israel's continued occupation, took center stage under George W. Bush. Despite becoming the first American president to officially endorse Palestinian statehood, Bush's alignment with Israeli Prime Minister Ariel Sharon following the 9/11 attacks and a wave of terrorist attacks by Palestinian militants gave Sharon a relatively free hand in his bid to quash the Second Intifada while systematically destroying Palestinian governing and security institutions along the way. The culmination of the Intifada and the election of Mahmoud Abbas in 2005 following Arafat's death did not lead to a revival of the diplomatic process. Instead, the Bush administration abandoned its own peace plan, the internationally backed roadmap, favoring Israeli unilateralism in Gaza and elsewhere, while providing Israel with "assurances" regarding the fate of Israeli settlement blocs in the West Bank, Palestinian refugees, and other issues (the 2003 Roadmap for Peace is discussed in more detail in chapter 6). Hamas's surprise victory in the January 2006 parliamentary elections and Washington's response to it marked the beginning of the slow demise of the peace process. American and Israeli refusal to recognize a government headed by Hamas or to consider any scenario short of Hamas's removal from government ensured a lose-lose outcome for Abbas and his leadership, ultimately paving the way for civil war and the current division between Gaza and the West Bank. Meanwhile, the decade-old schism has paralyzed Palestinian politics, fueled instability and repeated outbreaks of violence in Gaza, and undercut the legitimacy of Abbas's leadership.

Barack Obama's arrival in the White House provided an opportunity to arrest or even roll back the trends that threatened a two-state solution. And for a time, Obama seemed to be inclined to do so, taking a tough stance on Israeli settlement construction, insisting on the primacy of the 1967 border, and even hinting at a possible policy shift toward Gaza. When faced with resistance from Israeli leaders and their allies in Congress, however, the administration backed down, and Obama focused his energies on the path of least resistance: resumption of bilateral negotiations. Nor was Obama averse to preserving the massive power imbalance of the peace process. The Obama administration devoted considerable resources to defeating Abbas's mostly symbolic bids to gain recognition of a Palestinian state at the United Nations in 2011 and 2012, in glaring contrast to its lack of follow-through on Israeli settlements. The Obama administration approved a ten-year, $38 billion military aid package to Israel, the largest single pledge in U.S. history, despite the collapse of a second round of negotiations in 2014, fresh violence in Gaza and East Jerusalem, and its repeated warnings that Israeli actions were endangering a two-state solution. Even as the clock ran down on Obama's term, and with a Donald Trump presidency waiting in the wings, Obama continued to play it safe. Instead of breaking new ground, for example, by stipulating the need for a Palestinian capital in Jerusalem or taking the more radical step of recognizing a Palestinian state, the only action that Obama took was that he opted to abstain on an anti-settlements resolution at the Security Council.

The relative inertia of the Obama years left an opening for the incoming Trump administration, which has been far less committed to a two-state solution and far more blatant in its willingness to tip the scales in Israel's favor. Much as Lyndon Johnson had done more than a half century earlier, Trump seems determined to rewrite the basic ground rules of the peace process in Israel's favor. Just as Johnson denied both the centrality of the refugee problem and Israel's responsibility for its creation, the Trump administration has been largely oblivious to the central reality of Israel's half-century-old occupation and its role as the primary driver of the conflict. Trump's decision to break with seven decades of U.S. policy and international consensus by recognizing Jerusalem as Israel's capital surrendered a major point of American leverage over Israel and removed one of the few remaining incentives the Palestinian leadership had for participating in an American-sponsored peace process.

There are few world conflicts in which the United States has had more intensive involvement and met with less success than the Palestinian-Israeli dispute. The chronic failures of the Middle East peace process have had many authors over the years, including poor leadership and decision making on the part of both Israelis and Palestinians and Israeli intransigence. In light of Washington's virtual monopoly over the process and its insistence on remaining the sole mediator, however, its "blind spot" with respect to Israeli power and Palestinian politics has been a leading factor in those failures. So, although the United States remains uniquely suited to the role of brokering peace between Israelis and Palestinians, it is also uniquely hampered from doing so by its domestic politics and the nature of its relationship with Israel. Unless and until this fundamental paradox is resolved, an American-sponsored peace process holds little chance of success.

PART I
Origins of the Blind Spot: 1917–67

1

The Balfour Lens

Palestine . . . is in constant danger of conflagration.
Sparks are flying over its borders all the time and it may
be that on some unexpected day a fire will be started that
will sweep ruthlessly over this land.

—*Dispatch from Otis Glazebrook, U.S. consul*
general in Jerusalem, December 1919

In April 1922, the Foreign Affairs Committee of the U.S. House of Representatives convened a rather remarkable hearing to debate a joint congressional resolution endorsing the Balfour Declaration.[1] A little over four years earlier, in November 1917, Britain's foreign secretary, Arthur Balfour, had put the weight of the British Empire behind the creation of "a national home for the Jewish people" in Palestine, with the stipulation "that nothing shall be done which may prejudice the civil and religious rights of existing non-Jewish communities in Palestine." Palestine was then part of the crumbling Ottoman Empire; it came under British control following World War I, formalized in 1923 as a League of Nations mandate. As in other parts of the Levant (including Syria), however, Arabs, who then made up more than 90 percent of Palestine's population, also hoped for independence.

Ten outside witnesses were called to testify at the four-day hearing, including Fuad Shatara and Selim Totah, two Palestine-born U.S. citizens who spoke against the resolution and were the last witnesses to address the committee. "This is our national home, the national home of the Palestinians," said Shatara, a Brooklyn surgeon and native of Jaffa, "and I think those people are entitled to priority as the national home of the Palestinians and not aliens who have come in and have gradually become a majority."[2] Totah, a young law student originally from Ramallah, attempted a less confrontational approach: "You gentlemen and your forefathers have fought for the idea, and that is taxation with representation. We are asking for the same principles. By the operation of the Balfour Declaration a majority of Jews will be established in Palestine, and after a while by their majority they will govern the native people. Would you stand for things like that in California if the Japanese should come in and after 20 or 30 years become a majority and establish a republic of their own? Not for a moment. How would you expect 93 percent of the people in Palestine to stand for that?"[3]

Totah's words sparked a heated exchange with members of the panel. "Your point is that the people should be given control of the country and shut the Jews out," said New York Congressman W. Bourke Cockran, a strong supporter of the bill.

In particular, Totah's insistence that the Arab majority be given a say in determining the policies of the country was met with hostility and derision, as illustrated by the following exchange between Totah and Cockran and another strongly pro-Balfour lawmaker, Ambrose Kennedy of Rhode Island.

> MR. TOTAH: If they come to establish a majority, the natives have a right to limit immigration as this country has a right to control immigration.
> MR. KENNEDY: But we are an organized government. There is no one over there.
> MR. TOTAH: But that does not cut out the equities of the situation.

MR. KENNEDY: These Jews are making this land fertile where it was sterile.

MR. TOTAH: No, sir; I disagree with that in its entirety.

MR. KENNEDY: The places that are fertile are not sterile now. The lands that those Jews have taken, this report states, have been lands that were sterile when they got them and they have turned them into fertile lands.

MR. TOTAH: We could do that ourselves.

MR. KENNEDY: That is another matter. That is a fact that the Jews are doing that. There is no doubt. It is conceded that what you want is to be yourselves given control of this land.

MR. TOTAH: To develop it.

MR. COCKRAN: And not allow the Jew to enter in, peacefully or otherwise.

MR. TOTAH: We do not say that.

MR. COCKRAN: Peacefully or otherwise, even to buy it, no matter what the result, if they should become a majority.[4]

Cockran had the last word in the hearing.

And so began U.S. involvement in what is now the century-old conflict between Arabs and Jews in the Holy Land. A few months after the hearing, Congress voted overwhelmingly to endorse the goal of establishing a Jewish "national home" in Palestine. Although highly controversial both inside and outside American government circles, including within the American Jewish community, the Balfour Declaration became the primary lens through which American politicians viewed Palestine, the Zionist project, and Palestine's Arab inhabitants. Britain's experience as a superpower attempting to mediate between two groups with competing national claims while leaning heavily toward one of them in Palestine offered a preview of many of the problems that would later confront American peacemaking between the Israelis and the Palestinians. By the end of the Mandate in 1948, the basic elements of American policy toward the conflict and the Palestinians had begun to take shape: admiration, particularly on Capitol Hill, for Zionist economic, political, and even military power; a parallel antipathy toward a highly nationalistic and often opportunistic Palestinian political leadership; and a deeply conflicted attitude on the part of U.S. policymakers over how best to resolve the conflict.

BALFOUR AND ITS DISCONTENTS

The British began warming to the idea of a Western-oriented, Jewish outpost in the eastern Mediterranean during World War I, as a way both to strengthen the war effort and to advance their own colonial ambitions in the region.[5] Sentimental factors, including a religiously inspired fascination with the Holy Land and sympathy for the plight of Europe's persecuted Jews, also played a role in Britain's embrace of Zionism. As the land of the Bible and the birthplace of Christianity, Palestine was regarded by many as the natural birthright of Jews (and hence also Christians), which required that the land be "reclaimed" and "restored" to its "rightful owners."[6] Such views were prevalent in the United States as well, being held by many government officials, members of Congress, and even President Woodrow Wilson.[7]

For the country's Arab inhabitants, however, the designation of Palestine as a Jewish national home posed an irremediable threat. As in other parts of the Levant, nationalist sentiment in Palestine was expressed mainly through the language of pan-Arabism. But by the early 1920s, the focus of Palestinian political aspirations had begun to shift away from a unified Greater Syria to an independent Arab Palestine.[8] In addition to anonymizing the country's Arab majority as "existing non-Jewish communities," the authors of the Balfour Declaration were careful to confer only "civil and religious rights" on the Arabs while avoiding any reference to their political or national rights. The question was debated within official British circles prior to the Declaration's publication. When queried about the implications of a Jewish national home for the country's Arab inhabitants, Arthur Balfour famously replied, "In Palestine we do not propose even to go through the form of consulting the wishes of the present inhabitants of the country. . . . The Four Great

Powers are committed to Zionism. And Zionism, be it right or wrong, good or bad, is rooted in age-long traditions, in present needs, in future hopes, of far profounder import than the desires and prejudices of the 700,000 Arabs who now inhabit that ancient land."[9] The Zionists meanwhile had made no secret of their goal of making Palestine "as Jewish as England is English" through immigration and colonization. To most Palestinian Arabs, therefore, the Jewish national home was "an objective that, from its inception and logic, would lead either to the Palestinians' permanent subjugation in their own patrimony or, as it turned out, the destruction of their national existence."[10]

Although the idea of transforming Palestine into a Jewish national home remained highly controversial and the subject of intense debate both inside and outside of government, for a variety of sentimental, cultural, and political reasons both the White House and Congress came down in favor of the Balfour Declaration and Zionist plans to colonize Palestine. In keeping with the State Department's policy of neutrality, President Woodrow Wilson's administration stopped short of officially endorsing the Balfour Declaration, although the president personally communicated his sympathies to leaders of the Zionist movement, and occasionally did so publicly as well. Wilson's thinking was heavily influenced by prominent Zionist figures such as Louis Brandeis, a close confidant whom he later appointed to the Supreme Court, as well by his own religious upbringing.[11] Nevertheless, his views on the subject were not especially nuanced or consistent. Although an ardent believer in the liberation of colonized peoples and the right of self-determination, as a devout Christian and the son of a Presbyterian minister Wilson was also deeply attracted to the idea of the "rebirth of the Jewish people . . . as a blessing for all mankind."[12] Indeed, Wilson's concept of a Jewish homeland went beyond what was laid out in the Balfour Declaration; he informed Chaim Weizmann, the head of the World Zionist Organization, in January 1919 of his hope that "in Palestine shall be laid the foundations of a Jewish Commonwealth," for which he offered his "entire support . . . full and unhampered."[13]

Wilson's casual pronouncements about the Balfour Declaration irritated officials at the State Department, who cautioned him against being overly supportive of the Zionist cause. Officially, Palestine was regarded as a British affair and American officials were keen to avoid "foreign entanglements." American diplomats, particularly those based in the region, also understood the potential for bloodshed in the Holy Land. "There is no difference of opinion that the opposition of the Moslems and Christians to granting any exceptional privilege to the Jews in Palestine is real, intense and universal," the U.S. consul general in Jerusalem, Otis Glazebrook, told delegates at the 1919 Paris Peace Conference.[14] The King-Crane Commission, appointed by Wilson in early 1919 to ascertain the wishes of the local populations in Arab regions of the former Ottoman Empire, came to a similar conclusion. Among other things, the commission found Palestine's Arabs to be "emphatically against the entire Zionist program" and concluded that to "subject a people so minded to unlimited Jewish immigration, and to steady financial and social pressure to surrender the land, would be a gross violation of the principle" of self-determination. The King-Crane Commission's final report was completed in August 1919 but was not published until three years later, by which time the Mandate, incorporating the concept of establishing a Jewish national home in Palestine, had already been approved by the League of Nations, and the U.S. Congress had completed its deliberations on the subject.[15] Several of Wilson's advisers expressed similar concerns as those of the commission members. Secretary of State Robert Lansing asked how Wilson's commitment to self-determination could be "harmonized with Zionism, to which the President is practically committed."[16] The president's legal adviser, David Hunter Miller, argued similarly that "the rule of self-determination would prevent the establishment of a Jewish state in Palestine." Wilson heard similar warnings from members of his delegation to the Paris Peace Conference.[17]

However, members of Congress were even more enthusiastic in their support than Wilson. The American Jewish community at the time was still deeply divided over political Zionism and the question of whether Jews constituted a nation.[18] However, by this point "a pioneering Zionist lobby" with the ability to make support for a Jewish homeland into an election issue was already an established presence on Capitol Hill.[19] In

1919, a majority of American lawmakers were publicly supportive of Zionist objectives,[20] before the House and Senate gave their formal approval to the creation of a Jewish national home in September 1922. In approving the joint resolution, members of Congress made one modification to Balfour's original formula, stating that "nothing shall be done which may prejudice the civil and religious rights of *Christian and all other* non-Jewish communities in Palestine" (emphasis added).[21] Despite their strongly pro-Zionist leanings, members of Congress nonetheless engaged in a relatively lively debate over the issue—an increasingly rare occurrence on Capitol Hill today on matters concerning Israel. Although no members of Congress from either party spoke against it, five of the ten witnesses called before the House Foreign Affairs committee hearing in April 1922 testified against the Jewish national home, including two rabbis who represented the Reform movement and two Palestine-born American citizens. The arguments in favor of a Jewish homeland drew heavily on the Bible, the history of Jewish persecution, and notions of manifest destiny, all standard themes emphasized by the Zionist movement at the time.[22] Palestine was described as "a devastated and sparsely settled land," a country that was "underdeveloped and underpopulated" with "no civilization" to speak of. Meanwhile, Arab opposition to Zionism was attributed to ancient religious hatreds, outside agitators, or a stubborn resistance to "civilization."[23]

The two Palestinian witnesses, Shatara and Totah, spent much of their time attempting to refute these claims, though they met with little success. The most passionate voice of opposition to the measure came from Edward Bliss Reed, a professor of English literature who had spent several months in Palestine as a volunteer with the American Red Cross. In Bliss's view, the Balfour Declaration clearly gave one group preference over another and was therefore "thoroughly un-American." Bliss doubted whether "any State will ever prosper founded by such means because people are the same all over. . . . How would you feel if the German troops were holding you down until enough Frenchmen came in to take possession of the State."

The counterargument was put forward by Louis Lipsky of the Zionist Organization of America. According to Lipsky, the Arabs in Palestine "were entitled to what is called 'individual rights,'" but "the self-determination principle certainly has no application" to them, since "the inherent right of self-determination had to do not with groups of people who happened by accident to be occupying a certain territory; it had to do with races, with nationalities."[24] The claim that Palestinians were not a "real" nation, and thus not entitled to self-determination, has proved to be remarkably durable, as illustrated by Newt Gingrich's 2011 reference to "an invented Palestinian people." A few of the bill's more strident supporters, including Congressman Walter Marion Chandler of New York, a Republican, went even further. Despite having skipped the hearing, Chandler delivered a passionate and long-winded defense of the resolution on the House floor later that summer. The Arabs, Chandler insisted, should be given a choice: "If they will not consent to Jewish government and domination, under conditions of right and justice, or to sell their lands at a just valuation and to retire into their own countries, they shall be driven from Palestine by force."[25]

AN UNWORKABLE MANDATE

Following the Allied victory, the newly formed League of Nations awarded Britain a "mandate" over Palestine, Transjordan, and Iraq, with the stated aim of preparing the local populations for independence. Lebanon and Syria became French mandates. (Palestine, Iraq, Syria, Lebanon, and Transjordan were designated Class A mandates, meaning that they were considered "independent nations" in all but name, subject only to the "administrative advice and assistance" by the mandatory power.) In Palestine, however, instead of preparing the local Arab population for an independent state in Palestine, the British continued to maintain their commitment to establishing a Jewish national home there. This led to periodic unrest and outbreaks of violence, in 1920, 1921, 1929, and 1933, culminating in the Arab Revolt of 1936–39.

Although the British had officially ruled out the eventuality of a Jewish state in the whole of Palestine, the goal of creating a Jewish national home was incorporated into the terms of the Mandate, thus ensuring Palestinian political opposition to British rule as well as to the

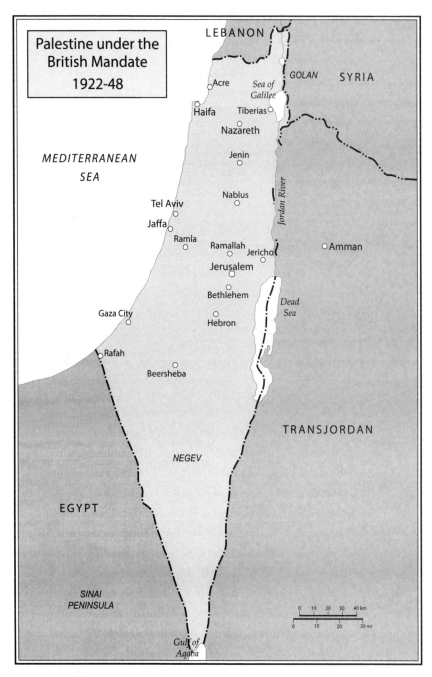

Palestine under the British Mandate 1922-48

LEBANON

Acre

Sea of Galilee

GOLAN

SYRIA

Haifa

Tiberias

Nazareth

MEDITERRANEAN SEA

Jenin

Nablus

Tel Aviv

Jaffa

Ramla

Ramallah

Jericho

Amman

Jerusalem

Bethlehem

Gaza City

Hebron

Dead Sea

Rafah

Beersheba

TRANSJORDAN

NEGEV

EGYPT

SINAI PENINSULA

0 10 20 30 40 km

0 10 20 30 mi

Gulf of Aqaba

Jordan River

Source: Adapted from United Nations map

Zionist project. The Palestine Arab Congress, the earliest attempt at forging a national leadership for the Arab population, sent delegations to various foreign capitals to plead the Arab case. Representatives of the Arabs also lodged legal challenges to the Mandate on the ground that the Balfour Declaration violated their right to self-rule.[26] Meanwhile, British authorities and members of the growing Jewish community in Palestine became targets of mass protests, general strikes, boycotts, and periodic violence. The British in turn dismissed the Palestine Arab Congress and its leadership, the Arab Executive, as unrepresentative and refused to recognize them until they explicitly accepted the terms of the Mandate, including the Jewish national home.[27] The commitment to developing Palestine as a "national home" for the Jewish minority also conflicted with the Mandate's ostensible mission of preparing the local population for self-rule.[28] British attempts to reconcile these two essentially irreconcilable ends resulted in confusion and frequent policy reversals, earning the enmity of both communities and ultimately making the Mandate unworkable.

The conflict was accentuated by the vast gap between a Palestinian Arab society that was traditional and largely agrarian and a Jewish community made up primarily of Western-educated European immigrants, differences that were also reflected in the political trends of the two communities.[29] The fact that the Zionists also enjoyed the financial backing of wealthy European and American Jews and the patronage of the powerful British Empire added to the imbalance, despite the Arabs' demographic advantage. In addition to establishing in 1922 the Jewish Agency, the proto-government of the growing Jewish community in Palestine, the British also provided training, arms, and other support to Zionist paramilitary groups.[30] British offers to set up a parallel "Arab Agency" were rejected outright by the Arabs, who instead insisted on the creation of a representative assembly, a privilege they had enjoyed under Ottoman rule. But both the British and the Zionists opposed the idea of representative government until such time as a Jewish majority could be achieved through immigration.[31]

The most dominant Palestinian political figure to emerge at the time was Amin al-Husseini (1897–1974), a charismatic activist from a prominent Jerusalem family, who in 1921 was installed by the British as the grand mufti of Jerusalem but later fell out with the mandatory government. By the mid-1930s, al-Husseini, a nationalist with shrewd and often ruthless political instincts, had emerged as the undisputed leader of Palestine's Arab community and continued to dominate Palestinian politics even after his exile in 1937. The dilemma facing al-Husseini and the Arab Executive was one that would confront future generations of Palestinian leaders as well: acquiescing in a political process seen by most Palestinians as fundamentally unfair would leave them vulnerable domestically, while boycotting the process altogether would only cement their political marginalization. Publicly, Arab leaders felt compelled to reject anything that could be seen as legitimizing the Jewish national home, including the Mandate itself. As a practical matter, most of the Arab leadership maintained relatively friendly ties with British officials.[32] Their ability to maintain this delicate balance would ultimately depend on the extent to which they were seen as successfully confronting the Zionist project and its British sponsors. But by adopting such a public stance of rejection, particularly given their relative weakness vis-à-vis the British and the Zionists, the Arab leadership in Palestine overlooked more pragmatic, if less dazzling, policy options, and ultimately set themselves up for failure.

Each round of violence was followed by a new British commission of inquiry, most of which attributed the unrest to Arab fears of losing their land or livelihoods to Zionist immigration. The inquiries typically led to new policy statements, or white papers, that recommended changes to the Mandate regime but that were very often ignored or suppressed. The first of these, the Palin Commission, attributed the unrest to the Arabs' "sense of betrayal" at the nonfulfillment of British promises of independence and their ongoing fears of Jewish political and economic domination. The commission's final report was never published, in anticipation of Zionist objections.[33] The Passfield White Paper of 1930—issued following the mini-rebellion of August 1929 that had been triggered by a dispute between Muslims and Jews over the Western Wall in Jerusalem's Old City—recommended putting limits on Jewish immigration and land purchases while downgrading the Jewish national home to "a consideration that would enjoy continued support but was not central to mandate governance." Several days of violence left 153 Jews and 116 Arabs dead, leading to two new inquiries, the Shaw Commission (March 1930) and the Hope Simpson Commission (October 1930). Given the emotions surrounding the holy site of the Wailing Wall and the potential for broader conflagration, the League of Nations launched a separate investigation into the competing claims of Muslims and Jews over the Wall.[34] Under pressure from Zionists and their supporters in Parliament, however, British authorities disavowed the white paper. While Zionists breathed a sigh of relief, the episode convinced the Arabs of the futility of continuing to engage in the political process.[35]

It was also through the violence of 1929 that many in Washington and the broader American public were first introduced to Palestine and the Palestinians. Until then, American interests in Palestine had been viewed mainly in terms of American charitable activities or the small number of (mostly Jewish) U.S. citizens in Palestine. Even American consular officials in Jerusalem had very little to say about Palestinians or their political concerns for the first decade or so of British rule.[36] In contrast, the August 1929 disturbances were covered fairly extensively by the American consul general in Jerusalem, Paul Knabenshue, who reported that the "basic cause of the serious troubles . . . arises out of the Balfour Declaration." Knabenshue's report went on to state, "It is quite evident that the Zionists' ambition was, and still is, to convert Palestine into . . . a Jewish state and by economic pressure to force out the Arabs, or reduce them to impotency, until Palestine should become as Jewish as England is English."[37] In contrast to the relatively nuanced dispatches of U.S. diplomats, American press accounts, which were heavily influenced by Zionist accounts, characterized the unrest as "race riots" or the result of religious fanaticism. For example, a report by the *Washington Post* editorial board described the violence as "a fanatical outbreak of holy-war fervor originating in incidents at the century-old Wailing [Western] Wall."[38] A handful of Arab American organizations attempted to provide an alternative perspective, but their efforts were negligible in comparison to the information put out by American Zionists.[39]

American interest in Palestine intensified following the Arab Revolt of 1936–39.[40] It also marked a decisive moment for the Mandate, Palestinian politics, and the Zionist movement. By 1933 the Jewish sector of the economy had surpassed that of the Palestinians.[41] At the same time, the rise of Nazi Germany and the persecution of European Jews led to a massive influx of Jewish immigrants into Palestine. Between 1932 and 1937, approximately 184,000 Jews arrived in Palestine, doubling the size of the Jewish population.[42] As a result, "the possibility that they could be outnumbered in their own country came to be a growing concern for the Palestinians, even as that same outcome promised security, victory and absolute sovereignty to the Zionists."[43] Unlike earlier disturbances, which had mainly targeted the Jewish community, the 1936 uprising was directed at British rule. Among the first casualties of the rebellion was the old leadership of the Arab Executive, which was replaced by the Arab Higher Committee (sometimes referred to as the Higher Arab Committee), an umbrella comprising local committees and political parties headed by the grand mufti, Amin al-Husseini. In mid-1937 the Royal Peel Commission report for the first time proposed partitioning the country into separate Jewish and Arab states, reigniting the uprising. The British responded with unmitigated force, demolishing large sections of Jaffa, Palestine's largest city and the epicenter of the rebellion, while dismantling the Arab leadership. The Arab Higher Committee was outlawed and most of its leaders were jailed, executed, or deported. Al-Husseini had managed to flee the country in October 1937 and remained in exile for the remainder of the Mandate, which ended on May 14, 1948.

For the Zionists, the rebellion gave new urgency to the goals of establishing a Jewish state and creating a Jewish army. The Zionist leadership inside and outside Palestine had conditionally accepted Peel's partition proposal, and by 1939 the latter was also within reach. The Haganah, the armed wing of the Jewish Agency and the largest of the Zionist militias, had a trained force of roughly 20,000 men.[44] This was in addition to smaller, more radical "revisionist" groups such as the Irgun Zvai Leumi (National Military Organization, the Irgun for short) and the Stern Gang (also called Lehi, from Lohamei Herut Israel,

Fighters for the Freedom of Israel), the forebears of today's Likud Party. Unlike the more pragmatic "labor" Zionists who dominated the Jewish Agency, who were prepared to accept a Jewish state in any portion of Palestine, the Revisionists sought to establish Jewish sovereignty over the whole of Eretz Yisrael, "the Land of Israel," including the territory east of the Jordan River known as Transjordan, which later became Jordan.[45] The revolt had also galvanized Arab solidarity in support of Palestine. The Pan-Arab Congress of September 1937, in which delegates from across the Arab world convened in Bloudan, Syria, to reject partition and demand an end to Jewish immigration, marked the unofficial entry of the Arab states into the conflict.

In the meantime, al-Husseini turned his attention to another rising power on the regional and global scene, the United States. In August 1937, just as the rebellion was starting up again and a few weeks before he went into exile, al-Husseini paid a visit to the American consul general in Jerusalem, George Wadsworth II, on behalf of the Arab Higher Commission. Husseini sought the meeting following reports that the United States planned to invoke its right under the 1924 Anglo-American Treaty to be consulted on changes in the Mandate, a sign that it was potentially moving away from its official position of neutrality—in which case, al-Husseini hoped to dissuade the Americans from weighing in on behalf of the Jews. "If the United States is upholding the Jews out of sympathy for them," al-Husseini stated, "it should be remarked that the Arabs are more deserving of that sympathy as they are in the right and are the owners of the country and the victims of aggression." Al-Husseini went on: "The United States enjoys in Arab countries great respect and affection and a moral standing of great value which are a result of the accomplishments of groups of Americans over a great number of years." Wadsworth explained that the policy of consulting with the mandatory authorities in Palestine applied to all of the mandate regimes, including Iraq, Syria, and Lebanon. Wadsworth further reassured al-Husseini that the United States "was not departing from that impartiality which has for many years characterized the various good works of the United States in the Near East for which the Arabs had every cause to be gratified."[46]

Despite the severity of the crackdown, the revolt produced a major shift in British policy. Acknowledging that it could not "both concede the Arab claim to self-government and secure the establishment of the Jewish National Home," the 1937 Peel Commission declared the Mandate to be "unworkable." But the commission's findings were not a vindication for the Arabs. Despite concluding that the "Arabs of Palestine . . . are as fit to govern themselves as the Arabs of Iraq or Syria," the Peel Commission also recommended partitioning the country into separate Jewish and Arab states, with the latter incorporated into Transjordan.[47] The Arabs saw partition as a reneging by Britain on its pledge not to support Jewish statehood, but they also had another reason to reject Peel's proposal. The partition scheme was framed as a "transfer of land and population," which in practical terms meant uprooting hundreds of thousands of Arabs. In contrast to the tiny proportion of Jews, numbering a little more than a thousand, who fell inside the borders of the proposed Arab state, the proposed Jewish state would have included close to a quarter million Arabs, or roughly half its total population.[48]

Unsurprisingly, the Peel Commission was not the last word. Peel's findings were later overturned by the Woodhead Commission of 1938, which paved the way for a new British white paper. The May 1939 white paper shocked the Zionists by declaring "unequivocally" that Palestine should not become a Jewish state and imposing tight restrictions on Jewish immigration. Instead of partition, Britain would help set up a unitary state to be established in ten years. The Zionists' denunciation of the new policy was understandable; Palestinian leaders' rejection of the white paper was more difficult to comprehend. The decision undoubtedly reflected the Arabs' intense distrust of the British, who had rarely followed through on their pledges. But it was also a question of leadership—or, in the case of the Palestinians, the lack of one. With most of their leaders in jail or in exile, the Palestinians had no competent authority that could adequately assess and represent the needs of the people on the ground. Even so, many if not most of the Arab Higher Committee's members were inclined to accept the white paper, as were most Arab states. Al-Husseini himself had briefly toyed with the idea before finally rejecting it out of deference to the guerrilla leaders in the field.[49] The decision nonetheless proved extremely costly in the long run.

Notwithstanding Wadsworth's assurances to al-Husseini in the summer of 1937, American political attitudes toward Palestine increasingly aligned with those of the Zionist movement, including on such controversial ideas as transfer. The possibility of inducing the Arab population to leave Palestine, voluntarily or otherwise, had always been part of Zionist thinking. Theodore Herzl, the father of modern Zionism, had written of a desire "to spirit the penniless population across the border by procuring employment for it in the transit countries whilst denying it any employment in our own country." By 1932 the Jewish Agency was also discussing the "transfer of the Arabs of Palestine." A few Zionist thinkers opposed transfer on moral grounds.[50] However, following the Peel Commission report, transfer became part of the official policy debates in London and Washington. "Let the Arabs be encouraged to move out, as the Jews move in," declared a December 1944 statement by Britain's Labour Party, which also publicly condemned the 1939 white paper.[51] Representatives of the World Zionist Organization and the Jewish Agency openly discussed it with U.S. officials.[52] A 1942 postwar planning paper by the State Department concluded, "For the Jewish State to be successful, it might also be necessary for large numbers of the Arabs living there at present to be transplanted elsewhere."[53] One senior State Department official even proposed the use of American military power to help carry it out.[54] Others within the State Department found the idea of forcible removal to be morally abhorrent as well as a violation of international law. For example, the American envoy to the Vatican, Myron Taylor, cited the 1941 Atlantic Charter, which he argued "refers to the protection of peoples in their home and in their not being forcibly moved about at the will of anyone else. That is quite a hurdle to get over if you are going to eject a million people from Palestine."[55] Even President Franklin Delano Roosevelt toyed with the idea of relocating several hundred thousand Arabs from Palestine, occasionally broaching the topic with others, including Chaim Weizmann and Justice Louis Brandeis.[56] Ironically, it was British officials who attempted to disabuse the president of the idea on both practical and moral grounds.[57] In 1945, former president Herbert Hoover proposed relocating Palestine's Arab population en masse to Iraq.[58] Hoover, who was closely associated with the Revisionist wing of the Zionist movement, touted his proposal as a "constructive humanitarian solution.

A GROWING DISCONNECT

In the late 1930s, as the British were beginning to reconsider their commitment to the Zionist project, American politicians were moving in the opposite direction. But whereas the British, administering the Mandate, were compelled to address Palestinian concerns on some level, American politicians remained conveniently detached from realities in Palestine. By the early 1940s, the prospect of Jewish statehood began to take on an air of inevitability in Washington. The atrocities perpetrated against European Jews by Nazi Germany led hundreds of thousands to flee the continent, many of them to Palestine, as well as to an outpouring of American sympathy and mounting political pressure on Congress and the White House to support a Jewish state and to reject the 1939 white paper. By this time the United States had eclipsed Britain as the world's leading political and military power; before the end of the Mandate in 1948, it would also replace Britain as the principal power broker in Palestine. President Roosevelt and his successor, Harry S. Truman, despite their personal sympathy for the plight of the Jews and the cause of a Jewish homeland, attempted to walk a delicate line between maintaining American neutrality in the name of protecting U.S. interests in the region and trying to defuse mounting political pressure at home to support Zionist ambitions in Palestine. The fact that both presidents also had personal reservations about the prospect of a Jewish state further complicated their ability to spell out a clear American position on Palestine. By attempting to straddle otherwise incompatible positions or to split the difference between them, Roosevelt and Truman ended up diluting the official U.S. policy, which inevitably drifted toward the path of least resistance as dictated by domestic politics.

By the 1940s the British Empire, battered both physically and economically by World War II, and with the costs of maintaining its
imperial domains draining its resources, was in decline. As British international power waned, the focus of Zionist lobbying and advocacy
shifted from London to Washington, and the United States became the
epicenter of political, financial, and military support for the Zionist
project. In the period before 1948, the American Jewish community had
funneled nearly $250 million—roughly equivalent to $2.75 billion
today—along with another $73 million investment into the growing
Jewish community in Palestine. From 1901 to September 1946, contributions from American Jews to the Jewish National Fund, the agency
responsible for acquiring land for colonization in Palestine, totaled
£7,863,200, or more than half of the agency's net income. At the same
time, the Jewish National Fund helped underwrite the annual budget
of the American Zionist Emergency Council, the main Zionist lobby in
Washington, to the tune of more than $500,000.[59] The Jewish Agency
and other elements of the Zionist movement had also developed an elaborate arms procurement and smuggling network in the United States,
bypassing a government-imposed embargo on arming either side of
the conflict.[60] In May 1942, Zionist leaders from around the world convened in New York City's prestigious Biltmore Hotel to lay out their
political program. The Biltmore Program, as it became known, called
for unlimited Jewish immigration to Palestine and the creation of a
Jewish army, and demanded that "Palestine be established as a Jewish
Commonwealth." As the scale of the Nazi genocide against European
Jewry became known, Roosevelt came under increasing pressure from
American Zionists and their allies in Congress to publicly denounce the
white paper and support a Jewish state. The State Department and the
British urged Roosevelt not to take an overly pro-Zionist stance, which
they feared could undercut the Allied war effort and drive the Arabs
into the arms of the Germans and the other Axis powers, which were
aggressively courting the Arabs with promises of independence and ex-
ploiting the issue of American support for Zionism.

Like others in Washington, Roosevelt viewed Britain's white paper
of 1939 as reneging on the Balfour Declaration, which in Roosevelt's

estimation had always been intended "to convert Palestine into a Jewish Home which might very possibly become preponderantly Jewish within a comparatively short time."[61] Nevertheless, Roosevelt had also come to believe that the Mandate was "impossible due to the two strongly competing nationalistic movements there present" and that a Jewish state "could only be established in Palestine through force."[62] As a result, Roosevelt personally favored the idea of a "trusteeship," an idea promoted by many in the State Department, in which Jews, Christians, and Muslims in Palestine lived together on an equitable basis.[63] Much as the British had done throughout the Mandate, however, the American administration made conflicting promises to the Zionists and the Arabs.

In May 1943, Roosevelt formalized the policy of American neutrality by giving formal assurances to King Abdul-Aziz of Saudi Arabia and other Arab leaders that "no decision altering the basic situation of Palestine should be reached without full consultation with both Arabs and Jews."[64] In early 1944, an election year, the administration succeeded in shelving a congressional resolution endorsing Jewish statehood as a "security-military" threat.[65] In a message to House Speaker Sam Rayburn, Roosevelt expressed his satisfaction at the tabling of the resolution, which he said "merely illustrates what happens if delicate international situations get into party politics."[66] Ironically, that same day Roosevelt met with Rabbi Stephen Wise and Rabbi Abba Hillel Silver of the American Zionist Emergency Council to reassure them, and authorized them to say publicly, that his administration had never officially endorsed the 1939 white paper.[67] Later that year, in the midst of his own reelection campaign, Roosevelt conveyed to Zionist leaders his full support for the Palestine plank of the Democratic Party platform, which favored "the opening of Palestine to unrestricted Jewish immigration and colonization. . . . Such a policy is to result in the establishment there of a free and democratic Jewish commonwealth." Roosevelt promised that "if reelected I shall help to bring about its realization."[68] After his reelection, Roosevelt renewed the pledge of "full consultation" with the Arabs during a meeting with Abdul-Aziz aboard the king's private yacht and again in writing just before his death in April 1945.[69]

The equivocation of American policy toward Palestine intensified under the Truman administration. Like Roosevelt, Truman was torn between upholding America's commitment to consult fully with both sides on matters related to Palestine and his own personal preferences, and mounting political pressure from Zionist groups and key White House advisers to back Jewish statehood and partition. Officials at the State Department continued to argue that supporting Zionist ambitions in Palestine would undermine U.S. interests in the Middle East and be seen as a breach of America's moral commitment to self-determination.[70] As World War II came to a close, however, the plight of a quarter million Jewish refugees displaced by the Holocaust also weighed heavily on Truman's thinking. A few months after renewing Roosevelt's pledge to the Arab states in May 1945, in defiance of the State Department Truman demanded that Britain allow immediate entry of 100,000 refugees into Palestine, which angered the Arabs.[71] Although Truman was genuinely distressed by the plight of Jewish refugees in Europe, he also hoped to deflect some of the pressure he faced to support Jewish statehood.[72] As both a U.S. senator and vice president, Truman had been vocal in his support of Zionism. Although he became more circumspect after succeeding Roosevelt in the White House, domestic political considerations remained ever-present in Truman's mind. As Truman explained to a group of American diplomats posted in the Middle East in November 1945, "I have to answer to hundreds of thousands who are anxious for the success of Zionism; I do not have hundreds of thousands of Arabs among my constituents."[73]

Hoping to forestall, or at least delay, Truman's instinctive urge to adopt pro-Zionist positions, the British proposed a joint commission, the Anglo-American Committee of Inquiry, to look into the issue of the Jewish refugees, immigration, and the overall fate of Palestine, which released its findings in April 1946. It recommended that Palestine "be neither a Jewish state nor an Arab state" and that the country instead be placed under a United Nations trusteeship that "accords to the inhabitants, as a whole, the fullest measure of self-government." Attempts to partition the country, the commission warned, "would result in civil strife such as might threaten the peace of the world."[74] A follow-up commission, the 1946 Morrison-Grady Committee, recommended the creation of an Arab-Jewish federation under temporary British tutelage. Truman viewed the idea of a federated state as the single best option for resolving the Palestine question, but this idea was rejected by the Zionists and the Arabs alike.[75] Ironically, despite the pivotal role he played in Israel's creation, Truman's own thinking on the subject of Jewish statehood was itself rather conflicted.[76] According to the historian John Judis, Truman personally was "as put off by the idea of a Jewish state as he was of a Protestant or Catholic state."[77]

Congress's passage of a joint resolution endorsing Jewish statehood and unlimited Jewish immigration in late 1945, along with Truman's concerns over his party's fortunes in upcoming midterm elections, made it increasingly difficult for Truman to straddle the two positions. In a statement commemorating Yom Kippur in October 1946, a few weeks before the election, Truman formally rejected the Morrison-Grady Committee's proposal and reiterated his support for the immediate entry of 100,000 displaced Jews into Palestine. The statement also alluded to a "viable Jewish state" along the lines of the Jewish Agency's partition proposal, which he described as something to which "our Government could give its support." After receiving an advance copy of the statement, Prime Minister Clement Attlee of Britain sent an angry message to Truman expressing frustration at his "refusing even a few hours' grace to the Prime Minister of the country which has the actual responsibility for the government of Palestine in order that he may acquaint you with the actual situation and the probable results of your action. These may well include the frustration of the patient efforts to achieve a settlement and the loss of still more lives in Palestine"— where the British had become targets of Zionist terror.[78]

Truman's carefully crafted statement had been intended to appease the Zionists without explicitly endorsing partition.[79] Instead, it was widely seen as marking a decisive shift in America's posture toward Palestine, as one scholar put it, "injecting what heretofore had been a mere Presidential preference with the stuff of decision-making power."[80] Even so, Truman continued to advocate for federation until the end of his presidency while blaming the defeat of the Morrison-Grady proposal on "British bullheadedness and the fanaticism of our New York Jews." "When it came to Palestine," writes Judis, "the man known for the motto 'The buck stops here' had had trouble making up his mind, and even when he did, he denied responsibility for his decisions."[81]

That many of the lost lives alluded to in Attlee's message to Truman were British was no doubt at the center of Britain's frustration with the Americans. Since 1939, the Zionist underground, led by Menachem Begin's Irgun and Yitzhak Shamir's Stern Gang, had stepped up their campaign of violence against British authorities as well as Arab civilians in Palestine. By 1945, the Haganah had joined in the insurgency as well. In November 1944, in Cairo, the Stern Gang assassinated Walter Guinness, also known as Lord Moyne, the British secretary of state for the colonies and the highest-ranking British official in the Middle East. Following the assassination, the director of the State Department's Office of Near Eastern and African Affairs, Wallace Murray, lamented that such "ill-considered statements in this country for political purposes have indirectly contributed to the present insecurity by giving encouragement, albeit unwittingly, to the more extreme Zionist elements such as the assassins of Lord Moyne represent."[82] Two years later, the Irgun orchestrated the bombing of the King David Hotel in Jerusalem, which housed British government headquarters, killing ninety-one Britons, Arabs, and Jews.[83] The Irgun and its affiliates worked openly in the United States to raise funds and lobby members of Congress. The Zionist terror campaign, which peaked from 1944 to 1947, did little to dampen support for the Zionist cause in Washington. The British were especially riled by what they viewed as American tolerance for Zionist terrorism. "It is no secret that the terrorists in Palestine have received the bulk of their financial and moral support from the United States," Foreign Minister Ernest Bevin told senior American officials in London in September 1947. According to Bevin, "Organizations based in the United States have carried on extensive publicity campaigns with the purpose of encouraging the Palestinian terrorists and the smugglers of illegal immigrants and of discrediting the attempts of the British Government to maintain law and order. The American Government has to an extent subsidized these activities by exempting from income tax donations to organizations so engaged."[84]

The Zionist insurgency was one manifestation of the new balance of power in Palestine. By 1946 the military arm of the Jewish Agency had a force of 62,000 well-equipped and well-trained fighters. "There is no doubt that the Jewish force is superior in organization, training, planning and equipment," Haganah commanders told the Anglo-American Committee of Inquiry in 1946, "and that we ourselves will be able to handle any attack or rebellion from the Arab side without calling for any assistance from the British or Americans. If you accept the Zionist solution [partition and a Jewish state in the greater part of Palestine] but are unable or unwilling to enforce it, please do not interfere, and we ourselves will secure its implementation."[85]

A very different picture was emerging on the Arab side. The Palestinian leadership vacuum was partially filled by the Arab states. The Saudis had taken the lead in securing assurances from the Americans. The newly established Arab League, whose formation was prompted in large part by the crisis in Palestine, helped set up a new Arab Higher Committee to represent Palestine's Arabs in the league's proceedings and other international forums. As an externally created body, however, and with most of its members in exile, the Arab Higher Committee lacked the organizational or military capacity to adequately deal with the end of the Mandate and the impending confrontation with the Zionists.[86] In May 1946, Arab League member states resolved to support the Palestinians "with arms and manpower" and threatened to impose sanctions against Western commercial and oil interests in the Middle East. Although very little came of these pledges, they laid the foundation for Arab military intervention two years later and ensured Arab control over the Palestinian cause.[87] Meanwhile, the exiled grand mufti, Amin al-Husseini, had been thoroughly discredited by his decision to join forces with Nazi Germany and the Axis powers. For many radical nationalists in the Arab world at the time, the Germans were seen, as one American diplomat put it, as the "less objectionable of two imperialisms."[88] Al-Husseini had begun making overtures to Germany in 1940, once it became clear that there was no possibility of restoring ties with the British, although he denied having any knowledge of the Nazis' genocidal plans for the Jews.[89] Al-Husseini continued to hold out the possibility of restoring ties with the British after his exile but by 1940 had concluded that there was no going back.[90] Despite its opportunistic nature, al-Husseini's alliance with the Nazis made him an international pariah in the eyes of British and American officials and greatly harmed his cause.

In the wake of World War II, the United States had eclipsed Britain as the leading political and military power in the world, and by the 1940s it had replaced Britain as the principal power broker in Palestine. With Britain's announcement in early 1947 that it planned to terminate the Mandate and turn the matter over to the United Nations, the fate of Palestine was now largely in American hands. Truman's interventions at key moments leading up to the historic United Nations vote of November 1947 proved to be decisive in ensuring partition. While the State Department continued to maintain that partition was "certain to undermine our relations" with the Arab and Muslim world and to insist that any plan adopted by the UN "be able to command the maximum cooperation of all elements in Palestine," the administration moved inexorably toward endorsing Jewish statehood and away from the American commitment to mutual consultation.[91] In August the Truman administration declared that the United States attached "great weight" to the United Nations Special Committee on Palestine's preliminary finding in favor of partition, even as it continued to reassure the Arabs that it was keeping an open mind.[92] The tide officially turned in October, when Truman instructed his UN envoy, Herschel Johnson, to announce that the United States supported the UN Special Committee's partition plan. Under the plan, the Jews, who made up one-third of Palestine's population and owned 6 percent of the land, were allotted 56 percent of the country's territory; the Arab state, with twice the population, was allotted 44 percent of the land. Complicating matters further, roughly half of the population of the proposed Jewish state would be Arab.[93] Jerusalem and its surroundings would be placed under a separate international regime. The decision to divide Palestine represented a clear victory for the Zionists and an unmitigated defeat for the Arabs. As the historian Walid Khalidi writes, "For the Zionists, partition was three-quarters of a loaf; for the Palestinians, partition was half a baby."[94]

In the weeks leading up to the General Assembly vote, Truman took a number of steps to tip the scales in the Zionists' favor. Hoping to blunt Arab and Palestinian opposition, the State Department had proposed amending the plan to make partition "as equitable and just as possible."[95] However, following an "extensive campaign in Congress and the President against the scheme" by the Jewish Agency and its lobbying arm in Washington, the American Zionist Emergency Council, Truman pressed the State Department to withdraw the proposal.[96] With only days before the November 29 vote and support for partition just shy of the required two-thirds majority, Truman reversed an earlier pledge not to "use improper pressures of any kind" to sway UN delegations.[97] As the State Department and the CIA continued to warn of imminent war, the White House began actively lobbying UN members to back partition.[98] "During this time, we marshalled our forces," recalled Rabbi Hillel Silver of the American Zionist Emergency Council. "Jewish and non-Jewish opinion leaders and masses alike converged on the Government and induced the President to assert the authority of his Administration to overcome the negative attitude of the State Department which persisted to the end, and persists today. The result was that our Government made its intense desire for the adoption of the partition plan known to the wavering governments." Eddie Jacobson, a lifelong friend of Truman's who served as a go-between with Zionist leaders, later wrote in his diary of how the president was "fighting [the] entire Cabinet and State Department to put over Partition."[99] The American envoy to the UN at the time, Herschel Johnson, later recalled how David Niles, a close aide of Truman's, had pressured them "to get busy and get all the votes that we possibly could; that there would be hell if the voting went the wrong way."[100]

According to the scholar Michael E. Jansen, "[The] vote on partition in the Assembly is famous for the pressure, bribery, cajoling and use of pull which were employed . . . by the Jewish Agency and high-ranking pro-Zionist and Zionist Americans, including officials, to secure the necessary two-thirds vote."[101] As the consequences of his policy reversals became clear, Truman still tried to have it both ways, blaming his repeated wavering on the "unwarranted interference of the Zionists," even as he continued to maintain that he was immune to Zionist influence.[102] Truman's equivocation on Palestine was only just beginning.

2

From Deferral to Denial

In the event that partition is imposed on Palestine, the resulting conflict will seriously disturb the social, economic, and political stability of the Arab world, and US commercial and strategic interests will be dangerously jeopardized.

—*"Consequences of Partition of Palestine," Central Intelligence Agency memo, November 28, 1947*

Truman regretted his decision almost immediately.

Within days of the General Assembly vote, violence erupted between Arabs and Jews in Palestine. With their earlier warnings now validated, in January 1948 the State Department, the CIA, and other intelligence agencies urged Truman to "consider abandoning support of partition as being unworkable." The CIA described the partition plan as "hopeless. . . . Such a plan cannot be implemented without Arab cooperation, and it is inconceivable that the Arabs will abandon their present violent opposition to partition."[1] The State Department similarly concluded, "U.S. support of partition has already brought about loss of U.S. prestige and disillusionment among the Arabs and other neighboring peoples as to U.S. objectives and ideals."[2]

Department analysts further warned that given the Arabs' "unequivocal opposition to any form of partition, . . . one of the major premises on which we originally supported partition has proved invalid," and thus attempting to impose partition against the wishes of the Arab majority would most likely constitute a violation of their right to self-determination.[3] Truman concurred, and fearing the possibility that American troops would be drawn into the conflict, authorized the State Department to explore the possibility of a "temporary trusteeship" under which the UN would administer the country until a permanent solution could be found. Draft "Articles of Trusteeship" were drawn up by the State Department on April 2 and circulated to U.S. missions in the region and around the world.[4] In March, the American envoy to the UN, Warren Austin, formally notified the Security Council that "partition of Palestine is no longer a viable option" and requested that the plan be shelved.[5] The attack on Deir Yassin in April 1948, in which 250 unarmed Palestinian villagers were killed by Zionist militias on the outskirts of Jerusalem, reinforced Washington's move away from partition and marked a turning point in the civil war. In the wake of Deir Yassin, the trickle of Palestinian refugees that had begun in late 1947 now became a full-blown flood.[6]

Once again Truman tried to have it both ways. In explaining the reversal of American policy Truman noted, "It has become clear that the partition plan cannot be carried out at this time by peaceful means. We could not undertake to impose this solution on the people of Palestine by the use of American troops, both on [UN] Charter grounds and as a matter of national policy."[7] Meanwhile, with only months remaining until the election in which Truman would be seeking his first full term, Truman privately assured American Jewish groups and the Zionist leadership in Palestine of his continued support for partition.[8] As the May 15 deadline for the expiration of the British Mandate neared, the Zionist leadership in Palestine made it known that it would sidestep the UN and unilaterally declare the independence of the Jewish state. Clark Clifford, a senior White House adviser, urged the president to announce his intention to recognize

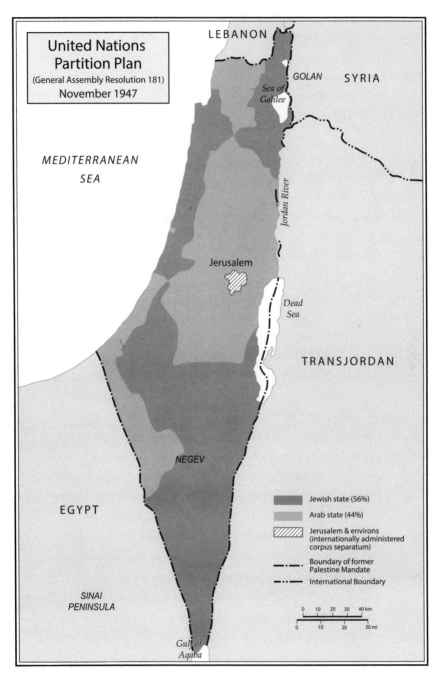

United Nations Partition Plan
(General Assembly Resolution 181)
November 1947

LEBANON

GOLAN   SYRIA

Sea of
Galilee

MEDITERRANEAN
SEA

Jordan River

Jerusalem

Dead
Sea

TRANSJORDAN

NEGEV

Jewish state (56%)

Arab state (44%)

Jerusalem & environs
(internationally administered
corpus separatum)

Boundary of former
Palestine Mandate

International Boundary

EGYPT

SINAI
PENINSULA

0   10   20   30   40 km

0   10   20   30 mi

Gulf of
Aqaba

Source: Adapted from United Nations map

the Jewish state after the declaration. Secretary of State George Marshall argued against such a move, describing it as a "transparent dodge to win a few votes. . . . The counsel offered by Mr. Clifford was based on domestic political considerations, while the problem which confronted us was international." As a result, Marshall added, the "great dignity of the office of the President would be seriously diminished."[9]

At 6:11 p.m. Washington time on May 14, eleven minutes after the Jewish Agency proclaimed the independence of the State of Israel, President Truman announced that the United States recognized the provisional government of Israel on a de facto basis. The news came as a shock to American diplomats, so much so that Marshall had to send a State Department official to the United Nations to prevent the entire American delegation from resigning en masse.[10]

Truman's frequent policy reversals reflected a deeper ambivalence within the U.S. policymaking establishment in the aftermath of the 1948 war and the massive Palestinian refugee crisis that accompanied Israel's creation. In addition to Truman's characteristic indecisiveness over the Palestinian conflict and his constant fretting over his electoral prospects, competing priorities between the State Department and officials at the Pentagon also pulled America's Palestine policy in different directions. In the wake of the war, American policymakers from the president on down had a firm grasp of the nature and scale of the Palestinian refugee problem, including Washington's own moral responsibility for its creation and the likely destabilizing effects of leaving it unresolved. Although successive U.S. administrations continued to officially uphold UN resolutions and a solution to the refugee issue as the keys to an Arab-Israeli peace settlement, the United States steadily gave in to Israel's refusal to allow refugee repatriation and other Israeli-imposed realities on the ground, while deferring a political resolution of the problem. Deferral soon gave way to denial. Within less than a generation, as the U.S.-Israel "special relationship" took hold and Israel's value increased in both domestic political and geopolitical terms, both the political significance of the refugee crisis and the roots of the Israel-Palestine conflict were all but forgotten in Washington. The reasons for this dramatic turnaround in U.S. policy were relatively straightforward. As the political, diplomatic, and other costs of challenging Israeli actions increased, so too did Washington's incentive to align its policies with those of Israel. The fact that Israel was increasingly tied to the United States while most of its Arab adversaries were gravitating toward the Soviet Union reinforced the view that the Arabs were on the "wrong" side of the emerging Cold War rivalry.

DEFERRING A POLITICAL RESOLUTION

The war that led simultaneously to the creation of Israel and the destruction of Arab Palestine began as a civil war between Arabs and Jews and was later subsumed under a broader regional war following the declaration of the Israeli state and Britain's departure from Palestine on May 14. The Arabs briefly held their own in early 1948, but the tide turned decisively against them in the spring of 1948 when Zionist forces launched a major offensive, known as Plan Dalet (Plan D), that sent hundreds of thousands of Arabs fleeing across the borders.[11] By the time Egyptian, Syrian, Jordanian, and Iraqi forces entered Palestine on May 15, roughly a quarter million Palestinians had fled the country.[12] The Arab states' stated aim was to crush the Jewish state in its infancy. Realizing they could not prevent the emergence of a Jewish state militarily, Arab armies focused their efforts on securing areas within the allotted Arab state.[13] The combined Arab forces totaled around 20,000 men.[14] Jewish forces stood at roughly 50,000 at the start of the war and swelled to nearly 120,000 by war's end.[15] The Arabs' paltry troop deployment was less a reflection of their military capabilities than of the "half-hearted and poorly conceived" nature of the Arab intervention and the fact that Arab states were working at cross purposes.[16] While Egyptian and Syrian forces focused on salvaging what was left of Arab Palestine, the Arab Legion of the Hashemite Kingdom of Transjordan (created in 1946), the largest and most effective of Arab armies, backed by their fellow

Hashemites in Iraq, set out to swallow up as much of Palestinian territory as it could.[17]

By early 1949 Israel had soundly defeated all four Arab armies, which left Israel in control of nearly four-fifths of the territory of former mandatory Palestine, including half the territory allotted to the proposed Arab state. In the process, 400 Palestinian towns and villages were destroyed and at least 750,000 Palestinians, roughly two-thirds of the country's Arab population, fled or were driven from their homes, with most taking refuge in neighboring Arab countries.[18] The two remaining parts of Palestine, the West Bank and Gaza Strip, came under Jordanian and Egyptian control, respectively. The largest number of refugees came under Jordanian control, including some 430,000 refugees on both sides of the Jordan River, joining the roughly 400,000 Palestinians of the West Bank, thus making Jordan's population overwhelmingly Palestinian. Only a small number took refuge in Egyptian territory, though around 230,000 fled to the Egyptian-occupied Gaza Strip, where they lived among the 100,000 local Palestinian residents. Another 200,000 refugees fled to Syria and to Lebanon. UN General Assembly Resolution 194, adopted in December 1948 and backed by the United States, called on Israel to allow the refugees to return to their homes "at the earliest practicable date" and to provide compensation for lost properties and other damages.[19] But Israeli leaders rejected calls for repatriation and compensation and denied any responsibility for the creation of the refugee problem, insisting that the refugees be resettled in Arab states instead.

American diplomats and intelligence officers closely monitored developments in Palestine, providing officials in Washington with regular reports and updates more or less as the crisis unfolded. Within days of the massacre at Deir Yassin, the American consul general in Jerusalem, Thomas Wasson, sent a cable to Washington describing how Irgun and Stern Gang members had "killed 250 persons of whom half, by their own admission to American correspondents, were women and children."[20] The Palestinian exodus was now in full swing. On April 23, consular officials in Jerusalem reported 6,000 to 7,000 Arabs fleeing Haifa. By May 3, Wasson relayed what appeared to be an imminent Zionist

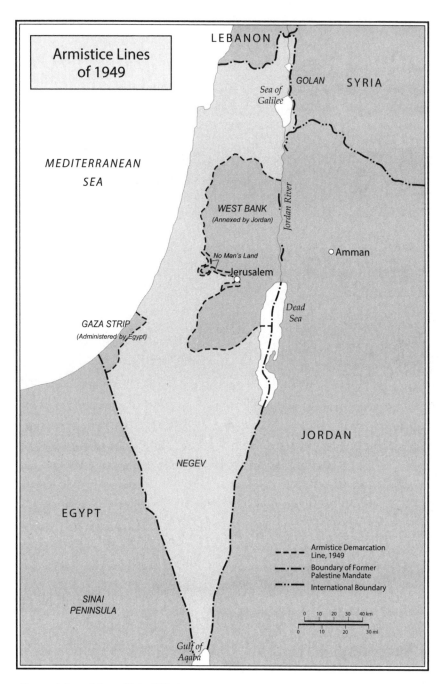

Armistice Lines of 1949

LEBANON

GOLAN

SYRIA

Sea of Galilee

MEDITERRANEAN
SEA

Jordan River

WEST BANK
(Annexed by Jordan)

○Amman

No Man's Land

Jerusalem○

Dead Sea

GAZA STRIP
(Administered by Egypt)

JORDAN

NEGEV

EGYPT

- - - - Armistice Demarcation Line, 1949
- ·- ·- Boundary of Former Palestine Mandate
- ··- ··- International Boundary

0 10 20 30 40 km
0 10 20 30 mi

SINAI
PENINSULA

Gulf of Aqaba

Source: Adapted from United Nations map

victory: "Morale following Jewish military successes is low with thousands Arabs fleeing country. . . . So far Arab resistance has been ineffective and GOC [General Officer Commanding] and others believe Jews will be able to sweep all before them unless regular Arab armies come to rescue." A few weeks later Wasson was gunned down by an unknown sniper in Jerusalem.[21]

Wasson's replacement, William Burdett, relayed similar stories of Palestinians "displaced either by force, or terrorism or have fled because of their own fear."[22] On June 28, the State Department reported a preliminary figure of 300,000 refugees, although the actual number was likely higher. By the end of October, the State Department estimated that a total of 468,000 refugees had fled and warned Truman that the "situation is daily more critical as cold weather sets in." On March 15, 1949, U.S. government sources put the total number of refugees at 725,000.[23] A State Department study found that "Israeli authorities have followed a systematic program of destroying Arab houses," leaving "in many instances, literally no houses for the refugees to return to."[24] Truman's peace envoy and the U.S. representative on the UN Palestine Conciliation Commission, Mark Ethridge, was among the most outspoken in asserting that Israel bore "particular responsibility for those who have been driven out by terrorism, repression and forcible rejection."[25]

As a result, senior American policymakers, including the president and secretary of state, had a firm understanding of the nature and scope of the Palestinian exodus and the conditions under which Palestinians fled, as well as the political implications of the exodus. An August 1948 State Department report to President Truman described the dire conditions of the refugees and warned that America's failure "to render substantial assistance in this emergency is jeopardizing our relations with the Near Eastern states."[26] The American consul general in Jerusalem expressed a similar view, noting that "the United States has accumulated an enormous moral and even financial responsibility in the situation in our justifiable zeal for creation of a [Jewish] state."[27] In the meantime, Ethridge warned of "unrest among refugees growing and likely to explode if idleness continues."[28] Whether the Palestinian exodus was the result of a deliberate plan to clear areas of the country of Arabs to make room for incoming Jews remains the subject of intense debate, even among Israeli historians. According to the Israeli-British political scientist Ahron Bregman, there was at least a tacit agreement among Zionist leaders to do so.[29] And there is little doubt that Israel's leaders welcomed the new demographic reality, which Chaim Weizmann described to the first American ambassador to Israel, James McDonald, as "a miraculous simplification of our tasks."[30]

American officials took particular exception to Israeli claims that Palestinians fled at the urging of Arab leaders or that the mass flight of refugees was triggered by the invasion of Arab armies. When Ambassador McDonald repeated these claims in his correspondence with Washington, it was Marshall himself who set him straight: "Arab refugee problem is one which . . . did develop from recent war in Palestine but which also began before outbreak of Arab-Israeli hostilities. A significant portion of Arab refugees fled from their homes owing to Jewish occupation of Haifa on April 21–22 and to Jewish armed attack against Jaffa April 25." Marshall went on to warn that the "leaders of Israel would make a grave miscalculation if they thought callous treatment of this tragic issue could pass unnoticed by world opinion. Furthermore, hatred of Arabs for Israel engendered by refugee problem would be a great obstacle to those peace negotiations you say PGI [Provisional Government of Israel] immediately desires."[31] Marshall had correctly assessed the impact of Israel's disregard for the refugees on the diplomatic process but, as later events demonstrated, misjudged the extent to which there would be a price to pay for it.

The events of 1948 resulted in two parallel, and almost mutually exclusive, national narratives. For Israelis it was a war of independence waged against a singular Arab enemy determined to destroy the nascent Jewish state in the cradle. For the Palestinians, it was the Nakba (meaning "calamity"), which resulted in the physical destruction of Arab Palestine and the dispossession of most of its people at the hands of the Zionists. Washington's understanding of the events of 1948 involved elements of both narratives. For most American officials, the central story of 1948 revolved around the creation of Israel and the regional war that followed—even as they frequently took issue with Israeli actions and their characterizations of events. The flight of hundreds of thousands of Palestinians from their homes, while tragic in human terms, was first and foremost a humanitarian problem, albeit one that had political implications. Once Israel declared its independence and was recognized by the United States, the Soviet Union, and other countries, the political dimension of the Palestinian question—at least as it was understood during the Mandate period as a struggle between two national groups vying for political and territorial control—ceased to be relevant. Thus, what had been the defining moment in the Palestinian national movement remained for most American officials an "unrecognizable episode."[32] That American officials had embraced the political significance of the Israeli narrative while disputing its factual basis was bound to lead to confusion and contradictions in American policy.

Officially, American policy continued to be based on UN General Assembly Resolution 181, the UN partition plan, which in addition to defining Israel's borders had called for placing Jerusalem and its immediate environs under a special international regime, and Resolution 194, which provided for the return and compensation of Palestinian refugees. As a practical matter, however, the United States and the international community effectively abandoned both resolutions while deferring to Israel-imposed realities on the ground. The first component of Resolution 181 to be abandoned, of course, was the proposed Arab state. A secret arrangement between the Jewish Agency and King Abdullah of Transjordan ensured that Arab Palestine—or what remained of it after the war—would be annexed by Transjordan. Meetings between the Hashemite king and the Zionist leadership began in November 1947, even before the UN voted to partition Palestine, and continued right up until May 1948.[33] The plan was supported by the British, who had invested heavily in the Hashemite monarchy and had never seriously considered the possibility of an independent Palestinian state.[34]

Despite some initial hesitancy on the part of the State Department, Washington eventually signed off on the plan as well.[35] By November 1948, Marshall concluded, "Arab Palestine standing alone could not constitute a viable independent state. It is desirable, therefore, that Arab Palestine be transferred to one or more of the neighboring Arab states . . . taking into account the wishes of the inhabitants of Arab Palestine."[36] The latter had not been consulted, of course. Moreover, British and American officials had already seen to it that Transjordan's annexation of the Arab state, along with other modifications to the UN partition plan, were incorporated into the peace plan put forward by the UN mediator, Count Folke Bernadotte, in mid-September. The administration saw little downside to the plan, which not only provided a way out of Truman's partition/trusteeship debacle without committing U.S. troops but also had the added advantage of "effectively eliminat[ing] the Grand Mufti of Jerusalem and his followers."[37]

As the Zionists, Hashemites, and British worked to prevent the emergence of an Arab state in Palestine, Arab rulers scrambled to bring one about. The creation of the All Palestine Government (APG) in September 1948 by Egypt and the Arab League was designed to fill the Palestinian leadership void as well as derail Hashemite ambitions in Palestine and deflect popular anger over the Arabs' poor performance during the war.[38] Under the leadership of Amin al-Husseini, the former grand mufti, who staged a triumphant return to the Egyptian-controlled Gaza Strip on September 27, the APG marked the first attempt to create a Palestinian governing entity. This challenge would continue to consume Palestinian politics and Arab states throughout the 1950s and '60s.[39]

The creation of the APG was welcomed by Palestinians inside and outside the country, and, with the exception of Transjordan, was universally recognized by the Arab states. But it was already too late. Al-Husseini's stature among Palestinians was unmatched, a fact recognized by the American consul general in Jerusalem, Robert Macatee, who wrote that "no Arab approaches the Mufti's stature in the eyes of Palestinian Arabs."[40] As the largest and best-trained Arab military contingent in the war, however, King Abdullah had the advantage of controlling large swaths of Palestinian territory, in which the APG's supporters and its activities were banned. Moreover, without an army, a budget, or a functioning administration inside the country, the APG collapsed within just a few weeks. It continued to exist in name only until Egypt's Gamal Abdel Nasser finally closed its offices in 1959.[41]

The United States dismissed the APG as a ruse devised by Arab states, at best to undermine friendly regimes in Israel and Transjordan and at worst to provide a platform for the hated former grand mufti. An official State Department directive circulated in a cable to U.S. missions abroad declared, "US Govt considers establishment of 'Arab Palestine Govt' under present circumstances prejudicial to successful solution Palestine problem as well as to best interests Arab States and Arab inhabitants Palestine." Without irony or apparent self-awareness, the directive further accused the APG of having been "set up without prior consultation wishes Arab Palestinians."[42] The emergence of the APG only reinforced American support for the annexation of Arab Palestine by Transjordan, which was seen as a more acceptable peace partner for Israel than angry and disenfranchised Palestinians.[43] As a result, the "Jordanian solution"—the idea that Jordan could serve as a substitute for a credible Palestinian interlocutor—would remain a cornerstone of U.S. Middle East policy for the next forty years.

Meanwhile, Israel's rapid territorial expansion during the summer and fall of 1948 had complicated American and international peace efforts and created a new dilemma for Truman. Since Israel's independence had been declared and recognized on the basis of the UN partition plan, American and UN officials considered Israeli conquests beyond its UN-defined boundaries to be occupied territory to which it was not entitled.[44] The United States was not opposed to changes to Israel's UN-defined boundaries in accordance with new realities on the ground but insisted that they be part of a broader diplomatic arrangement involving the UN and relevant Arab states. Angered by the territorial concessions laid out in the UN mediator's peace plan, Irgun terrorists assassinated Bernadotte in mid-September; nevertheless the UN peace plan remained the focal point of U.S. policy, which if abandoned, according to the State Department, "could be absolutely disastrous to us in the U.N. and elsewhere."[45] During the war, Ben-Gurion had confided to his followers that no aspect of partition would be considered final, "not with regard to the regime, not with regard to borders, and not with regard to international agreements."[46] After Israel conquered the northern Galilee in late October 1948, in violation of an earlier truce agreement and causing another 130,000 Palestinians to flee the area, Secretary of State Marshall joined other world powers in calling for censuring Israel in the Security Council. In the midst of a tight presidential race and only days before the election, however, Truman came under intense pressure from members of his party to rein in his secretary of state. As the Security Council prepared to vote on the matter, Truman sent a cable instructing the U.S. delegation to do all it could to "avoid taking position on Palestine prior to Wednesday," the day after the election. If the matter came to a vote before then, the American delegation was to abstain.[47] As a result, American support for the censure was withdrawn and the measure was subsequently dropped. "It is to be doubted if there has ever been, before or since, such a direct interplay between domestic politics and foreign affairs," wrote Truman's biographer Michael Cohen of the incident.[48]

Even as the territorial dimension of the conflict remained fluid, U.S. officials focused their energies on the growing refugee problem. Although the Truman administration, in accordance with Resolution 194, continued to view refugee repatriation and compensation as the key to an Arab-Israeli settlement, it eventually backed down amid stiff Israeli resistance and opposing priorities within the administration. Despite their repeated attempts, American officials failed to convince Israel to take back even a limited number of refugees. In its one and only offer at the Lausanne peace conference of 1949, Israel agreed to take back up to 150,000 refugees from the Gaza Strip, but only on the condition that Israel be allowed to annex the territory. An American proposal that Israel allow the return of refugees who fled areas outside the proposed Jewish state was similarly rejected.[49] Israel's provisional government considered the refugees a "formidable fifth column" and took immediate steps to prevent their return.[50] As a result, Ethridge pinned much of the blame on Israel for the failure of the Lausanne peace conference in August 1949.[51] In a strongly worded message to Truman, Ethridge complained of having "repeatedly pointed out political weakness and brutality of their position on refugees but it has made little impression."[52] While the State Department continued to press the Israelis on refugee repatriation and compensation, officials at the Pentagon took a different view. The Joint Chiefs of Staff were impressed with the effectiveness of Israel's military and was keen to preserve Israel's pro-Western orientation.[53] "For reasons unrelated to domestic politics," writes Boston University's Irene L. Gendzier, "the JCS concluded that Israel's military justified U.S. interest, and such interest merited lowering the pressure on Israel to ensure that it turned away from the USSR and toward the West and the United States."[54]

Truman shared Ethridge's frustration, conceding that he was "rather disgusted with the manner in which the Jews are approaching the refugee problem."[55] Truman attempted to ratchet up the pressure by putting a hold on Israel's application for UN membership while threatening "a revision of attitude toward Israel" if the Israeli government "continues to reject the basic principles set forth" in Resolution 194 "and the friendly advice offered by the US Govt."[56] The State Department backed up the president's ultimatum with a threat to withhold $49 million in loans from the Export-Import Bank unless Israel agreed to take back 200,000 refugees. This figure was based on the number of refugees estimated to have come from areas conquered by Israel beyond the borders defined by the UN partition resolution.[57] However, the Israelis called Truman's bluff. The American coordinator for Palestine refugees, George McGhee, later recalled how the Israeli ambassador "looked me straight in the eye and said, in essence, that I wouldn't get by with this move, that he would stop it. . . . Within an hour of my return to my office I received a message from the White House that the president wished to dissociate himself from any withholding" of the loan.[58] The funds were subsequently released and the United States even helped push through Israel's application for UN membership.

The episode marked the end of Truman's attempts to influence Israeli behavior and the start of the steady erosion of American policy toward the refugees. Frustrated by what he termed "an abortion of justice and humanity to which I do not want to be midwife," Ethridge resigned, predicting a "complete destruction of all faith in an international organization and creation of a very dangerous flame against US in this part of world." Looking back at the experience many years later, Ethridge recalled, "Truman let me down on two phases of the Palestine thing."[59] Others in the State Department echoed those concerns. "Israel is convinced of its ability to 'induce' the United States to abandon its present insistence on repatriation of refugees and territorial changes," observed Consul General William Burdett. Burdett further cautioned that unless the United States and the UN were prepared to impose "the necessary punitive measures against Israel to force Israel to consent to a reduction in territory—and repatriation of refugees," they should "admit that the US and UN are unable or unwilling to take the required measures; and therefore that US policy on boundaries and refugees cannot be carried out."[60]

ECONOMIC SOLUTIONS

As it became clear that a political settlement between Israel and the Arabs was not in the offing, American policymakers shifted their focus to managing the conflict. A March 1949 State Department analysis warned that a failure to "liquidate or materially reduce the magnitude of the Arab refugee problem" would greatly increase instability in the region, opening it to possible Soviet penetration and even the toppling of Arab governments.[61] Recognizing the potential for radicalization and instability posed by the presence of several hundred thousand destitute refugees scattered throughout the region, Truman sent his new peace envoy, Gordon Clapp, head of the Tennessee Valley Water Authority, to lead a UN mission to the Middle East to identify ways "to facilitate the repatriation, resettlement and economic and social rehabilitation of the refugees and the payment of compensation."[62] The mission's findings became the impetus for the creation of the United Nations Relief Works Agency for Palestine Refugees in the Near East (UNRWA) in December 1949 as well as other American-sponsored development projects aimed at resettling Palestinian refugees in neighboring Arab states.[63] In addition to meeting the basic needs of the refugees, UNRWA also served as a sort of welfare agency providing education, employment, and other social services.[64] However, the emphasis on development and resettlement alarmed the Arabs, especially the Palestinians, who viewed it as an attempt to liquidate the refugee problem and bypass Palestinian rights. The pursuit of economic and other temporary solutions nonetheless remained a focal point of U.S. policy toward the Palestinians. Like Truman, Presidents Eisenhower and Kennedy and later presidents appointed Middle East peace envoys and gave them economic mandates.

But Washington's desire to defer a political resolution of the refugee problem came with a price, as a newly educated and highly politicized generation of Palestinian activists came to the fore. The loss of Palestine and the Arabs' humiliating military defeat shook the foundations of the Arab world, culminating in the overthrow of several Arab rulers by military juntas—President Shukri al-Quwatli of Syria in 1949, King Farouk of Egypt in 1952, and King Faisal II of Iraq in 1958—and leaving Jordan's Hashemite monarchy even more isolated and exposed. The assassination of King Abdullah by a Palestinian nationalist on the steps of Jerusalem's Al-Aqsa Mosque in 1951 was the opening shot in the protracted struggle between the nascent Palestinian national movement and the Hashemites of Jordan. The rise of socialist, pan-Arab regimes also posed a unique challenge to Truman's successor, Dwight D. Eisenhower, who saw Soviet penetration and communist subversion as the dominant threat to the stability of the Middle East and its vast oil resources, on which Western nations depended. Although an Arab-Israeli settlement was not a top priority for Eisenhower, the administration felt compelled to take up the matter "insofar as the failure to do so might damage U.S. and Western relations with the Arab world, make Arab states susceptible to Soviet influence, and risk the security of Middle Eastern oil sources."[65]

Eisenhower took a markedly different approach to the Arab-Israeli conflict from that of his predecessor. Conscious of the damage caused to America's standing in the Arab world and "the deep resentment against it that has resulted from the creation of Israel," Eisenhower and his secretary of state, John Foster Dulles, expressed the U.S. desire to maintain favorable relations with both Israel and the Arab states.[66] In contrast to Truman's sense of "historic responsibility" toward Israel, the

Eisenhower administration made clear "that Israel will not, merely because of its Jewish population, receive preferential treatment over any Arab state."[67] Like its predecessor, the Eisenhower administration expressed sympathy for Palestinian refugees. In a June 1953 radio address to the American people shortly after returning from his introductory tour of the region, Dulles spoke passionately of the plight of the refugees and of the challenges it posed for American interests:

> Closely huddled around Israel are most of the over 800,000 Arab refugees, who fled from Palestine as the Israeli took over. They exist mostly in makeshift camps, with few facilities either for health, work, or recreation. . . . Today the Arab peoples are afraid that the United States will back the new state of Israel in aggressive expansionism. They are more fearful of Zionism than of communism, and they fear lest the United States become the backer of expansionist Zionism.[68]

But the administration's sympathy for the refugees did not translate into a willingness to deal with the political roots of the problem.

Although decidedly less sentimental toward Israel and, on the whole, more balanced in his approach to the conflict than Truman, Eisenhower invested even more heavily in resettlement and other economic solutions to the refugee problem. American officials had come to the realization fairly early on that Israel would never willingly allow a meaningful repatriation of refugees, and neither Truman nor Eisenhower was inclined to compel it to do so. As early as March 1949, State Department officials had already concluded that "the majority of these unfortunate people will soon be confronted with the fact that they will not be able to return home."[69] Faced with the threat of growing Soviet influence in the region and other more pressing priorities, Eisenhower was even less inclined to push for repatriation than was his predecessor. For the Eisenhower administration, Israel's existence was an irreversible reality with which Arab states ultimately would have to come to terms. Moreover, while the administration insisted that the "Arab refugee problem" required a political settlement between Israel and the Arab states, the onus was primarily on the latter. The aim was to encourage

Israel to take back a limited number of refugees, perhaps no more than 100,000, while the rest would have to be resettled in neighboring Arab states.[70] In response to Arab calls for repatriation, administration officials maintained that "the clock could not be turned back."[71] Regarding those Palestinians who had been uprooted, U.S. officials insisted that there was simply "no room" for them, and that the Jews "who were now in territory originally allotted to the Arabs could not be thrown out."[72] Arab proposals for a Palestinian state based on the 1947 partition plan similarly failed to gain any traction in Washington. Appeals by Arab leaders for a return to Resolutions 181 and 194, on which U.S. policy was still ostensibly based, were dismissed by American officials as "unrealistic" and tantamount to calling for "the destruction of Israel."[73]

The centerpiece of Eisenhower's peace strategy was a regional water-sharing and development scheme spearheaded by his special envoy to the Middle East, Eric Johnston. The Johnston Plan was in large part based on the 1949 Clapp report, which had concluded that in the absence of a comprehensive peace settlement on all outstanding issues, "It is unrealistic to suppose that agreement on the complex question of international water rights could be negotiated among the parties."[74] Launched in October 1953, the Johnston Plan proposed the employment and resettlement of some 300,000 Palestinian refugees in the Jordan valley, by means of which the administration hoped "the back of the Palestine refugee problem will have been broken."[75] The Johnston Plan, which bore a striking resemblance to the "transfer" schemes of the 1930s and '40s, was based on the belief that given the promise of land, jobs, and other economic benefits, Palestinian refugees would agree to be resettled in neighboring Arab states "by preference."[76] The plan stalled after two years but remained a focal point of U.S. policy until the early 1960s. The Israelis continued to push various proposals of their own for resettling Palestinian refugees in Libya, Somalia, Brazil, and other countries.[77]

A handful of American diplomats warned of the futility of relying on an exclusively economic approach to dealing with the refugees. Among them was Talcott Seelye, the U.S. chargé d'affaires in Amman, who provided a more sober assessment of the plan's prospects among Palestinians. Seelye cabled Washington on the eve of Johnston's arrival in the Jordanian capital:

> Jordan Government and public opinion channels are presently dominated by the Palestinian. He is bitter, emotional, and he has not forgotten. An appeal to his economic reason, without in any way attempting to satisfy his psychological (pathological, if you will) complex, risks not only failure, but may prejudice any future US efforts to solve Palestine problem *in toto*. An appeal to his sense of dramatics (e.g., espousal of his "right to return"), mixed with fair amount of justice (e.g., promise of compensation, territorial rectification of Jordan-Israeli border) has better chance of securing his recognition of economic facts of life. If [the Johnston] mission's proposal for joint control of Yarmuk-Jordan waters cannot now be made part of larger, overall political settlement, it would be better for US interests not to broach proposal at all.[78]

Dulles had heard similar warnings during his introductory tour of the region in spring 1953 from the Palestinians themselves. In a series of meetings held at the American embassy in Amman in May 1953, representatives of Palestinian refugee groups advised Dulles that the "refugee problem in its essence and as the refugees themselves see it is a political problem much more so than an economic or humanitarian one." Izzat Tannous of the Palestine Arab Refugee Organization likewise insisted that the refugee crisis "requires a political solution" without which there would be dire consequences: "Although we don't want war, we cannot overlook the fact that you have created a class of people who are so destitute that they are bound to want war."[79] Seelye's and Tanous's warnings proved prescient.

THE SEARCH FOR A PALESTINIAN "ENTITY"

The growing frequency of cross-border infiltrations by Palestinians in the years following Israel's creation underscored the consequences of leaving the refugee issue unresolved. These infiltrations began as individual efforts by Palestinian refugees attempting to recover lost property, tend to their crops, or visit relatives, where they were often met with deadly force by Israeli authorities, which resulted in the deaths of several thousand mostly unarmed Palestinians in the first few years of Israel's existence.[80] As the infiltrations became armed and more organized, a familiar pattern emerged. Arab leaders began to recruit and train Palestinian commando fighters, known as fedayeen ("self-sacrificers"), to launch cross-border raids on Israel, which were usually followed by massive Israeli military retaliation against the fedayeen and those who sponsored or hosted them. The October 1953 Israeli raid on the West Bank border village of Qibya, which resulted in the death of sixty-nine Palestinian villagers, earned Israel rebukes from both the UN Security Council and the Eisenhower administration. The United States temporarily suspended economic aid to Israel, while Dulles warned that Israel's policy of using excessive force risked destabilizing the region.[81] The assault on Qibya, which was led by a young IDF commander named Ariel Sharon, was an early example of Israel's "doctrine of retaliatory action," which called for the use of massive, disproportionate force as means of deterring future attacks. However, as Ahron Bregman has pointed out, "Israel's retaliatory doctrine neither curbed infiltration nor eased public insecurity. In fact, it achieved precisely the opposite effect for, by reacting massively and disproportionately to even minor Palestinian provocations, the Israeli leadership instilled in the public a mistaken impression that a big and continuous war was being waged between Israeli troops and the fedayeen."[82]

For Egypt's Gamal Abdel Nasser, in particular, the fedayeen proved to be a double-edged sword. Cross-border raids by the fedayeen from the Egyptian-administered Gaza Strip allowed President Nasser to put pressure on Israel while boosting his nationalist credentials, but they also exposed him to the severity of Israeli reprisals and the risk of full-scale war. The line was crossed in October 1956, when Israel, along with Britain and France, invaded and occupied Egypt's Sinai Peninsula and the Gaza Strip. For Eisenhower, who subsequently forced the three U.S. allies to withdraw, the tripartite invasion posed a direct threat to the newly established international order and risked pushing the Egyptians further into the arms of the Soviet Union. In ignoring the political dimension of the Palestinian refugee issue, however, American policymakers failed to fully appreciate the dangers of allowing the problem to fester in the Gaza Strip, the West Bank, and southern Lebanon, which would soon become hotbeds of fedayeen activity and wellsprings of instability.

The Sinai War produced two seemingly contradictory trends: it convinced Arab leaders of the need to control (or, in the case of Jordan, eliminate) Palestinian activism, while simultaneously fueling the desire among Palestinians in the diaspora for an autonomous political leadership. Both of these trends played out in the arena of intra-Arab rivalries and the growing rift between revolutionary pan-Arab regimes, led by Nasser's Egypt, and the conservative monarchies of Jordan, Saudi Arabia, and other Gulf states, known as the "Arab cold war." Out of the teeming refugee camps and university campuses of Arab capitals emerged a new, educated, and socially mobile generation of Palestinian political activists. The most important group to emerge at this time was the Palestine Liberation Movement, better known as Fatah. Founded in 1959 by a small group of activists, including Yasser Arafat and Khalil Al-Wazir (aka Abu Jihad), Fatah's philosophy centered on two key principles: the need for independent Palestinian decision making free of the control of Arab governments and the primacy of armed struggle against Israel as the only means to liberate Palestine.[83]

For their part, Arab regimes sought to harness the power of the Palestinian cause both domestically and in the international arena while controlling Palestinian activism at home. For Arab leaders and citizens alike, the loss of Palestine had come to symbolize lost Arab dignity at the hands of Western imperialism and Zionism, all the more demeaning in light of the Holy Land's sacred status. Ownership of the Palestinian cause was therefore a highly coveted and much-fought-over prize in intra-Arab politics. By the late 1950s, intra-Arab competition over Palestine had produced something of a bidding war between rival Arab regimes over the shape of a future Palestinian "entity." Starting in 1959, Nasser began pushing the idea of a Palestinian "entity" to represent the Palestinian people in the international arena "as a unified people, and not mere refugees," through an elected legislative council.[84] Not to be outdone, Iraq's nationalist prime minister, Abd al-Karim Qassem, announced his own plans to form a Palestinian "republic" backed by a new "liberation regiment."[85]

After several fitful attempts by the Arab states, the long-awaited Palestinian "entity" finally came into being. On May 28, 1964, the Arab League, at Egypt's behest, announced the creation of the Palestine Liberation Organization (PLO) under the leadership of Ahmad Shuqeiri, a Palestinian lawyer who had briefly served as a minister in the defunct APG. The PLO's goal was straightforward: to replace Israel with an "independent Palestinian state" from the Jordan River to the Mediterranean Sea, presumably through its armed wing, the Palestine Liberation Army. This was mostly bluster, however, as Arab leaders, most notably Nasser, had neither the will nor the capacity to liberate Palestine. For the time being the PLO remained a tool of Arab leaders, particularly Nasser, who used it to claim ownership of the Palestinian cause and, more important, to control and coordinate Palestinian action, particularly military action, in order to limit the risk of being drawn into a new war with Israel. Key Palestinian groups, including Fatah and the leftist Arab Nationalist Movement founded in 1951 and the parent organization of the Popular Front for the Liberation of Palestine (PFLP) and its offshoot the Democratic Front for the Liberation of Palestine (DFLP), refused to join the PLO, which they accused of being a puppet in the hands of Nasser, unrepresentative and insufficiently revolutionary.

Like the fedayeen, the struggle for a Palestinian entity in the eyes of most American policymakers remained a distinctly Arab rather than a Palestinian phenomenon. Although government analysts had followed with great interest the intra-Arab debate over a Palestinian entity from the early 1950s up until the creation of the PLO in 1964, it would be several more years before the emergence of autonomous Palestinian groups appeared on their radar. For the most part, Arab proposals for a Palestinian entity were seen against the backdrop of the defunct APG and the "notorious ex–Grand Mufti of Jerusalem" or as manifestations of intra-Arab "intrigue," and thus were generally dismissed as a "gimmick" or attempts to put the "political squeeze on Israel."[86] King Abdullah of Transjordan had formally annexed the West Bank in 1950, thereafter renaming the country Jordan. Although the United States never officially recognized Jordanian sovereignty over the West Bank, which included the eastern portion of the divided city of Jerusalem, American officials treated it as a fait accompli. The very idea of a Palestinian government or political entity was seen as a direct challenge to Israeli and Jordanian territorial sovereignty and thus inherently destabilizing.[87] But the sheer persistence of the proposals to create a Palestinian entity eventually required that they be taken seriously. For example, a 1961 State Department memorandum denounced the notion of a "Palestine Government in exile [as] a retrogressive development in Arab-Israel relations," but advised against a "frontal attack" on the idea as being "only likely to give it more life."[88]

Such policies were not theoretical. As the United States and Israel grew closer politically and militarily under the Kennedy and Johnson administrations, American resistance to Palestinian political representation increased under various pretexts. For example, in 1961, American diplomats actively worked to block efforts by Egypt and other Arab states to form a Palestine Arab delegation at the United Nations, which U.S. officials said would "upset present calm" in the region.[89] Any Palestinian representation at the UN, U.S. officials insisted, should be "as individuals only and not officially recognized as 'The' delegation representing all Palestine Arabs."[90] These efforts were coordinated with and often undertaken at the behest of Israel.[91]

Only a small handful of American diplomats could see beyond the intra-Arab power plays to understand why Arab rulers felt a need to compete over Palestine in the first place. Among them was Jefferson Caffery, who served as the American ambassador to Egypt during Israel's early years. In a report to his colleagues in the State Department, Caffery explained: "Palestine refugees are a key group which must be taken into consideration in seeking a settlement" and "their assent is essential," particularly if one hoped to bring Arab governments on board with a future peace settlement. Caffery was far ahead of his time in recognizing not only the centrality of the refugee issue to a political settlement between Israel and the Arab states, but in the need for Palestinian involvement in bringing one about. In fact, Caffery's recommendations went even further; he proposed that the United States create a "hand picked and cooperative 'Palestine Goverment' [*sic*] . . . to replace the shadowy and dubious existing 'Government'"—the APG—which "could negotiate on behalf of the Palestinians and would be able to make bolder and more realistic decisions than could the Arab Governments."[92]

Caffery remained the exception, however. Most American officials paid very little attention to political developments among the Palestinians themselves, in contrast to their intense focus on Arab-sponsored initiatives to create a "Palestine entity." The emergence of Fatah and the various Palestinian leftist groups associated with the Arab Nationalist Movement around the same time period went largely unnoticed by American officials until several years after the fact. For example, it was not until May 1965, a few months after Fatah had officially launched the "armed struggle" against Israel and six years after its formation, that U.S. analysts began to report on the group.[93] By late 1966, Fatah was being described as the "most prominent Palestinian terrorist group."[94]

It was also during this period that the basic pillars of current U.S. policy toward the PLO were established. As with earlier attempts to create a Palestinian entity, the formation of the PLO in 1964 was initially dismissed as yet another ruse in the intra-Arab "struggle for power."[95] As it became clear that the PLO was more than just a "new and stronger refugee organization," as one State Department memorandum called it, U.S. officials began to look at it more seriously.[96] By March 1965 the State Department had developed formal guidelines for dealing with the organization, which were circulated to American missions overseas. According to the official guidance, the United States did not recognize the PLO "as the sole or even as an official representative of the Palestine people. It is the USG's view that it has no official status whatever."[97] Even so, U.S. officials still held out the possibility of maintaining unofficial ties with the group.[98] According to the State Department, "Productive relations can be established between PLO members and USG officers," if only as a "way of demonstrating to the Palestinians and other

Arabs our continuing friendship for the Palestinian people. There is of course the possibility of acquiring useful intelligence." The PLO's pariah status had little to do with terrorism or violence but rather was entirely political, since the PLO "did not represent a sovereign entity" and because it "was widely regarded in the United States as an organization dedicated to terminating the existence of a state that we recognized."[99] As a result, U.S. officials vowed "to head off" any attempts by the PLO to win recognition at the UN—a stance that would be played out repeatedly in one form or another over the next half century.[100]

The "terrorist" label soon followed, however. In December 1965 a CIA analysis described the PLO as one of a handful of "peaceful" Palestinian initiatives.[101] Just one year later, CIA analysts included the PLO as one of several "Palestine Arab Terrorist Organizations" active at the time, even though it had not engaged in armed operations against Israel at this stage.[102] Thus, on the eve of the 1967 War, well before the PLO's takeover by Fatah and other fedayeen groups and before the PLO joined the armed struggle, the main features of the American policy toward the PLO for the next quarter century—the denial of political recognition, arm's-length engagement on a strictly utilitarian basis, and an association with extremism and terror—were already in place.

DENIAL

Although not a top priority for his administration, John F. Kennedy was personally conflicted over how to deal with the Arab-Israeli dispute. For the Kennedy administration, a settlement of the Arab-Israeli conflict generally took a backseat to other priorities such as the growing rivalry with the Soviet Union and communist threats in Cuba and Southeast Asia. Nevertheless, Kennedy shared his predecessor's view of the need to foster friendly relations with both Israel and the Arab states. Given his anticolonialist instincts, however, Kennedy was more inclined to accommodate than to suppress Arab nationalism.[103] Yet like most U.S. officials at the time, Kennedy had no real appreciation for Palestinians as a national or political entity; the Palestinians, as one scholar put it, "were a problem, not a people."[104] At the same time, Kennedy also had an emotional attachment to the Jewish state and a keen sense of its value in domestic political terms. Consequently, Kennedy was the last U.S. president to make a serious attempt to resolve the refugee problem as well as the first to define the U.S.-Israeli partnership in strategic terms.

Under Kennedy, U.S. officials continued to press the Israelis to accept a limited form of repatriation, even as they continued to encourage resettlement through economic development programs for the bulk of the refugee population. Shortly after taking office in 1961, Kennedy wrote to the leaders of Egypt, Jordan, Saudi Arabia, and other Arab states promising to help resolve the Arab-Israeli conflict, including a resolution of "the tragic Palestine refugee problem on the basis of the principle of repatriation or compensation for properties."[105] Kennedy's Middle East peace envoy, Joseph Johnson, proposed that refugees be allowed to choose between returning to their homes in Israel and resettlement in Arab states or other countries; in the latter case they would be compensated from a special UN fund. Israel's willingness to accept some Palestinian refugees could be tied to the Arabs' recognition of Israel. The plan deeply unnerved the Israelis, who grew more adamant in their insistence that the only acceptable solution to the refugee problem lay in resettlement outside Israel. When his efforts finally ran aground in the summer of 1962, Johnson concluded that "Israel not only does not want any refugees back but would prefer no Arabs in Israel. Its drive is toward 'uncompromising exclusivity.'"[106] Thereafter Johnson's peace plan was shelved. Kennedy continued to half-heartedly promote the option of repatriation while privately signaling to the Israelis that such an outcome was unrealistic.[107]

Under Kennedy, U.S.-Israel relations reached unprecedented levels of cooperation. In addition to working to prevent a Palestinian presence at the UN, Kennedy became the first American president to sell weapons to Israel, as well as the first to describe the U.S.-Israel partnership as a "special relationship." The sale of Hawk missiles to Israel in 1963, which was billed as a means of restoring the regional balance of power in light of the Soviets' arming of Arab states, was originally aimed at persuading the Israelis to accept Joseph Johnson's refugee plan, but later it became an inducement for Israel to end its nascent nuclear arms program as well as a bid for Jewish votes ahead of the 1962 midterm election.[108] Whatever its main motivations, the Hawk sale marked the start of a new strategic partnership between the United States and Israel as well as an end to the pretense of American neutrality in the Arab-Israeli conflict.

As the U.S.-Israel partnership deepened throughout the 1960s, not only did Washington's commitment to resolving the Palestinian refugee problem begin to recede but even the reality of what had occurred in 1948 was eventually forgotten. Kennedy may have been the first to apply the term "special relationship" to Israel, but it was Lyndon Johnson who endowed the phrase with meaning as well as substantial U.S. resources. "You have lost a very great friend," Johnson told an Israeli diplomat shortly after Kennedy's assassination in November 1963, "but you have found a better one."[109] Like Truman, Johnson had a personal affinity for the Jewish state as well as a tendency to surround himself with friends and advisers with strongly pro-Israel leanings. Johnson vastly expanded American arms sales to Israel, putting an end to the U.S. policy of avoiding becoming a major arms supplier to either side in the Arab-Israeli dispute. Kennedy had been alarmed by Israel's determination to develop an atomic bomb and urged Israel to abandon its nascent nuclear program and sign on to the Nuclear Nonproliferation Treaty and allow inspections of the Israeli nuclear facility in Dimona. However, Johnson tamped down Washington's protests of Israel's nuclear program and declined to tie the sale of high-tech fighter jets to a commitment to denuclearize as the Pentagon had recommended. Moreover, Johnson steadily began to align U.S. policies with Israel's. In 1964 the State Department acquiesced in the Israeli government's March 1964 decision to stop recognizing American (and other) passports bearing the entry "Jerusalem, Palestine," marking the first major shift in U.S. policy on Jerusalem since 1947.[110] The Johnson administration also worked diligently to block measures opposed by Israel at the UN, including proposals aimed at protecting refugee property rights in Israel and any mention of Palestinian or refugee "rights."[111]

Apart from perfunctory calls for "justice for the refugees," Johnson showed little interest in the refugee problem and, much to the relief of Israel's leaders, made no serious attempt to deal with the issue. Despite their persistence in denying responsibility for the refugee problem, up until then Israeli officials had at least been willing to engage on the issue, often denying that they had ever adopted a policy of "not one refugee," as some had alleged.[112] After Johnson's arrival in the White House, however, Israeli officials simply dropped the pretense. In his June 1964 meeting with the U.S. president, Prime Minister Levi Eshkol explained to Johnson that Palestinian refugees "really are not people within the classic meaning of refugees. They are used by the Arab nations to develop enemies against Israel."[113] Whether Eshkol meant to cast doubt on their status as refugees or as a nation, the message was the same: the Palestinians had no legitimate claims or grievances against Israel. Two years later, Israeli officials informed Johnson's secretary of state, Dean Rusk, that Israel would no longer entertain any proposals that involved repatriation, which would henceforth be considered tantamount to calling for Israel's destruction.[114] Johnson's own views tracked closely with those of Israeli leaders, as illustrated in this passage from his memoirs:

> I was aware of the deep resentment Arab leaders felt over Israel's emergence as a nation-state. I knew that many Arab refugees in the area still had not been absorbed into community life. But I also knew that various Arab leaders had used the issue of Israel and the tragic plight of the refugees to advance personal ambitions and to achieve the dominance of Arab radicals over Arab moderates. I knew that resentment and bitter memories, handed down from generation to generation, could only endanger all those who lived in the Middle East. I was convinced that there could be no satisfactory future for the Middle East until the leaders and the peoples of the area turned away from the past, accepted Israel as a reality, and began working together to build modern societies, unhampered by old quarrels, bitterness, and enmity.[115]

Gone was any sense of Israel's responsibility in the creation of the refugee problem much less of Washington's involvement in it.

There was little doubt that Arab leaders had exploited the Palestinian cause and the plight of the refugees for their political purposes, though perhaps no more so than American politicians had used Israel to advance their own "personal ambitions" in the United States. Moreover, the "old quarrels" to which Lyndon Johnson alluded had occurred less than a decade and a half before he took office. The noted Palestinian historian Walid Khalidi ranks Johnson as one of the worst American presidents in terms of the damage caused to Palestinians by his policies, second only to Harry Truman.[116] Yet, unlike Johnson, Truman had at least understood the nature and the causes of the Palestinian refugee problem, even if he had failed to address them as a matter of policy. Within less than two decades, American policymakers had lost sight of the roots of the Israel-Palestine conflict, and allowed the basic guidelines for Arab-Israeli peace to be rewritten as well.

PART II

Evolution of the Blind Spot: 1967–93

3

Missed Opportunities

We cannot deliver the minimum demands of the PLO, so why talk to them.

—U.S. Secretary of State Henry Kissinger, August 1976

On September 6, 1970, commandoes belonging to the Marxist-leaning Popular Front for the Liberation of Palestine (PFLP) hijacked four U.S.-bound, commercial jetliners en route from various European airports.[1] One of the hijackings was foiled in midflight, resulting in the killing of one hijacker and the detention of another. A second plane was diverted to Cairo, where the passengers were allowed to deplane and then the plane was blown up by the hijackers. The two remaining planes were forced by hijackers to land at a remote desert airstrip north of the Jordanian capital, Amman. Days later, PFLP militants commandeered a fifth airliner over Lebanon and forced it to land in Jordan, where it joined the other two. Within a few days, most of the roughly four hundred passengers and crew members held hostage in Jordan were released and two more planes were blown up.

The audacious operation carried out by the PFLP triggered a major confrontation between Jordanian forces and Palestinian guerrilla groups that ultimately resulted in their expulsion, along with the entire PLO leadership, from the Hashemite kingdom, but not before putting the Palestinian question back on the international—and on Washington's—agenda. As Walter Cronkite reported on the *CBS Evening News* in the midst of the crisis, "Palestinian guerrillas, in a bold and calculated action . . . thrust back into the world's attention a problem diplomats have tended to shunt aside."[2] "We had to shock an indifferent world and a demoralized Palestinian nation," said the PFLP leader, George Habash. "The world has forgotten Palestine. Now it must pay attention to our struggle."[3] Habash's cynicism encapsulated the perennial dilemma of Palestinian politics: as destructive and as damaging as the hijackings were to their cause, insofar as they forced Israel, the United States, and the international community to take up the Palestinian issue, the tragic reality was that terrorism worked.

For the first two decades of Israel's existence, most U.S. policymakers viewed the conflict as one between Arab states and Israel. That began to change shortly after the 1967 war, when the Palestinian national movement literally exploded on to the scene. But as Washington's awareness of Palestinian nationalism grew, particularly after the 1973 Arab-Israeli war, so, too, did the drive to keep the Palestinians out of the diplomatic process. It was during the period between the 1967 Arab-Israeli war and the Israeli invasion of Lebanon in 1982 that the basic foundations of the current peace process were first laid. No American policymaker had a greater influence on shaping that process than Henry Kissinger, who was both the godfather of the Middle East peace process and the architect of U.S. policy toward Palestinians.[4] The three pillars of Kissinger's strategy—American and Israeli preeminence, incrementalism rather than a comprehensive approach to peacemaking, and, most important, the strategic exclusion of the PLO—would continue to define American diplomacy well beyond his time in office. Although Jimmy Carter did make a serious attempt to bring the PLO into the peace process, ultimately both his and Yasser Arafat's leadership were too constrained by their own internal politics to permit a mutual accommodation.

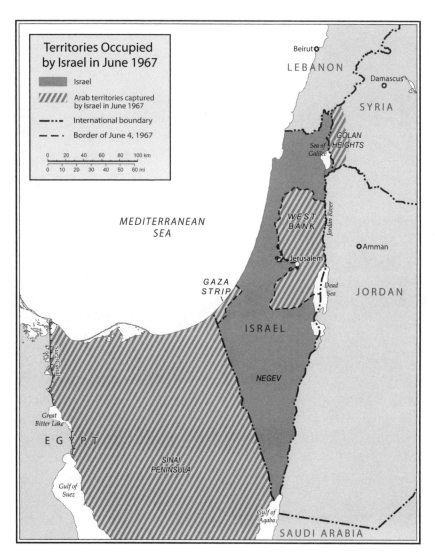

Territories Occupied by Israel in June 1967

▨	Israel
▥	Arab territories captured by Israel in June 1967
·—··—··—	International boundary
—·—·—	Border of June 4, 1967

```
0    20    40    60    80   100 km
0   10   20   30   40   50   60 mi
```

Beirut

LEBANON

Damascus

SYRIA

GOLAN HEIGHTS

Sea of Galilee

MEDITERRANEAN SEA

WEST BANK

Jordan River

Amman

Jerusalem

GAZA STRIP

Dead Sea

JORDAN

ISRAEL

NEGEV

Suez Canal

Great Bitter Lake

E G Y P T

SINAI PENINSULA

Gulf of Suez

Gulf of Aqaba

SAUDI ARABIA

Source: Adapted from United Nations map

THE TERRORISM PARADOX

Israel's lightning-fast victory over Egyptian, Syrian, and Jordanian forces in June 1967 redrew the political map of the Middle East and permanently altered the nature of the Israeli-Palestinian conflict. The Arabs' defeat in just six days left Israel in control of the West Bank and the Gaza Strip, Egypt's Sinai Peninsula, and Syria's Golan Heights. Israelis saw themselves transformed almost overnight from a tiny nation struggling for survival into a regional superpower. The routing of Arab armies, which the Arabs rather inadequately labeled *al-naksa*, "the setback," shook the Arab world to its core and set off a wave of anti-Americanism across the region. The loss of large swaths of sovereign Arab territory transformed the conflict from a solidarity-based struggle over Palestine and the plight of its refugees into a genuine regional conflict in which key Arab states now had their own claims and grievances against Israel.

In the aftermath of the war, UN Security Council Resolution 242, adopted on November 22, 1967, replaced the largely defunct Resolutions 181 and 194 as the framework for a new peace process now led by the United States. Resolution 242 called on Israel to withdraw from Arab territories occupied during the war in return for peace with Arab states, making the "land-for-peace" formula a cornerstone of American Middle East policy. The text of the resolution was deliberately vague, leaving the matter of whether Israel was required to relinquish all of the territories it occupied or merely most of them open to interpretation.[5] As a former American diplomat involved in the process later explained, Resolution 242 "meant one thing to the Israelis and their friends, and another thing to the Arabs and their friends. And that ambiguity probably made it possible to pass the resolution, but it has plagued peacemakers ever since."[6] Apart from calling for "a just settlement of the refugee problem," the resolution did not mention the Palestinians, particularly the 1.2 million then living under Israeli occupation in the West Bank and Gaza. This omission, along with the reframing of the conflict as a territorial dispute between sovereign states, was condemned by Palestinian political factions and became the basis of the PLO's opposition to it for years to come.

In addition to solidifying the U.S.-Israel special relationship, the war established the United States as the preeminent power in Arab-Israeli diplomacy. Despite Washington's opposition to the annexation of East Jerusalem and other Israeli actions after the war, the United States worked to ensure that the resolution adopted by the Security Council would not "tie Israel's hands before the negotiations."[7] American officials maintained that Israel should not have to withdraw from all of the territory it occupied, some of which could be retained as a "bargaining chip" in exchange for peace and recognition by Arab states.[8] Disagreement over how to interpret Resolution 242, including Washington's hedging on the scope of an Israeli withdrawal, ultimately doomed UN mediator Gunnar Jarring's mission to facilitate peace talks between Israel and Arab states, and marked the end of the UN's peacemaking role in the Middle East.

Washington's new role as chief arbiter in the conflict imbued the nascent Arab-Israeli peace process with the idiosyncrasies of U.S. policymaking, including its characteristic ambivalence. This was particularly true during the Nixon administration, which was torn between those players who focused on the particular needs of the conflict and those who viewed the Middle East peace process as a platform for advancing other U.S. interests—namely, attempting to weaken the influence of the USSR in the Arab world. On one side stood Secretary of State William Rogers, who put forward a peace plan in line with Resolution 242 that called for an Israeli withdrawal from the Sinai Peninsula and the West Bank, minus East Jerusalem and other areas unilaterally annexed by Israel; Gaza's fate was left to future negotiations. But Nixon's powerful national security adviser, Henry Kissinger, scoffed at both the "land-for-peace" formula and the State Department's contention that post-1967 realities were damaging America's standing in the Arab world.[9] Instead, Kissinger believed a "continuing [Arab-Israeli] deadlock was in our interest," and set out to undermine Rogers and his peace plan.[10] Nixon initially sought to keep Kissinger, who was both Jewish and a Holocaust survivor, out of the Middle East morass. As he became increasingly consumed by the war in Vietnam and the Watergate scandal, however, Nixon gradually ceded control over foreign policy, including the Arab-Israeli portfolio, to Kissinger. For the dyed-in-the-wool Cold Warrior Kissinger, the Arab-Israeli conflict was just another front in the global competition between the United States and the Soviet Union. Kissinger believed that "only the United States could bring about a settlement" of the conflict, but only on the basis of American and Israeli preeminence.[11] The main thrust of U.S. policy, therefore, was not to facilitate a settlement between Arab states and Israel but to support its Israeli ally against the USSR's Arab clients, such as Syria and the PLO, while working to pry other Arab states away from Soviet influence.

The war also radicalized Palestinian fedayeen groups, the largest of which was Yasser Arafat's Fatah. Fatah and other Palestinian guerrilla groups had carved out havens in the refugee camps of Arab host states, particularly Jordan and Lebanon, which they used to cultivate their political networks and to plan and carry out attacks on Israel. The fedayeen remained politically marginal in the Arab-Israeli conflict until March 1968, when Israeli troops invaded the town of Karameh on the East Bank of the Jordan River in a bid to end cross-border attacks by Palestinian guerrillas and crush the fedayeen once and for all. Despite suffering heavy losses, Palestinian guerrillas withstood the onslaught and managed to inflict losses on the Israeli army, turning a tactical defeat into a political victory. The battle of Karameh propelled Arafat's Fatah and the fedayeen into instant political stardom among Palestinians and put them "on the global map of Third World revolutionaries."[12] "After Karameh," observed one Israeli military commander, "we understood that we had on our hands a serious movement."[13] The fedayeen were now the dominant force in Palestinian politics and soon took control of the PLO's parliament-in-exile, the Palestinian National Council (PNC), pushing through a new covenant calling for the liberation of Palestine through armed struggle. By early 1969 Arafat had assumed the chairmanship of the PLO and transformed it into a genuinely independent vehicle for Palestinian political expression.[14]

The Palestinian havens were especially problematic for Jordan, where the fedayeen had established a virtual "state within a state" and, since Karameh, had assumed an air of untouchability. Fatah's main rival within the PLO, the Marxist-oriented PFLP, for whom the enemy was "Zionism, imperialism and Arab reaction," was particularly antagonistic toward the Hashemite throne.[15] For King Hussein, an armed Palestinian presence with statist ambitions in a country with a Palestinian majority posed an existential threat. At the same time, Palestinian guerrilla attacks on Israel subjected the kingdom to devastating Israeli reprisals that caused considerable human and physical damage.

Outraged by the multiple airplane hijackings orchestrated by the PFLP in September 1970, King Hussein set out to quash the fedayeen once and for all. Equally determined to preserve their base of operations against Israel, Palestinian factions closed ranks and called for the overthrow of the monarchy, which triggered civil war in Jordan. The PLO decision to overthrow the Jordanian monarchy was reached incrementally and, in the case of Fatah at least, reluctantly. It had less to do with ruling over the East Bank than with maintaining what Yezid Sayigh has termed the "duality of power" between the Hashemite throne and the PLO and preserving, in the fedayeen's words, the use of Arab territory around Israel as a "legitimate arena for Palestinian struggle." The differences were therefore irreconcilable: whereas Hussein's survival depended on avoiding confrontation with Israel, the PLO's survival hinged on promoting such confrontations.[16] A generation after Hussein's father had colluded with the Zionists and the British to swallow up Arab Palestine, the Palestinians were now in a position to return the favor. However, the fedayeen had vastly underestimated the Jordanian monarch's resolve and greatly overestimated their own capabilities. The bloody showdown between King Hussein and the fedayeen, dubbed "Black September," ended disastrously for Arafat and the PLO, who were forced to relocate to Lebanon. But the showdown succeeded in establishing Palestinian nationalism as a force to be reckoned with in the region.[17]

The violence undoubtedly sullied the image of Palestinians in the United States, but it also put the Palestinians squarely on Washington's and the international agenda as never before. Until Karameh, the Palestinians were still predominantly seen by American officials as refugees or in otherwise apolitical terms.[18] "The Palestinians were not seen as a separate party to the conflict in those days by very many people," recalled Alfred Leroy Atherton Jr., the State Department's deputy director for the Near East. As a result, there "was little talk in those days about a Palestinian political role."[19] The assertion of a distinct national or political identity by Palestinians was therefore seen as subversive, even radical. Even the largely ineffectual and soon-to-be-ousted PLO chief, Ahmad Shuqeiri, managed to earn the label "the radical leader of the Palestine Liberation Organization." A later CIA appraisal more accurately described Shuqeiri as an Egyptian puppet, "operating rather ineffectually behind a facade of militancy."[20]

Awareness of the political significance of the Palestinian issue within the policymaking establishment increased dramatically after Karameh. By 1968, CIA national intelligence estimates had identified the Palestinian issue as the heart of the Israeli-Arab conflict.[21] A Pentagon memo dated August 1969 similarly argued that the United States should be more concerned with the plight of the Palestinians.[22] At the same time, the Palestinians continued to be seen through the distortive lens of extremism and superpower rivalry.[23] In the increasingly polarized global order of the Cold War, the Palestinians fell squarely in the "radical" camp, alongside Syria, Iraq, Algeria, and other Arab nationalist, pro-Soviet regimes. The terms "terrorist" and "radical" were applied liberally to Palestinian factions, leaders, and politics,[24] which were seen collectively as "adamantly opposed to any solution other than the destruction of Israel."[25] Political and financial backing for Palestinian political groups by various Arab states was likewise seen as evidence of extremism, while the presence of a sizable Palestinian community in a given country was often considered a "radicalizing" influence. American officials were particularly baffled by the conservative Gulf state Kuwait, which despite its "traditional pro-Western pull" had become a major source of financing and organizational support for Palestinian fedayeen groups.[26]

A handful of officials inside the administration argued for taking a more serious look at Palestinian grievances and perhaps even speaking to the Palestinians directly, though their voices remained marginalized. Several months before the fedayeen's showdown with King

Hussein, the American ambassador in Amman, Harry Symmes, warned that betting on King Hussein was a losing bet for the U.S. government and urged Washington to begin looking seriously at the PLO as the true representative of the Palestinians.[27] Around the same time, Under Secretary of State Elliot Richardson made a similar plea, arguing, "The fallacy of the great-powers policy or the involved powers in dealing with the situation from the establishment of the state of Israel to date had been the failure to recognize that the aggrieved party were the Palestinians."[28]

The September 1970 PLO-Jordan civil war marked a watershed in U.S. policy that produced two opposing trends. Although much of the foreign policy establishment began to recognize the need to accommodate Palestinian nationalism on some level, others, most notably Kissinger, saw events in Jordan as a reason to double down on the "Jordanian solution." Assistant Secretary of State Joseph Sisco commented that a peace settlement would require "giving expression to the Palestinian movement and very likely in the form of an entity."[29] An internal assessment by the National Security Council advised that the United States would have no choice but to acknowledge "the Palestinians as a distinct and relevant political voice," either "through their own representation in negotiations—or perhaps through Israel and Jordan—but nevertheless deserving a separate political entity in the final outcome."[30] President Nixon, too, declared, "No lasting settlement can be achieved in the Middle East without addressing the legitimate aspirations of the Palestinian people."[31] But Kissinger remained unconvinced. With Nixon preoccupied with the Watergate scandal and Kissinger now firmly in charge of foreign policy, Kissinger's views carried the day.

If anything, events in Jordan reinforced Kissinger's "strategic opposition to the PLO" and his belief that a resolution of the Palestinian issue lay with the Hashemites alone.[32] Even as attitudes toward the Palestinians elsewhere in Washington and throughout much of Europe were beginning to change, in Kissinger's eyes the Palestinian problem remained first and foremost an "an inter-Arab concern" whose resolution lay with Jordan's King Hussein rather than the PLO.[33] In fact, Kissinger viewed the PLO war in Jordan as an attempt to turn the kingdom into "a national homeland for the Palestinians," an idea that actually was anathema to the Palestinian movement.[34] The PLO, in his view, was at best "overtly anti-American" and at worst a tool of the Soviet Union; either way, the PLO was irrelevant to the diplomatic process.[35] Kissinger's attitudes toward the Palestinians were deeply ideological. As a student of the realist school, Kissinger naturally believed in the primacy of sovereign states over nonstate actors such as the PLO. To the Israelis, the idea of engaging with the PLO or, for that matter, any form of Palestinian nationalism was a nonstarter. Israeli military and political leaders alike regarded Fatah and other fedayeen groups not as legitimate political actors but as agents of terror—a security problem to be contained or crushed. Moreover, as a Cold Warrior, Kissinger sought to forge an international balance of power based on the preeminence of the United States and its allies, which in the Middle East meant Israel. All of these factors precluded the possibility of any sort of political role for the PLO.

Kissinger feared that a protracted stalemate over the West Bank would ultimately work against Washington's key allies, Israel and Jordan. "The longer the delay of negotiations to relieve Israeli occupation of the West Bank," Kissinger said, "the more inexorable the growth of the political status and weight of the PLO." His hope was that Israel would return the West Bank to Jordanian rule. But the Israelis were not ready to discuss a withdrawal from the West Bank, an area rich in biblical symbolism with considerable natural resources and strategic potential. Instead, Israel's Labor government offered to give Jordan administrative control over the civilian population in the West Bank while Israel's army continued to control the land. But even Kissinger understood the limits of such a proposal: "It was, in fact, an amazing reflection of how little the Israelis understood Arab psychology that the proposal was continually put forward," Kissinger later wrote in his memoirs, since "not even the most moderate Arab head of government could accept administering the West Bank under Israeli occupation."[36] It was an interesting admission, given the nature of the Oslo Accords some two decades later, in which the PLO ultimately did consent to administering the West Bank under Israeli occupation.

KISSINGER OPENS A WINDOW . . .

As Kissinger thought about ways to keep the PLO out of the peace process, members of Arafat's leadership cadre had begun looking for ways to ingratiate themselves with the United States. In late 1969, Arafat authorized his security chief, Ali Hassan Salameh, to open a secret back channel with a CIA field agent, Robert Ames. Through the clandestine track, which took off after 1973 and continued on and off until Ames's death in 1983, Fatah agreed to provide security for American diplomats in Lebanon as well as valuable intelligence on a wide range of anti-American threats. Among other things, the Ames-Salameh track helped to thwart terror plots by rogue Palestinian factions, including a December 1973 assassination attempt on Kissinger.[37] But the Ames-Salameh track failed to open up a political channel as Arafat had hoped, and in July 1973 the PLO leader began making direct overtures to the United States.[38]

The timing was somewhat audacious on Arafat's part. Three months earlier, two American diplomats in Khartoum had been murdered by the Black September Organization, a Fatah terror cell under Arafat's direction. The Black September Organization was also responsible for the murder of eleven Israeli athletes at the 1972 Munich Olympic Games. American intelligence officials had little doubt as to Arafat's involvement in such operations.[39] Communicating through various intermediaries, Arafat promised to "put the lid on" fedayeen operations targeting Americans "as long as both sides could maintain a dialogue."[40] Arafat's messages also signaled a readiness to live in peace with Israel.[41] The move was part of a new PLO strategy aimed at cleaning up the group's image and transforming it into a legitimate political actor. Kissinger, having no interest in a political dialogue with the PLO but nonetheless intrigued by the gesture, instructed his people to respond to Arafat with a "nothing message." The administration's communication was vague and equivocal, but more substantive than Kissinger had let on: The United States was prepared to be part of "a far-reaching solution of the refugee problem" and also recognized that "some Palestinians have an interest in political self-expression of some kind." The carefully worded letter included an additional teaser: "If the Palestinians are prepared to participate in a settlement by negotiation, the US would be pleased to hear their ideas."[42]

The outbreak of war between Arab states and Israel in October 1973 created a new opportunity for U.S.-PLO engagement. The surprise attack by Egypt and Syria on Israel shattered the aura of Israeli invincibility, creating the possibility of a diplomatic settlement that Kissinger hoped to capitalize on. Following the war, UN Security Council Resolution 338 reaffirmed the land-for-peace formula and paved the way for a new Middle East peace conference in Geneva in December 1973. The new postwar dynamics posed several challenges for Kissinger, who had replaced Rogers as secretary of state shortly before the war. In retaliation for the U.S. decision to resupply the Israeli military during the war, the Arab Gulf states had imposed an oil embargo on the United States and its allies. In addition to lifting the Arab oil embargo, Kissinger was eager to pursue a diplomatic settlement that shored up Israel's position at the expense of Arab "radicals" while keeping both the Soviets and the UN from having any meaningful role in the peace process. At the same time, Kissinger found the renewed emphasis on comprehensive peace and the "Palestinian question" deeply unsettling. In keeping with his rather Machiavellian worldview, Kissinger devised a diplomatic process based on incrementalism and a hierarchy of power. Through Kissinger's "step-by-step" diplomacy, as it became known, Israel would deal with the Egyptian, Syrian, and Jordanian tracks separately. Palestinian participation would be decided at the end of the process, preferably after the PLO had been weakened.[43] To help get Arab leaders on board, Kissinger held out the prospect of U.S. recognition of the PLO or even the possibility of a Palestinian state, neither of which he ever seriously considered.[44] As Kissinger later wrote in his memoirs, "The idea of a Palestinian state run by the PLO was not a subject for serious discourse."[45]

President Anwar Sadat of Egypt was already predisposed to go along with Kissinger's approach. While Syria's Hafez Assad remained highly skeptical of American intentions, Sadat had concluded that the road to regaining Egyptian territory captured by Israel ran through Washington and that the United States in fact "held all the cards." Hoping to earn a seat at the table in the upcoming Geneva peace conference, Arafat stepped up his outreach to Washington after the war. This time Kissinger was more responsive, authorizing the first high-level contacts between the United States and the PLO. Arafat hoped to use the dialogue to convince the Americans that he was more like Sadat than like Assad, and that he was prepared to make far-reaching compromises. However, the PLO was not Egypt—least of all for Kissinger, who continued to view the Palestinian issue as a hindrance to his diplomatic strategy. According to Kissinger, "Once the PLO are in the peace process they can radicalize all others. They'll raise all the issues the Israelis can't handle, and no other Arab can raise any other issues once the PLO is raised."[46] Kissinger did agree to engage with the PLO but only as way to limit its ability to create problems for his diplomatic strategy and with the ultimate aim of sidelining it.

Kissinger's engagement with the PLO was designed to appease and pacify the PLO leadership while giving up nothing of substance. Kissinger arranged for CIA Deputy Director Vernon Walters to meet with a senior PLO official, Khalid al-Hassan, in the Moroccan city of Rabat in early November 1973. In keeping with his concede-nothing strategy, Kissinger restricted Walters to a "listening brief" while instructing him to inform his Palestinian interlocutors that the "United States has no proposals to make."[47] Walters told the Palestinians, "There are no objective reasons for antagonism between the United States and the Palestinians" and even thanked the PLO for adopting a "responsible position" during the war, but stressed that the United States would not take a position on Palestinian political claims.[48] Each side took away from the meeting more or less what it had put into it. From the American perspective, "The meeting yielded no lasting results."[49] Al-Hassan meanwhile described the encounter as "historic," adding "that everything the Palestinians had done had been to get the attention of the United States."[50] Walters and al-Hassan met a second time, in March 1974, but the meeting broke no new ground and the channel soon fizzled.[51]

Kissinger had no intention of including the Palestinians in the peace process. As he explained to his staff, "Anything including the PLO would run us into trouble with the Jews in the maximum conditions for irresponsibility."[52] Furthermore, Kissinger insisted, the PLO's radicalism made it incapable of compromise. Starting in late 1973, however, the PLO leadership began signaling its willingness to live in peace with Israel in return for a Palestinian mini-state in the West Bank and Gaza Strip. One early sign that Arafat's leadership was moving away from the PLO's traditional maximalist stance came during the Arab summit in Algiers of November 1973. The Algiers Declaration omitted two previously sacred clauses regarding the Palestinian struggle: the "indivisibility of Palestine" and the sanctity of "armed struggle" as the only path to liberate Palestine. While Israelis dismissed the new language as a restatement of PLO policy to destroy Israel in two phases instead of one, "Arab observers saw it for what it was: a step toward accepting Israel."[53] Within the Palestinian movement such ideas were still highly contentious and, to many, treasonous, although Arafat had begun gradually pushing the PLO in that direction. According to the CIA, even hardliners in the PLO leadership such as Salah Khalaf, Fatah's number two man and a key organizer of the Black September terror cell, were showing "elements of rather startling pragmatism."[54] Shortly before the Geneva peace conference—to which the PLO was not invited—Arafat sent a clear message to the U.S. administration: "The Palestine Liberation Organization in no way seeks the destruction of Israel, but accepts its existence as a sovereign state; the PLO's main aim at the Geneva conference will be the creation of a Palestinian state out of the 'Palestinian part of Jordan' plus Gaza." The message was delivered to U.S. officials by the Ivorian president.[55] This was the first, albeit unofficial, endorsement by the PLO leadership of a permanent settlement based on a two-state solution, some fifteen years before it became official PLO policy and a quarter century before either the Israelis or the Americans came around to the idea.

After being cut out of the Geneva process, Arafat moved to reinforce his pragmatic overtures by working to enhance the PLO's international profile and that of the Palestinians. In November 1973, the European Community called for respecting the "legitimate rights of the Palestinians" and acknowledging Palestinians as a party to the conflict for the first time.[56] The Russians soon followed, in March 1974, when Foreign Minister Andrei Gromyko held his first publicly acknowledged meeting with Arafat, which the CIA described as a "small step toward formal Soviet recognition of Arafat and his [PLO] as spokesman for the Palestinians."[57] Meanwhile, Arafat set out to bring the PLO's public posture more into line with its private messages to the Americans. In June 1974, the Palestinian National Council issued a declaration in which it adopted a new political program calling for the establishment of a "fighting national authority" on any liberated part of Palestinian territory. Arafat had attempted to enlist American support for the initiative two months earlier, to which Kissinger responded with a "bland reply," essentially reiterating previous formulations regarding Palestinian "legitimate interests."[58] The declaration riled Arafat's political opponents and intensified the debate within the administration over the possibility of a PLO role in the peace process.[59] According to the White House staffer William Quandt, despite its "heavily qualified language," the new PLO statement amounted to a recognition "that it was prepared to settle for a Palestinian state consisting only of the West Bank and Gaza."[60]

Arafat's political opponents understood it the same way. The Popular Front for the Liberation of Palestine suspended its membership in the PLO Executive Committee and formed a Rejectionist Front to oppose the PLO's "liquidationist" policies.[61] Meanwhile, Quandt and a fellow NSC staffer, Robert Oakley, continued in vain to press Kissinger to reassess his position. Despite his fiery rhetoric, they argued, "Arafat clearly wishes to move toward a political settlement recognizing, at least implicitly, Israel's right to peaceful existence," and warned that continuing to exclude the PLO would likely yield more terrorism.[62] Kissinger remained unmoved. Despite entreaties by Arab leaders as well as a growing chorus of voices within the administration to bring the PLO into the process, Kissinger still maintained that "involving the PLO was incompatible with the interests of any of the parties to the Middle East conflict."[63] If anything, the PLO's pragmatic gestures and growing international acceptability only strengthened Kissinger's determination to keep it out of the peace process. In a meeting with American

Jewish leaders in early 1974, a frustrated Kissinger warned that "if the Israelis don't make some sort of arrangement with Hussein on the West Bank in six months, Arafat will become internationally recognized and the world will be in a chaos."[64]

Kissinger's timing was off by only a few months. In October, the Arab League unanimously recognized the PLO as "the sole legitimate representative of the Palestinian people."[65] Kissinger blasted the decision as a "fit of emotional myopia" by Arab states for having "deprived Hussein of his negotiating role on the West Bank" and for identifying "the one group Israel was least likely to accept, as interlocutor."[66] The high point of Arafat's international strategy, however, came a few weeks later—appropriately enough, on U.S. soil. On November 22, 1974, despite stern U.S. opposition, the UN General Assembly voted overwhelmingly to recognize the PLO as "the representative of the Palestinian people" and granted it official observer status in the UN; a second resolution affirmed the "right of the Palestinian people to self-determination."[67] The first major UN action on Palestine since the 1947 partition resolution, it was a significant blow to American diplomacy, which had worked tirelessly to defeat it. Speaking against the measure, the American representative, John A. Scali, railed against the PLO's history of violence and terror, insisting that the "sole alternative to the sterile pursuit of change through violence is negotiation," in which "each party must remain committed to negotiations." Yet it was precisely his government's failure to recognize the Palestinians as a party to the negotiations that had brought the PLO to the UN in the first place.[68]

Scali's harsh words for the PLO seemed incongruous with the VIP treatment that had been afforded the Palestinian leader only a few days earlier. Upon their arrival in New York City ahead of the UN vote, Arafat and his entourage were greeted by members of the U.S. Secret Service and New York police. Two helicopters ferried Arafat and members of the PLO delegation to UN headquarters, while a motorcade decoy made its way from the airport to the Waldorf Astoria, with sharpshooters posted along the route. "They treated him just like a head of state," recalled one member of the Palestinian delegation.[69] In light of the number of death threats lodged against the PLO leader as well as a recent assault on a Palestinian official by members of the Jewish Defense League, authorities had reason to be concerned for Arafat's safety.[70] But there were also other explanations for the pomp and circumstance surrounding Arafat's arrival. The UN vote took place in the middle of sensitive Egyptian-Israeli disengagement talks and shortly after the Arab embargo had been lifted. Thus Arafat's warm welcome may have been a gesture to Washington's friends in the Arab world. Moreover, on the day of his speech, a meeting took place at the Waldorf Astoria between a senior CIA official and Arafat's security chief, Ali Hassan Salameh. The two men reportedly agreed to formalize the existing U.S.-PLO understandings on security and intelligence sharing, including cooperation against common enemies, although accounts differ as to what the United States agreed to provide the PLO in return (written records from this meeting remain classified).[71] Shortly thereafter the CIA began training Palestinian forces to provide security for U.S. diplomats in Beirut. For the Americans, the meeting was strictly utilitarian, reaffirming security cooperation as the bedrock of U.S.-PLO ties for the foreseeable future. Arafat, however, hoped that by ingratiating himself with the Americans and elevating the PLO's status, he would make it impossible for Washington to continue ignoring the PLO politically. He was wrong on both counts.

. . . AND CLOSES A DOOR

Arafat's red-carpet reception in November 1974 would be the high point of the U.S.-PLO relationship for some time to come. Not long after the delegation's departure, the State Department issued new guidelines instructing government officials to avoid "any statement or action which could be construed as implying official USG recognition of PLO as quote sole legitimate representative of Palestinian people unquote or in any other capacity."[72] A month later, the Immigration and Naturalization Service issued a blanket ban on visas to "past and present members" of the PLO. A number of State Department officials criticized the ban, which appeared to target Palestinians more generally and not just "PLO terrorists," as "highly questionable and offensive."[73]

Ironically, the period surrounding the PLO's christening at the UN was marked by unprecedented levels of openness and debate on the Palestinian issue in Washington. With the Palestinians now on the global agenda and Kissinger's shuttle diplomacy in the Middle East going nowhere, the new administration of Gerald R. Ford began a reassessment of U.S. policy toward the Palestinians. As part of the internal reassessment, a new interagency working group on the Palestinians was launched to explore the possibility of bringing the Palestinians, and perhaps even the PLO, into the peace process. The working group also commissioned two Washington think tanks to conduct their own studies of the issue. The better known of the resulting reports, published by the Brookings Institution in December 1975, called for a comprehensive peace settlement and an end to Kissinger's "step-by-step" approach as well as some form of Palestinian self-determination.[74]

Even Congress, where pro-Israel and anti-PLO sentiment ran high, had begun to show signs of change. Extensive hearings were held in the House of Representatives on the "Palestine issue" throughout the fall of 1975. The hearings covered the whole range of issues, from the origins of the conflict to the nature of Palestinian politics to the shortcomings of existing U.S. policy, and included such expert witnesses as Edward Said and Ibrahim Abu-Lughod, the first Palestinian voices to be heard from on Capitol Hill in more than a half century.[75] A handful of U.S. senators and representatives, including Senate Foreign Relations Committee Chairman J. William Fulbright, spoke openly for the first time about Palestinian rights and past suffering. "Israel, I am convinced can and should survive as a peaceful, prosperous society—but within the essential borders of 1967," Fulbright stated. "That much we owe them, but no more. We do not owe them our support of their continued occupation of Arab lands. . . . The Palestinian people have as much right to a homeland as do the Jewish people."[76] A number of lawmakers, including Senators James Abourezk of South Dakota and Howard Baker of Tennessee, even dared meet with Arafat at his headquarters in Beirut, increasing the Palestinian leader's legitimacy and opening up new channels of communication with Washington.[77]

For reasons of both domestic politics and ideological rigidity, however, the newly opened political space in connection with the Israeli-Palestinian conflict did not translate into a more accommodating policy toward the PLO or the Palestinians. In fact, the reverse occurred. For one, Washington's policy reassessment remained firmly anchored in Kissinger's approach. The new policy was unveiled in September 1975 at the House hearings on Palestine. Speaking for the administration, the State Department's Hal Saunders laid out the new U.S. approach to the Palestinians. The United States would no longer treat the Palestinians solely as a refugee problem but recognized that they were a "political factor which must be dealt with if there is to be a peace between Israel and its neighbors. . . . In many ways, the Palestinian dimension of the Arab-Israeli conflict is the heart of that conflict."[78] Despite drawing angry cries from Israel and its supporters in Congress, Saunders's testimony marked more of a shift in tone than in actual policy. The statement acknowledged the need to take the "legitimate interests of Palestinians" into account, while saying nothing about their rights. Moreover, the statement still spoke of "bringing issues of concern to the Palestinians into negotiation," rather than bringing the Palestinians themselves into negotiations, while allowing others, including the Israelis, to determine what those issues and interests were and which ones could be brought into the process. Despite having vetted the statement beforehand, Kissinger still saw fit to publicly disavow it.[79]

To the extent there was a shift in U.S. policy toward the PLO, it was in the opposite direction. Kissinger's primary focus was on drawing Israel into negotiations with Egypt, which remained the centerpiece of his diplomatic strategy. In an effort to push Egyptian-Israeli disengagement talks, the Ford administration leaned heavily on the Israelis, hinting at a possible reduction in Israel's massive aid package if it did not make further withdrawals in Sinai.[80] The threat earned Kissinger a considerable amount of grief from the Jewish community.[81] To provide some incentive to the Israelis, in September 1975 Kissinger signed a secret memorandum of agreement with the Israelis pledging not to "recognize or negotiate with" the PLO until it recognizes Israel's right to exist and accepts UN Security Council Resolution 242 (which Israel had accepted but interpreted very narrowly), and promising to "consult fully" with Israel beforehand.[82] Significantly, despite the U.S. focus on PLO terrorism, the memorandum of agreement made no mention of terrorism. Just as terrorism had not prevented the U.S. from engaging with the PLO, it also was not the reason for excluding it from the peace process. For Arafat, however, who had already incurred the wrath of hard-line Palestinian factions with his implicit acceptance of Israel, formal recognition was out of the question. The same went for Resolution 242, which the PLO continued to reject for its failure to address the Palestinians' right to self-determination.[83] Kissinger's 1975 pledge was the first of many restrictions placed on the PLO in the decades ahead.

In the meantime, Kissinger continued to ignore the PLO's pragmatic gestures while working to undermine the PLO in the diplomatic arena and in the field. After the UN General Assembly, over American opposition, invited a representative of the PLO to address the Security Council "on an equal footing with other parties" in late 1975, the administration promised the Israelis that it would veto any attempt to alter the terms of the peace process or "force PLO participation in negotiations in any form."[84] Meanwhile, as the State Department continued to debate the idea of a Palestinian mini-state in the West Bank and Gaza, signals of a moderating stance from the PLO leadership became more explicit.[85] In February 1976, Arafat announced a new peace initiative calling for a gradual Israeli withdrawal from the West Bank and Gaza leading to the creation of a Palestinian state.[86] A *Washington Post* editorial urged the Ford administration to test the offer by the PLO, which it said "should be encouraged, not ignored or dismissed at every turn."[87] However, Kissinger continued to maintain that the PLO was a "Soviet Trojan horse" that was incapable of moderating.[88]

Despite Kissinger's overall aversion to the PLO, even he recognized the utility of dealing with the organization. Since its founding in 1964, the PLO had maintained a presence in New York in connection with the United Nations, but never in the American capital. As a gesture to

Sadat, Kissinger had agreed to allow the PLO to open an office in Washington in late 1976.[89] However, when the Israelis and American Jewish groups protested, Kissinger promptly ordered deportation of the two PLO representatives, Issam Sartawi and Sabri Jiryis, who had just arrived in Washington.[90] More important to Kissinger was preserving the PLO's security cooperation, which he had exempted from the memorandum of agreement. The start of the Lebanese civil war in 1975 increased American dependence on PLO security coordination.[91] Fatah security forces had helped to coordinate the evacuation of American citizens from Beirut in the summer of 1976, for which President Ford personally thanked the PLO in a letter delivered by Kissinger via Egyptian intermediaries.[92] At the same time, the American ambassador in Beirut, G. McMurtrie Godley, had been urging Kissinger to open a dialogue with the PLO to assess its suitability as a negotiating partner and help strengthen Palestinian moderates. "However inconvenient its existence or repugnant its behavior," Godley stated, the "PLO has become a reality" and has the sympathy and support of millions of Palestinians and Arabs."[93] Kissinger had a different objective in mind, and instead viewed the Lebanese crisis as an opportunity "to help weaken the PLO without losing the PLO."[94] His hope was that an intervention in Lebanon by Syria and the Syria-backed Saiqa faction of the PLO would weaken Fatah and keep the PLO divided, allowing Kissinger to continue promoting Jordan as the representative of the Palestinians.[95]

It is not entirely clear whether Kissinger genuinely believed he could undermine the PLO in the political and diplomatic realms without seriously diminishing its security value to the United States or was simply prepared to sacrifice the latter in order to attain the former. Either way, the result was to embolden Palestinian rejectionists at the expense of PLO moderates, paving the way for increased instability. A CIA analysis at the time concluded, "Yasir Arafat's relatively moderate policies favoring Palestinian participation in Middle East peace negotiations have so far brought few tangible gains for the Palestinians." As a result, "Arafat recently has shown a heightened awareness of the need to protect his personal position and to prevent the erosion of Palestinian popular support in the direction of the radicals."[96]

TYING CARTER'S HANDS

Jimmy Carter's approach to the Middle East conflict was almost the polar opposite of Kissinger's. In addition to putting greater emphasis on human rights and international law, Carter and his new secretary of state, Cyrus R. Vance, had a deeper appreciation for the plight of the Palestinians. "The continued deprivation of Palestinian rights was not only used as the primary lever against Israel," Carter later wrote, "but was contrary to the basic moral and ethical principles of both our countries."[97] Much of the new thinking that had been generated in the preceding years was now incorporated into the administration's policies. The Carter administration revived the long-dormant policy of affirming the illegality under international law of building Jewish settlements in the Israeli-occupied territories. Most important, Carter sought to bring the Palestinians into the peace process and was prepared to apply pressure on all sides, including on Israel, to advance the peace process. A resolution of the Palestinian question became an essential requirement for Middle East peace, alongside an Israeli withdrawal from the territories it occupied and a final peace settlement between Israel and its Arab neighbors. Despite the best efforts of Carter's peace team to put together a formula that would enable the PLO to join the peace process, each side remained too politically constrained to meet the other's minimal demands. Moreover, while Carter proved to be an effective mediator between Israel and Egypt, the combination of Kissinger's 1975 memorandum of agreement, domestic political pressures, and the absence of a strategic imperative effectively tied Carter's hands when it came to the Palestinians.

Eager to capitalize on the change of administration in Washington, Arafat used his CIA back channel to request an official dialogue with the new administration.[98] For their part, Carter and Vance hoped to revive the Geneva peace process, while avoiding the errors of their predecessors. Their primary challenge was to find a way to bring the Palestinians into the process while working within the constraints imposed by Kissinger's pledge and the pro-Israel lobby. Those constraints became evident early in Carter's presidency. Carter's impromptu endorsement of a "Palestinian homeland" in March 1977 sent shockwaves throughout the Middle East and Washington.[99] He was later forced to clarify that this would have to be "in the framework of the nation of Jordan or by some other means."[100] The 1975 memorandum of agreement in effect became a "no contact" pledge that tied the hands of Carter's and subsequent administrations.[101] Although forced to reaffirm that he would "never negotiate or recognize the PLO" until it accepted Israel's right to exist and Resolution 242, Carter later complained that it was "absolutely ridiculous that we pledged under Kissinger and Nixon that we would not negotiate with the PLO."[102]

The first order of business for Carter's peace team, which included National Security Adviser Zbigniew Brzezinski and the NSC staffer William Quandt, was to devise a formula by which the PLO leadership could accept Resolution 242, thus allowing them to participate in the peace process. A clear and unambiguous acceptance of Resolution 242 would be considered by the administration tantamount to a renunciation of PLO calls for destroying Israel. This was no easy task, given Arafat's position among the various Palestinian factions in Lebanon. In addition to the PLO's rejectionist factions, such as the PFLP and Saiqa, Arafat also had to contend with their Syrian sponsors, who now occupied much of Lebanon. After an intensive exchange throughout the summer of 1977 involving multiple third parties, including Saudi, Egyptian, and various American intermediaries, the administration arrived at what it felt to be a workable formula. If the PLO could accept Resolution 242 "with clarification"—for example, by stipulating its desire for an independent state—the Palestinians would be allowed to participate in an anticipated Geneva II conference, slated for December 1977, as part of a unified Arab delegation. The PLO could select the Palestinian participants, provided they were not official office holders in the organization.[103] The proposal showed considerable creativity and pragmatism on the part of the administration's Middle East team. The administration also recognized the inherently political nature of the Palestinian question, which was "not just a refugee issue but one involving the political status of the Palestinians" and, as such, was a "co-equal core issue" to those raised in Resolution 242.[104]

Arafat and others in the PLO leadership agreed in principle with the administration's formulation of accepting Resolution 242 with modifications, but requested additional assurances to help neutralize opposition back home.[105] Arafat asked the administration for a gesture of American "intentions toward the concept of [a] Palestinian state" or "some similar moral commitment to the idea of a Palestinian state."[106] The thinking was that if Palestinians were being asked to endorse land-for-peace they should also be allowed to reap its benefits in the form of actual territory. The American formulation had stopped short of acknowledging a Palestinian right to self-determination, falling back on what would now become a standard formula calling for "self-determination by the Palestinians in deciding on their future status." In other words, the Palestinians should be just one of the parties that could decide on their future, alongside Israel, Arab states, the United States, and others. It was, as one American scholar noted, an attempt "to split an unsplittable difference" by in effect trying to separate "self" from "determination."[107]

Still hoping to find a workable compromise, Arafat proposed various alternative formulations involving "reserved acceptance" of Resolution 242 in return for U.S. recognition of the PLO as the "legal representative" of the Palestinian people or a "guarantee" of PLO participation in the Geneva II conference, none of which were acceptable to U.S. officials.[108] While the Egyptians, Saudis, and Russians all urged Arafat to accept the proposal, the Syrian regime opposed it and pressed him to hold out for something more tangible than a dialogue.[109] With both statehood and recognition of the PLO off the table, the PLO's Central Council voted down the American proposal in late August.[110]

The Carter administration's communications with the PLO, however indirect, alarmed the Israelis, particularly the newly elected prime minister, Menachem Begin of the hard-line Likud Party. For Begin—who had been a leader of the terrorist Irgun gang—the PLO was "the most barbaric organization since the Nazis."[111] Although Israel had accepted Resolution 242 in principle, Begin refused to accept U.S. arguments that its withdrawal-from-territory clause also applied to the West Bank and Gaza Strip.[112] Instead, Begin's government proposed a form of autonomy for Palestinians in the West Bank and Gaza that would be limited to the people but not the land. Israel responded to the U.S.-PLO dialogue and the PLO's possible acceptance of Resolution 242 by launching a major offensive against Palestinian targets in August 1977 and announcing a series of new settlement plans in the West Bank and Gaza.[113] Begin pulled back Israeli forces from Lebanon, but only after a stern warning from Carter that Israel was in violation of the 1976 Arms Export Control Act prohibiting the use of American weapons for offensive purposes.

The fallout from an October 1977 joint U.S.-Soviet communiqué further slowed the momentum toward a U.S.-PLO arrangement. The communiqué's reference to the "legitimate rights of the Palestinian people" angered the Israelis and triggered a backlash from the Jewish community in the United States. After being inundated with angry letters from American Jewish leaders, Carter backtracked, reverting to the customary language of "legitimate interests" favored by previous administrations.[114] To mollify the Israelis, the administration proposed a joint working paper to agree on various procedural and substantive aspects of the peace talks ahead of the Geneva II conference. Among other items, the U.S.-Israel working paper gave Israel the ability to veto participation of additional parties in the negotiations and agreed to treat the issue of Jews who fled Arab states after the creation of the Jewish state as being equivalent to the issue of Palestinian refugees.[115]

Sadat's surprise visit to Israel in November 1977 put an end to U.S. attempts to bring the PLO into the peace process and preempted the planned peace conference in Geneva. Sadat's initiative also forced Arafat to end the PLO's delicate balancing act between Egypt and Syria. "I was on the mountaintop," Arafat complained, "but Sadat threw me into the valley."[116] The PLO's opposition to Sadat's peace overtures was not merely ideological. As Kissinger was fond of pointing out, there could be no war without Egypt and no peace without Syria. A separate Egyptian peace deal with Israel would take Egypt out of the military equation, hence eliminating a key source of leverage for the Palestinians vis-à-vis Israel while leaving them vulnerable and exposed. Without the threat of war, Israel would be free to sideline the Palestinian issue while swallowing up as much of the West Bank as it could. Out-wardly, Arafat had little choice but to join Palestinian rejectionist fac-tions and other Arab rejectionists in denouncing both Sadat's "high treason" and American diplomacy. Palestinian rejectionists were now allowed back into the PLO fold. Initially taken by surprise by Sadat's initiative, the Carter administration quickly adapted its strategy. In a sort of modified version of the old "step-by-step" approach, Brzezinski described the new U.S. Middle East peace strategy in terms of three concentric circles: an Egyptian-Israeli deal, an Israeli-Jordanian-Palestinian agreement on the West Bank, and an Israeli-Syrian agreement.[117]

In the meantime, the two sides resorted to mutual recriminations. The Carter administration accused Arafat and the PLO of intransi-gence, which in Brzezinski's words effectively meant "bye bye PLO."[118] Arafat responded in kind, accusing Israel and America of "trying to eliminate the Palestinian factor, the Palestinian people. . . . When he says, 'Farewell to the PLO,' what he really should be saying is 'Fare-well to his interests in this area.'"[119] Despite the mutual goodbyes, how-ever, neither side was prepared to close the door completely.

Meanwhile, as the September 1978 Camp David summit drew near, the situation on the ground continued to deteriorate. In March 1978, PLO militants from Arafat's Fatah movement hijacked a bus along Israel's coastal highway, and killed thirty-eight Israelis, including thir-teen children. In retaliation for the massacre, in early March the Israelis launched another large-scale invasion of Lebanon; they killed more than a thousand Lebanese and Palestinian civilians and displaced tens of thousands more. The Israelis eventually withdrew, but only after the Carter administration forced their hand by pushing through a Secu-rity Council resolution condemning the action and setting up a new United Nations peacekeeping force in Lebanon. What Israel's leaders regarded as restoring its "deterrent" capability was viewed by much of the international community as an attempt to pound the Palestinians into submission. Carter expressed sympathy for the Israeli victims of terror but, as he later wrote in his memoirs, also felt that Israel had "grossly overreacted in Lebanon to the terrorist attack on some Israeli citizens, destroying hundreds of villages, killing many people, and making two hundred thousand Lebanese homeless." What was more, Carter continued, "They are using American equipment for invasion of a foreign territory, which is illegal."[120]

For the administration, the question was no longer how to bring in the Palestinians, but what Sadat could secure on their behalf.[121] Sadat had continued to insist that he would not pursue a separate peace and that it was necessary to secure some tangible achievement toward justice for Palestinians. Carter's answer to the Egyptian leader's concerns was embodied in his January 1978 declaration that a peace settlement should "enable the Palestinians to participate in the determination of their own future." The statement, as one scholar described it, represented a "codification of American ambivalence."[122] In the lead-up to the September 1978 Camp David peace summit, Carter worked to bridge the differences between Sadat and Begin, both of whom subsequently gave in to American pressure. Unable to fully appreciate Sadat's insistence on a linkage between an Egyptian-Israeli settlement and progress on the Palestinian issue, Carter convinced him to drop his demand for some sort of statement on Palestinian self-determination.[123] In return, Begin relented on the questions of Israel's withdrawal from the Sinai and the applicability of Resolution 242 to the West Bank.

In addition to laying out the broad outlines of an Egyptian-Israeli peace treaty at Camp David, American, Israeli, and Egyptian negotiators also agreed on a separate framework for a comprehensive Middle East peace. While giving a nod to "the legitimate rights of the Palestinian people," the centerpiece of the agreement was a proposal for limited Palestinian autonomy in the West Bank and Gaza. The result was a vaguely defined Palestinian "autonomy" plan that did not provide for a freeze on Israeli settlement construction or Palestinian control of land and resources and included no means of enforcement. Hence, it held few incentives for Palestinians in the occupied territories.[124] Continued settlement activity, which the administration regarded as a form of "creeping annexation," remained a consistent source of tension between Carter and Begin throughout the Camp David talks.[125] The failure to secure a written commitment from Israel to freeze settlements was, according to William Quandt, the "biggest error of Camp David."[126] Had U.S. officials secured such a commitment at the time, it might have set a precedent for subsequent administrations and perhaps mitigated the kind of attrition that took place in U.S. settlements policy after Carter.

Palestinian and Arab reaction to the summit was swift and severe. A unified PLO Central Council rejected the West Bank and Gaza autonomy plan and adopted a joint program to oppose the Camp David Accords. The Arab League voted to freeze relations with Egypt and later suspended Cairo's membership. Meanwhile, the Carter administration and the PLO leadership seemed intent on keeping the door open for some type of mutual accommodation, even as circumstances were forcing it shut. Having lost faith in Sadat, Arafat requested a direct dialogue with Washington in late 1978.[127] The Carter administration could not agree to direct contact but quietly enlisted the help of Edward Said, a prominent Palestinian American intellectual and a member of the PNC, to probe Arafat's receptiveness to the "242 with reservations" formula. By the time Said was able to convey the message directly in early 1979, Arafat's disposition toward the Americans had changed significantly. According to Said, Arafat rejected the offer. "I want you to tell Vance that we're not interested," Arafat informed Said. "We don't want the Americans. The Americans have stabbed us in the back. This is a lousy deal. We want Palestine. We don't want to negotiate with the Israelis. We're going to fight."[128]

Arafat's sudden unresponsiveness may have been due to the mounting pressure he faced internally from Palestinian rejectionists and especially from the Syrians, at whose mercy the PLO operated in Lebanon. Arafat may have also felt betrayed by Washington's inability to protect his security chief and long-time CIA asset, Ali Hassan Salameh, who had been assassinated in Beirut a few weeks earlier by means of an Israeli car bomb in January 1979. As the former CIA analyst Bruce Riedel explains, the Israelis "viewed Salameh as a threat in two ways. First, he was a terrorist. But second, he was in a clandestine relationship [with the Americans via the CIA]. They thought such a relationship was the first step to seeing Arafat in the White House. So they would have wanted him dead just for that reason alone."[129] Violence in Lebanon caused by the Israeli-PLO clash continued to escalate over the next several years. In August 1980, Israel carried out its largest operation in two years, taking its war against the PLO deep into Lebanese territory and setting the stage for the next major war.

It is impossible to know whether Arafat's acceptance of the American formula regarding Resolution 242 before and after the Camp David summit would have brought the Palestinians into the peace process, particularly given the Begin government's continued rejection of any accommodation with Palestinian nationalism. Eventually the two main sticking points—the PLO's inability to explicitly accept Resolution 242 and the United States' inability to explicitly accept Palestinian statehood—would be overcome, but only after many years and considerable bloodshed.

4

Abnormal Normalization

No matter that some Israelis believe that the PLO can
and must be totally and visibly smashed into oblivion—
we will pay a great price in terms of our broad interest
and international image.

—Philip Habib, U.S. presidential peace envoy to the
Middle East, June 27, 1982

On May 17, 1987, Secretary of State George Shultz took the podium
before an admiring audience of the American Israel Public Affairs
Committee, the powerful pro-Israel lobby group also known as AIPAC,
in Washington, DC. In his address Shultz spoke of the deepening ties
between the United States and Israel, which had expanded
considerably under the Reagan administration, before addressing
prospects for Arab-Israeli peace. Taking aim at the Palestinian
leadership, Shultz denounced Arafat and the PLO, which he declared
were "not qualified" to be part of the peace process. As Shultz railed
against the PLO, he found himself unwittingly leading the audience in
a chant of "PLO? Hell, no!"[1] The somewhat awkward moment was
more than just a testament to the remarkable influence of the pro-
Israel lobby in Washington. Eighteen months later, in the final weeks

of Ronald Reagan's second term in office, Shultz shocked both AIPAC's leaders and the Israeli government by authorizing the first-ever official dialogue between the United States and the PLO.

Shultz's apparent change of heart had less to do with a strategic reorientation in the U.S. approach to the Palestinians or the peace process than with the slow, halting, and reluctant realization that there was no alternative to dealing with the PLO. This rather abnormal process of normalization with the PLO began in the lead-up to Israel's 1982 invasion of Lebanon and continued in various forms during and after the crisis. That this process of quasi-normalization occurred alongside a parallel process of growing Palestinian political weakness and fragmentation was not entirely coincidental. Internal PLO weakness and division in the aftermath of the Lebanon War led Arafat to become more moderate and more eager to enter into Washington's good graces and to accommodate U.S. demands, even as it remained a source of overall violence and instability in the region. But as the PLO's moderation and visibility increased, so too did the attempts by Israel and its allies in Congress to keep the PLO out of the peace process. It was only after the Palestinian uprising of 1987 and the collapse of the "Jordan option" a year later—both of which coincided with the PLO's desire to reassert its relevance—that the Reagan administration began to actively seek a dialogue with the PLO. Ironically, although the launching of an official U.S.-PLO dialogue opened the door to Palestinian participation in the peace process, it did so while formally precluding a formal role for the PLO.

"AMBER LIGHT": THE LEBANON WAR

Israel's invasion of Lebanon, launched on June 6, 1982, did not come as a surprise either in the region or in Washington. The immediate trigger for the invasion was a failed assassination attempt in London on Israel's ambassador to the UK by the Abu Nidal network three days earlier (though it had been in the planning for at least a year).[2] Israeli officials had briefed the Reagan administration on their war plans in

December 1981, and the PLO had received prior intelligence on the planned invasion as well. However, no one fully grasped the true scope of Israel's war aims.[3] Once the invasion began, Prime Minister Menachem Begin and Defense Minister Ariel Sharon assured American officials that the operation would extend no further than 40 kilometers into Lebanon and last no more than forty-eight hours. Within a week, however, Israeli forces had reached the outskirts of Beirut. After reaching a truce with the Syrians, the Israeli Defense Force (IDF) turned its attention to the PLO. Now besieged in predominantly Muslim West Beirut, the PLO was subjected to fifty days of fierce bombardment by air, land, and sea.

The stated purpose of the operation, code-named "Peace for Galilee," was to put an end to rocket fire by Palestinian fedayeen on population centers in the north of Israel, but its real aims were more political than military. On reaching Beirut, Sharon demanded the total evacuation of PLO personnel from the city. His primary objective was "not to halt Palestinian attacks on northern Israel. Rather, it was an attempt to produce a weakened, more radical PLO under Syrian dominance . . . which would pose a lesser political threat to Israel, and one with which Israel would feel less international pressure to eventually negotiate."[4] In addition to eradicating the "PLO's infrastructure" in Lebanon, Sharon hoped to install a friendly government in Lebanon dominated by his Maronite Christian allies, the Phalange. Sharon also set his sights on Palestinian refugee camps, which were hotbeds of Palestinian guerrilla activity in which Palestinian grievances against Israel were kept at a boil.[5] The Lebanon crisis marked the first instance of American mediation between Israel and the PLO. However, Washington's inability to influence Israeli behavior before and during the war ultimately derailed its mediation efforts during one of the bloodiest episodes of the Israeli-Palestinian conflict and eventually led to U.S. troops being drawn into the conflict.

Senior Reagan administration officials, including Secretary of State Alexander Haig and the president's Middle East peace envoy, Philip Habib, made their opposition known as soon as they were briefed on the Israeli plan.[6] According to Habib's deputy, Morris Draper, American officials spent the next six months "trying to head off what we perceived to be a catastrophe not only for Israel, but also for the West and the United States."[7] The Pentagon took an equally dim view of the planned invasion.[8] In late May 1982, less than two weeks before the invasion, Sharon again pitched his war plans to senior administration officials. Habib "firmly, loudly and unambiguously opposed Sharon's agenda." Haig, on the other hand, was more equivocal, informing Sharon that the "U.S., as an ally, cannot tell Israel not to defend its interests," while stipulating that there needed to be "a recognizable provocation . . . that will be understood internationally, and any reaction must be in proportion to the provocation."[9] Although the Pentagon and other American officials had made clear the administration's opposition to an Israeli invasion, Haig's words represented "a clear, strong amber light," according to Samuel Lewis, the American ambassador in Tel Aviv. Haig has since rejected that charge.[10] Whatever his intentions, Haig's response clearly was not a red light. Once again, the lack of clarity in Washington played into Israel's hands. As Robert Dillon, who served as the U.S. ambassador to Lebanon during the war, later explained, "Sharon didn't care whether Americans approved or disapproved of whatever he wanted to do. He just wanted to know whether the US would take any punitive action. He had sat and looked at the Secretary [Haig], who was a distinguished military officer himself, and immediately understood that the Americans were not going to take any action if Israel were to invade Lebanon. He saw that there would be no political costs to Israel."[11]

Internal divisions within the administration over how to respond to the invasion only added to the confusion surrounding U.S. policy. Most of Reagan's national security team, including Secretary of Defense Caspar Weinberger, Vice President George Bush, and National Security Adviser William Clark, favored an immediate Israeli withdrawal backed by a credible threat of sanctions. However, Haig and a handful of others wanted to give Israel more time to complete its mission and ultimately convinced Reagan not to pressure Israel to withdraw until PLO and Syrian fighters did the same.

Haig was a staunchly anti-Soviet conservative who shared the president's view of the Middle East as a key battleground in the struggle against global communism and Soviet expansionism. At the center of Reagan's Middle East policy was the notion of "strategic consensus," according to which key American allies, such as Israel and Saudi Arabia, would set aside their differences, particularly with regard to the Palestinians, to join the U.S.-led struggle against the Soviet menace.[12] Israeli leaders embraced their status as a "strategic asset" to the United States, recasting the century-old territorial dispute with the Palestinians as an extension of the struggle against the Soviet Union and its Arab clients. "Palestinian terrorism, PLO terrorism, has been one of the main means by which the Soviets are preparing the ground for further extension into the Middle East," Sharon told the *Wall Street Journal* shortly before the invasion.[13] In other words, Israel's enemies were also America's enemies. Reagan's own understanding of Palestinian history and politics was rather limited. John L. Helgerson, a CIA analyst, recalls briefing Reagan shortly after his election on the inner workings of Palestinian politics, at which point President-elect Reagan looked up and said, "'But they are all terrorists, aren't they?'" Helgerson added, "My heart just sank."[14]

Notwithstanding Reagan's crude stereotypes, Haig's views were considerably more developed and ideological than the president's. Habib's biographer, John Boykin, describes Haig as "the most fervent supporter of Israel ever to serve as America's secretary of state."[15] In addition to seeing Israel as a bulwark against Soviet-inspired radicalism, Haig also shared the Kissingerian view that weakening the PLO, mainly through the destruction of its military power in Lebanon, would be an asset to the peace process. Other senior administration officials shared this view, including Reagan's UN ambassador, Jeanne Kirkpatrick.[16] According to Wat Cluverius, who served as the U.S. consul general in Jerusalem shortly after the war, Haig considered the Palestinians to be "kind of a phony issue" and was "intrigued by the idea that the Palestinian problem could be made to just disappear by force, the Sharon thesis."[17]

Indeed, Haig's primary interest was to get the issue of the Palestinians "off the table."[18] This could be achieved in one of two ways: talk to the PLO in order to find some mutually beneficial accommodation, or defeat it—and Palestinian nationalism—once and for all. Haig began with the former and eventually settled on the latter. The administration's top priority in the region remained the Egypt-Israel treaty and the delicate normalization process between the two countries, which U.S. officials hoped to insulate from the ongoing cross-border violence in Lebanon. Shortly after Habib was recruited to broker a ceasefire between Israel and the PLO in Lebanon, Haig authorized two senior Middle East hands, Nick Veliotes and Wat Cluverius, to conduct "a totally private, indirect negotiation with Arafat" through John Mroz, the head of the EastWest Institute, a New York–based think tank.[19] Mroz had been tapped by Arafat to convey the message to the new administration that the PLO might be ready to recognize Israel in exchange for American recognition of the PLO.[20] "We got very close, until the Israelis invaded Lebanon," said one of the American diplomats involved. "But that, too, was part of our multifaceted attempt to protect the Egyptian-Israeli Treaty." After the Israeli invasion, Arafat became convinced that the Mroz dialogue had been a ruse by Haig as part of his collusion with Israel to destroy the PLO.[21]

The sheer scale and brutality of the IDF operation in Lebanon shocked the administration. Three weeks into the Israeli offensive, more than 10,000 Lebanese and Palestinians had been killed and some 19,000 wounded, the vast majority of them civilians, while IDF losses stood at 300 dead and 1,200 wounded.[22] The high civilian toll as well as Sharon's apparent obsession with killing Arafat incensed Washington's Arab allies, including President Hosni Mubarak of Egypt, who came under intense pressure to abrogate the new peace treaty with Israel. Meanwhile, Habib complained bitterly at being repeatedly misled by Sharon; he blamed the IDF's frequent truce violations for preventing him from brokering an end to the carnage. Reagan was personally taken aback by the ferocity of the IDF offensive. "I was angry," Reagan wrote in his diary of his phone call to Begin, "I told him it had to stop or our entire future relationship was endangered. I used the word holocaust deliberately & said the symbol of war was becoming a picture of a 7-month-old baby with its arms blown off."[23] Reagan went on to warn Begin that Israel's continued shelling of Beirut would put U.S.-Israel relations "in the balance," although the administration later vetoed a

UN Security Council resolution calling for military sanctions against Israel.[24] Habib urged Reagan and his new secretary of state, George Shultz, to follow through on their threats by suspending weapons shipments to Israel. Shultz had replaced Haig as secretary of state a few weeks into the crisis. Apart from a brief delay in the delivery of aircraft and cluster bombs, however, American weapons continued to flow to Israel throughout the war.[25]

The mixed signals from the U.S. administration allowed Sharon to prosecute the war in Lebanon more or less on his terms and ultimately doomed American mediation efforts. Communicating with the PLO through Lebanese security officials, Habib finally secured a comprehensive ceasefire arrangement in mid-August. Under the U.S.-brokered agreement, Palestinian fighters and other PLO personnel would be evacuated from Beirut in exchange for an Israeli pledge not to invade West Beirut and American guarantees to protect the tens of thousands of Palestinian civilians left behind. The United States would also contribute troops to a multinational force to serve as a buffer and oversee the plan's implementation. With the crisis seemingly under control, Reagan announced a new peace initiative on September 2 that called for a "just and lasting peace," while Habib received a hero's welcome in Washington and was awarded the Presidential Medal of Freedom.

The celebrations were premature, however. One week after the PLO's evacuation in early September, American and other international forces were suddenly withdrawn. Days later, on September 14, Bashir Gemayal, the Israeli-backed Christian leader of the right-wing Phalange Party, was assassinated just as he was about to become the president of Lebanon. The following day, on September 15, under various and conflicting pretexts, the Israeli army entered West Beirut and surrounded the Palestinian refugee camps of Sabra and Shatila. Over the next three days, under the watchful eyes of the IDF, Phalangist militiamen set about "liquidating whatever humanity came in their path."[26] At the end of the killing spree, between 1,000 and 2,500 women, children, and elderly men lay dead.[27] Despite Sharon's insistence that "2,500 terrorists" had been hiding out in the camps, American officials found no evidence to back his claim. Recently declassified transcripts of meetings between U.S. and Israeli officials as events were unfolding suggest that the administration could have done more to prevent the massacre but allowed itself to be browbeaten by Sharon. "Working with only partial knowledge of the reality on the ground," the Middle East scholar Seth Anziska wrote in the *New York Times*, "the United States feebly yielded to false arguments and stalling tactics that allowed a massacre in progress to proceed."[28] Before withdrawing from the city, the IDF occupied a number of PLO offices and institutions, including the Palestinian Research Center, which Israeli soldiers ransacked, looted, and defaced. The center housed thousands of books, land deeds, photos, maps, and other documents related to the lives and properties of Palestinian refugees before Israel's creation.[29]

The very outcome that Habib had worked to avoid—and that the United States had pledged, in writing, to prevent—had now happened. President Reagan expressed "outrage and revulsion over the murders" in Sabra and Shatila and ordered the Marines back to Lebanon under a new multinational force. A few members of Congress again raised the threat of cutting aid to Israel before promptly abandoning it. Expressing the sense of betrayal felt by many of his colleagues in the administration, Morris Draper accused the Israeli prime minister of telling "a straight-out, 100 percent, bald-faced lie to the United States government, his great friend."[30] A few senior officials went further, acknowledging American culpability. "The brutal fact," Shultz would later acknowledge, "is we are partially responsible."[31]

In the end, Israel's Lebanon war produced no winners, only degrees of losers. Ultimately, the highest price was borne by Palestinian and Lebanese civilians, with more than 19,000 killed and another 30,000 wounded (not including the Sabra-Shatila massacre) and dozens of villages and neighborhoods damaged or destroyed. The PLO, which had now relocated to Tunis and was greatly weakened both militarily and politically, estimated its own losses at around 1,000 killed and 6,000 captured.[32] For its part, the invasion cost Israel some $3.5 billion in direct and indirect economic costs, and the lives of roughly 650 Israeli soldiers.[33] Israel's conduct in the war badly tarnished its image around the world and divided Israeli society. Begin was forced to resign in October 1983 and left public life soon afterward. Israel's Lebanon debacle became Israel's "Vietnam," a mistake that even Begin came to regret a few years later.[34] The architect of Israel's Lebanon war, Ariel Sharon, was forced to step down as defense minister, and an official Israeli inquiry later determined that he bore "personal responsibility" for failing to prevent the massacre in Sabra and Shatila. Most Palestinians and Arabs, meanwhile, continued to believe that the massacre had been part of Sharon's plan all along.[35] (Although he continued to be dogged by allegations of war crimes, Sharon would be politically rehabilitated in the 2000s.)[36]

Despite paying a toll in human and material terms, Israel had been largely spared any political, much less legal, consequences for their actions, much of which was borne by the United States. If Lebanon was the first test in the U.S.-Israel strategic partnership, it is difficult to imagine a less propitious outcome. That the United States had so little sway over its Israeli ally in a crisis that most administration officials agreed was detrimental to American interests raised serious questions about Washington's ability to serve as an effective mediator. Philip Habib resigned in July 1983, citing the damage done to his and America's credibility.[37] Not only was the United States now fully identified with Israel, but, following the redeployment of U.S. Marines to Lebanon in the wake of the Sabra and Shatila massacre in September 1982, it also became party to the conflict, as well as a ready target for a wide variety of armed groups operating out of Lebanon. The Israeli invasion and subsequent occupation of southern Lebanon became an incubator for several new radical groups, including the Iranian-backed Shia militia, Hezbollah. The bombings of the U.S. embassy and Marine barracks by pro-Iranian radicals in April 1983 and October 1983, respectively, claiming the lives of more than 240 Americans, served as grim reminders of the perils of ill-conceived American intervention and marked "the beginning of America's deadly encounter with a political Islamist movement."[38]

THE KISSINGER TEST

The administration's anger over Israel's conduct throughout the Lebanon crisis quickly subsided, highlighting the extent to which the basic premises of the U.S.-Israel relationship were immune from developments on the ground. Even as U.S. troops remained bogged down in Lebanon, the U.S.-Israel strategic partnership was greatly expanded throughout the 1980s. Reagan formalized Washington's commitment to maintaining Israel's "qualitative military edge" over any potential adversaries. Meanwhile, Israel became the first nation to sign a free trade agreement with the United States. Thanks in large part to AIPAC and its army of activists and campaign donors, Congress did its part to boost Israel's sagging economy in 1985 by doubling its annual economic aid package to nearly $2 billion, all of it in the form of a grant, alongside the $1.4 billion it received in military grants.[39]

Meanwhile the diplomatic process remained stalled. The Reagan Plan had been put together by a core group of experienced Middle East hands from the State Department and the intelligence community and billed as a "fresh start" to the peace process. More than anything, however, it embodied the administration's deep ambivalence about the conflict and about Palestinian leaders. The plan called for granting Palestinians in the West Bank and Gaza "full autonomy" in association with Jordan, while explicitly ruling out the possibility of a Palestinian state and precluding a role for the PLO. Shultz later acknowledged that he briefly considered dealing directly with the PLO during the Lebanon war in return for its public acceptance of Resolution 242 and Israel's right to exist. "I decided it was a bad idea," Shultz wrote in his memoir, "The Lebanon crisis was one problem; an Arab-Israeli solution for the West Bank and Gaza was another. I would not try to bargain one for the other." To help instill confidence in the plan, Reagan called for "the immediate adoption of a settlement freeze by Israel" in the occupied territories. At the same time, however, he "assured the Israelis and informed the Arabs . . . of the U.S. view that Jews must have the right to live on the West Bank, historically Judea and Samaria," employing the term favored by the settler movement and the Israeli right.[40] In any case, a resolution of the Israeli-Palestinian conflict was not a top priority for Reagan or Shultz. The Reagan Plan, as one American diplomat explained, was designed "to recapture the momentum of Camp David and the Egyptian-Israeli Treaty, which was our first priority to implement."[41]

It was just as well. Although the PLO had signaled a readiness to work with the Reagan Plan, Israel opposed the proposal in its entirety. Committed to the vision of Greater Israel, encompassing the whole of the land between the Mediterranean Sea and the Jordan River, Begin's Likud government firmly opposed an Israeli withdrawal from the West Bank and Gaza; nor was it prepared to grant Palestinians meaningful self-rule, insisting that "autonomy is for people not territory."[42] Israel's rejection of the plan effectively rendered it "dead on arrival." The Reagan Plan "failed literally the day we presented it to the Israelis," recalled Daniel Kurtzer, a former American diplomat then stationed in Tel Aviv.[43] In place of a political settlement, Shultz proposed focusing on improving the "quality of life" of Palestinians in the occupied territories through economic and humanitarian assistance plans. While conceding that "problems in the West Bank and Gaza" could not be fully resolved without an end to the Israeli occupation, Shultz hoped that funneling aid money and promoting private investment into the occupied territories would stem the spread of extremism.[44] The program never got off the ground, thanks to resistance from Israel's Likud government, while Palestinians largely viewed it as an attempt to make the occupation more palatable.[45]

If Shultz had failed to see the connection between the Lebanon crisis and the occupied territories, Israeli leaders had not. For Begin and Sharon, Lebanon and the West Bank and Gaza were two fronts in the same struggle against Palestinian nationalism. Begin breathed new life into Israel's settlement project in the occupied territories, which had languished under a decade of Labor Party rule, while simultaneously cracking down on Palestinian institutions and leaders, particularly those deemed to be "PLO sympathizers."[46] Both efforts were spearheaded by Ariel Sharon. As Israel's minister of agriculture from 1977 to 1981, Sharon had overseen implementation of an ambitious settlement "master plan" aimed at intensifying settlement construction in areas adjacent to the Israeli border, called the Green Line, and other strategic parts of the West Bank. The plan helped produce a nearly 150 percent increase in Israel's settler population in under a decade, from 106,600 in 1983 to 258,400 in 1992.[47] As defense minister, meanwhile, Sharon set out to create an alternative leadership in the West Bank. The plan was to assemble various rural and tribal elders in the West Bank into various "village leagues" to serve as a counterweight to the "radical" nationalist leadership of the PLO and eventually to assume the role of the self-governing authority called for in the Camp David Accords.[48] It was classic colonial-style "divide and rule." Lacking any legitimacy, Sharon's village leagues proved to be a spectacular failure. "They were quislings," recalled Brandon Grove, the American consul general in Jerusalem. "Some, if not all, were in the pay of the Israelis. They were a mediocre lot, whose experience had little to do with skills in governing, and whose backgrounds were often shady."[49]

On the Palestinian side, the war had left the PLO leadership severely weakened and divided and thus provided the first real test of Kissinger's hypothesis. Kissinger, along with his ideological fellow travelers such as Al Haig, had operated on the assumption that a weakened PLO would be a boon for peace and stability. Precisely the opposite occurred. The Lebanon crisis did not radicalize the PLO leadership but instead reinforced Arafat's moderate inclinations and his desire to get into Washington's good graces. To compensate for his weakness, Arafat's leadership was compelled to seek an alliance with Jordan's King Hussein as well as a rapprochement with Egypt. Despite the PLO's exclusion and the Reagan Plan's explicit rejection of Palestinian statehood, Arafat was keen not to reject the plan outright. Instead, the PLO pushed the Arab League to put forward its own initiative, the Fez Declaration, which called for an independent state in the West Bank and Gaza. It was the first iteration of what later became the Arab Peace Initiative of 2002. The cornerstone of Arafat's post-Lebanon strategy, however, was the alliance with Jordan's King Hussein, which began in late 1982 and culminated with the signing of the Amman Accord in February 1985. Paradoxically, the PLO's weakness and internal fragmentation gave Arafat's leadership the space to pursue his moderate agenda, since he was no longer bound by the need to achieve a political consensus. At the same time, however, a weaker and less cohesive leadership was far less able to rein in rogue elements and violent spoilers within the Palestinian camp. The period from 1982 to 1987 was therefore a time of considerable instability, violence, and terror.

Arafat went to some lengths to demonstrate moderation in order to earn a place at the negotiating table, even at the risk of triggering civil war. Under the Amman Accord, the PLO would join negotiations as part of a joint Palestinian-Jordanian delegation. The accord provided for a future Palestinian state to be part of a confederation with Jordan. In this way Arafat would ensure Palestinian inclusion in the peace process while preempting Washington's preference for the "Jordan option." However, by making Palestinian self-determination contingent on Jordanian approval, the PLO was also undermining its own claim to be the "sole" representative of the Palestinians. Arafat's alliance with the PLO's former nemesis deepened the polarization within the Palestinian camp and led to a formal break of the PLO with Damascus, which now became host to a wide variety of anti-Fatah and anti–peace process Palestinian factions.

An internal CIA assessment in 1984 warned that the "decline and probable eventual eclipse of the moderate Palestinian center represented by Arafat, together with the Palestinians' refusal to compromise on their demands for self-determination will leave the Palestinians susceptible to the appeal of extremist elements."[50] Palestinian political fragmentation and the absence of a credible diplomatic process proved a highly volatile combination, especially in 1985. Intra-Palestinian rivalry erupted into open fighting between pro- and anti-Arafat Palestinian forces in Lebanon in April 1985, starting the intermittent civil war known as the "camps wars." Following an attack by Fatah's Force 17 on an Israeli yacht in Larnaca, Cyprus, that left three Israelis dead in late September 1985, Israel sent war planes to bomb the PLO's headquarters in Tunis, killing sixty. The Security Council denounced the Israeli raid as a violation of international law and of Tunisian sovereignty (the U.S. abstained).

The Cyprus attack was followed by a string of terror attacks throughout late 1985. In early October, Mohammed Zaidan's Palestine Liberation Front hijacked an Italian cruise liner, the *Achille Lauro*, and in the process killed an elderly wheelchair-bound U.S. citizen, Leon Klinghoffer.

Several weeks later, the Abu Nidal group hijacked an EgyptAir jetliner in Malta. It resulted in the deaths of sixty passengers following a botched rescue attempt by Egyptian commandos. In late December, Abu Nidal struck again, launching simultaneous bombings of the El Al counters at the Rome and Frankfurt airports, killing a total of eighteen and wounding more than a hundred. It mattered little to the international public that such atrocities were mostly the work of rogue elements hostile to Arafat's leadership. Despite Arafat's attempts to distance himself from the attacks, the terror wave further damaged the PLO's already battered image in Washington and eventually led to the collapse of the PLO-Jordan alliance in early 1986.

Back in Washington, the post-Lebanon period became a time of intensive debate over whether and how to include the Palestinians and their leaders in the peace process. Although Sharon's Village Leagues had a few supporters within the administration, most Middle East experts at the State Department did not take the initiative seriously and worked to convince Shultz not to encourage it. "Had it been implemented," recalled Brandon Grove, "the 'Village Leagues' proposal would have been the final coffin nail for the Camp David Accords."[51] Another Foreign Service officer, Daniel Kurtzer, then stationed in Tel Aviv, used the Village Leagues controversy to press for a change in what he and many of his colleagues considered to be an outdated policy. Kurtzer sent a formal dissent memo to Secretary Shultz urging him to open a direct channel with the PLO. By refusing to talk to the PLO, Kurtzer later explained, "not only had we denied ourselves the ability to talk to the Palestinians who actually mattered, but we were also complicit in the idea of empowering the Palestinians who really don't matter." Kurtzer hoped to generate a debate on the importance of including the PLO. "There was never an expectation that I was going to change policy," he said, "but I felt it was necessary to say it. The Palestinians were a central player in the conflict and we weren't talking to them."[52] Kurtzer's memo reflected the sentiment of many inside the State Department's Near East Bureau, including Assistant Secretary of State Richard Murphy, but faced intense hostility from Israeli officials and pro-Israel activists. Ultimately it went nowhere.

"This was a missed chance," Murphy said. "It could have moved things much earlier."[53]

Shultz remained unconvinced, insisting that the PLO could "have no place in our diplomacy" and that its refusal to accept Resolution 242 and Israel's existence was a sign that the group had a "reality problem."[54] To buttress the argument that the PLO could not be part of the peace process, senior U.S. policymakers, including Reagan, Shultz, and various members of Congress, regularly cast doubt on the legitimacy of the PLO's claim to represent Palestinians.[55] Such claims were rather striking, not only because they ran counter to the assessments of the intelligence community and American diplomats in the region but also because the administration's peace plan did not allow Palestinians to choose their own representatives to future negotiations.[56] Many within Washington's policy community still harbored hopes of establishing an alternative leadership to the PLO. Among them was Dennis Ross, who served on Reagan's national security staff before joining a Washington think tank. According to a policy paper authored by Ross in 1985, Palestinian opposition to Camp David could be overcome by working with Israel to "create a credible alternative Palestinian leadership." Whether such a leadership would be viewed as legitimate in the eyes of ordinary Palestinians seemed to matter little to Ross, who went on to explain: "Initially, West Bankers will be reluctant to go along with this, but the demands of daily life will make autonomy a fact at some point."[57] Ross would later join George H. W. Bush's Middle East peace team before going on to serve as Bill Clinton's peace envoy throughout the Oslo process in the 1990s.

What was most striking about the administration's official stance toward the PLO, however, was that U.S. officials had consistently engaged with the group before, during, and after the Lebanon war. Despite the administration's subsequent denials, the Mroz backchannel of 1981–82 had been personally approved by Reagan.[58] Likewise, even as Habib negotiated with the PLO via Lebanese security officials in Beirut in the summer of 1982, Arafat had his own emissary, Nabil Shaath, conducting parallel discussions in Washington. Although barred from speaking directly to the administration, Shaath communicated with

White House and State Department officials via the Egyptian and Saudi ambassadors, and was free to meet with members of Congress, journalists, and think tanks. According to Shaath, his channel was even used to deliver an advance copy of the Reagan Plan to Arafat, as well as the PLO's non-rejection of it.[59] Such under-the-radar contacts continued after the Lebanon war, including at least half a dozen visits by PLO representatives to Washington between 1982 and 1985.[60] According to a former Shultz aide, Charles Hill, "Our internal discussion at that time was how do we talk with the Palestinians in a way that was disavowable?"[61] In other words, the problem wasn't so much in talking to the PLO as it was in being *seen* talking to them.

American engagement with the PLO was not limited to times of crisis. The announcement of the Jordanian-Palestinian joint delegation, approved and mandated by the PLO, in the summer of 1985 had greatly limited the administration's options. Realizing it could not circumvent the group entirely, the administration privately indicated that it was prepared to allow the PLO to select the Palestinian side of the delegation, provided its members were residents of the West Bank and Gaza and were not PLO members. "PLO members" was interpreted narrowly to mean members of the PLO's Executive Committee or senior Fatah officials, thus exempting from the ban members of the PNC, with whom Shultz and other U.S. officials were in frequent contact. The limits of the administration's flexibility were exposed when a meeting between the Palestinian delegates and Assistant Secretary of State Richard Murphy was scheduled for August 1985. The meeting might have been a first step toward unofficial American recognition of the PLO as an interlocutor but was abruptly canceled by the State Department. The administration gave no explanation for the last-minute cancellation, though Palestinians suggested the meeting fell apart when U.S. officials made new demands on who could or could not be a Palestinian delegate.[62] Concern over a political backlash in Washington may have also contributed to the cancellation.

Even the prospect of an indirect PLO role in the peace process seemed to be too much for Israel and its powerful supporters in Washington. Although many American and Palestinian officials considered the façade of non-dealings with the PLO to be absurd and counterproductive, the frequency of U.S.-PLO contacts set off alarm bells for Israel and its friends on Capitol Hill. In particular, leaked reports in early 1984 about Mroz's secret dialogue with the PLO set off a firestorm of outrage among Israel's supporters in Congress and spurred the pro-Israel lobby into action.[63] In October 1984, Congress passed the first of several laws aimed at keeping the PLO out of the diplomatic process. The new law reaffirmed Kissinger's 1975 memorandum of agreement prohibiting contacts with the PLO until it recognized Israel's right to exist and accepted Resolution 242, to which it now added a third condition requiring the PLO to "renounce the use of terrorism." The three conditions were enacted into law in August 1985, shortly after the Amman Accord between Jordan and the PLO and just as State Department officials were beginning to flirt with the idea of an indirect PLO role in the peace process.

The fact that these new restrictions on the PLO, including the condition to "renounce terrorism," were enacted before the terror wave of late 1985 further suggested that they were not a response to PLO violence but to its growing political stature. Although the terrorist attacks were not the immediate or even the primary trigger for the PLO's exclusion from the diplomatic process, they did harden anti-PLO sentiment in Washington and inspired a new crop of anti-Palestinian measures in Congress. Pro-Israel activists had long set their sights on shutting down the PLO's information office in Washington and its mission at the UN.[64] The State Department opposed such measures, insisting that they tied the hands of American diplomats and impaired their ability to persuade the PLO to accept the very conditions Congress had mandated, but it was powerless to prevent them. Given the U.S.'s treaty obligations as the host country, there was little the administration could do against the PLO's mission at the UN. However, hoping to preempt even tougher actions demanded by the pro-Israel lobby and U.S. lawmakers, in September 1987 the State Department ordered the closure of the PLO's information office in Washington.[65] In December 1987, shortly after the outbreak of the Palestinian uprising in the occupied territories, Congress formalized the closure of the PLO office with the passage of the Anti-Terrorism Act, which for the first time defined the PLO as a "terrorist organization" and barred it from operating in the United States. The laws restricting contacts with the PLO and designating it a terrorist organization would eventually come back to haunt American peace efforts. In the meantime, U.S. officials continued to focus on circumventing the PLO.

GETTING TO "UNCLE"

The outbreak of the Palestinian uprising, or Intifada, in early December 1987 dramatically changed the political calculus on all sides, paving the way for the first official dialogue between the United States and the PLO a year later. But the initiation of an official dialogue did not signal a strategic shift in Washington's approach to the conflict or to the Palestinians; rather, it was a tactical adjustment to changed circumstances, namely, the Palestinian uprising and the need to fill the vacuum left by the collapse of the "Jordan option."

The spontaneous uprising caught virtually everyone off guard, including the Israeli government of Yitzhak Shamir and even the PLO leadership in Tunis. Israeli attempts to quash the popular revolt through sheer military force ultimately failed but exacted a heavy toll. During the first two years of the rebellion, more than 600 Palestinians were killed by Israeli soldiers and settlers and some 13,000 were wounded.[66] The April 1988 assassination in Tunis of Khalil al-Wazir (aka Abu Jihad), Arafat's deputy and head of the PLO's military wing, by Israeli commandos only fueled the uprising.[67] Images of heavily armed Israeli soldiers battling Palestinian teenagers armed with rocks and Molotov cocktails tarnished Israel's image and put Israeli leaders on the defensive. Meanwhile, a new generation of Palestinian leaders, born and raised under Israeli occupation rather than in the refugee camps of the diaspora, came to the fore. In place of the khaki-clad guerrilla fighters that usually appeared on American TV screens, well-dressed and articulate men and women such as Faisal Husseini, Hanan Ashrawi, and Saeb Erekat became the new face of the Palestinian struggle.

For Arafat and his top lieutenants, the Intifada presented both an opportunity and a challenge. The uprising had put the Palestinian question and Israel's military occupation squarely on the international agenda, but it also shifted the center of gravity of Palestinian politics away from the diaspora to those inside occupied territories. The PLO could provide financial support and political guidance for the uprising in the West Bank and Gaza, but the day-to-day operations of managing the mass mobilization fell to the young activists on the ground. The nearly simultaneous emergence of the Islamic Resistance Movement, better known as Hamas, marked the first direct, non-PLO-affiliated challenge to Arafat's leadership in many years. The growing prominence of local Palestinian leaders in the West Bank and Gaza along with the rise of a credible Islamist opposition fueled the PLO's fears of being sidelined by the Intifada.

The Palestinian rebellion had a profound impact in Washington as well. In addition to challenging assumptions regarding Israel's ability to maintain indefinite control over the occupied territories through military means alone, the Intifada "made mainstream American policymakers recognize the Palestinian issue as the central and core issue."[68] In contrast to the administration's halfhearted peace plan a few years earlier, Shultz launched a major diplomatic push in early 1988. The U.S. plan called for convening an international peace conference to oversee negotiations between Israel and a joint Jordanian-Palestinian delegation to hammer out an interim autonomy arrangement in the occupied territories. The plan gained little traction in the region. Prime Minister Yitzhak Shamir, of the Likud party, opposed the idea of an international conference. Meanwhile, Shultz's visit to the region in February 1988 was boycotted by local Palestinian leaders as a protest of Washington's continued refusal to deal with the PLO.

The decisive shift for Washington occurred later that summer when Jordan's King Hussein officially severed legal and administrative ties to the West Bank. Hussein's announcement threw the administration's peace efforts into disarray and upended a major pillar of America's Middle East policy. By formally renouncing the Hashemites' claims to the West Bank, Hussein put an end to the "Jordan option" as a solution to the Palestinian problem as well as to Washington's futile search for alternatives to the PLO. After the announcement, "There was a great silence in Washington," recalled Richard Murphy. "There was a sense then that maybe we missed opportunities years earlier."[69] Resigned to the inevitability of dealing with the PLO, Shultz tapped multiple channels simultaneously to communicate with Arafat's leadership on the precise terms for initiating a formal dialogue. The most important of these was the Swedish foreign minister, Sten Andersson.[70] At the same time, Shultz was wary of appearing overeager to deal with the PLO. "We had to be careful," recalled Dan Kurtzer, then on Shultz's staff, "because we could not convey interest, and we could not convey commitment. But the very fact that Shultz didn't stop [the secret channel] was important."[71]

By the autumn the PLO had signaled a readiness to meet U.S. conditions, although Shultz was determined not to make it easy for Arafat. On November 15, 1988, the Palestinian National Council, the PLO's parliament-in-exile, voted to declare an independent Palestinian state in the West Bank and Gaza defined by the 1967 borders. Although the declaration included an explicit acceptance of UN Resolutions 242 and 338 and disavowed terrorism, it failed to satisfy the U.S. administration. When Arafat announced his intention to clarify the PNC statement in a speech before the UN General Assembly in New York, the State Department denied him a visa. "It was politics," Kurtzer surmised. If there was going to be "some hell to pay with the Israelis and with the American Jewish community, the pro-Israel community, then maybe he could establish a little bit of a firewall for having proved his credentials."[72] In response to the visa denial, the world body took the unprecedented step of moving its proceedings to Geneva to allow Arafat to address the General Assembly. In his Geneva speech Arafat reiterated the PLO's rejection of terrorism while hailing the right of all peoples to resist occupation. Yet once again Arafat's words failed to satisfy the Americans, who insisted that the PLO leader "read the script which we had crafted for him."[73] Finally, on his third attempt, Arafat uttered the magic words in precisely the manner the Americans had demanded. On December 14, 1988, with a little more than one month left in his term,

President Reagan announced that the United States would open a "substantive dialogue" with the PLO.

Shultz later explained why it took so many attempts for Arafat to satisfy U.S. conditions: "In one place Arafat was saying, 'Unc, unc, unc' and in another he was saying, 'cle, cle, cle,' but nowhere will he yet bring himself to say 'Uncle.'"[74] Shultz's choice of words was telling. Whereas Arafat and the PLO had pursued the United States in the hope that it would eventually "deliver" Israel, the Reagan administration now boasted that it had effectively "delivered" the PLO to Israel. "I did not change my mind," declared Shultz. "They changed theirs."[75] In response to Shamir's vociferous opposition to the decision to talk directly to the PLO, Reagan assured the Israeli prime minister that neither the dialogue nor the peace process would alter America's "unshakable" commitment to Israel's security and well-being, and added that "a major reason for our entry into this dialog is to help Israel achieve the recognition and security it deserves."

A "VERY SHORT LEASH"

The launching of an official U.S.-PLO dialogue had enormous symbolic value and was a crucial step in opening the door to Palestinian participation in the peace process—which, interestingly enough, still did not include a role for the PLO in the peace process, nor even a recognition of the group as the official representative of the Palestinians.

The Palestinians had welcomed the new administration of George H. W. Bush and his secretary of state, James Baker, which, despite their continued opposition to Palestinian statehood, took a firmer line against Israeli settlement construction in the occupied territories. Nevertheless, the official dialogue remained highly restricted and tightly controlled and ultimately went nowhere. The dialogue was conducted by Robert Pelletreau, the American ambassador in Tunis, who held a total of four face-to-face meetings with mid-level PLO officials over a period of roughly eighteen months. Pelletreau's main point of contact was Yasser Abed-Rabbo, a relatively junior member of the PLO Executive Committee. Arafat "was pointedly excluded" from the exercise, according to Baker, due to "his reputation as a terrorist."[76] The PLO resented the tight controls imposed by Washington but went along in the hope of that they would gradually loosen. Instead, the opposite occurred. Congress placed additional restrictions on the dialogue with the PLO while adding new sanctions on the group. In addition to requiring the administration to verify the PLO's compliance with U.S. conditions every three months, Congress enacted new legislation requiring the United States to defund any UN organization or agency that recognized the PLO.[77] The latter was a clear attempt to tie the group's hands diplomatically.

Unlike his other diplomatic duties, Pelletreau's contacts with the PLO were tightly controlled by Washington. As the ambassador to an important Arab nation, Pelletreau had broad authority to shape U.S. policy as developments required. "You tell *us* what to do. Don't ask us to tell you what to do," Pelletreau recalled being told by his superiors prior to his deployment to Tunis. Thus, when insiders within the Tunisian regime resolved to quietly "retire" the country's aging and increasingly erratic dictator, Habib Bourguiba, after more than thirty years in power—the so-called Velvet Coup of 1987—Washington turned to Pelletreau to shape the direction of U.S. policy. "I almost dictated the U.S. response on that," Pelletreau recalled. "But then, when we opened the dialogue the PLO, that very long leash snapped back into a very short leash. And every day I would have a secure telephone conversation back to Washington . . . so that I could understand the pressures in Washington and what was happening there. And it was through that channel that I would report who I was going to be meeting with."[78]

Once the dialogue began, the discussions focused primarily on two issues. The first was security cooperation. According to Pelletreau, "We were very interested in not only having further assurances that the PLO was not involved [in terrorism] but that the PLO would condemn and . . . help suppress any such actions."[79] The other issue was Shamir's autonomy plan for the West Bank and Gaza, under which Palestinians would elect a "council" to negotiate on the shape of future self-rule. Although Shamir later backed away from his own proposal, the plan became the basis of U.S. peace efforts for the first two years of the Bush administration. The administration also gave in to Shamir's demands that Palestinians from East Jerusalem, the diaspora, and the PLO be excluded from the process.[80] "In effect," Baker wrote in his memoir, "we were asking Arafat to disenfranchise himself on the grounds of political expedience."[81]

Baker later authorized Pelletreau to speak with Arafat's deputy, Salah Khalaf (Abu Iyad), the reputed ringleader of the notorious Black September Organization. Leaks of Khalaf's involvement embarrassed the administration and triggered a major outcry on Capitol Hill. According to Pelletreau, Khalaf's inclusion in the dialogue was due in part to the belief that he would be more flexible than anyone else inside the PLO on proposals for electing non-PLO negotiators in the West Bank and Gaza.[82] Khalaf had also become an important intelligence asset and was working simultaneously with the CIA to shut down the Abu Nidal terror network. When word got out of his meetings with Khalaf, however, Pelletreau "was instructed, in very straight language, no further meetings with Abu Iyad." Moreover, both men were now physically, as well as politically, vulnerable. According to Pelletreau, "Word was also out that Abu Nidal had known that we were meeting and was going to put a contract on both of us. And the State Department was concerned enough that I received a reinforced security detachment in Tunis, which included some Delta Force folks. And my own security and movements became a lot tighter and more unpredictable."[83]

By the spring of 1990, it was clear that both the dialogue and Baker's peace initiative were going nowhere. Attempts by the Palestinian side to broaden the discussion proved fruitless.[84] Members of Pelletreau's team who wanted to engage the PLO more seriously complained of being "hogtied" by the administration and of its inability to appreciate changes in PLO positions.[85] The Palestinians did little to hide their frustration with Washington. "What is most surprising and painful," Khalaf wrote in *Foreign Policy* magazine, "is not the position of Shamir or those of a similar bent in Israel, but rather that of the United States." Despite the PLO's displays of goodwill and flexibility, he continued, "The United States appears unwilling or unable to distance itself from the more extreme Israeli positions and policies. . . . As a result, the PLO still has no clear or serious understanding of why the United States itself—as distinct from Israel—does not support the two-state solution or on what its objections to such a solution are based."[86] Several months later, Khalaf was assassinated by an Abu Nidal operative.

The dialogue officially ended following an abortive attack at a Tel Aviv beach in May 1990 by the Palestine Liberation Front, an Iraqi-sponsored PLO faction headed by Mohammed Zaidan (Abul-Abbas). Although unsuccessful, the attack was seen by U.S. officials as a breach of the PLO's commitment to refrain from terrorism. Unsatisfied with Arafat's condemnation of the attack, the administration demanded he take more serious action against Zaidan. Arafat was in Baghdad at the time and was under pressure from Saddam Hussein. Moreover, two-thirds of the PLO's fighters were based in Iraq, and Arafat had grown heavily reliant on Iraqi financial and military support. Meanwhile, American officials had been in contact with senior PLO figures who were eager to preserve the dialogue in the hope of persuading Arafat to make a clear statement distancing himself from Zaidan. Faced with mounting pressure of his own, however, Bush decided to suspend the dialogue even before hearing from Arafat.[87] Baker insisted that "Arafat had squandered any chance of establishing his credibility or even a scintilla of moral authority by refusing to renounce the terrorist attack," but the Palestinians viewed the decision as a convenient pretext to suspend a dialogue that was no longer useful for Washington. According to Baker, Bush was reluctant to end the dialogue, which "was now all that remained of the tattered peace process."[88]

BAKER'S BADLY TAILORED SUIT

The PLO's apparent siding with Saddam Hussein following Iraq's invasion of Kuwait in August 1990 ended any hope of resuming the U.S.-PLO dialogue. The invasion of Kuwait confronted the PLO leadership with a "dilemma of unprecedented proportion."[89] In addition to the PLO's heavy reliance on Iraqi financial and strategic support, pro-Saddam sentiment ran high among Palestinians in the occupied territories and Jordan. Arafat also hoped to avoid burning his bridges with Kuwait, home to some 300,000 Palestinians, and other wealthy Gulf states. As a result, the PLO leader attempted to hedge. Arafat, like Jordan's King Hussein, had called for an "Arab solution" to the crisis while linking an Iraqi withdrawal from Kuwait with an Israeli withdrawal from the West Bank and Gaza. But Arafat's failure to call unequivocally for an Iraqi withdrawal from Kuwait was seen as siding with Saddam Hussein. A few senior PLO figures, including Khalaf, tried unsuccessfully to dissuade Arafat from his support of Iraq regarding withdrawal from Kuwait, for which the PLO and the Palestinians paid dearly. The PLO lost $100 million in annual support from Arab Gulf states, while tens of thousands of Palestinians were expelled from Kuwait.[90] What was more, according to Kurtzer, "The PLO was finished in the Bush administration's playbook. . . . Not only had they not done what we'd asked them to do, but they went over to the enemy as far as we were concerned."[91]

In response to the Iraqi occupation and subsequent annexation of Kuwait, the United States assembled a broad international coalition, which included several key Arab states, including Saudi Arabia, Egypt, and Syria, aimed at ousting Saddam's forces from the oil-rich emirate. After a two-month bombing campaign, the U.S.-led coalition successfully expelled Iraqi forces from Kuwait in March 1991. The United States emerged from the First Gulf War with its stature in the Middle East and around the world greatly enhanced. Iraq's defeat by the American-led coalition in early 1991 presented Baker with "an historic opportunity" to pursue Israeli-Arab peace.[92] Baker's plan was to bring Israel, Arab states, and the Palestinians into direct negotiations under the auspices of an international conference. On the thorny matter of Palestinian representation, Baker turned to a group of prominent Palestinian leaders from the occupied territories with whom he held a series of meetings in preparation for what became the 1991 Madrid peace conference. The group comprised roughly a dozen Palestinians selected by the PLO in Tunis and headed by Faisal Husseini, a leading figure of the Intifada and the PLO's unofficial representative in Jerusalem. Husseini's team made it a point to open each meeting by asserting that they were acting under the authority and at the behest of the PLO—something Baker already knew but preferred not to hear.[93] Despite such modest acts of defiance, Husseini and the others held Secretary of State Baker in high esteem for his willingness to treat them as equal participants in the peace process. "He was the one U.S. official who took us seriously," recalled Hanan Ashrawi, who worked closely with Baker in the lead-up to Madrid.[94] According to Ashrawi, "Baker was the only person who engaged with us and wanted to learn. We could discuss and argue with him, and he didn't hide behind his talking points. And he didn't allow the team to take over—even though they tried; Dennis Ross was always trying to take charge and hijack the policy."[95]

But even Baker had his limits. The Shamir government had conditioned its participation in the upcoming peace conference on the usual Israeli demands: the Palestinians could participate only as part of a joint delegation with Jordan, and the delegation could not include Palestinians from East Jerusalem, the diaspora, or (of course) the PLO. Otherwise Israel would not attend. The administration accepted Shamir's conditions, which the Palestinians found galling—particularly since Baker's two primary interlocutors, Faisal Husseini and Hanan Ashrawi, were themselves Jerusalemites. Husseini likened the myriad restrictions placed on the Palestinians to a badly tailored suit whose sleeves and pant legs were severely twisted and uneven and forced Palestinians to contort themselves to fit the shape of the suit. "So, Mr. Baker," Husseini would say, "if you see us behaving in strange or inappropriate ways, it is not because we were born that way, or because it is our nature, but because the suit you have tailored for us doesn't fit!"[96] Baker urged the group not to put "symbolism over substance," and reminded them that Palestinians had more to lose from the absence of a peace process than anyone else.[97] Many within the Palestinian leadership were inclined to agree. As Farouk Kaddoumi put it, the PLO would have either to join the peace process or to exit history.[98]

Baker may not have been able to offer the Palestinians a new suit, but he was willing to make the one they had a bit less constricting. In exchange for dropping their claim to East Jerusalem as the capital of their future state, Baker promised to take a tougher stance on Israeli settlements.[99] Shamir's commitment to accelerating the settlement project in the West Bank and Gaza, which included plans to settle thousands of Soviet Jewish immigrants there, was a constant source of friction between Shamir and Baker. In the lead-up to the Madrid conference, Baker rankled the Israeli government and its supporters in Congress by urging lawmakers to delay action on Israel's request for $10 billion in loan guarantees to help with the absorption of Soviet immigrants until it agreed to freeze settlement construction in the occupied territories. Baker later worked with U.S. lawmakers to pass legislation requiring the United States to deduct the amount estimated to have been spent by Israel on settlement construction in the occupied territories from U.S. loan guarantees provided to Israel. Although the loan guarantees deduction was largely symbolic, it was the first time an American administration had linked the issue of Israeli settlements directly to Israeli aid. "Baker and President Bush stared down the supporters of Israel in Congress, they took on AIPAC and basically beat them," recalled a former U.S. diplomat. "The crisis caused a lot of turmoil in Israel politically because one of the most important tasks I think the Israeli public believed that any Prime Minister has to do is to maintain a very good working relationship with the government of the United States."[100] In addition, Baker provided each side with written assurances outlining American commitments during the negotiations, thus elevating the Palestinians to virtual co-equals with the Israelis. Among other things, Baker's letter of assurances to the Palestinians promised the Palestinians that their participation in the process would not affect their claim to East Jerusalem and stipulated that the United States was "opposed to the Israeli annexation of East Jerusalem and extension of Israeli law on it and the extension of Jerusalem's municipal boundaries."[101]

The Madrid peace conference, convened in late October 1991, marked a major milestone in the pursuit of Arab-Israeli peace. Although the talks did not produce any agreements, the process brought Lebanon, Syria, and Jordan into direct negotiations with Israel for the first time. Baker's approach also succeeded in bringing the Palestinians directly into the peace process for the first time and to a certain extent helped to normalize the PLO's participation as well. Although officially not invited, PLO officials were physically present—oftentimes in the same hotel—throughout the Madrid conference, and it was clear to almost everyone, including the Israelis, that Arafat's leadership in Tunis was calling the shots. Subsequent peace talks held in Washington throughout 1992 eventually dispensed with the pretense of a joint delegation, even with the understanding that the Palestinian team was fully delegated by the PLO. Baker was certainly no fan of the PLO or of Arafat—as he makes clear in his memoir, where he expresses the hope that if local Palestinian leaders "decided to do something for themselves, the PLO's authority might be diminished."[102] But Baker also understood there was no realistic way to avoid the PLO and Arafat. In the end, the relative success of the Madrid conference was possible because Baker understood whom to push on or to prop up, and when, in order to achieve his objectives and because he sought out creative ways to circumvent his own government's limitations.

As the peace process was about to enter a new phase, the Palestinians' dilemma remained. "The Baker suit not only did not fit but was unbefitting," wrote Hanan Ashrawi. "How many disadvantages and handicaps could we bear to bring with us to a process whose scales were already weighted in favor of our adversary? . . . Could we afford the price of a no? And if we said yes it would bring not only serious suffering, but also a certain amount of negation and denial."[103] Bush and Baker had helped to offset some of the imbalance in their quest to build a credible peace process. But they were the last American administration that was prepared to do so.

PART III

Consequences of the Blind Spot: 1993–2018

5

The Oslo Trade-Off

Mr. Chairman, I am not a great man. I am a failure, and you have made me one.

—President Bill Clinton to Yasser Arafat, January 2001

On July 12, 1994, thousands of exuberant Palestinians poured into the streets to greet Yasser Arafat upon his arrival in the Gaza Strip. The Palestinian leader's triumphal return to the homeland after a quarter century of exile was a personal victory for Arafat as well as a vindication of his political strategy. After years of bloodshed and failed diplomacy, the PLO had finally established the long-awaited "national authority" on Palestinian soil—all without firing a shot. For those few Palestinians old enough to remember, Arafat's return must have seemed like something of a déjà-vu moment. Forty-five years earlier, another exiled Palestinian leader, Amin al-Husseini, had similarly mounted a triumphal return to Gaza to establish a provisional government for a would-be state—the ill-fated All Palestine Government. But this time things would be different. Whereas al-Husseini's political career had ended unceremoniously in defeat, humiliation, and international pariah status, Arafat had managed to reverse his political fortunes. His return was not the final, desperate act of a leader in decline; rather, he saw his return as the opening act of a leader determined to reinvent himself and to turn the page on his people's tragic history. In the end, both Arafat's fate and that of the prospective state he sought to lead had more in common with their 1948 counterparts than he could have realized at the time.

Arafat's return to Palestinian soil had been made possible by another historic moment ten months earlier. The signing of the Oslo Declaration of Principles in Washington, DC, on September 13, 1993, by Prime Minister Yitzhak Rabin and the PLO leader Yasser Arafat laid the groundwork for Palestinian self-rule in the occupied territories with the aim of reaching a permanent peace settlement within five years. The sight of the two former enemies shaking hands on the White House lawn, flanked by a smiling U.S. President Bill Clinton, has since become one of the most iconic images of the twentieth century. That the man who had been shunned by successive U.S. presidents as a terrorist was now an honored guest of the White House was a testament to Arafat's dramatic transformation in the eyes of American officials. But Arafat's newfound VIP status was still entirely dependent on Israel and the peace process, the product of an unspoken trade-off between the Palestinian leadership and the peace process's American sponsors. In return for a seat at the negotiating table, the PLO was expected not only to live up to its security and other obligations under the Oslo Accords but also to work to neutralize political opponents of the peace process and other problematic aspects of their politics. For their part, Palestinian leaders were prepared to give up a degree of control over their internal politics and decision making in the hope that the United States would ultimately prevail on Israel to end its occupation of the West Bank and Gaza to enable the creation of a Palestinian state. However, this highly precarious arrangement would not last. Ironically, even as the Clinton administration came to terms with Palestinian political leaders, and eventually even the idea of Palestinian statehood, it proved to be far more deferential to Israeli demands and far less willing to pressure its leaders than previous U.S. administrations. Arafat, too, did not live up to his end of the bargain, as the failed Camp David summit and the outbreak of the Al-Aqsa Intifada demonstrated. Just as it was through Israel that Arafat was welcomed in Washington, it was also Israel that later kept him out.

OSLO AND ITS DISCONTENTS

The Oslo Declaration of Principles, the result of secret negotiations held between Israel and the PLO in the Norwegian capital, caught almost everyone by surprise. Not least of these were American and Palestinian negotiators in Washington. After the Madrid conference, U.S. officials oversaw bilateral talks between the Israelis and each one of the Syrian, Jordanian, and Palestinian tracks. The Israeli and Palestinian teams were about to enter their eleventh round when news of the deal was leaked in August 1993. The two sides had been hopelessly deadlocked for weeks over the nature of the "Palestinian interim self-governing authority" in the West Bank and Gaza. Yitzhak Shamir's Likud government had stuck to the old Begin formula that Palestinian autonomy applied solely to people and not land. He later confessed that he "would have carried on autonomy talks for ten years and meanwhile we would have reached half a million Jews" in the West Bank. Although Shamir's defeat in June 1992 by Yitzhak Rabin's Labor Party brought a more peace-oriented government to power in Israel, the Palestinian side faced its own limitations imposed by the PLO leadership in Tunis. Fearing being upstaged by Palestinian negotiators in Washington and resentful of their direct access to the U.S. administration, Arafat worked to obstruct the process in order to force the Americans to deal with him directly.[1] The news from Oslo blindsided members of the Palestinian delegation, who had been in serious negotiations with U.S. and Israeli officials for nearly two years, along with most members of the PLO Executive Committee and Fatah's Central Committee, neither of which were consulted beforehand.[2] Clinton administration officials had known about the Oslo channel since early 1993 but put little stock in its success.[3] Among other things, members of the American team were surprised to find that Israel had agreed to things that they themselves had deemed unworkable, such as allowing former PLO fighters to serve as the core of the new Palestinian internal security force in the West Bank and Gaza.[4]

The Oslo agreement fundamentally challenged longstanding assumptions on both sides—particularly the widely accepted notion that progress in the peace process could only occur with active American involvement. This fact, however, did not fundamentally alter the political calculus of American and Palestinian decision makers toward the peace process or one another. For all intents and purposes, Oslo represented a reversal of Arafat's traditional formula—instead of relying on Washington to help bring the Israelis on board, Arafat used Israel's recognition of the PLO to force the United States to follow suit. However, this did little to alter the PLO leader's basic strategic calculation that the road to a Palestinian state necessarily ran through Washington. For U.S. policymakers, the success of the Oslo back channel ran against two basic axioms of U.S. Middle East policy: that the United States was indispensable to the Arab-Israeli peace process and that it was possible, if not preferable, to exclude the PLO from that process.

While Arafat continued to bank on the United States, many U.S. officials remained highly distrustful of the PLO and its leaders. Even the question of whether Arafat would be allowed to attend the signing ceremony in Washington was the subject of considerable controversy and debate within the administration.[5] Few U.S. officials were more distrustful of Arafat than Dennis Ross, Clinton's newly appointed Middle East peace envoy. "I was never convinced that the PLO should be involved in this process," a Palestinian official reported hearing Ross say as they awaited Arafat's arrival at Dulles International Airport in September 1993.[6] The new envoy had unparalleled influence in shaping U.S. policy throughout the Oslo years. Distrust of Arafat and the PLO was even more pronounced in Congress. The large corpus of anti-PLO legislation accumulated over the years, including the 1987 law labeling the group a "terrorist organization," remained on the books. To allow the peace process to continue, Congress enacted waivers granting the president the ability to temporarily suspend specific provisions such as the ban on dealings with the PLO and allowing U.S. funds to flow to the Palestinian Authority.

Like the Camp David–inspired autonomy talks of the 1980s, the Oslo Declaration of Principles envisioned a two-tier process. In the first phase, Israel's military government in the occupied territories would transfer powers to the newly formed Palestinian Authority, which would govern Palestinians in the West Bank and Gaza for a period of five years. A resolution of the more difficult core issues of the conflict—including the future of Jerusalem, Israeli settlements, security arrangements, final borders, and the fate of millions of Palestinian refugees—would be put off until a later stage, with so-called permanent-status negotiations between Israel and the PLO to be completed by the end of the interim period in May 1999. In the meantime, Israel would retain overall security responsibility for the whole of the occupied territories while gradually transferring powers and limited territory to the Palestinians. The nature of the transition, including where and how much land Israel would cede to the newly formed Palestinian Authority, was left to subsequent agreements. The Oslo process was premised on the notion that confidence-building measures and incremental progress on day-to-day issues, including improved economic conditions for Palestinians, enhanced security for Israelis, and the gradual transfer of administrative responsibility and territory to the Palestinian Authority, would enable the parties to tackle the more difficult core issues of the conflict further down the road. Much to their regret, the Palestinians failed to secure an explicit reference to a freeze on settlement construction in the occupied territories during the interim period in either the Declaration of Principles or sequent agreements. PLO negotiators had reportedly attempted to include such a clause in Oslo, which the Israelis refused. Instead, the Palestinians relied on a vaguely worded provision in the Oslo Accords to treat "the West Bank and the Gaza Strip as a single territorial unit, whose integrity will be preserved during the interim period," though this, too, was repeatedly violated.

The timing of the agreement reflected a convergence of interests between the PLO leadership in Tunis and Israel's Labor government led by Rabin, although both sides had very different understandings of what the agreement meant and where it should lead. For the PLO, the Oslo Accord fulfilled two long-standing strategic aims: achieving formal recognition by Israel and the United States and gaining a foothold in the homeland on which to build the long-awaited Palestinian state. At a more practical level, Oslo also provided a way to ensure the PLO's bureaucratic survival and continued political relevance, as well as Fatah's continued dominance, at a moment when Arafat's leadership faced a severe political and financial crisis. For Arafat, it was "the PLO's political survival, rather than any specific provision in the accord, that provided the real guarantee of eventual statehood."[7] The PLO had been crippled by the loss of funding from Arab Gulf states and increased political isolation following the 1991 Gulf War, while the collapse of the Soviet Union later that year only reinforced Arafat's conviction that Washington was the key to Palestinian statehood. Internally, the winding down of the Intifada, the growing prominence of Palestinian leaders from the "inside," and the rise of Hamas, which was now second only to Arafat's Fatah movement in strength and popularity, posed an immediate threat to the PLO's primacy and drove Arafat's desire to gain access to Palestinian territory at any cost.[8]

In return for preserving the PLO's leadership and representative status, Arafat was prepared to make far-reaching concessions, including several he had previously rejected, such as holding elections under occupation and putting off dealing with crucial issues such as sovereignty and the status of both Jerusalem and refugees until the end of the process. The fact that the PLO leadership in Tunis had a limited understanding of the physical and political conditions in the occupied territories, both in terms of Israel's settlement enterprise and Palestinian civic and political life, also did not help matters. This, combined with the PLO's weakness, would explain why, for example, the PLO negotiators in Oslo did not insist on including an Israeli commitment to freeze settlement construction in the West Bank, a lapse that they would later come to regret. To Arafat and the small coterie of PLO figures who negotiated the Oslo Declaration of Principles, what mattered most was to preserve the central role and relevance of the PLO while issues such as the settlements, jurisdiction, and security were, according to one former member of the Palestinian delegation in Washington, "just details."[9]

The weakened state of the PLO leadership was not entirely lost on Israeli leaders.[10] For Prime Minister Rabin, however, the overriding priority was to end the Intifada, which had cost the lives of over 1,100 Palestinians and 160 Israelis, sapped Israeli resources, and battered Israel's image around the world.[11] In addition to forcing Israeli society to come to terms with Palestinian nationalism, the uprising had convinced Rabin of the need for a new security paradigm for the occupied territories. Oslo provided a way to operationalize "autonomy" in the West Bank and Gaza, relieving Israel of the burden of having to govern millions of hostile Palestinians, without relinquishing overall control over the territories. The fact that progress toward ending the occupation would be conditional on Palestinian performance while thorny issues like Jerusalem and settlements would be put off until the end of the process helped to mitigate the risks for Israeli leaders. Meanwhile, the promise of potential normalization of relations with Arab and Muslim countries and in the broader international arena provided additional political and economic benefits for Israel.

The inherent vagueness of the Oslo Accords, which laid out a detailed blueprint of the transitional period without defining what it was transitioning to, produced very different expectations on each side. The expectation among Palestinians was that Israel would gradually withdraw from all of the occupied territories with the exception of those areas reserved for permanent status negotiations—namely East Jerusalem and the settlements—leading eventually to an independent state at the end of the interim period, in May 1999. For the Israelis however, Oslo represented a sort of expanded autonomy focused more on relinquishing control over people rather than of territory, with no commitment to Palestinian statehood. The result fell somewhere in the middle, reflecting the asymmetry of the two sides. At the height of the Oslo process, in 1999, the PA had jurisdiction over some 95 percent of the Palestinian population in some 39 percent of the West Bank, plus Gaza. All of East Jerusalem remained off limits to the PA.[12] Neither the 1993 Declaration of Principles nor any of the half dozen or so interim agreements signed in subsequent years called for the creation of a Palestinian state or even an end to the occupation. In the words of one Israeli scholar, "The two sides could not march forward together because they were intent on marching in different directions."[13]

Even as Clinton and other world leaders hailed Oslo as a triumph for peace, the accord met with fierce opposition among large segments of Palestinian and Israeli societies. In Israel, the opposition leader Benjamin Netanyahu of the Likud blasted Rabin for violating the political consensus against negotiating with the PLO and likened the agreement to British Prime Minister Neville Chamberlain's appeasement of the Nazis. Leaders of Israel's settler movement denounced the "extreme treacherous acts against Eretz Yisrael" and threatened that there would be "war over Judea, Samaria and Gaza."[14] Opposition to Oslo was equally severe among Palestinians. The Popular Front for the Liberation of Palestine, the Democratic Front for the Liberation of Palestine, and other rejectionists within the PLO, along with the Islamist factions Hamas and Islamic Jihad, accused Arafat and the PLO of "selling out" the Palestinian homeland and of abandoning the rights of Palestinian refugees. Critics also accused the agreement of institutionalizing the power imbalance between the two sides. Thus while the Palestinians had recognized the "right of the state of Israel to exist in peace and security," Israel had agreed simply to recognize "the PLO as the representative of the Palestinian people." Nor was opposition to the accord limited to hardliners—some of Oslo's fiercest critics came from within the Palestinian mainstream. Chief among them was Edward Said, who railed against Oslo as an "instrument of Palestinian surrender, a Palestinian Versailles," while accusing the PLO of having "transformed itself from a national liberation movement into a kind of small-town government."[15]

Palestinian opponents of Oslo also took issue with the authoritarian manner in which the deal was sprung on the Palestinian public. In contrast to Israel, where Oslo's provisions were subjected to heated and often incendiary political debate, Arafat had presented the Oslo Declaration of Principles as a fait accompli, with virtually no internal debate, much less an attempt at building a political consensus, around the more controversial provisions of the agreement. The PLO's leftist factions were too weak and fragmented to mount a credible fight against the agreement, while the largest opposition force, Hamas, was not part of the PLO. The PLO's highest decision-making body, the Palestine National Council, never took up the matter in any case and by this time had become "largely formalistic and ceremonial [in] nature," convening only periodically to rubber-stamp decisions of its Fatah-dominated leadership.[16] Despite having been kept in the dark, Fatah's ruling body, the Central Committee, gave the accord its grudging approval. The PLO's Executive Committee eventually ratified the Declaration of Principles as well, but only by the thinnest of margins, thanks largely to the resignations and boycotts of several Oslo opponents.[17] The failure to build a minimal political consensus around the agreement became one of the "original sins" of the Oslo era, one that would haunt Arafat's leadership, Palestinian politics, and the peace process for a generation.

The euphoria that followed the celebrated handshake on the White House lawn came to an abrupt and violent end in February 1994 when Baruch Goldstein, a radical Jewish settler and former Brooklyn resident who opposed the Oslo agreement, gunned down twenty-nine Palestinian worshipers at the Ibrahimi Mosque, known to Jews as the Cave of Machpelah, a shrine sacred to both Muslims and Jews, in the southern West Bank town of Hebron. Even as Prime Minister Rabin and other Israeli officials condemned the massacre, radicals in the Israeli settler movement hailed Goldstein as a hero and a martyr. Although Goldstein did not succeed in derailing the Oslo Accords as he had hoped, his bloody act set off a chain reaction of extremism, violence, and terror that permanently altered the course of the peace process. In the wake of the Hebron massacre, Hamas shifted its focus from mainly targeting Israeli soldiers and police to deliberate attacks on Israeli civilians, launching the first of what would become a pattern of deadly suicide bombings in April 1994.[18] Determined to forge ahead, in September 1995 Israeli and Palestinian negotiators agreed on the terms for the redeployment of Israeli soldiers outside most major Palestinian cities in the West Bank with the promise of several further redeployments down the road. The new interim agreement, known as Oslo II, further delineated the Palestinian Authority's powers and areas of jurisdiction as well as a timetable for electing a new Palestinian legislative council. A few weeks later, on November 5, the peace process suffered its most serious blow yet when another Jewish extremist, Yigal Amir, gunned down Prime Minister Yitzhak Rabin at a peace rally in Tel Aviv.

Rabin's murder cast a pall over the peace process, arresting Oslo's momentum even if it did not completely halt its forward movement, and for many it marked the moment to which many would later trace the death of the peace process.[19] Despite the assassination, the Israeli army completed its redeployment from West Bank cities in December 1995 in time for Palestinian legislative and presidential elections in January 1996. The elections were a crowning moment in the Oslo process, as well as for Arafat, who handily won election as president of the Palestinian Authority, while his Fatah faction took control of the newly seated Palestinian Legislative Council. Celebrations were short-lived, however, as another deadly wave of suicide attacks by Hamas killed scores of Israeli civilians in early 1996. Israel responded to the attacks by sealing off the West Bank and Gaza and imposing harsh movement restrictions and other repressive measures on the Palestinian population. The closures, which were reinstated after each attack, wreaked havoc on the Palestinian economy, thus undermining a central pillar of the Oslo process. On the Israeli side, the growing frequency of terrorist attacks soured public opinion on the peace process, paving the way for the election in May 1996 of a government headed by Likud's Benjamin Netanyahu, a vocal opponent of the Oslo Accords.

The Oslo process, along with the violence and terror that accompanied it, badly polarized Israeli and Palestinian politics and opened up deep rifts within both societies. Yet while both sides had their violent spoilers, only the Israeli side had the institutional capacity to accommodate political opposition. The Israeli polity could withstand a catastrophic event like Rabin's assassination not only because it had strong state institutions and a well-developed constitutional order but also because it enjoyed a deeper societal consensus on the underlying rules of the political game. Consequently, Israeli opponents of Oslo who resorted to violence remained relatively marginalized in large part because opportunities for political dissent, and even course correction, were available through normal political channels, as the election of Netanyahu following the rash of suicide bombings in 1996 clearly demonstrated. The same did not hold true of the Palestinians, who lacked not only a state and properly functioning governing institutions but also the means for ensuring meaningful representation and political dissent. Thus, not only was there no minimal political consensus on the difficult compromises that Oslo entailed—recognition of Israel, giving up armed struggle, and accepting a two-state solution—but also, in the absence of genuinely representative institutions, there was no credible way to bring one about. In the absence of meaningful avenues for political dissent and possible course correction, both of which were strongly discouraged by the Oslo framework and the PA leadership, political actors found other ways to assert themselves politically—very often through violence.

THE NATURE OF THE TRADE-OFF

Despite its emphasis on state building, the peace process did not provide Palestinians with either the means or the incentives to rectify this situation. If anything, the Oslo process helped to accelerate the decline of Palestinian institutional politics that began in the 1980s while reinforcing the exclusionary and authoritarian impulses of the PLO leadership. This outcome was a product of the peculiar political and power dynamics between the United States, Israel, and the Palestinians as well as of the nature of the Oslo Accords themselves. Oslo was in fact not one process but two, combining traditional conflict resolution between two parties with a process of "state building" for one of them. The implications of this were enormous, particularly given the status of the United States as the world's sole remaining superpower, the exceptionally close bonds between the U.S. and Israel, and the PLO's internal and external weakness. For one, this meant that outside actors, including the United States, foreign donors, and even Israel, now had a direct say in—and in some cases an effective veto over—key aspects of Palestinian political life. This also meant that Palestinian politics and the peace process were now inextricably linked. Exclusion from one almost invariably meant exclusion from the other; if one failed the other was likely to suffer as well. The challenge for the PLO leadership, as one Palestinian reformer observed at the time, would be to "prove that it is still able to represent, defend, and further the interests, aspirations, and rights of the entire Palestinian people, and not just a portion of them."[20]

As it turned out, all three sides—the United States, Israel, and the PLO—had an interest in curtailing or suppressing various aspects of Palestinian politics, albeit for different reasons. The PLO leadership was fixated on three overriding goals: ensuring the PLO's institutional survival, preserving Fatah's continued dominance within Palestinian politics, and winning American favor. Thus, for reasons of both pragmatism and parochialism, the Palestinian leadership was prepared to give up a degree of control over its internal decision making and to suppress certain aspects of Palestinian politics in return for a seat at the table and the expectation that the United States would apply sufficient pressure on Israel to compel it to meet its obligations in the interim period and ultimately to end its occupation and allow the establishment of a Palestinian state.

For their part, U.S. officials tended to view the peace process through the lens of the special relationship with Israel and American domestic politics as well as to conflate their own priorities with the needs of the peace process. As a result, Oslo became a vehicle not just for resolving the conflict but for transforming the Palestinians into a suitable peace partner as well as a platform for promoting Israeli normalization in the region and projecting American power and influence in the region and beyond. The United States was the "indispensable nation," in the words of Secretary of State Madeleine Albright. All the more so since the collapse of the USSR left the United States as the world's only remaining superpower. The Middle East was an area of strategic importance where U.S. officials felt they could have more influence.

In the meantime, the Oslo process had fundamentally reorganized and redefined Palestinian politics and governing institutions, including their main sources of legitimacy as representative and inclusive of all

Oslo Jurisdiction Areas
As per Wye River Agreement
October 1998

■ Area A (Palestinian security & civilian control)
▨ Area B (Israeli security/Palestinian civilian control)
░ Area C (full Israeli control)
▨ Nature Reserve (Israeli control)
– – – 1949 Armistice Line (1967 border)
–··– International Boundary

Sea of Galilee

MEDITERRANEAN

SEA

Jordan River

WEST BANK

East Jerusalem
West Jerusalem

ISRAEL

GAZA STRIP

Dead Sea

JORDAN

EGYPT

Source: Adapted from United Nations, with additional detail from other sources.

Palestinians, in the occupied territories and the diaspora. The creation of the Palestinian Authority in 1994 marked the first step in the PLO's institutional reincarnation, although the process of restructuring Palestinian political institutions remained ad hoc and non-inclusive. While the PLO remained the official political address of the Palestinian national movement in the international arena and in negotiations with Israel, its bureaucratic and administrative infrastructure was gradually transferred to the newly formed PA. Even as the PA replaced the PLO as the locus of Palestinian politics, the lines between the two bodies continued to be blurred.[21] In the process, the PLO's secrecy, nepotism, and corruption were now extended to the PA, alienating large segments of the local population, many of whom derisively referred to their newly transplanted overlords as "the Tunisians." The authoritarian and elitist tendencies of the PLO were at odds with the more grassroots and decentralized civic and political culture of the West Bank and Gaza, which despite restrictions imposed by the occupation had remained relatively vibrant.[22]

Oslo did introduce positive elements into Palestinian politics, most notably an elected parliament and president, effectively replacing the PLO's elaborate and antiquated quota system. However, these came at the expense of the PLO's claims to be representative of all Palestinians. Although elections for PA president and the new Palestinian Legislative Council in January 1996 were widely viewed as free and fair, the vote was boycotted by the largest opposition group, Hamas. Moreover, the roughly 60 percent of the Palestinian population who were refugees were not eligible to vote in PA elections and were effectively cut out of the Oslo process.

The implicit trade-off of Oslo rested on two essential pillars: security and aid. The underlying theory was that improving the economic conditions of Palestinians would reduce public support or sympathy for violence and increase confidence in the PA and the peace process. On the Israeli side, meanwhile, the expectation by the Americans was that enhanced security would boost the public's confidence in the process, thereby increasing the willingness of Israeli leaders to make concessions such as turning over territory to the Palestinians. "The Palestinians wanted land; the Israelis wanted security," observed Clinton's secretary of state, Madeleine Albright. "The question was how much land Israel would return and what kind of security assurances the Palestinians would provide." In Albright's view, Jewish settlements in the occupied territories were a constant reminder of what were essentially Palestinian socioeconomic grievances: "Within the gated settlement walls were people with money living well. Outside were shacks and Palestinians living miserable, impoverished lives."[23]

Of the two pillars, security came first. Like the Israelis, the Clinton administration believed that security was paramount and hence the key to political progress. A major portion of international aid therefore went to support Palestinian security forces. The CIA began providing counterterrorism and intelligence training and other assistance to PA security officials in 1994, progressively expanding overt and covert assistance to Palestinian security services in subsequent years.[24] So long as the PA performed well in the security realm, Washington was prepared to overlook abuses and other governance problems. "Neither we nor the Israelis questioned what Arafat was doing internally," observed the U.S. peace envoy, Dennis Ross. "At this point, we both felt he was the only one who could manage the Palestinians. As we would hear often from Rabin, we shouldn't be pressing Arafat on human rights or even corruption."[25]

The ability to "manage the Palestinians" rested mainly on the influx of unprecedented levels of international aid to the PA. From 1993 to 1999, international donors channeled more than $2.7 billion in reconstruction and development assistance to the PA, making Palestinians the largest per capita recipients of international donor aid in the world.[26] As the largest single donor and the peace process's main sponsor, the United States spearheaded the donor effort by pledging $500 million to the PA while bringing others on board. Internationalizing the donor aid effort also helped to insulate the process from Oslo's many opponents on Capitol Hill, where pro-Israel lobbyists and American lawmakers had worked to ensure that the continuation of U.S. aid was conditioned on PA compliance with its security and other obligations.[27] Aid played an essential role in the creation and maintenance of the PA, enabling it

to pay salaries, particularly for its security services, and serving as a crucial buffer against the negative effects of Israel's frequent closures of
the territories and various other economic impediments of the occupation. Its main purpose, however, was to help transform the PA into a
suitable "partner for peace" while building a "peace constituency"
among Palestinians.[28]

The reality proved to be very different. International aid did lead
to significant improvements in the occupied territories, including
large-scale infrastructure projects, increased access to education and
health services, and the creation of thousands of new public-sector
jobs. However, the influx of large amounts of donor funds also helped
fuel PA corruption and reinforce the leadership's authoritarian tendencies by underwriting Arafat's patronage networks and facilitating the
PA's suppression of political dissent. International donors, including
the United States, gave Arafat considerable leeway to stack the PA's
ballooning bureaucracy with Fatah loyalists and to curtail the activities of civil society organizations affiliated with his opponents.[29] Providing Arafat with what American officials called "walking around
money" was considered a necessary evil in order to help strengthen the
PA and its ability to implement agreements, fight terrorists, and neutralize Oslo's opponents.[30]

Meanwhile, the anticipated "peace dividend" never materialized.
Israeli closures and other restrictive measures in the West Bank and
Gaza in response to terrorist attacks led to a precipitous decline in
Palestinian economic conditions during the Oslo period. Thus, between 1992 and 2001 Palestinian living standards declined by approximately 20 percent.[31] Unemployment rates tripled as the economic
growth rate stood at half what it had been prior to Oslo.[32] As a result,
the focus of donor aid shifted from encouraging economic growth to
merely keeping the PA—and the Oslo process—afloat.[33] Foreign aid,
as one U.S. official observed, "quickly became life support, not development aid."[34] The PA's growing dependency on international aid also
raised questions as to whether Palestinian leaders should be more responsive to the needs of its donors and benefactors than to those of its
constituents.[35]

The central flaw of Oslo, according to Nigel Roberts, the former World Bank country director, was that it "required that the PLO turn protector of Israel at a time when Israel was still in occupation of territories the PLO was committed to liberating."[36] Repressive measures by the PA and Israel led to temporary lulls in violence but failed to put an end to terror attacks by Hamas and other militant groups. Not only did the "security first" doctrine fail to curb attacks on Israelis, it is likely that Hamas and other militant groups became stronger as a result of "the economically regressive and politically stifling atmosphere of Oslo."[37] As the same time, the securitization of Palestinian governance under Oslo helped to deepen the rift between the PA and Hamas while steadily eroding the credibility of the PA and the peace process. To be sure, relations between Fatah and Hamas had long been strained, but the relationship became considerably more antagonistic and confrontational during the Oslo years.

Arafat preferred to deal with Hamas through a combination of carrots and sticks, alternating between repression and attempts at cooptation, an approach American and Israeli officials strongly disapproved of. Although Hamas mostly refrained from violent reprisals against the PA, it still had the ability to hit Arafat where it hurt most—the peace process and his budding relationship with the United States. A relentless series of suicide bombings in Israeli cities in early 1996 following the assassination of the Hamas military commander Yahya Ayyash in January 1996 claimed the lives of fifty-nine Israelis and brought intense American and Israeli pressure on Arafat to take firm action. The PA's subsequent crackdown on Hamas and other militant groups led to a period of relative calm in the second half of 1997, although Hamas suicide bombings resumed in early 1997. Human rights groups accused the PA of torture, arbitrary arrests, and other abuses, but Clinton administration officials largely looked the other way and occasionally even voiced their approval. When human rights groups accused the PA of violating basic due process by using special "security courts" to try suspected terrorists, Vice President Al Gore defended the practice, claiming "the accusations are misplaced and that they are doing the right thing in progressing with prosecutions."[38] The PA's repressive measures also played into the hands of Arafat's domestic political opponents. "If you were Hamas," observed Bruce Riedel, who served in the Clinton White House during the latter years of Oslo, "how could you design a scenario more to your liking, in which the father of the Fatah security service is going to be the Central Intelligence Agency working with the Israelis? It's like it's setup to undermine these people. And yet that's how we ended up."[39]

THE PRICE OF AMBIVALENCE

As in the past, the White House and Congress managed to work both for and against the goals of the peace process at the same time. Bill Clinton came to office determined to undo what he viewed as the overly critical approach to Israel taken by his predecessors. A former administration official and peace process veteran, Aaron David Miller, recalled, "That several of us happened to be Jewish was less important than the prevailing climate of pro-Israel sentiment that mushroomed under Bill Clinton."[40] That climate was quickly translated into policy. The Clinton administration backed away from the assurances provided to the Palestinians by James Baker ahead of the Madrid conference, which according to Dennis Ross had created "needless suspicions on the Israeli side, and raised expectations on the Palestinian side."[41] Within months of taking office, Clinton also became the first U.S. president since 1948 not to reaffirm UN General Assembly Resolution 194 on the rights of Palestinian refugees. Although the refugee issue remained unresolved, U.S. officials characterized Resolution 194 as "obsolete and anachronistic" following the signing of the Oslo Declaration of Principles, mirroring the language of the Israeli government.[42] In addition, the Clinton administration for the first time lent tacit U.S. approval to Israeli settlement construction in the occupied territories.[43] The Clinton White House did away with language referring to Israeli settlements as "obstacles to peace"; instead they were now downgraded to a "complicating factor" in the peace process.[44]

Congress responded to Oslo by passing new legislation with the barely concealed aim of tipping the scales in Israel's favor and handicapping the Palestinians politically and diplomatically. The new laws were the product of a Congress controlled by a Republican leadership that was highly skeptical of Oslo and by pro-Israel lobbyists who were well to the right of the Israeli government—some of whom were openly committed to defeating the peace process. Despite objections from both the Rabin government and the Clinton administration, Congress passed a new foreign aid bill in 1994 backed by the anti-Oslo Zionist Organization of America that prevented the transfer of aid to the Palestinians until the president certified that the PLO was complying with signed agreements.[45] No similar provisions were put in place regarding Israel's compliance. That same year, Congress passed new laws requiring the United States to defund UN agencies—and potentially the UN as a whole—that admitted the Palestinians as a full member. Another Oslo-era piece of legislation with an embedded "poison pill" was the Jerusalem Embassy Act of 1995—the same law invoked by President Donald Trump in December 2017. In addition to recognizing "undivided" Jerusalem as Israel's capital, the law required the United States to move its embassy from Tel Aviv to Jerusalem by 1999, while allowing the president to waive implementation every six months. Although opposed by the Clinton administration on both diplomatic and constitutional grounds, the law passed by wide bipartisan majorities in both houses of Congress. Trump eschewed the customary waiver, thus giving the act force for the first time.

The Oslo process suffered from a number of deficiencies, including the absence of an implementation mechanism and a lack of accountability. In addition, Oslo's focus on incremental progress left too many opportunities for extremists on either side to derail the process. As a result, gestures intended as confidence-building measures did not actually build confidence but ended up expending large amounts of political capital just to keep the process afloat. Given the high domestic political costs entailed in such concessions, the two sides had few incentives to do more than what was minimally required to keep the process alive.[46] This was compounded by the Clinton administration's reluctance either to pressure Israel to meet its obligations or to accommodate Palestinian domestic political constraints. The failure of Israel to follow through on its commitments, particularly after Netanyahu came to power, badly damaged Arafat's credibility and that of the peace process as a whole. By the end of Clinton's presidency, Israel had carried out only two of the three withdrawals agreed to in the 1995 Interim Agreement, reflecting mainly Netanyahu's reluctance to upset his right-wing coalition. Even when Netanyahu's cabinet voted not to carry out the withdrawals called for in the October 1998 Wye Memorandum, Clinton still asked Congress to approve $900 million in supplemental aid to implement an agreement that Israel had failed to implement.[47]

The two issues that ultimately doomed the Oslo process in the eyes of ordinary Israelis and Palestinians—terrorism by Palestinians and continued Israeli settlement expansion—received very different treatment by the administration. The administration had consistently pressured Arafat to crack down on Palestinian militants, which while politically understandable was ultimately ineffective. On the other hand, American officials did very little to curb the growth of Israeli settlements, an area where they could genuinely have affected the outcome were it not for a lack of political will. Israeli settlements were considered an "obstacle to peace," but apparently not a big enough obstacle to warrant any sort of cost for Israel. The former Clinton peace team member Aaron David Miller stated, "I don't recall a single tough, honest conversation in which we said to the Israelis, 'Look, settlements may not violate the letter of Oslo, but they're wreaking havoc with its spirit and compromising the logic of a gradual process of building trust and confidence.'"[48] Instead, the Clinton administration urged the Israelis to refrain from building in the settlements while carving out various exemptions for East Jerusalem, large "settlement blocs," "natural growth," and other loopholes. As a result, during the Oslo years, from 1993 to 2000, the Israeli settler population in the West Bank, East Jerusalem, and the Gaza Strip grew from roughly 270,000 to more than 370,000, nearly three times the growth rate inside Israel.[49]

The announcement in February 1997 by the Netanyahu government of plans to build a new settlement, Har Homa, on the outskirts of Jerusalem illustrated the very different responses by the administration to the political pressures facing both sides. The new settlement,

strategically situated between East Jerusalem's Palestinian neighborhoods and the West Bank town of Bethlehem, was seen by Palestinians
as a major blow to their hopes of establishing a future capital in East
Jerusalem. The administration expressed its objection to the new settlement but declined to pressure the Israeli government to halt the project
out of deference to Netanyahu's precarious coalition. "Prime minister," Ross told Netanyahu, "you will have to do what you have to do, but
there will be a problem and you should not kid yourself."[50] Clinton took
the additional step of vetoing a Security Council resolution calling on
Israel to abandon its plans for the new settlement.[51] In response to the
announcement and Netanyahu's reluctance to move forward with further withdrawals, Arafat attempted to shield himself politically by suspending peace talks with Israel and making overtures to his political
opponents, including releasing prisoners and inviting Palestinian
factions to a "national dialogue." The administration condemned
the inclusion of Hamas and other militant groups in the internal dialogue. According to Ross, such gestures were evidence of Arafat's du-
plicitous character and his "preoccupation . . . with how he looked to
his public . . . Defiance being so much a part of Arafat's appeal to Palestinians, always took precedence over accommodation, particularly if
he judged the mood to be negative in the street."[52]

The administration's ambivalence on issues such as settlements and
Jerusalem, while reflective of Clinton's and the Democratic Party's
strong political and ideological attachment to Israel, nonetheless had serious consequences for the success of the Oslo process. The emphasis
on improving security and combating terrorism was understandable but
was ultimately fruitless in the absence of a similar effort to deal with the
highly corrosive effects of Israeli repression, internal closures, and settlement expansion policies. "It was almost impossible to even discuss
the implications with [U.S. officials] at a senior level," recalled Joseph
Saba, the World Bank's country director for the West Bank and Gaza in
the 1990s. According to Saba, Clinton administration officials "some-
how did not appreciate, or chose not to appreciate, their significance for
a Palestinian state or the consequences of the suffocation of Palestinian political and economic aspirations."[53] The failure to deal with the

increasingly explosive conditions on the ground would have serious consequences. Instead of building a peace constituency among Palestinians, the Oslo process seemed to produce the opposite. By the end of 2000, there had been a marked increase in support among Palestinians for violence while only a minority of Palestinians still supported the Oslo process; the two primary reasons cited were a lack of improvement in living standards and increased settlement activity.[54]

THE CLINTON PARADOX

Although his personal and political leanings were clearly aligned with Israel, few presidents showed a greater willingness to break with old taboos and break new ground with regard to the Palestinians and the peace process than Clinton. When controversy broke out over Arafat's attendance at the signing ceremony in September 1993, it was Clinton who decided that he needed to be there.[55] In addition to hosting Arafat at the White House a dozen times, Clinton skillfully used his soft power to bolster the Palestinian leader while subtly bearing down on the Netanyahu government. Clinton also went out of his way to connect with Palestinians on a human level. "If ever there was a president who could be both pro-Israel and pro-Palestinian, it was Clinton," observed William Quandt.[56]

Indeed, for a time, the "trade-off" appeared to be working well for both sides, particularly after Netanyahu came to power in 1996. That same year, the United States extended its free trade agreement with Israel to include Palestinian products originating in the West Bank and Gaza, ostensibly laying the groundwork for an independent bilateral relationship. In the spring of 1998, an increasingly frustrated Clinton indirectly accused Netanyahu of "a deliberate strategy of delay."[57] Hillary Clinton's public observation in May 1998 that it was in the interests of all sides "for Palestine to be a state" roiled the Netanyahu government. Although the White House walked backed the first lady's statement as a slip of the tongue, the president had already arrived at the same conclusion, even if he would not say so officially.

The real high point in U.S.-Palestinian relations occurred in the lead-up to and just after the signing of the Wye River Memorandum, an agreement negotiated between Israel and the Palestinian Authority at a summit in Wye River, Maryland in October 1998. Under Oslo II, Israel was to carry out three substantive redeployments of Israeli forces from West Bank territory. The first phase was completed in January 1997, when Secretary of State Warren Christopher successfully brokered a deal on Israel's redeployment from most of Hebron. Since then, however, the Netanyahu government had dragged its feet on carrying out any further withdrawals. Instead of compelling the Israeli prime minister to live up to his obligations, the Clinton administration agreed to renegotiate the terms of the withdrawal. The Palestinians had been pushing for a withdrawal from an additional 30 percent of West Bank territory while Netanyahu was prepared to offer only 9 percent. Ross basically split the difference, proposing that Israel withdraw from 13 percent. The transfers would occur in parallel with antiterrorism measures by the PA. Despite his bitterness over Netanyahu's intransigence, Arafat went along with the U.S. proposal. According to Ross, "This reflected the weakness of his position, because our proposals were far closer to the original Israeli concepts than to his."[58] The arrangement was formalized at a three-way summit between Clinton, Netanyahu, and Arafat held at the Wye River Plantation in Maryland.

Upon returning to Israel, however, Netanyahu suspended implementation of the Wye Memorandum while making new demands of the PA. "This was unfortunate," explained Ross, "because the Palestinians were working diligently to carry out most of their commitments under Wye, particularly in the area of making arrests and fighting terror."[59] The administration was much less pleased with Netanyahu. After Wye, according to the PLO's Ahmed Qurei, "The Americans began to display an unprecedented level of sympathy with our aspirations. This change in American attitudes resulted in part from the sustained diplomatic effort by my Palestinian colleagues at Wye River and elsewhere, but also because of Netanyahu's bad management and mistakes."[60]

The crowning moment for Arafat came in December 1998 during the president's historic visit to Gaza and Bethlehem. Palestinian officials saw the visit "as a boost for us and as a rebuke to Netanyahu for his provocation of the Americans," including his lack of compliance with agreements he had signed.[61] The stated purpose of the visit was to allow Clinton to oversee the removal of objectionable passages from the PLO's charter, a key demand of the Netanyahu government. However, Clinton used the visit to send a clear message to leaders on both sides. After presiding over the PNC vote amending the PLO charter in Gaza City, Clinton addressed the hundreds of delegates assembled: "For the first time in the history of the Palestinian movement, the Palestinian people and their elected representatives now have a chance to determine their own destiny on their own land." It was the closest a U.S. president had come to supporting a Palestinian state. During his short visit to Gaza, Clinton took the time to meet with Palestinian children whose fathers had been killed or imprisoned by Israel. "Those children brought tears to my eyes," he declared. "We have to find a way for both sets of children to get their lives back and to go forward."[62] Arafat's many risky ventures since 1973—the intelligence and security cooperation with the CIA, the countless third-party dialogues, the various UN initiatives, the decision to recognize Israel—all seemed to be leading to this moment.

BLAME GAME: CAMP DAVID AND THE INTIFADA

Arafat's moment lasted until roughly May 1999, when Ehud Barak of the Labor Party defeated Netanyahu for Israel's premiership. Barak had come to office with a highly ambitious diplomatic agenda, promising to conclude comprehensive peace agreements with both Syria and the Palestinians within fifteen months and to end Israel's occupation of southern Lebanon. Barak's bold ideas appealed to Clinton, who was now in the final year of his presidency. Arafat, however, distrusted Barak, who like his predecessor had reneged on his commitments to hand over territory and release prisoners. The Palestinian leader was also troubled by Barak's determination to pursue the Syrian track first, which had the blessing of the Clinton administration. A separate peace agreement between Syria and Israel, much like the Egypt-Israel treaty of 1979, would leave the Palestinians more isolated and exposed. After Israeli-Syrian talks collapsed in early 2000, Barak shifted back to the Palestinian track and convinced Clinton of the need to convene a high-stakes peace summit between Israelis and Palestinians. Although Arafat resisted the idea as premature and highly risky, Clinton embraced Barak's plan and remained highly deferential to the Israeli prime minister throughout the process, from the timing and structure of the summit in Camp David to the fateful decision to lay blame for its failure solely on the Palestinians.[63]

On July 11, President Clinton hosted Ehud Barak and Yasser Arafat at the Camp David presidential retreat in Maryland. Over the course of the next two weeks, the Israeli and Palestinian leaders, along with their respective teams, held intensive negotiations on all of the core issues, including security, territory, Jerusalem, and refugees. The talks were punctuated by periodic interventions by President Clinton with the active support of the U.S. peace team, most of whom remained at the compound for the duration of the summit as the president shuttled back and forth between Camp David and Washington. The negotiations adopted an all-or-nothing approach, based on the principle that "nothing is agreed until everything was agreed." The stakes were therefore exceptionally high, particularly for Arafat, who feared being entrapped by his two more powerful counterparts. The talks made some progress in the area of security and to a lesser extent on territory, but wide gaps remained on the central issues of Jerusalem and refugees. When Clinton proved unable to bridge those gaps, the summit ended in failure. The collapse of the Camp David summit in July 2000, which was soon followed by the outbreak of the Palestinian uprising, the Al-Aqsa Intifada, became the first real demonstration of how the power and political dynamics of the American-led peace process operated in times of crisis. Although all three leaders were guilty of missteps and miscalculations during and after Camp David, it was easier and less costly politically for Clinton and his ally, Barak, to shift the costs of failure onto the Palestinians in general and Arafat in particular. However, this came at the expense of broader U.S. goals of stability and diplomacy.[64] In addition to narrowing the political space for an agreement during

Clinton's remaining time in office, the decision helped to fuel the cycle of violence in the months and years that followed and to cement the "no partner" narrative later seized on by Prime Minister Ariel Sharon.

According to the Israeli narrative, which gained wide currency in Washington, the Camp David talks failed when Arafat unreasonably rejected a "generous offer" by Barak and then instigated a violent Intifada in an attempt to squeeze more concessions out of the Americans and Israelis.[65] However, accounts by various Palestinian, American, and Israeli former negotiators, scholars, journalists, and other observers told a different story.[66] Arafat had been reluctant to go along with the idea of a "make or break" summit out of a fear that Clinton and Barak would team up against him and attempt to squeeze the Palestinians and then blame them for the summit's failure. Despite a prior pledge by the president not to blame Arafat in the event of failure, however, Clinton joined Barak in publicly holding Arafat responsible for the summit's collapse. Clinton's interests in pursuing an Israeli-Palestinian peace deal were not driven solely by calculations of American national interests or the strategic, diplomatic, or humanitarian benefits that resolution of the conflict might bring. His motivations were also rooted in more parochial concerns, such as the primacy of U.S.-Israel relations, Clinton's personal admiration for Barak and his desire to help him politically, and the president's own desire to enhance his legacy.[67]

The summit itself was plagued by a variety of deficiencies related to all three sides, including a lack of preparation on the part of its American hosts and internal dynamics that were notoriously "dysfunctional."[68] A lack of cohesion on the Palestinian side also hampered the process and greatly limited Arafat's flexibility.[69] Compounding the problem was a distinct knowledge and expertise gap on the American team. According to one American negotiator, Clinton and the U.S. team began the summit already predisposed "to consider Israeli needs and requirements as the standard by which to judge what we could live with." In contrast, the U.S. team's understanding of Palestinian needs or claims was far more limited, particularly on the crucial questions of sovereignty and the future of Jerusalem.[70]

In the end, the problems with Camp David came down to substance. The climax of the summit was Barak's proposal for a Palestinian state on some 80 to 90 percent of the West Bank (depending on the method of calculation) along with limited autonomy in Arab East Jerusalem. Under the proposal tabled by Barak, the Palestinians would have sovereignty over Arab suburbs of Jerusalem but only "functional autonomy" in the city's Palestinian neighborhoods, including the Old City, where most Christian and Muslim holy sites are located, as well as "custodianship" over the Al-Aqsa Mosque compound (Haram al-Sharif, the Temple Mount). Clinton and the American team hailed Barak's offer as a "far reaching and brave" proposal.[71] While certainly unprecedented and politically risky from the standpoint of Israeli politics, Barak's offer fell well short of the Palestinian's minimal demands. Among other things, the proposal seriously undervalued the importance of Palestinian sovereignty in Jerusalem and the depth of Arab and Muslim attachment to the Holy City. "At Camp David we never got close," said one member of the U.S. team. "Despite the mythology that's been created since then, we weren't even in the ballpark."[72]

The Palestinians rejected the Israeli proposal in its entirety but declined to make a counteroffer. Like Barak, Arafat was under enormous domestic pressure not to concede too much at Camp David.[73] Popular frustration in the occupied territories had been running high, while Hamas leaders seized every opportunity to denounce Arafat for participating in the peace summit.[74] Moreover, as the weakest party in the equation, the Palestinian leader was even more circumspect in his approach to the summit than his American and Israeli counterparts. The exceptionally high stakes for both sides may also explain why Barak, perhaps feeling overly exposed by the extent of his unrequited offer, chose to lash out at Arafat. In the wake of the failed summit, the Israeli prime minister mounted a media campaign denouncing Arafat as a nonpartner who had no interest in peace.

The fact that the most significant progress occurred after the summit suggested that Barak's offer at Camp David was not in fact the best offer the Palestinians could hope to get from the Israelis, as Barak and the American team had claimed, but rather was a basis for more serious negotiations in the months that followed. Despite Barak's campaign to paint Arafat as "not a partner" for peace, Israelis and Palestinians continued to negotiate in the weeks and months after the summit, both with and without American mediation. However, the outbreak of the Al-Aqsa Intifada in late September 2000 made the ongoing peace talks both more urgent and less likely to succeed.

The uprising was triggered by the visit of Ariel Sharon, the leader of the Likud opposition, to the Al-Aqsa Mosque compound in Jerusalem in late September, but it reflected deeper Palestinian frustrations that had been simmering beneath the surface for some time.[75] Israeli and Palestinian leaders both sought to leverage the violence politically, even as they continued to negotiate: Arafat often approved of armed attacks on Israelis, either directly or by turning a blind eye; Barak gave the Israeli army a free hand in the occupied territories in a bid to crush the uprising in its infancy. Human rights groups and other international observers attributed the rapid escalation of violence to Israel's use of lethal force against both unarmed protesters and armed militants, leading to extensive civilian casualties and contributing to the militarization of the Intifada at an early stage. An official fact-finding commission appointed by Clinton in October 2000 and headed by former Senate majority leader George Mitchell later found that "for the first three months of the current uprising, most incidents did not involve Palestinian use of firearms and explosives."[76] Israeli, Palestinian, and international human rights groups came to similar conclusions.[77]

The administration responded to the violence with characteristic ambivalence. Despite occasional rebukes by the U.S. State Department of Israeli use of "excessive force," the administration put the onus for the violence on the Palestinians. In an interview with a Sunday morning news program, CNN's *Late Edition*, Secretary of State Madeleine Albright complained that "the Palestinians in many ways are putting the Israelis under siege," and accused Palestinian stone-throwers of provoking a "siege mentality" among Israeli soldiers.[78]

By the time the Americans put forward a serious peace proposal in late December, the political environment was far less hospitable to peacemaking. Unlike at Camp David, Clinton's "parameters" for a final status peace deal, which envisioned a Palestinian state in roughly 95 percent of the West Bank plus Gaza with Palestinian sovereignty over most of East Jerusalem, including much of the Old City, were by all measures "in the ballpark." Sovereignty over the highly contentious Al-Aqsa Mosque–Temple Mount would be divided between Palestinians and Israelis. The bulk of Palestinian refugees would be resettled in the Palestinian state with a limited number allowed to return to Israel. After three months of bloodshed and with less than a month remaining in Clinton's term, however, the political calculus on all sides had changed. The narrow window of opportunity that emerged after the collapse of Camp David in late July effectively closed following the outbreak of violence in late September. Moreover, with Israeli elections only weeks away, Barak's defeat at the hands of Sharon looked increasingly imminent. Arafat, too, faced growing public anger over the mounting civilian casualties as well as the growing appeal of Hamas and other "resistance" elements, and was steadily losing control over dynamics on the ground.

Clinton's offer was take-it-or-leave-it, and the two leaders were given just four days to respond. Although both sides had serious misgivings about the plan, neither rejected it outright. Barak and Arafat each gave what amounted to a highly qualified yes. This seems to have been Clinton's interpretation as well, and a January 7 statement issued by the White House acknowledged that "both Prime Minister Barak and Chairman Arafat have now accepted these parameters as the basis for further efforts. Both have expressed some reservations."[79] Ross saw things differently, however, and convinced Clinton that whereas Barak's reservations were "within" the parameters, Arafat's were not and, hence, were "tantamount to rejection."[80] It is not clear why Clinton shifted his stance regarding Arafat's response. Although it is reasonable to assume that with the clock running down and the realization slowly setting in that a conflict-ending peace deal was not in the offing, the urge to assess blame increased in parallel—if only to help ensure that the failure did not end up as part of Clinton's legacy.

Since then a debate has raged over whether Arafat's failure to give an unequivocal yes was motivated by political considerations or something more nefarious. Israeli leaders have suggested that it was because

Arafat was not genuinely interested in peace—his true aim was "the elimination of Israel," if not through violence and terror then by seeking to flood Israel with millions of refugees.[81] Administration officials attributed Arafat's response to his failure to "pivot from being a revolutionary and the leader of a movement to being a statesman and the leader of a country."[82] Such explanations however seem to overlook the more basic factors of power and politics. It should not come as a surprise that the weakest and most politically disadvantaged actor would also be the most risk-averse. And after the Camp David blame game, Arafat likely understood where he stood vis-à-vis Clinton.

Timing and political environment were also likely critical factors in shaping Arafat's decision making. By the time Clinton left office, nearly 300 Palestinians and 43 Israelis had been killed in the Intifada.[83] The mounting Palestinian death toll, public anger at both Israel and the United States, and the growing appeal of Hamas and other "resistance" elements, would have limited what Arafat could agree to explicitly. "If they had offered [the Clinton Parameters] in the first or second week of the Intifada, it could have changed history," observed a veteran Palestinian negotiator.[84] With Clinton on his way out and Barak's chances for defeating Sharon in upcoming elections growing slimmer by the day, "The likelihood of reaching a deal was remote at best; if no deal could be made, the Palestinians feared they would be left with principles that were detailed enough to supersede international resolutions, yet too fuzzy to constitute an agreement."[85] Arafat may have also believed that he would fare better under the incoming administration of George W. Bush, an impression that seems to have been encouraged by his friends in Saudi Arabia.[86] In other words, Arafat may have rationally assessed the potential costs of an unequivocal acceptance as too high and the expected return too low.

In the eyes of American officials, however, Arafat would remain the "artful dodger" and "master manipulator" who had failed to prepare his people for the hard choices necessary for peace.[87] That the same could be said of Barak—who after all did not fully understand the requirements of peace until after the collapse of the Camp David summit—was less compelling to American officials in light of the political dynamics between the two countries. As the Camp David negotiator Bruce Riedel explains, "When the moment of truth came, there was no doubt whose side we were going to come down on."[88] According to Clinton's national security adviser, Sandy Berger, Arafat's chief failing was that he "had not built the framework into which he could try to sell an agreement."[89] But building such a political framework would have likely required a far more cohesive and inclusive brand of Palestinian politics than either Arafat or the Oslo process were prepared to tolerate. Clinton unloaded his anger with Arafat onto the incoming Bush administration. "Don't ever trust that son of a bitch," he warned. "He lied to me, and he'll lie to you."[90] Although far less interested in peacemaking than his predecessor, Bush nonetheless heeded the advice. The peace process was failing, and for that someone would have to pay a price.

6

The Price of Failure

I believe that there could be no greater legacy for America than to help to bring into being a Palestinian state for a people who have suffered too long, who have been humiliated too long, who have not reached their potential for too long, and who have so much to give to the international community and to all of us.

—Condoleezza Rice, keynote address at American Task Force on Palestine inaugural gala, October 11, 2006

Ariel Sharon was known as many things during his long political and military career, but "a man of peace" was seldom one of them. Yet these were the words President George W. Bush used to describe the Israeli prime minister in April 2002. At the time, the statement drew a mix of outrage and bewilderment both at home and abroad, including a phone call from the president's father, George H. W. Bush, who telephoned "to complain vociferously about the president's choice of words."[1]

The timing of Bush's comment was especially awkward, coming as it did in the midst of a massive Israeli military offensive in the West Bank that had destroyed much of the Palestinian Authority's security apparatus and governing institutions and resulted in the deaths of hundreds of Palestinians and dozens of Israeli soldiers. A week earlier, in one of the bloodiest episodes since the start of the Al-Aqsa Intifada, IDF soldiers had raided the Jenin refugee camp, leaving fifty-two Palestinians and twenty-three soldiers dead and triggering allegations of war crimes. A report by Human Rights Watch accused the IDF of the "deliberate killing of civilians."[2] The day after Bush's comments on Sharon, the administration voted in favor of a UN Security Council resolution calling for a fact-finding team to investigate events inside Jenin refugee camp, although Israel subsequently blocked the team from entering the country. The series of events was emblematic of the Bush administration's highly conflicted approach to the Israeli-Palestinian conflict, which even more than Clinton's simultaneously worked both for and against the goals of the peace process.

One aspect of Bush's approach that was rather consistent however was in working to ensure that the costs of repeated political and diplomatic failures were borne primarily by the Palestinians. Both the horrific violence of the Intifada in the early 2000s and Hamas's surprise election victory of 2006 posed serious challenges for U.S. policymakers and for the peace process as a whole as well as major opportunities for course correction. But instead of addressing the many longstanding contradictions that had accumulated within the Oslo process, including their own roles in creating them, American and Israeli decision makers consistently put the onus for absorbing the fallout from these challenges onto the Palestinians. Like any fragile object subjected to persistent pressure, the Palestinian Authority eventually broke, further crippling both the peace process and Palestinian politics for the foreseeable future.

1982 REDUX

In contrast to his predecessor, who had invested considerable time and energy in the pursuit of Israeli-Palestinian peace, George W. Bush significantly scaled back American involvement in the peace process.

Bush shared Clinton's assessment that Arafat and the Palestinians were largely to blame for the collapse of peace negotiations and the ongoing violence but saw little value in wading into the troubled waters of Arab-Israeli peacemaking despite early opportunities to do so.[3] When Israeli and Palestinian negotiators held a final round of peace talks in Taba, Egypt, in late January, the Bush administration largely stayed away from the proceedings. A single State Department official was dispatched to Taba for the purpose of reporting back to Washington. The election shortly after Bush took office of Ariel Sharon, who shared the new president's tough stance on terror and his penchant for unilateralism, only reinforced the president's aversion to the peace process.

Like Ronald Reagan, Bush came to office with a limited knowledge of foreign affairs and a tendency to view the world in stark, black-and-white terms.[4] Moreover, his administration was plagued by internal divisions and infighting between two opposing camps with very different approaches to the Middle East and the world. Secretary of State Colin Powell and CIA director George Tenet favored a balanced approach to the Israeli-Palestinian conflict as well as active American involvement in dealing with the crisis. On the other side were Vice President Dick Cheney and Defense Secretary Donald Rumsfeld, along with a cadre of neoconservatives, who preferred to give Sharon a free hand in dealing with the uprising. As Condoleezza Rice later wrote in her memoirs, "The differences in the administration between the decidedly pro-Israel bent of the White House and the State Department's more traditional pro-Arab view percolated beneath the surface."[5] Bush vacillated between the two camps throughout his presidency, which led to a pattern of indecision, inconsistency, and lack of follow through.[6]

Bush's attempts to steer clear of the conflict would not last, however, as the violence of the Intifada continued to spiral out of control. Sharon's determination to crush the Intifada through military force had helped to fuel the militarization of the uprising, leading to a sharp rise in attacks on Israeli civilians as well as a growing humanitarian crisis in the West Bank and Gaza. Roughly half of the Israelis killed during the first four months of the Intifada (September 29, 2000, to January 20, 2001) were civilians. However, that proportion shot up to around

80 percent in the four-month period that followed (January 21 to June 1, 2001).[7] Mounting casualties and growing Arab anger over Washington's hands-off approach spurred the administration to act. After a Hamas suicide bombing at a Tel Aviv nightclub killed scores of Israelis in June 2001, Bush sent CIA Director George Tenet to the region to arrange the first of several abortive ceasefires. Sharon simply ignored the truce, preferring instead to keep up the pressure militarily. Arafat, too, was not inclined to fully assert his authority by clamping down on groups such as Hamas and Islamic Jihad. The spike in terror attacks galvanized Israeli public support for Sharon's crackdown in the occupied territories, while Washington's Arab friends viewed Bush's inaction as an endorsement of Sharon's war on the Palestinians.

The administration's tepid response to the violence strained its ties with its key Arab ally, Saudi Arabia, whose de facto ruler, Crown Prince Abdullah, repeatedly turned down Bush's invitations to visit Washington. In late August 2001, Abdullah sent a strongly worded message to President Bush warning that unless the United States found "a way to separate the actions of the Israeli government and its own interests in the region," the kingdom would be forced to reevaluate its relationship with the United States.[8] Rattled by the threat from its Saudi ally, and with the backing of Secretary of State Colin Powell, Bush sent a private message to the Saudi ruler pledging to take concrete steps to advance the peace process while affirming that "the Palestinian people have a right to self-determination and to live peacefully and securely in their own state, in their own homeland, just as the Israelis have a right to live peacefully and safely in their own state."[9] In his message to Abdullah, the president also promised to make a similar public declaration in support of Palestinian statehood the following month.

The terrorist attacks of September 11, 2001, on Washington and New York exacerbated divisions within the administration, which were now reflected in its increasingly discordant policies. Bush continued to adhere to Secretary of State Powell's moderate, multilateralist approach to the peace process for the first few months after the attacks but gradually began to publicly align with Sharon. In the wake of the attacks, the White House rejected Sharon's characterization of Arafat as "our Bin

Laden," and further angered the Israeli prime minister by refusing his repeated requests for permission to "go after" Arafat.[10] Bush also kept his promise to the Saudis, affirming for the first time official American support for Palestinian statehood. In a speech before the UN General Assembly on November 10, 2001, Bush declared, "We are working toward the day when two states—Israel and Palestine—live peacefully together within secure and recognized borders, as called for by the Security Council resolutions."[11] The speech infuriated the Israeli government and conservatives within the administration, who viewed it as a "significant departure" from past U.S. policy.[12] Clinton had attempted to delineate the contours of a Palestinian state in the negotiations, but Bush's statement for the first time made a two-state solution official U.S. policy.

The statement was a major victory for Powell, who now led the international effort to reengage with the Israelis and the Palestinians diplomatically. Working with representatives of the European Union, the United Nations, and Russia, who joined the United States in the newly formed Middle East Quartet, Powell coordinated the Quartet's efforts to end the violence and reestablish a diplomatic process. With only limited engagement by the president, however, the peace process remained Powell's domain. Bush resisted calls to appoint a special envoy for the Middle East, as past presidents had done, leaving Powell to name his own special adviser for the peace process, General Anthony Zinni.

Powell's approach would not last. The United States was now engaged in a war in Afghanistan against the Taliban as part of the broader global fight against terrorism. Bush came under mounting pressure from the Israeli government and administration hardliners, as well as his own conservative base, to reorient his approach to the Israel-Palestine conflict as well. Their efforts were unwittingly aided by Arafat, who had failed to fully appreciate the new realities of the post-9/11 era and continued to green-light violence and attacks on Israelis, either directly or with a wink and a nod. The decisive moment came on January 3, 2002, following Israel's seizure of a Gaza-bound ship, the *Karine A*, in the Mediterranean that was carrying weapons. Although Arafat denied involvement, the incident convinced Bush that Arafat was a "failed leader" and that peace would require a transformation of Palestinian politics.[13] Sharon, who had already declared Arafat "irrelevant" and severed ties with the Palestinian Authority shortly after 9/11, welcomed the shift in the administration's position.

In the meantime, the situation on the ground went from bad to worse. On March 29, 2002, following a pair of deadly suicide bombings in Israel for which Hamas claimed responsibility, including an attack on a Passover celebration that left thirty Israelis dead, Sharon launched a major offensive in the West Bank, operation "Defensive Shield." During the operation—the largest military offensive since Israel captured the territory in 1967—the IDF reoccupied Palestinian cities while Israeli tanks surrounded Arafat inside his Ramallah headquarters, the Muqataa. The nature and scale of the Israeli offensive was reminiscent of Sharon's invasion of Lebanon two decades earlier. As in the 1982 war, the IDF's targets extended well beyond armed militants and the "infrastructure of terrorism" to include a wide range of Palestinian institutions and national symbols. Having already closed down Palestinian institutions in Jerusalem, including the PLO's unofficial headquarters, known as Orient House, the previous year, Sharon now set his sights on those in the West Bank and Gaza.[14] In addition to destroying Gaza's international airport, Israeli forces targeted numerous Palestinian Authority ministries, including Health, Education, Finance, and Agriculture, along with the Central Bureau of Statistics and several municipalities, and seized or destroyed official computers, public records, and cultural works.[15] Terje Rød-Larsen, the UN special coordinator in the occupied territories, warned that events were "moving in the direction of state destruction and not state building."[16]

The White House responded to the invasion with conflicting messages, affirming Israel's "right to defend itself from terror" while simultaneously warning Sharon "to halt incursions into Palestinian-controlled areas and begin the withdrawal from those cities it has recently occupied."[17] The president's mixed message amounted to a green light for Sharon to quash the Intifada while systematically destroying Palestinian governing and security institutions along the way. In an attempt to defuse the crisis, Powell traveled to Ramallah to meet

with Arafat in his besieged and partially demolished presidential compound. However, Bush prevented Powell from making any offers to
Arafat, so his mission ended in failure.[18] Meanwhile, Sharon brushed
aside the administration's warnings and pressed on with the operation,
which continued for another month and ended only after Bush threatened to publicly criticize Israel "in the harshest terms."[19] The six-week
offensive left nearly 500 Palestinians dead and most of the PA's institutions damaged or destroyed.

"I was appalled by the violence and loss of life on both sides," Bush
later wrote in his memoirs, "but I refused to accept the moral equiva-
lence between Palestinian suicide attacks on innocent civilians and
Israeli military actions intended to protect their people."[20] The suicide
bombings in Israel were intolerable. But Israel's use of disproportionate military force had killed many more Palestinian civilians and had
made life unbearable for Palestinians in the West Bank and Gaza. As
Rice later wrote, "The President and Colin said yet again that Israel had
a right to defend itself . . . But the Israelis always seem to go too far."[21] In
addition to the moral and humanitarian dimensions, there was also the
question of the political and security costs wrought by the wholesale
destruction of Palestinian security and governing institutions, and of
who would pay them. Sharon continued to insist that the offensive was
no different than the U.S. war on al-Qaeda in Afghanistan, but many in
Washington took a different view. An editorial by the *Washington Post*
noted: "The problem with equating Israel's campaign against terrorism with that of the United States, as Mr. Sharon and some of his American supporters do, is that it overlooks this contest for territory and
sovereignty underlying the Israeli-Palestinian bloodshed. . . . In the
name of uprooting terrorism, they have systematically destroyed the institutions and infrastructure of Palestinian self-government. To back
the Israeli invasion, as the Bush administration has mostly done, is not
just to back the cause of counterterrorism; it is also to abet Mr. Sharon's
drive to suppress Palestinian national rights."[22]

Inside the administration, however, there was one group that was
almost totally in sync with Sharon's thinking, which included Vice President Dick Cheney, Secretary of Defense Donald Rumsfeld, and NSC

staffer Elliott Abrams. The Cheney camp had been in the ascendant
since early 2002, but by June it was firmly in charge of U.S. Middle East
policy. On June 24, in a speech he delivered in the White House Rose
Garden, Bush stated: "Peace requires a new and different Palestinian
leadership, so that a Palestinian state can be born."[23] Under the new
policy Palestinians would need to "elect new leaders . . . not compro-
mised by terror" before there could be movement toward a political
resolution. The speech "was music to Sharon's ears," recalled Condoleezza Rice. Reactions to Bush's speech were considerably more negative in Europe and the Arab world, as well as in much of the State
Department. While most welcomed Bush's call for a Palestinian state,
the speech was widely seen as relieving Israel of any of its own obligations in the peace process.

The speech effectively designated Arafat an unofficial member of
Bush's "axis of evil," alongside the leaders of Iran, Iraq, and North
Korea, while the Intifada and the decades-old Israeli-Palestinian conflict were subsumed under a broadly defined and open-ended war on
terror.[24] For administration hawks, the Palestinians were just one
manifestation of a much broader problem of extremism and terrorism
which were at the heart of the violence and instability in the Middle
East and which, in the wake of 9/11, were also a clear threat to the
American homeland. Terrorism had to be uprooted at its source,
which, in the view of Cheney and other neoconservatives, was the lack
of freedom and democracy. The administration's "war on terror" was
framed in distinctly ideological, even civilizational, terms. The goal
was not simply to end repression or tyranny—otherwise it might also
have taken aim at Israel's occupation—but to restructure the political
and ideological underpinnings of societies where terrorism prevailed
to bring them in line with those of self-described free societies and
Western democracies. It was the same reasoning that propelled the
decision to invade Iraq and overthrow Saddam Hussein in 2003 and
the administration's "freedom agenda," through which the United
States would help transform the region's autocratic regimes into liberal democracies. As the former deputy national security adviser
Elliott Abrams writes, "The president was using Palestine, like Iraq

and Lebanon, as an example of how democracy might be coming to the Arab world."[25]

Politically and rhetorically, Bush and Sharon were now in virtual lockstep. But this did not mean that American and Israeli interests were also in alignment, as the IDF's repeated assaults on Arafat's Ramallah compound throughout 2002 demonstrated. Sharon had openly expressed his desire to expel or kill Arafat, later admitting that he was "sorry that we did not liquidate him," but was prevented from doing so by Bush.[26] Despite their denunciations of Arafat as an unrepentant terrorist and an obstacle to peace, U.S. officials understood that allowing Sharon to "eliminate" him would likely plunge the region into further chaos. Having all but endorsed Sharon's offensive, however, the administration now found it exceedingly difficult to rein it back in. The administration's frustration with Sharon finally boiled over in September 2002, shortly after the Rose Garden speech, during the third and largest assault on the Muqataa. The State Department spokesman Richard Boucher urged Israel "to consider carefully the consequences of its recent actions and their effect on the goals of Palestinian security cooperation and reform of Palestinian institutions in preparation for Palestinian statehood."[27] Even so, it took an American abstention from a Security Council resolution demanding an end to the Arafat siege and a stern warning from the White House for Sharon to comply. "This needs to end now," Rice warned the Israeli ambassador. "If you and I are having this same conversation a week from now, you are going to have a serious problem in this building, and you're going to have that serious problem with me."[28]

In her memoirs, Rice lamented the fact that Israel's repeated attacks on Arafat's compound allowed a "smiling Arafat to emerge to a hero's welcome." Indeed, the Bush administration's hopes for advancing the peace process while denying Arafat's legitimacy and relevance would prove to be a difficult task, not only because of the natural impulse of people to rally around their leaders in times of crisis and his stature among Palestinians as the father of the national movement, but because Arafat himself would not allow himself to be marginalized. Years later a senior Palestinian official described how Arafat would allow "Hamas and others to carry out [armed] action. Not because Arafat was sitting back and thinking 'Now I'll use violence.' But because he thought he can prove he's needed to counter violence."[29] To be sure, many within the PA leadership and even inside Fatah had grown frustrated with Arafat's rule and hoped to loosen his stranglehold over power, including his deputy and longtime rival, Mahmoud Abbas (Abu Mazen). But their task became appreciably more difficult in the context of Israeli siege and perceived American dictates.

A ROADMAP TO NOWHERE

Bush's June 2002 Rose Garden speech effectively modified the original trade-off of the 1990s by adding new conditions on the Palestinians while simultaneously downgrading what they could expect to receive in return. In addition to fighting terror, which of course was even more paramount than before, the Palestinians would also need to elect new leaders and enact democratic reforms to be eligible for statehood. In a sense, Bush's Rose Garden speech marked a return to the Kissinger and Haig school of Arab-Israeli diplomacy, which viewed Palestinian politics as a kind of pathology that needed to be transformed or defeated before peace could be achieved. According to Deputy National Security Adviser Abrams, one of the principal architects of Bush's Palestine policy, peace would require a complete "transformation of Palestinian attitudes and self-identity." The same did not hold true for Israel, however. According to Abrams, Israelis had been engaged in "a decade-long untrammeled debate over the conditions of a final status agreement, but nothing of this sort has occurred on the Palestinian side. The PA and PLO have not prepared the Palestinian people for the national concessions that any final status agreement with Israel will require." In other words, for Abrams and other administration hardliners, the real source of the conflict was not Israel's ongoing military occupation, which still controlled most aspects of Palestinian life in the West Bank and Gaza, or the still unresolved fate of Palestinian refugees, but the fact that Palestinian politics still placed a premium on resolving these issues. The reality, of course, was that Palestinians had been engaged in a highly contentious—often violent—internal debate over the two-state solution dating back to the 1970s, well before such ideas were taken up seriously by Israeli or American politicians. Certainly aspects of Palestinian politics were no doubt distasteful and problematic, but the same could be said of Israeli politics, where settler extremists and other champions of Eretz Yisrael, "Greater Israel," wielded growing influence over the Israeli government and its treatment of Palestinians.

For Abrams and other administration hardliners, Bush's vision was straightforward: "Get rid of Arafat, abandon terror, start building a democracy, and then—but only then—the United States will support creation of a state—and even then, a state 'whose borders and certain aspects of its sovereignty will be provisional' until there was a wider peace agreement in the region." In other words, says Abrams, "Statehood would be the Palestinians' reward for ridding themselves of a corrupt leadership, ending terrorism, and becoming capable of self-government." Abrams had been critical of the president's unconditional embrace of Palestinian statehood earlier on since in his view, "the Palestinian side was not ready for statehood."[30]

In the meantime, Bush's Middle East policy continued to operate on two parallel and increasingly contradictory tracks. Despite the ascendancy of the Cheney camp, Powell continued to pursue his peacemaking agenda through the Middle East Quartet. The Quartet was in many ways an ideal forum for dealing with the seemingly intractable conflict between Israelis and Palestinians. Its small but powerful membership gave it political heft and a degree of authority in dealing with both sides of the conflict, while its informal structure afforded it the flexibility to navigate crises and adapt to changing developments. Since Israel's incursion into the West Bank in the spring of 2002, American, European, Russian, and UN officials had been working on a plan to pave a way out of the violence and back to a diplomatic process—the Roadmap to Peace in the Middle East.

After several delays, the Quartet's roadmap was officially released on April 30, 2003. The authors of the roadmap had sought to correct what they viewed as the primary deficiencies of the Oslo process that ultimately led to its collapse in 2000, including the absence of implementation mechanisms and the overall lack of accountability.[31] The plan's emphasis on parallel implementation and mutual accountability was fundamentally at odds with the one-sided conditionality and implicit unilateralism contained in Bush's Rose Garden speech. The roadmap laid out parallel steps for both sides to rein in violence and end incitement to violence. In addition, the Palestinians would be required to reform their security and governing institutions, including consolidating PA security services and appointing an "empowered" prime minister to help curb Arafat's influence. For its part, Israel was required to freeze "all settlement activity (including natural growth of settlements)" as well as ease movement restrictions in the West Bank and reopen Palestinian institutions in Jerusalem. In terms of implementation, Quartet members discussed the need for a formal monitoring mechanism but instead left the task of ensuring each side's compliance with the roadmap to the United States.

Despite reservations over the roadmap's intrusive nature, the Palestinian leadership had little choice but to embrace it. In contrast, Sharon's government refused to engage with either the plan or its sponsors.[32] Although attempts by the Sharon government to derail or change the roadmap were unsuccessful, they did succeed in delaying its release for several months until after the Israeli election in early 2003, as well as in redefining its provisions more to its liking. The delay in the roadmap's release also gave the administration time to build up international, particularly Arab, support for its impending invasion of Iraq. It also allowed time for the appointment of the PA's first prime minister in the hope of gradually "easing Mr. Arafat out."[33] After hastily amending the Palestinian Basic Law, Arafat reluctantly appointed his longtime deputy Mahmoud Abbas to the post. When Abbas resigned after just five months in office, citing internal opposition and a lack of international support, it became clear that Arafat was still calling the shots and that "the effort to sideline Arafat had failed."[34]

Meanwhile, Israeli officials worked behind the scenes with the White House to negotiate a separate arrangement that was more in line with their concerns, particularly when it came to the settlements and the emphasis on "security first." As a result, the Bush administration agreed to make Israel's implementation of the roadmap conditional on the Palestinians' meeting their obligations first. In addition, instead of a total freeze, Israel could continue building in the occupied territories subject to a much less stringent set of "restrictions on settlement growth."[35] The two main elements of the roadmap—mutual accountability and parallel implementation—had now been eliminated. By July 2003, the roadmap—and for some, the Quartet itself—was already being pronounced dead. "The reason the Roadmap was accepted by the Palestinians was because it specified obligations for both sides, and the Quartet was involved," said one senior Palestinian official. However, he added, "The Quartet is now dead, and there are no Israeli obligations. The Roadmap is being used as a carrot and stick, but only on the Palestinian side." An Israeli official likewise conceded that "the Quartet has been sidelined, and that means that a part of the Roadmap doesn't exist."[36] Although effectively stillborn, at a rhetorical level the roadmap remained official U.S. policy, leading to considerable confusion, even among U.S. officials, regarding when, how, and even if its provisions went into effect.[37]

The sidelining of the roadmap spelled the end of the Powell approach and cemented the Bush-Sharon alignment, which was no longer limited to simply fighting terror. As Sharon continued to insist that Israel had "no partner" for peace, the Israeli prime minister outlined two short-term strategic priorities. The first was to complete construction of the 400-mile-long barrier that snaked through the West Bank, which had been begun in 2002. The barrier, a complex of barbed wire and electrified fences in some places and a twenty-five-foot concrete wall in others, was routed in a way that incorporated most of the major settlement blocs, often extending several miles deep into West Bank territory. Sharon justified the barrier as a security measure designed to prevent terrorists from entering Israel. But Palestinians and Israeli and other rights groups saw the barrier's tortuous route, which incorporated around 10 percent of West Bank land, as a land grab.[38] The Bush administration initially feared that the barrier might be used as a unilateral demarcation of a border but eventually accepted Israel's security rationale. The Palestinians took the matter to the International Court of Justice, which ultimately ruled in their favor in July 2004. In a non-binding advisory opinion, the ICJ determined that the "wall" was part of Israel's settlement enterprise and therefore illegal under international law. But this did nothing to prevent its continued construction.[39]

The second component of Sharon's strategy was to "disengage" unilaterally from the Gaza Strip, where some 8,000 Israeli settlers had been living among 1.5 million Palestinians. Once again, the administration hesitated before eventually embracing the plan. Sharon's Gaza Disengagement plan raised immediate red flags for the Palestinians, who feared that by cutting Gaza loose, Israel would then be free to consolidate its control over the West Bank, particularly around Jerusalem. The Palestinian leadership also worried about the implications of being cut out of the process politically, a situation that could play into Hamas's hands. Sharon trumpeted his plan as "a blow to the Palestinians, in that it will force them to give up on their aspirations for many years to come."[40] Sharon's chief of staff, Dov Weissglass, described the disengagement plan as the "formaldehyde that is necessary so there will not be a political process with the Palestinians." The White House understood the risks of a unilateral withdrawal as well, and Rice and other U.S. officials were keen that the United States not be seen as legitimizing settlements or as endorsing Israeli attempts to preempt future negotiations.[41] Despite the administration's initial reservations, however, Bush hailed the initiative as a "courageous and historic step" on the path to peace, while administration officials attempted to convince the Palestinians that the planned evacuation from Gaza was in line with the roadmap.[42]

In return for Sharon's plans to quit Gaza Bush gave Sharon formal "assurances" regarding Israeli positions on several core issues of the conflict. In a letter dated April 14, 2004, Bush assured Sharon that Israel would not have to withdraw fully from the occupied territories in the event of a peace deal and that Israel should be allowed to keep "existing major Israeli population centers"—a reference to the major settlement blocs in the West Bank. In addition, Bush stated, Palestinian refugees should not be allowed the right to return to their former homes in Israel but only to a future Palestinian state. Since 1948, successive

Israeli governments have rejected any form of return of Palestinian refugees, fearing that they would dilute the Jewish character of the state or even become a majority. While Sharon hailed Bush's statement as yet another victory, the Palestinians denounced the statement in the harshest of terms. Although Bush's letter stopped short of explicitly legitimizing Israeli settlement expansion, the fact that Israel already controlled these areas, and in the context of the administration's overall support of Israeli unilateralism, meant it would inevitably be seen as an endorsement of settlements and a departure from longstanding American policy.

STILL NOT A PARTNER

The year 2005 proved to be pivotal in the peace process, and in Palestinian politics. Yasser Arafat died on November 11, 2004. On January 9, 2005 the Palestinians elected a new leader, Mahmoud Abbas, to succeed Arafat as president of the PA and chairman of the PLO. Violence had declined sharply, and for the first time in more than four years the popular mood among both Palestinians and Israelis had begun to show signs of optimism. These trends, combined with Israel's anticipated evacuation from Gaza later that summer, had opened a narrow window of opportunity to move past the bloodshed and political deadlock of previous years.

Abbas came to power on a platform of unifying the Palestinians' badly fractured political system under his leadership and securing a conflict-ending peace agreement with Israel that would pave the way for an independent Palestinian state. A critic of Arafat's handling of the Intifada, the new Palestinian leader seemed to grasp that Palestinian statehood would to a large extent depend on fixing the Palestinians' broken politics. After concluding a ceasefire agreement with Sharon on February 8, 2005, Abbas brought the Palestinian factions together in Cairo to solidify the truce with Israel, quietly ending four years of violence. Hamas, after carrying out dozens of suicide attacks that killed hundreds of Israelis during the previous several years, all but ceased its attacks on Israelis. A report by Israel's internal security agency, Shin

Bet, credited the intra-Palestinian accord for the dramatic reduction in violence against Israelis, underscoring the extent to which Palestinian political cohesion had a direct bearing on Israeli security.[43] The Cairo Declaration also laid out a framework for reforming Palestinian politics, including a timetable for holding legislative elections and a commitment to reform and restructure the PLO to bring in groups like Hamas, Islamic Jihad, and others.

The first seven months of Abbas's presidency brought a sense of cautious optimism.[44] As the violence and chaos subsided, Palestinian security forces gradually resumed control over major Palestinian towns from the IDF. Unfortunately for Abbas, however, the Israeli-Palestinian conflict was no longer a top priority in Washington. Ironically, the sharp decline in violence seemed to remove the sense of urgency that had kept U.S. officials focused on the issue during the worst years of the Intifada. Moreover, the administration had other more pressing matters to tend to, including the ongoing wars in Afghanistan and Iraq. The U.S. occupation of Iraq in particular was going badly and the United States was becoming increasingly bogged down with the growing anti-U.S. insurgency there. The failure to capitalize on the election of Abbas and the reduction in violence—the two main conditions outlined in Bush's 2002 Rose Garden speech—and the planned Gaza withdrawal undercut Abbas's rule at a critical moment and marked the start of his steady decline.

The stakes for Abbas were particularly high in Gaza, politically, economically, and security-wise. On the eve of Israel's withdrawal, Gaza "was almost a failed entity" with a poverty rate of 65 percent and 35 percent unemployment, with high instability both inside and outside its borders.[45] For the evacuation to be a success it would need to deliver tangible economic benefits to Gaza's 1.5 million Palestinians, which in turn would require internal stability and access to the outside world, particularly the West Bank and Israel.[46] In addition, Abbas hoped to use the disengagement from Gaza, a traditional Hamas stronghold, to demonstrate the efficacy of his negotiations approach, thereby weakening Hamas. Conversely, if the evacuation went badly, Hamas stood to gain at Abbas's expense. On its face, Sharon's disengagement plan

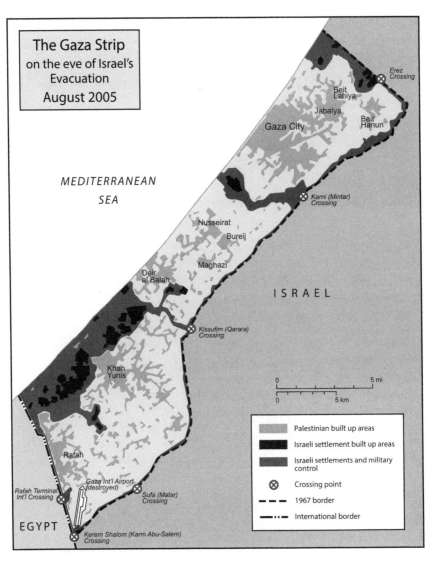

The Gaza Strip
on the eve of Israel's
Evacuation
August 2005

MEDITERRANEAN
SEA

Erez
Crossing

Beit
Lahiya

Jabalya

Beit
Hanun

Gaza City

Karni (Mintar)
Crossing

Nusseirat

Bureij

Maghazi

Deir
al Balah

I S R A E L

Kissufim (Qarara)
Crossing

Khan
Yunis

0   5 mi

0   5 km

Rafah

Gaza Int'l Airport
(destroyed)

Sufa (Matar)
Crossing

Rafah Terminal
Int'l Crossing

EGYPT

Kerem Shalom (Karm Abu-Salem)
Crossing

	Palestinian built up areas
	Israeli settlement built up areas
	Israeli settlements and military control
⊗	Crossing point
– – –	1967 border
–·–·–	International border

Source: Adapted from United Nations Office for the Coordination of Humanitarian
Affairs (OCHA), Occupied Palestinian Territory (oPt) map

offered little improvement over the status quo.[47] Sharon remained adamant about avoiding a negotiation of any kind. Under pressure from the administration he agreed to coordinate the process with Abbas's PA while making it clear to the Americans and the Palestinians that he "wanted the withdrawal defined entirely as an Israeli move made for Israeli interests."[48]

Meanwhile, Abbas continued to press the administration to ensure that the Gaza withdrawal produced tangible political as well as economic rewards. For Abbas, this meant two things: Gaza needed to be accessible to the outside world and could not become a "prison" following the evacuation of Israeli soldiers and settlers and, secondly, the evacuation needed to be linked to a broader "political horizon" for the day after. Administration officials made no promises, suggesting only that the disengagement might offer a "way back" to the roadmap and that they would do their best to make the process a success. In an attempt to boost the Palestinian leader ahead of the withdrawal, Bush welcomed Abbas at the White House in May 2005 while pledging $50 million to help "transform and professionalize" Palestinian security forces and build trust between the PA and Israel. International donors promised another $1.2 billion to support the effort. Bush appointed the former World Bank president James Wolfensohn to oversee the evacuation and spearhead Gaza's economic recovery on behalf of the Quartet.

The administration was willing to marshal economic and security resources to ensure a smooth evacuation, but was not prepared to make a significant political investment in Abbas or the planned withdrawal. Little thought was given to what was to come after Israel's evacuation. According to the USAID mission director for the West Bank and Gaza at the time, Howard Sumka, administration officials were not seeking to normalize economic operations on Gaza's borders but only to "maintain a sufficient flow of goods so that you wouldn't have any humanitarian problems."[49] Moreover, the president shared Sharon's skepticism of Abbas, whom he considered "well-meaning, but [he] had little confidence in his ability to force change and lead to statehood."[50] The perception of Abbas as too weak to be a peace partner would soon become self-fulfilling.

The one person in the administration who was prepared to help the withdrawal plan succeed was Condoleezza Rice, who had now replaced Powell as secretary of state. Rice's personal involvement in the process helped to secure a commitment from Israel to keep Gaza's borders open, but it was not enough to ensure its implementation, and the arrangement quickly collapsed. The ambitiously named Agreement on Movement and Access (AMA) of November 15, 2005, outlined a detailed plan to allow limited movement of people and goods in and out of Gaza and between Gaza and the West Bank. In keeping with Sharon's insistence that it was not a negotiation, Israel had refused to sign the document, which bore only Rice's signature. The United States assumed responsibility for overall implementation of the agreement, and EU monitors were put in place to ensure daily compliance at key crossings. However, the AMA was suspended within weeks of its signing, leading to the closure of Gaza's borders.[51] "In the end," recalled Sumka, "the Israelis had no interest really in the AMA, and they were not cooperative with us in trying to increase the flow of commodities back and forth," and Washington did little to follow through.[52] The closure of Gaza's borders precipitated a "sudden economic free fall" and an upsurge in rocket attacks into Israel, which in turn triggered Israeli military reprisals and tighter border restrictions.[53] Hamas quickly capitalized on the situation, claiming credit for having driven the Israelis out of Gaza through "resistance" and pointing to the AMA's collapse as further of evidence that Abbas's negotiations were futile.

ALL STICK AND NO CARROT

The collapse of the AMA and the closure of Gaza's borders could not have occurred at a worse time for Abbas, coming as they did just two months before planned legislative elections. Unlike the first PA elections held in 1996, Hamas had decided to contest a race for the Palestinian Legislative Council, now slated for January 25, 2006. Hamas's participation in the elections had been the subject of intense debate beforehand, both inside and outside the organization. Internally, Hamas's decision to enter the race, despite its longstanding and often violent opposition to the Oslo Accords, reflected a change in strategy on the part of the group's leaders. The Intifada had exacted a heavy toll on the organization, including the assassination of its two top leaders, Sheikh Ahmed Yassin and Abdel Aziz al-Rantisi, by Israel in 2004. Moreover, Hamas saw an opportunity to capitalize on Abbas's new and untested leadership and the growing popular discontent with Fatah and the peace process. Having concluded that the Oslo paradigm was dead, Hamas leaders no longer sought to replace the PLO or the PA but would now work within the existing political structures to reorganize Palestinian politics. The Israelis sought to have Hamas barred from the elections until it had recognized Israel and laid down its weapons, but Abbas maintained that banning the group would undermine the legitimacy of the election and further aggravate internal tensions. Although many within the Bush administration shared the Israeli view, Bush ultimately accepted Abbas's reasoning. "Whatever the outcome, free and fair elections would be the truth," the president wrote in his memoirs.[54] That truth turned out to be considerably more complicated and taxing than anyone expected.

Hamas won a clear majority of seats in the PLC, giving it the ability to form a government on its own (it won a slim plurality of the popular vote, 44 percent compared to Fatah's 41 percent). This created an immediate crisis for all sides, including Hamas. The election dealt a major blow to Abbas's fragile leadership and ended nearly a half century of Fatah dominance of Palestinian politics. Hamas, too, was surprised by its electoral success and was wholly unprepared to govern, particularly in light of Israel's and much of the international community's aversion to dealing with the group. Israeli leaders had no desire to legitimize a group that was responsible for the deaths of hundreds of Israeli civilians and was rhetorically committed to its destruction and vowed to boycott any government headed by Hamas. As a result, Israel suspended transfers of customs revenues (value added tax) collected on the PA's behalf, which accounted for roughly two-thirds of its budget. Given Hamas's official designation as a terrorist organization by the United States and the European Union, the PA's two largest donors, these donors had little choice but to suspend their Palestinian aid programs as well.

The United States and its partners in the Quartet called on the new Hamas-led government to lay down its arms, recognize Israel, and abide by previous agreements.[55] American officials took the lead in urging the international community to suspend its diplomatic and financial ties to the Palestinian government until it accepted the Quartet's three conditions. After having jettisoned the Quartet's official peace plan, the Roadmap for Peace, the Bush administration now treated the Quartet conditions as immutable and binding. The Bush administration had decided fairly early after the elections that its preferred outcome, short of Hamas's compliance with the conditions, was to ensure that the Hamas government failed. Other Quartet members, particularly the UN and Russia, disapproved of the U.S. approach but could do little to steer things in a different direction. The Quartet's envoy, James Wolfensohn, criticized the policy as "a misguided attempt to starve the Hamas-led Palestinians into submission."[56] Wolfensohn's office closed down shortly thereafter. For its part, Hamas rejected the Quartet's conditions as "blackmail" but offered no alternative way out of the crisis.[57]

Hamas's election prompted several additional changes in the administration's policy. The previous policy of working for an "empowered" prime minister, a post now held by a member of Hamas, was quickly abandoned. Instead, the focus shifted to the office of the president, held by Abbas, who was encouraged to issue decrees to limit the authority of the government, particularly authority over the PA's security forces. A new U.S. Security Coordinator, Lieutenant General Keith Dayton, had arrived in the West Bank only weeks before the election. Dayton abruptly shifted his mission from security reform to ensuring that a new Hamas-led government did not take control of the PA's security forces.[58] On the political front, Secretary of State Rice became convinced of the need to restart negotiations between Abbas and Israel's new prime minister, Ehud Olmert, who had recently taken over from Sharon, who had suffered a stroke in January.

Meanwhile, the international boycott of the PA combined with Israel's decision to withhold tax revenues sent the Palestinian economy into a tailspin and virtually paralyzed the government, jeopardizing the very institutions the United States and other international donors had

helped rebuild.[59] Eager to relieve the pressure on the PA, Abbas proposed a national unity government between Hamas and Fatah, an option favored by Palestinian political factions and the public. The UN's
Middle East envoy, Álvaro de Soto, explained: "As Abu Mazen [Abbas]
saw it, the alternative was for Hamas to remain in the cold, where it
would always have the means and incentive to blow up any moves he
might make towards a deal with Israel."[60] Despite assurances by Abbas
that any unity government would have to accept his program of two
states and "one gun, one authority," the Bush administration continued to view any option that allowed Hamas to remain in the government as a nonstarter. Instead, U.S. officials pressed Abbas to take the
extraordinary—and extraconstitutional—step of dissolving the government and calling for fresh elections. Such a step had no legal basis in
the Palestinian Basic Law and would almost certainly lead to civil war,
an outcome U.S. officials were not entirely averse to.[61]

Even though there were bound to be negative repercussions following Hamas's election victory, given the group's bloody past and its official terrorist designation, the election also presented an opportunity to
reexamine the developments that led to it, including whether and how
U.S. and Israeli policies may have contributed to such an outcome. The
election outcome—Hamas's decisive victory—had less to do with the
group's Islamist agenda or its violent tactics than with widespread frustration with Fatah and the PA. Indeed, even after the election most
Palestinians continued to voice support for a negotiated settlement with
Israel.[62] Moreover, after years in power, Fatah and the PA had failed to
deliver tangible improvements in the lives of most Palestinians. Fatah's
history of mismanagement, corruption, and bad governance had undoubtedly played a major role in the party's electoral defeat. Thus, the
announcement of $2 million in U.S.-funded aid projects to help boost
Fatah in the days leading up to the election may have done it more harm
than good.[63] However, the PA's failings also could not be divorced from
the chronic failures in the peace process. The closure of Gaza's borders and the marginalization of the PA during the disengagement process, the proliferation of military checkpoints, physical barriers, road
closures, and other restrictions on Palestinians' movement within the

West Bank, and ongoing Israeli settlement construction in the West Bank and East Jerusalem reflected as much on the PA leadership's credibility as they did on Israel and the peace process.[64]

Furthermore, Hamas leaders had also begun to show signs of moderation as well as a desire for political normalization and international legitimacy, which many believed were worth exploring. The group's 2006 electoral program had also notably omitted language calling for Israel's destruction and other offensive passages contained in its infamous charter of 1988.[65] Moreover, while the party still refused to recognize Israel, various Hamas leaders, including its founder and spiritual leader, Sheikh Ahmed Yassin, and its prime minister, Ismail Haniyeh, had expressed a willingness to accept a Palestinian state based on the 1967 borders.[66] Despite ample cause for skepticism, many observers believed that Hamas had evolved enough to at least warrant a reconsideration of the existing approach. For example, the UN's de Soto believed that Hamas "can potentially evolve in a pragmatic direction that would allow for a two-state solution—but only if handled right."[67] But these opportunities were never seized upon or even explored in any meaningful way. Instead, administration officials continued to ramp up the pressure on the Palestinians.

Faced with a choice between overturning the results of a democratic election—and a likely civil war—and the possibility of indefinite international isolation, Abbas opted for latter. In February 2007, amid sporadic street battles between Fatah and Hamas in Gaza and elsewhere, Abbas stunned the U.S. administration by signing an agreement with Hamas in Mecca on the formation of a national unity government. Upon learning of the Saudi-brokered reconciliation deal, said one State Department official, "Condi was apoplectic."[68] In her memoirs, Rice described the Mecca Accord as a "devastating blow" to the peace process that rendered her plans to relaunch Israeli-Palestinian peace negotiations "dead on arrival."[69] Abbas tried to emphasize the positives of the national unity government: Hamas would lose control over thirteen portfolios, including the foreign, finance, information, and interior ministries. Russian and UN representatives welcomed the unity deal while EU officials indicated a willingness to work with non-Hamas members of the government. A few isolated voices in Washington, such as that of Senator Chuck Hagel of Nebraska, urged the administration to engage with the Palestinian unity government because it was democratically elected. However, the Bush administration continued to work behind the scenes to bring it down. Washington stepped up the pressure on Abbas to "collapse the government" and call for early elections.

Like any fragile object subjected to persistent pressure, the Palestinian Authority eventually broke. American officials put together a detailed "action plan" to oust Hamas from power and pledged to support Abbas's Fatah forces with arms and training—a promise they could not keep.[70] Even as Hamas continued to receive military and financial support from Iran, Abbas's security forces were crippled by the many U.S. and Israeli sanctions imposed on the PA. The American-led boycott of the PA had prevented Abbas from paying the salaries of his security forces, which had never fully recovered from Israel's 2002 offensive. Meanwhile, Congress had put a hold on $86 million in pledged aid to the PA.[71] At the same time, Israel would not allow anything but small arms to reach PA forces in Gaza. When word of the U.S. plan to provide arms and training to Fatah forces was leaked in June 2007, Hamas launched a "preemptive" move to thwart what it saw as an American-backed plan to forcibly remove it power, in the process routing Abbas's PA and seizing control of the Gaza Strip. Hamas's rapid takeover of Gaza raised questions about the efficacy of what had been the centerpiece of U.S. policy since the start of the Oslo process. As one Palestinian analyst observed, "It took [Hamas] just a few days to flush away a 53,000-strong PA security apparatus which was a fourteen-year Western investment." American officials drew a very different conclusion from Hamas's takeover. "We didn't regard this as proof the project wasn't working," observed Elliott Abrams, "but rather that the project was needed"—that is, the United States had not done enough.[72] Whether or not Abrams and other administration officials genuinely believed their "regime change" strategy was working, or could work, the fact remained that the United States was now working at cross-purposes with its own stated objectives of ending Israel's occupation and building a Palestinian state.

FROM GAZA TO ANNAPOLIS AND BACK

Whereas most ordinary Palestinians saw the physical and political division between the West Bank and Gaza as a blow to the national project, Bush administration officials saw it as an opportunity to work with Abbas's leadership on laying the foundations of a Palestinian state without the negative influences of Hamas. Following the takeover by Hamas, Abbas dissolved the unity cabinet and appointed Finance Minister Salam Fayyad, a former IMF economist, to head a new caretaker government, allowing the resumption of American and European aid to the PA in the West Bank. Likewise, Israel released the PA's frozen tax revenues while sealing off Gaza's borders. Following the loss of Gaza, Abbas became more dependent than ever on the United States and his fate ever more tied to the peace process. The administration began working aggressively with the new Fayyad government to promote "state building" and economic prosperity in West Bank areas under PA control while isolating Hamas in Gaza, which was now subject to an Israeli blockade by air, land, and sea. The theory behind the unspoken policy, often referred to as "West Bank first," was to promote stability and prosperity in the West Bank with the expectation that while life improved under the PA, there would be a simultaneous decline in economic and political conditions in Gaza that would eventually prompt Palestinians there to rise up against Hamas. At the same time, the administration announced plans to relaunch negotiations between Israel and Abbas's leadership in the West Bank before the end of the year. "We'd always argued that the Palestinians needed new leadership before they could have a state," Rice later explained. "Now they'd fulfilled their part of the bargain; we needed to fulfill ours."[73]

The Americans took the lead on security, allocating $86 million to Dayton's program to train and equip PA forces in the West Bank. To spearhead Fayyad's economic revitalization and institution-building efforts, Bush tapped former British premier Tony Blair to serve as the Quartet's new envoy. The Quartet had already been in decline since the sidelining of the roadmap in 2003. With its members hopelessly divided over the abortive Palestinian unity government, the Quartet was now effectively paralyzed. The appointment of Blair and his decidedly nonpolitical mission marked the unofficial end of the Quartet's diplomatic or political role in the process.[74] Unlike his predecessor, James Wolfensohn, who had attempted to expand his largely technical role into the political realm and was promptly swatted down by the Bush administration, Blair remained loyal to his narrow economic mandate throughout his tenure.

In the end, the West Bank first policy did not dislodge Hamas from power. Instead, the Israeli blockade, combined with repeated military confrontations, exacerbated the dire economic and humanitarian situation in Gaza. By 2008, reliance on food aid increased from approximately 60 percent to 80 percent, while 90 percent of Gaza's 400 factories were forced to shut down as a result of the ban on exports.[75] Among the critics of the policy was Howard Sumka, who at the time was responsible for overseeing USAID projects in the occupied territories. "I believed it was fanciful then, and expressed that, quietly, to people in Washington," said Sumka of the idea that Gaza's isolation was likely to foment a rebellion against Hamas. In fact it may even have helped to consolidate Hamas's grip on the impoverished enclave: "The combined U.S.-Israeli policy has just destroyed the private sector in Gaza. It was the bulwark against radicalism there," said Sumka.[76] The results in the West Bank were not much better. Although the Israelis agreed to ease some movement restrictions in the West Bank, Fayyad and Abbas continued to complain that Israeli settlement construction, home demolitions, and IDF incursions were undercutting the institutional and security reform effort.[77] Moreover, the split between Fatah and Hamas had paralyzed the PA's most important institution, the Palestinian Legislative Council, thus removing parliamentary checks and balances and leaving Abbas to rule by presidential decree.

Ironically, the most successful component of the administration's strategy, albeit in relative terms, was the negotiation track, which was relaunched in November 2007 at the Annapolis Conference. Like the state-building project, the conference was intended to strengthen Abbas politically against Hamas, but ultimately ended up weakening him further. Rice's preparations for resuming Israeli-Palestinian negotiations had begun the previous year as a result of a reordering of American priorities in the Middle East in 2006, which had become the administration's annus horribilis. The anti-U.S. insurgency in Iraq had gone from bad to worse. Moreover, the electoral success of Hamas and other Islamist parties around the region put an end to the administration's Freedom Agenda, and the idea that free elections around the region would bring pro-Western forces to power. The war between Israel and Hezbollah in the summer of 2006 had shaken Bush's confidence in Prime Minister Ehud Olmert and convinced the president that unilateralism had run its course. The administration returned to the roadmap but abandoned the sequential and conditional approach that prevailed during Bush's first term. Moreover, under Rice's direction, U.S. officials had begun to emphasize the need to return to negotiations to achieve a two-state solution, which was now defined in terms of American national security interests. According to Rice, the creation of a Palestinian state alongside Israel would "strengthen peace and security, not just in the region but the peace and security of us all."[78]

The Annapolis negotiations, which began in November 2007 and continued throughout most of 2008, were the first substantive talks between Israelis and Palestinians in nearly seven years. On the surface, most of the key ingredients for a successful negotiations process seemed to be in place: Israeli and Palestinian leaders who were eager to make an agreement and were prepared to make the necessary compromises, and an American secretary of state who was equally determined to make an agreement, even if her boss remained somewhat disengaged. Just beneath the surface, however, the picture looked very different. The success of any negotiation process depends on three basic factors: the substance of the talks; the process—how those talks are structured; and the political dynamics within and between the parties. The Annapolis talks were quite promising on substance, highly flawed on process, and virtually hopeless in terms of the internal politics of both sides, especially as concerned Abbas.

In November 2005 Olmert had joined Ariel Sharon in defecting from the Likud Party to form Kadima, a new, centrist party that supported a two-state solution. Unlike Sharon, however, Olmert acknowledged Abbas as a peace partner and was eager to relaunch negotiations on a permanent peace deal with the Palestinians. But by the time of the Annapolis talks, Olmert was under criminal investigation on various corruption charges and was facing imminent indictment. Meanwhile, Olmert's chief rival within Kadima, Foreign Minister Tzipi Livni, also a key participant in the Annapolis talks, was eagerly waiting in the wings to replace him. Abbas's internal political weaknesses were more structural in nature. Olmert could be replaced by a new prime minister with a fresh electoral mandate, but this was not necessarily true of Abbas. The PLC and other Palestinian political institutions were paralyzed. Moreover, Abbas had just lost control of Gaza, home to roughly 40 percent of the Palestinians in the occupied territories. Given the division within the Palestinian polity, the proposition that Abbas would be in a position to negotiate far-reaching compromises with Israel was highly questionable at best.

The negotiations themselves got off to a rocky start. Within days of launching the negotiations at Annapolis, on November 27, 2007, the announcement of a raft of new Israeli settlements in East Jerusalem and elsewhere led to a public outcry in the West Bank and triggered a crisis on the Palestinian side. A debate ensued within Abbas's inner circle over whether to quit the process. In the end, Abbas opted to continue. Once the talks were under way, the sides established a highly elaborate, three-tiered negotiation structure. At the top of the pyramid were Olmert and Abbas, who held a series of one-on-one meetings. In the middle were the somewhat arbitrarily named "plenary" negotiations between Ahmed Qurei, the chief negotiator on the Palestinian side, and Foreign Minister Livni on the Israeli side. The plenary talks were supported by a dozen different technical committees, each of which also met separately. The highly ornate negotiation structure, which was often beset by communication problems both within and between the two sides, was largely illusory. The plenary and technical committees, which were part side show and part testing ground, were for the most part disconnected from the leadership talks. The only meaningful negotiations of the Annapolis process took place in the Abbas-Olmert tier.

By all accounts, the two leaders held highly substantive negotiations covering all of the core issues of the conflict, with each putting forward serious proposals of their own. Olmert's proposal was detailed in some areas, namely on territory, and less so in others, such as Jerusalem and refugees. In terms of borders, Olmert's proposal was consistent with the 2000 Clinton Parameters. Israel would annex 6.5 percent of the West Bank in return for a similar (but not equivalent) amount of Israeli territory—an improvement over Barak's proposal at Camp David, but less far-reaching than the Israeli proposal at Taba.[79] Areas annexed by Israel would include all of the Jewish settlements in East Jerusalem, while the city's Arab areas would be under Palestinian sovereignty. One of the more noteworthy aspects of Olmert's proposal was to place the Old City and its surroundings, known as the Holy Basin, under an international trusteeship made up of five states: Saudi Arabia, Jordan, Palestine, Israel, and the United States. Abbas also tabled his own counterproposal in May 2008—a first by a Palestinian leader. Abbas's proposal, which received far less publicity than Olmert's, would allow Israel to annex 1.9 percent of the West Bank, encompassing around 65 percent of the settler population, including East Jerusalem, in exchange for territory in Israel equivalent in size and value.

What value there was to a peace offer made by a lame-duck leader who was about to be indicted and another who had just lost a civil war and a major election is anyone's guess. What was clear, however—at least to other Palestinians—was that Abbas suffered from a serious legitimacy crisis that hampered his ability to make meaningful concessions. Palestinian negotiators emphasized this point during secret backchannel talks that ran parallel with the Annapolis negotiations. "Abu Mazen [Abbas] can't sign [an agreement], even if he wants to," they informed their Israeli counterparts. "Any agreement will become an instrument for internal political struggle, and even a unity government with Hamas won't put aside the disagreements between Fatah and Hamas on diplomatic decision-making."[80]

Despite the talks' slim prospects for success, Abbas had other reasons to participate in the Annapolis process. For one, the negotiations allowed him to assert his and Fatah's continued relevance on the international scene, particularly after the loss of Gaza to Hamas. According to Ahmed Qurei, the PLO's chief negotiator during the Annapolis talks, the Palestinian leadership saw Annapolis as a "lifeline" that would allow it to "renew its legitimacy at both the Arab and international levels, and to strengthen its position that had been badly shaken by the bloody coup carried out by Hamas in mid-June 2007."[81] Abbas had also internalized key lessons from the ill-fated Camp David summit, particularly the need to avoid being blamed for the failure of the negotiations at all costs. Hence Abbas's decision to put forward a formal map proposal in May 2008, something Arafat had strenuously avoided in 2000, and to remain in the process even after the new settlement announcements in December 2007. Finally, the Annapolis talks provided an opportunity to educate American officials, particularly Rice, whom the Palestinians had come to respect. The PLO's Ahmed Qurei considered Rice different from previous secretaries of state, not because she accepted the Palestinian perspective but because "she listened very carefully to the views we put forward and was willing to discuss them with us."[82] Like James Baker nearly two decades earlier, Rice had earned the respect of her Palestinian counterparts simply by acknowledging their voice and agency. Another of Rice's Palestinian interlocutors, Hanan Ashrawi, offered an even more glowing appraisal of Rice's role. "Condi Rice was smart, quick and decisive," observed Ashrawi. "She also checked whatever information she was given by the Israelis. This verification process was unique and indicated a sense of integrity and reliability."[83] Although Ashrawi was not directly involved in the Annapolis talks, she and Rice had developed a close working relationship over the years, which Ashrawi saw as vital to countering the inordinate influence wielded by Israeli officials and administration hardliners. "I could see there was a struggle in her because she was getting to know the facts and getting beyond the incessant Israeli hammering of the Israeli agenda, and discourse, and priorities. And as much as she tried to hold on to them, we kept coming back," said Ashrawi.[84]

Whatever value one attached to the Annapolis talks, negotiations were not necessarily what the peace process had been lacking in that particular moment in time. In the end, the Annapolis process was derailed by the same set of issues that had led to its launch. The start of Operation Cast Lead, in late December 2008, the biggest and most devastating Israeli military campaign in the Gaza Strip to date, dealt another major blow to Abbas's beleaguered leadership. The Bush administration had repeatedly failed to grasp a basic principle of conflict resolution, which is that peace negotiations are unlikely to succeed as long as those with the ability to derail the process through violence remain outside of that process.[85] Whether American policymakers would finally be able to break from this pattern would now be left to the next U.S. president.

7

Less of the Same

What matters to us, and what matters, we think, to the process that we are trying to keep on track here is that Abbas remains the president, that Fayyad remains the prime minister.

—Victoria Nuland, State Department spokesperson, February 9, 2012, commenting on Fatah-Hamas reconciliation efforts

After the twenty-four-day Gaza war in January 2009, a cease fire in Gaza finally went into effect on January 17, 2009, three days before Barack Obama's swearing in as the forty-fourth president of the United States. The operation had begun on December 27 with a massive air campaign followed a week later by an Israeli ground invasion. At the end of the fighting, nearly 1,400 Palestinians had been killed, most of them civilians, some 15,000 homes had been damaged or destroyed, and more than 50,000 Palestinians had been internally displaced.[1] Ten Israeli soldiers and three civilians were also killed. The fallout from the 2009 Gaza war was among the first major foreign policy challenges to confront Obama when he took office. "Our hearts go out to Palestinian civilians who are in need of immediate food, clean water, and basic medical care, and who've faced suffocating poverty for far too long," declared the president shortly after the war. At the same time, Obama hinted at a possible shift in U.S. policy by endorsing UN calls for opening Gaza's borders to allow the "regular flow of goods and people" and "unimpeded" humanitarian aid.[2]

Change did not come, however. Gaza remained physically cut off from the world and politically disconnected from both the Palestinian Authority and the peace process. After convening an international donors' conference in Egypt in March, where an estimated $4.5 billion was pledged in humanitarian and reconstruction aid to Gaza, the administration shifted its focus back to restarting negotiations between Israel and Abbas's leadership in the West Bank. The Obama administration was able to adapt U.S. policies to keep pace with changing realities elsewhere in the region, most notably during the tumultuous Arab Spring uprisings of 2011. But when it came to the Israeli-Palestinian conflict and the peace process, the administration fell back on the largely ineffective and outdated policy formulas developed by previous administrations. Despite adopting a more balanced approach than either Bush or Clinton, Obama refrained from directly challenging the increasingly destructive dynamics on the ground or the growing power asymmetry between the two sides. Unlike his two immediate predecessors, Obama did not actively contribute to the trends that were harming the peace process and prospects for a two-state solution, but neither did he seriously challenge them or attempt to break new ground. Obama's attempts to hold the line, namely by reasserting the primacy of the 1967 border and the illegitimacy of Israeli settlements, were necessary but ultimately insufficient, given the pernicious threats by a deepening Israeli occupation, a highly destabilizing siege in Gaza, and a divided and dysfunctional Palestinian leadership.

THE PATH OF LEAST RESISTANCE

Barack Obama entered office amid exceptionally high expectations both at home and around the world. Casting himself as a transformational figure, Obama began his presidency promising to right the wrongs of his predecessor, from ending America's highly unpopular military presence in Iraq and Afghanistan to shutting down the notorious prison camp at Guantanamo Bay. The contrast between Obama's image and self-presentation with that of his predecessor was sufficiently stark that less than nine months into his presidency Obama was awarded the Nobel Peace Prize "for his extraordinary efforts to strengthen international diplomacy and cooperation between peoples." As part of his efforts to lay out a "new beginning" in America's relations with the Muslim world, Obama pledged to adopt a more balanced U.S. approach to the Israeli-Palestinian conflict and to make a two-state solution a top priority of his administration. In his celebrated "Speech to the Muslim World," delivered at Cairo University on June 4, 2009, Obama spoke passionately about "the pain of dislocation" of Palestinian refugees and "the daily humiliations" of life under occupation. Obama pledged to make resolution of the conflict a top priority of his administration while alluding to the possibility of a more even-handed U.S. approach to Middle East peacemaking. "If we see this conflict only from one side or the other," the president cautioned, "then we will be blind to the truth."

The peace process Obama inherited was anything but promising. The return of Netanyahu to power in Israel, shortly after Obama's arrival in the White House, consolidated the rightward shift in Israeli politics that had been under way since at least the collapse of the Oslo process and the start of the Intifada. The arrival of more than a million immigrants from the former Soviet Union since the 1990s and the rapid growth in the Orthodox Jewish community combined with widespread disaffection with the Oslo process and mistrust of Palestinian intentions also helped to fuel illiberal and pro-settlement trends within Israeli politics. This was reflected in the increased prominence and assertiveness of the Israeli settler movement, many of whose members were now part of Netanyahu's ruling coalition.

On the Palestinian side, Hamas was no longer merely a renegade opposition movement that could be squeezed or co-opted, but a powerful political and military force nearly equal in stature to Fatah and, in Gaza at least, a government in its own right. In addition, Hamas now boasted a larger and more sophisticated military arsenal, thanks in part to the growing influence of its primary sponsor, Iran, since the 2003 U.S.-led invasion of Iraq. Hamas's growing stature, which received an additional boost following the Arab uprisings of 2011, stood in marked contrast to the declining fortunes of Abbas's Palestinian Authority, whose governing and security apparatus remained heavily dependent on the political patronage and financial largesse of the United States and other Western donors. Meanwhile, the 2008–09 Gaza war had helped to deepen the split between Hamas and Fatah while badly damaging Abbas's domestic standing. With his popularity in decline, and few if any institutional checks on his power, Abbas's rule became increasingly autocratic.

Changes in the physical landscape were equally dramatic. Israel's settler population in the occupied territories, which stood at nearly 270,000 at the start of the Oslo process, had nearly doubled to 490,000 when Obama entered office. Settlement growth was heavily concentrated in and around Jerusalem. In the decade or so since Clinton had proposed dividing Jerusalem along demographic lines, the Israeli settler movement, with government support, had worked frantically to fill in the blanks. The case of Har Homa, the strategically situated East Jerusalem settlement inaugurated by the first Netanyahu government at the height of the Oslo process in the late 1990s, stood as a testament to the enormous success of the settlement enterprise, particularly in Jerusalem. First populated in 2002, Har Homa had a population of around 1,600 at the end of 2003. But by 2009 its population had increased sevenfold, to nearly 12,000. With a highly unnatural growth rate of around twenty times that of Israel's overall population, the mainly government-sponsored building frenzy in Har Homa illustrated how settlement construction was driving settlement growth, rather than the other way around. By 2017 Har Homa's population had reached 21,000.[3] Meanwhile, by 2009 close to two-thirds of Israel's separation barrier had been

The West Bank
Israeli Settlements &
Separation Barrier

Jenin

Tulkarm

Nablus

Qalqiliya

Salfit

JORDAN VALLEY

Jordan River

JORDAN

Ramallah

Jericho

ISRAEL

East
Jerusalem

Bethlehem

DEAD
SEA

Hebron

- - - 1967 border
Palestinian autonomy (Areas A & B)
Full Israeli control (Area C)
Palestinian built up areas
Israeli settlement (built up/outer limit)
Route of Israeli barrier/wall
Israeli settlement bloc areas (including
Israeli-defined municipality of Jerusalem)

0   5   10 mi
0   5   10 km

Source: Adapted from United Nations Office for the Coordination of
Humanitarian Affairs (OCHA), Occupied Palestinian Territory (oPt) map

completed. The combination of the barrier, Israeli settlements, and an array of checkpoints and other internal closures had carved up West Bank territory into hundreds of isolated Palestinian pockets surrounded by a sea of Israeli-controlled areas—what George W. Bush had famously referred to as "Swiss cheese."[4]

The political and physical realities on the ground reinforced two seemingly paradoxical trends that worked in tandem to stymie progress toward a peaceful settlement. In times of violence Israeli leaders lacked the will to engage in serious negotiations with the Palestinians, but during times of relative calm they felt no urgency to do so. Palestinian leaders had the opposite problem; although they generally had the will—perhaps even a need—to achieve a peace agreement with Israel, they lacked the capacity, both politically and materially, to bring one about.

The Palestinian leadership might have helped offset some of its structural weaknesses by, for example, developing a broader diplomatic strategy that appealed to a wider set of international actors. Instead, Abbas chose to use international action sparingly, and for the most part tactically, while continuing to bank almost entirely on the United States to deal with the power asymmetry for him. For a time, it looked as though Obama was inclined to do so. Unlike Bill Clinton and George W. Bush, both of whom had become serious about peacemaking at the end of their presidencies, Obama tackled the issue at the beginning of his first term, fulfilling a promise he had made during the campaign.[5] Whereas Bush had resisted naming a peace envoy, on his first full day in office Obama appointed former Senate majority leader George Mitchell to serve as special envoy for Middle East peace. Obama officially did away with Bush's policy of conditionality and even hinted at a possible change in policy toward Gaza. Even Hamas leaders seemed encouraged by the apparent shift in Washington, addressing a letter to the new president in which they urged him to visit the war-ravaged Gaza Strip.[6]

Perhaps most significant, Obama took an unusually tough stance on Israeli settlements. The president stopped short of declaring settlements illegal but insisted that the United States would "not accept the legitimacy of continued Israeli settlements." Whereas previous presidents had given Israeli leaders considerable latitude to continue building in the occupied territories, the Obama administration made it clear to the Israelis that it expected "to see a stop to settlements—not some settlements, not outposts, not natural growth exceptions."[7] As part of his efforts to undo Bush's legacy, Obama instructed Mitchell to inform the Israelis that prior assurances made by Bush were not binding on the new administration.[8] Obama's corrective on settlements stemmed from his view that settlements posed a direct threat to a two-state solution, which U.S. officials characterized as a "vital national security interest of the United States."[9]

The administration viewed the ongoing conflict between Israelis and Palestinians as the primary source of anti-American sentiment and a leading source of instability in the Arab and Muslim worlds.[10] In parallel with his calls for a settlement freeze, Obama called on Palestinian leaders to continue to fight terror and incitement to violence and urged Arab states to take steps toward normalizing relations with Israel. "The case he was trying to make was that the United States will be a better partner to Israel if it has more credibility with the Arab states, that we will be a better, more useful friend to Israel if we have more friends in the Arab world," explained Obama's deputy national security adviser, Ben Rhodes.[11] Although welcomed by the Palestinians, the shift in Washington's tone, combined with the broader perception that Obama was personally sympathetic to the Palestinians, alarmed the Netanyahu government and many American Jewish leaders.

During the first several months of the administration, U.S. officials focused most of their energies on getting the parties to restart negotiations, which had long been the path of least resistance for Americans, while devoting much less attention to the environment surrounding the talks or what might come out of them. As Mitchell pressed the two leaders to go back to the negotiating table, the administration coaxed Netanyahu into making a public endorsement, albeit a highly conditional one, of Palestinian statehood. However, since the collapse of the Annapolis process and the Gaza war, Abbas had become reticent about entering into direct negotiations. Mitchell also faced a number of additional challenges, particularly finding a way to translate the administration's lofty rhetoric on settlements into something more concrete. Netanyahu would not agree to a full settlement freeze, and Abbas would not negotiate without one. There was also the question of how or whether to enforce whatever arrangement was put in place. The old Baker-era loan guarantees deduction, last invoked by George W. Bush in 2005, had gone from being a symbolic sanction to a nonexistent one—mainly because Israel had not borrowed any funds from U.S. banks since then.[12] Moreover, despite hints by Mitchell that the administration would "keep open whatever options" in relation to settlements, it did not propose any other mechanisms for countering Israeli settlements. In the meantime, Obama continued to hear from American Jewish leaders and members of Congress regarding his handling of the issue, including AIPAC-initiated letters signed by 76 senators and 328 representatives expressing concern over what they regarded as the deterioration in U.S.-Israeli relations.[13] These problems were complicated by sharp disagreements within the president's peace team, as Mitchell butted heads with Dennis Ross, who had recently joined the administration and had been given a broad Middle East portfolio.

Throughout the summer of 2009, administration officials met with Israel to work out a package on settlements that would allow a resumption of negotiations. The Palestinians were not included in these discussions. In lieu of a full freeze on settlements, American and Israeli officials agreed on a ten-month moratorium on new settlement construction in the West Bank— but not in East Jerusalem, where some 200,000 Israeli settlers lived among roughly 230,000 Palestinians. Having taken Obama's tough talk at face value, Palestinian officials were taken aback by the administration's rapid climb-down on settlements. "You put me in this position! It's like having a gun to my head—damned if you do and damned if you don't," declared Saeb Erekat, the chief Palestinian negotiator, to Assistant Secretary of State David Hale. "We have had to kill Palestinians to establish one authority one gun and the rule of law. We continue to perform our obligations. We held the Fatah conference—our country remains divided."[14]

The president seemed to have his own questions about the process as well, repeatedly asking his advisers, "What's the strategy here?" Obama wanted to know how the settlement moratorium would "get us where we want to be? Tell me the relationship between what we are doing and our objective."[15] Abbas continued to insist that he could not enter direct negotiations without adequate preparations, though he eventually agreed to participate in proximity talks—that is, indirect negotiations with a third party, in this case with the United States serving as intermediary. Aides of the Palestinian leader warned the Americans that Abbas could not afford to engage in negotiations for their own sake or that lacked clear aims or ground rules. Without a halt in settlement construction and a commitment that the talks would be based on the 1967 lines, Erekat warned, "we will have the same result as Camp David."[16]

Abbas's troubles were only just beginning, however. The release in September 2009 of a report by a UN-commissioned investigation into the 2008–09 Gaza war, headed by the South African jurist Richard Goldstone, knocked the wind out of Abbas and threatened to wreck the administration's plans for restarting negotiations. The Goldstone Report accused both Israel and Hamas of having committed war crimes during the recent conflict.[17] But given the lopsided death toll, the bulk of the report's criticisms fell on Israel. Israeli officials dismissed the commission's findings as "distorted, falsified and not balanced."[18] Palestinians welcomed the Goldstone Report as a rare opportunity to hold Israel accountable for its actions during the war.

In the West Bank and Gaza, the Goldstone Report became a rallying cry for civil society groups and ordinary citizens alike, increasing the pressure on Abbas to embrace Goldstone's findings. The UN Human Rights Council was set to vote on the report's recommendations in early October. Although the vote would have been largely symbolic, Palestinian officials came under "heavy and ongoing pressure" from the Obama administration to delay the vote.[19] Washington had long had a zero-tolerance policy for Palestinian actions outside the confines of the U.S.-led peace process, particularly when they were strongly opposed by Israel. Moreover, for U.S. officials, such strong-arming was necessary to safeguard efforts to relaunch negotiations. Abbas, who had been widely criticized for his perceived impotence during the war, relented and agreed to have the vote delayed. Back home, the decision led to a popular outcry against the Palestinian leader, whom many now branded as a traitor.[20] A senior Hamas official called the decision "a very big crime against the Palestinian people" and called on Abbas to resign.[21] In an attempt to contain the damage, the embattled Abbas appointed an official PLO commission of inquiry to look into the events that led the UNHRC vote to be delayed. Abbas even offered to resign, although he quickly backtracked on the idea and said instead that he would not seek reelection for another term. The Goldstone affair badly wounded Abbas domestically and marked a turning point in his presidency, from which he would never fully recover.

The controversy over the Goldstone Report was soon followed by a new crisis. On March 10, 2010, just days after the administration announced that Palestinians had agreed to take part in proximity talks without a full settlement freeze, Israeli authorities announced plans to build 1,600 new settler homes in the East Jerusalem settlement of Pisgat Zeev. Although technically not a violation of the U.S.-Israel arrangement, which had exempted Jerusalem from the settlement moratorium, the announcement threatened to derail the negotiations even before they began. The timing of the announcement just as Vice President Joe Biden embarked on a three-day visit to Israel had further angered the White House. Secretary of State Hillary Clinton called the announcement "an insult to the United States." An outraged Biden reportedly told Netanyahu, "What you're doing here undermines the security of our troops who are fighting in Iraq, Afghanistan, and Pakistan. That endangers us and it endangers regional peace."[22] Despite Abbas's threats to walk away, the administration ultimately prevailed on the Palestinians to remain in the process.

After several rounds of mostly fruitless indirect talks, Mitchell finally convinced Abbas to resume direct talks with Israel. On September 1, 2010, amid much fanfare, President Obama hosted Prime Minister Netanyahu and President Abbas, along with Egypt's Hosni Mubarak and Jordan's King Abdullah, at the White House to officially relaunch Israeli-Palestinian negotiations. But with only three weeks left before the expiration of the moratorium on settlement construction, the decision to go ahead with the talks despite the looming deadline suggested that the administration had not fully thought the matter through. Netanyahu had made clear that he would not renew the moratorium, and Abbas had been equally clear that he would not remain in the talks without one. In a final bid to salvage the process, the Obama administration offered the Israelis an unprecedented multi-billion-dollar incentives package, including twenty F-35 fighter jets, various security guarantees, and an American pledge to block any UN action directed at censuring Israel, in return for a ninety-day extension of the moratorium—to no avail. It finally abandoned the effort in December 2010. The end of the moratorium put an end to the administration's attempts to constrain Israeli settlements, and to Obama's enthusiasm for the peace process.

"THE CURRENT PEACE PROCESS IS OVER"

Following the collapse of negotiations in late 2010, both Obama and Abbas began to disengage from the peace process. It seemed to Obama that he had done more than past presidents to restrain Israeli settlements while shielding Israel from any potential UN action stemming from the Goldstone Report, and had gotten only ingratitude from both leaders. Obama had essentially washed his hands of the issue. Abbas's pivot away from the peace process was more calculated and tactical in nature. After the expiration of the moratorium, Abbas announced plans to push for a Security Council resolution condemning Israeli settlements as a prelude to gaining formal recognition of a Palestinian state by the UN before the end of 2011.

The failed peace talks were the first in a series of setbacks for Abbas in the winter of 2010–11. On January 23, 2011, Al-Jazeera and *The Guardian* released hundreds of confidential Palestinian documents purporting to detail "unprecedented concessions" made by Palestinian negotiators to Israel. The release put Abbas on the defensive and rekindled questions about whether his leadership had a mandate to negotiate such crucial matters. The controversy over the leaks was soon eclipsed by mass protests in Egypt that led to the ouster of President Hosni Mubarak on February 11, 2011. The overthrow of Mubarak, a key ally of Abbas and the second Arab leader to be forced out of power in as many months, set off a wave of popular rebellions across the region that would soon redraw the political map of the Middle East.

The second clarifying moment for Abbas occurred a week later, on February 18, when the Obama administration vetoed an anti-settlements resolution in the Security Council that mostly mirrored the administration's own language. The American veto removed any lingering expectations Abbas might have had of the Obama administration as a fair-minded broker in the peace process. A few weeks later, the Palestinian foreign minister, Riyad al-Maliki, declared, "The current peace process, as it has been conducted so far, is over," and reiterated the PLO's plans to seek full UN membership.[23] Maliki's words proved to be more prescient than he may have realized.

The Arab uprisings exposed Abbas's domestic vulnerability and pushed him further away from an American-sponsored peace process. In a bid to shore up his sagging legitimacy Abbas moved to reconcile with Hamas while accelerating his international campaign for recognition of the Palestinian state.[24] The toppling of Mubarak and other Arab dictators was especially jarring for Abbas, who had serious legitimacy problems of his own. The same economic, institutional, and political stagnation that had spurred the region's youth into rebellion was also felt by Palestinians in the occupied territories. Even before the Arab uprisings, Palestinian officials had privately acknowledged that the PA's legitimacy was "hanging by a thread."[25] The PA's parliament had not convened in nearly four years, leaving Abbas, whose own presidential term had officially expired two years earlier, to rule by decree. The PA continued to be plagued by corruption, while Abbas's rule had grown more repressive and authoritarian. At the center of all these disruptions was the ongoing political division between the West Bank and Gaza.

Within twenty-four hours of Mubarak's resignation, Abbas had announced a slew of political reforms, including holding long-delayed local, legislative, and presidential elections before year's end. Within a few weeks, the revolutionary fervor sweeping the region, then optimistically known as the Arab Spring, had reached the West Bank and the Gaza Strip. Inspired by the successful uprisings in Tunisia and Egypt, young Palestinians began to mobilize their own revolution of sorts—except that the kind of "regime change" they sought was not aimed at bringing down their government but at putting it back together.

In March 2011, thousands of Palestinians gathered in public squares across the West Bank and Gaza to call for an end to the split between Fatah and Hamas. In response, Abbas asked the PLO's Constitution Committee to begin drafting amendments to the group's charter to allow for the inclusion of all Palestinian factions and announced that he would soon seek full membership of a Palestinian state in the UN. Despite his own misgivings over sharing power with Hamas, Abbas declared, "National unity supersede[s] all other considerations."[26] A few weeks later, on May 4, Palestine's two warring factions met in Cairo to sign a reconciliation agreement calling for the formation of a new government of "national consensus," new PA presidential and legislative elections, and reform of the PLO. Unlike the National Unity Government of 2007, the new "government of national consensus" would not include members of Hamas or any other faction but would instead by made up of technocrats and independents approved by all the factions. Abbas also believed the reconciliation pact would strengthen Hamas's pragmatic wing and reinforce de facto acceptance by Hamas of a state limited to the West Bank and Gaza.[27]

The new Egyptian-brokered reconciliation deal, the first of several in the years to come, also reflected shifts in the regional balance of power. Both the PA and Hamas had come to the arrangement from positions of weakness. Although Hamas was initially buoyed by Mubarak's ouster and the subsequent rise of the Muslim Brotherhood, the bloody crackdown on the nascent protest movement in Syria by the regime of Bashar al-Assad ultimately led Hamas to sever its ties with Damascus and strained its relations with Iran, its two principal allies in the region. Hamas's subsequent turn to Qatar and Turkey for support helped to confer a degree of legitimacy on Hamas within the region, while further alienating Abbas. Neither Fatah nor Hamas was in a hurry to share power, however; despite a number of follow-up agreements, the main components of the deal remained unimplemented as the two factions continued to jockey for position over the next several years.

The dramatic changes unfolding across the Arab world also offered an opportunity for the Obama administration to recalibrate its approach to what had become a stagnant and outmoded peace process, one that it nevertheless declined. Like most everyone else, the Obama administration was taken by surprise by the intensity of the Arab protests, which spread quickly from one country to another. Forced to adapt to fast-moving events around the region, Washington cut loose longtime American allies in Tunisia and Egypt, readjusted U.S. priorities in the region, and gradually came to terms with an array of new political actors. Among other things, the rapid rise and subsequent electoral success of groups affiliated with the Muslim Brotherhood and other Islamist movements in several Arab states forced the United States into an accommodation, albeit a reluctant one, with mainstream political Islam. In a May 19, 2011, speech on the Arab Spring, President Obama praised the political transformations under way in the Arab world and signaled that the United States, too, would have to alter its dealings with the region. The president pledged to put freedom, democracy, and respect for human rights at the center of U.S. policy while warning that "a failure to change our approach threatens a deepening spiral of division between the United States and the Arab world."[28]

The same could be said of the peace process. The Oslo process, originally envisioned as a five-year interim arrangement, was now nearly two decades old. Meanwhile, the only real attempt to update the process, the Quartet's Roadmap for Peace, had long since been abandoned, while the Quartet itself had ceased to play any meaningful political role. In his speech Obama spoke passionately of the "lack of self-determination" and "longing for freedom that has been building up for years" among Tunisians, Egyptians, Libyans, Syrians, and Bahrainis, but he mentioned the Palestinians only as a matter related to "the pursuit of peace," not political aspirations. At the same time U.S. officials were calling on governments in these divided Arab societies to "seek inclusive dialogue at home," the administration continued to oppose efforts by Palestinians to do the same.[29] "What matters to us and what matters, we think, to the process that we are trying to keep on track here is that Abbas remains the president, that Fayyad remains the prime minister," stated a State Department spokesperson in relation to Fatah-Hamas reconciliation efforts.[30]

The two previous presidents had both left their imprints on the peace process, in ways that were both constructive and not constructive. Both Clinton's "Parameters" of December 2000 and Bush's controversial Rose Garden speech of 2002, despite their differences and many shortcomings, nonetheless expanded U.S. policy into previously uncharted territory and at least attempted to respond to existing realities on the ground. Obama's May 19 speech was a chance to do the same. The question of whether and how to deal with the Palestinians in the speech was the subject of intense debate among members of Obama's Middle East team, especially between Mitchell and Ross, who had frequently butted heads over the peace process. Mitchell wanted the president to present positions on all four core issues of the conflict—borders, refugees, security, and Jerusalem—particularly the highly contentious issue of Jerusalem. According to Obama's deputy national security adviser, Ben Rhodes, Mitchell wanted the president "to be as bold as possible, to send a signal to the parties and the Arab world more broadly that the United States wanted change on this core issue of historic contention."[31] Ross advised against it, urging the president to focus on resolving the issues of borders and security, both of which had been discussed extensively in previous negotiating rounds, while putting off the more difficult issues of Jerusalem and refugees.[32] Obama sided with Ross. A few days before the speech, Mitchell announced his resignation.

The May 19 speech also underscored the political constraints on Obama and the extent to which the American political landscape had shifted in recent years. In the speech, Obama had reiterated the principle that the "borders of Israel and Palestine should be based on the 1967 lines, with mutually agreed swaps." This was a basic tenet of U.S. policy that had been acknowledged by both of the previous administrations, even if they did not always abide by it themselves. Obama's statement, "Changes to the 1949 Armistice lines must be mutually agreed to," was not substantively different from the formulation used by George W. Bush in 2005, although he used a different term for the 1967

lines. Yet Obama's statement drew angry responses from Israeli leaders and congressional Republicans, including accusations that the president had thrown Israel "under the bus."[33]

As Obama steadily disengaged from the peace process, Abbas
stepped up his efforts to gain international recognition of the Palestinian state. Gaining full Palestinian membership in the UN required
the approval of the Security Council, where a U.S. veto was all but assured. To help minimize the backlash, Abbas proceeded cautiously,
teasing the process out over the span of two years. His first step was to
deposit the formal application for full UN membership with the Security Council in September 2011, where it remained in bureaucratic
limbo for more than a year. Abbas planned to return to the UN in 2012
to take up the matter in the General Assembly, where he would only
need a simple majority to get Palestine recognized as a "nonmember
observer state," similar to the status of the Holy See. Although it would
change nothing on the ground, Palestine's recognition as a nonmember observer state would give the Palestinians access to a wide range of
international agencies and mechanisms, including the UN's human
rights bodies, the International Court of Justice, and the International
Criminal Court. In addition to gaining some negotiating leverage with
the Israelis and Americans, the UN bid provided Abbas with an opportunity to shore up his sagging popularity back home, where public
skepticism vis-à-vis an American-led peace process ran high.[34] The UN
bid did give Abbas a boost domestically even as it marked a low point in
his relations with Washington.[35]

Contrary to what many in Washington may have believed, Abbas's
pursuit of reconciliation with Hamas and recognition by the UN were
not a substitute for negotiations but his way of gaining some badly
needed leverage in any future negotiations. "Negotiations remain our
first option," wrote Abbas in the *New York Times* in May 2011, "but due
to their failure we are now compelled to turn to the international community to assist us in preserving the opportunity for a peaceful and just
end to the conflict."[36] Moreover, Abbas had gone to some lengths to
ensure the reconciliation pact with Hamas and his statehood bid at the
UN in a way that would cause the least amount of disruption to future

negotiations or his relations with Washington. By ensuring that Hamas members were not directly involved in the government Abbas hoped to avoid a repeat of 2007, when the PA had been boycotted by Israel, the U.S., and much of the international community. Likewise, by teasing out his bid for UN recognition over the span of two years, Abbas hoped to minimize the potential backlash from the U.S. and Israel. Abbas was now operating on all three tracks simultaneously—internal reconciliation, internationalization, and negotiations—not as part of some overarching strategy but as a survival tactic. When any one of them was exhausted or reached a dead end, Abbas would simply pivot to the next one.

Despite Abbas's rather cautious approach, neither the Obama administration nor the Israelis seemed willing to afford the Palestinian leader much leeway. Both the reconciliation deal with Hamas and the planned UN bid drew fierce opposition from Israel and the United States and badly strained Abbas's relations with the Obama administration. Israeli leaders decried Palestinian attempts to "delegitimize" Israel at the UN while warning of an "impending diplomatic tsunami."[37] In addition to suspending $100 million in tax transfers to the PA, Israeli officials threatened a range of other retaliatory measures, from revoking existing agreements with the PLO to annexing parts of the West Bank. The reactions in Washington mirrored those in Israel. Congress put a hold on $375 million in aid to the PA, though U.S. lawmakers later released the funds when Israeli military officials and others warned that it would threaten Israeli security by jeopardizing security cooperation between Israel and the PA.[38] Even as the administration scaled back its involvement in the peace process, the administration directed considerable energy and resources to defeating what President Obama described as "symbolic actions to isolate Israel at the United Nations."[39] Insisting that direct negotiations were the only path to Palestinian statehood, the president personally phoned Abbas in September 2011 to warn him that it would be "better for you and for us and for our relations" not to pursue the matter in the Security Council. Obama reportedly again phoned Abbas prior to the General Assembly vote in November 2012 and threatened him with consequences if the vote went ahead.[40] Meanwhile, a State Department spokesperson announced "a very broad and very vigorous démarche of virtually every capital in the world, that this is high on the agenda for every meeting the secretary [of State Hillary Clinton] has with every world leader."[41]

Abbas's May 4 reconciliation agreement with Hamas raised several legal and other complications for Washington in light of Hamas's involvement in violence against civilians and its official designation as a terrorist organization. Although Abbas had structured the agreement to avoid running afoul of U.S. law by ensuring that Hamas members were not part of the government, the sentiment inside the Israeli government and Congress was that even a government that was approved by Hamas was unacceptable.

Washington's response to the UN bid was more difficult to explain, at least from the standpoint of the peace process. Despite the administration's repeated denunciations of the move as disastrous for peace, Abbas maintained that UN recognition of Palestinian statehood was intended to affirm a two-state solution and would not necessarily foreclose the possibility of negotiations. Indeed, Abbas continued to pursue negotiations before, during, and after the UN bid, even when U.S.-led peace talks had become extremely unpopular back home. In fact, the only real threat posed by the UN bid was to the increasingly lopsided power dynamics of the peace process. In addition to providing the Palestinians with some modest leverage over Israel, Abbas's UN bid also threatened Washington's role in the international arena. Any attempt to internationalize the conflict was a direct challenge to the United States' monopoly over the peace process. Moreover, since U.S. law required defunding any UN agency that admitted Palestine as a full member, Palestinian leaders now had a potentially major source of leverage over the United States as well. In other words, the raft of anti-PLO laws adopted by the Congress over the years at Israel's behest had now become potential weapons in the hands of Palestinian leaders. Theoretically, the Palestinians could force the United States to defund agencies such as the World Trade Organization, World Health Organization, or even the International Atomic Energy Agency, any of which would have serious implications for U.S. business, economic, or strategic interests. For the time being, however, Abbas chose to tread lightly. His first stop after depositing his statehood application with the Security Council was UNESCO (United Nations Educational, Scientific and Cultural Organization), which voted in October 2011 to admit Palestine as its 195th member. The United States was forced to cut off funds to the UN agency. (In November 2015, Secretary of State John Kerry convinced Netanyahu to drop Israel's opposition to U.S. funding of UNESCO, allowing for its resumption).[42]

GAZA AND THE HAMAS CONUNDRUM

In November 2012, after nearly three years of relative quiet, Gaza once again erupted in violence. The eight-day conflagration between Hamas and Israel, which resulted in the deaths of 174 Palestinians and six Israelis (four of them civilians), was relatively contained, in part due to the new balance of power in the region.[43] Hamas had been emboldened by the electoral success of fellow Islamists in various Arab states, particularly in neighboring Egypt, where the Muslim Brotherhood's Mohammed Morsi had become the country's first democratically elected president. Solidarity visits by Egyptian, Tunisian, and other dignitaries to Gaza during the crisis also helped to buoy Hamas. A new cease fire with Israel was signed on November 21. Yet most of the underlying causes of the conflict remained unresolved, particularly the ongoing closure of Gaza's borders. Moreover, this latest Gaza war served as yet another reminder that the besieged enclave could not be ignored or isolated from the peace process.

In the aftermath of the first major Gaza war, in 2009, Israel had abandoned its policy of overthrowing the Hamas government, fearing that what came after would likely be worse. Despite officially endorsing UN calls for opening Gaza's borders, the Obama administration continued to adhere to the Bush-era policy of isolating Gaza and Hamas more or less indefinitely. According to Robert Danin, a former State Department official who also served in the Bush White House, it was a mistake for the United States to assume it could "broker peace between Israel and the Palestine Liberation Organization (PLO) as if Gaza and

Hamas do not exist" and that attempting to do so "only strengthens Hamas' grip, perpetuates Palestinian political stagnation, and helps preclude the creation of a Palestinian state and peace with Israel."[44] Moreover, since the original logic behind the regime change policy no longer applied, it was not even clear what it would take to lift the siege or bring about a political change with regard to Gaza.

Israel maintained that the blockade was necessary for security. Since September 2007, when Israel declared Gaza a "hostile territory," its official policy has been "to restrict the passage of various goods to the Gaza Strip and reduce the supply of fuel and electricity" as a means of pressuring Hamas.[45] Israel's closure of Gaza was not limited to restricting the flow of food and other materials. The Israelis also imposed severe restrictions on Palestinian exports out of the Strip. In all of 2012 a meager 252 truckloads of goods made their way out of Gaza, as compared with more than 11,500 during the first half of 2007.[46] The blockade, along with the destruction wrought by repeated military confrontations, decimated the Gaza economy and kept it on the brink of humanitarian crisis, with nearly 40 percent unemployment and roughly 80 percent of the population dependent on international food aid.[47]

Although violent attacks on Israelis emanating from Gaza no doubt exacted a heavy toll on Gaza's civilian population in the form of Israeli reprisals, it was also through bloodshed that any meaningful changes to the blockade regime came about. The first major change occurred in June 2010, following the deadly Israeli raid on an international aid flotilla attempting to break the Israeli siege. The attack, which occurred in international waters, resulted in the death of nine Turkish activists, one of whom was also an American citizen. In the wake of the flotilla incident, the Obama administration sent the Quartet representative, Tony Blair, to Israel to negotiate measures to ease the blockade. As a result, Israel agreed to lift restrictions on commercial goods entering Gaza by land and allow the delivery of limited construction materials under UN supervision. Where international diplomacy, PA advocacy, and Hamas "resistance" had all failed, a few hundred international activists succeeded in securing the most significant easing of the blockade in nearly four years, though at considerable cost.

The disastrous conditions in Gaza were as much a result of failure in Palestinian leadership and politics as of Israeli policies and American inertia. The internal division helped to perpetuate justifications for the blockade, and thus the blockade itself. So long as Hamas maintained control over Gaza and the PA did not operate there, neither Israel nor Egypt would be inclined to normalize their borders with Gaza. In the meantime, neither Abbas's PA nor Hamas could offer any way out of the Gaza conundrum. Hamas's involvement in rocket attacks on Israeli towns, abductions of Israeli soldiers, and other armed attacks, while momentarily boosting its popularity, brought little relief from Israel's punishing blockade and more often invited military action that brought even greater misery. Abbas, meanwhile, remained reluctant to inherit responsibility for Gaza's myriad social, economic, and security problems, for which he had no solutions.

Although both Hamas and Fatah bore a measure of responsibility for the tragedy in Gaza and the sorry state of Palestinian politics, they did not necessarily bear the burdens of failure equally. Despite facing more formidable immediate challenges, including a crippling siege and the persistent threat of Israeli military action, Hamas had the benefit of lower expectations among Palestinians as well as greater freedom of action. For Hamas to succeed it had to do little more than survive, whereas President Abbas was responsible for the well-being of all Palestinians, including those in Gaza, as well as for ending the occupation, establishing an independent state, and finding an equitable solution for Palestinian refugees. Keeping Hamas outside of the peace process gave it a freer hand both diplomatically and militarily. In contrast, Abbas's options—even nonviolent ones such as recognition by the UN—remained heavily constrained by his dependence on the United States and Israel. Contrary to what many American and Israeli officials seemed to believe, worsening conditions in Gaza did not enhance Abbas's and Fatah's standing among ordinary Palestinians, but instead helped to further erode their credibility. Meanwhile, PA failures in the West Bank very often helped Hamas.

8

The End of the Peace Process

"Useless, useless, useless."

—Palestinian official, describing the mission of the
Quartet representative, Tony Blair

On September 5, 2012, thousands of Palestinians took to the streets to demand the resignation of the Palestinian prime minister, Salam Fayyad.[1] Fayyad was best known for his state-building project, designed to lay the institutional foundations of a future Palestinian state in parallel with the diplomatic track. Fayyad's success in scaling back corruption and restoring basic law and order had earned him widespread admiration and praise from international donors, U.S. officials, and Israelis alike. The program was successful enough for the World Bank to conclude in April 2011 that the PA was "well positioned to establish a state at any time in the near future."[2] Yet Fayyad had always been more popular abroad than he was at home. Fayyad's international prominence had made him a target for Fatah cadres, who viewed him as a threat to Abbas's leadership. Moreover, ordinary Palestinians had not seen the tangible benefits of "Fayyadism," as the state-building project became known.

221

The protests began as a relatively limited display of anger over rising prices and unpaid salaries but soon metamorphosed into what was reported to be "the largest show of popular discontent with the Palestinian Authority in its 18-year existence."[3] For ten straight days, the unrest virtually paralyzed life in Palestinian cities across the West Bank, with scenes reminiscent of the first Intifada: burning tires, shuttered shops, and general strikes, punctuated by occasional clashes between rock-throwing Palestinian youths and uniformed security forces. Activists from Abbas's Fatah faction had initially encouraged the anti-Fayyad protests in the hope of sidelining their leader's longtime rival, until protesters began calling for his ouster, too. Many Palestinian demonstrators began calling not only for the resignation of key political figures but also for the nullification of the Paris Protocol, the Oslo-era agreement that had governed economic relations between Israel and the Palestinian Authority since 1994, as well as the Oslo Accords themselves.[4] The peculiar nature of the protests reflected more than just frustration with particular policies or leaders. The ease with which Palestinian anger had shifted from Fayyad to the Oslo Accords to Abbas's leadership reflected the growing sense among Palestinians that both the PA and the process that had created it had nothing left to offer.

The physical and territorial fragmentation fostered by the Israeli occupation was now also mirrored in the peace process and Palestinian politics. Gaza and East Jerusalem remained outside the scope of the peace process, as well as physically isolated from the West Bank, which was itself a patchwork of PA-controlled "islands" surrounded by areas of Israeli settlement and military control. Progress made in the economic, security, and institution-building spheres seemed to have no bearing on the political negotiations or on the day-to-day lives of Palestinians. Rather than attempting to reverse these dysfunctional trends, the peace process had simply incorporated and normalized them. As Abbas's leadership continued to pull away from the increasingly onerous constraints of the U.S.-led peace process, pro-Israel forces in the U.S. Congress worked to further limit his political and diplomatic options. The peace process had become little more than a way of maintaining the status quo and was now beginning to unravel one piece at a time.

FAYYAD VS. "FAYYADISM"

Salam Fayyad's resignation in April 2013 was the first tangible sign that the Oslo process had run its course. To many outsiders, the fact that Palestinian protesters had directed so much of their anger at Salam Fayyad, given his reputation as a clean and effective administrator and his impressive record of PA reforms, seemed misplaced. Fayyad's philosophy of self-empowerment, which his admirers affectionately termed "Fayyadism," had earned him universal praise and admiration in the United States, Europe, and even Israel. The *New York Times* columnist Thomas Friedman, who is credited with coining the term, defined Fayyadism as "the simple but all-too-rare notion that an Arab leader's legitimacy should be based not on slogans or rejectionism or personality cults or security services, but on delivering transparent, accountable administration and services."[5] President Shimon Peres went so far as to dub Fayyad the "Palestinian Ben Gurion."[6]

Fayyad's state-building plan was based on the belief that "building strong, sustainable, competent and effective democratic institutions" was first and foremost a Palestinian interest, and that, in addition, doing so would help eliminate international, especially Israeli and American, pretexts for failing to make progress on the political track.[7] Fayyad's philosophy was grounded in a firm belief that the Palestinians' emancipation begins with embracing their own agency. "I don't see Israel, with all its might, as something that cripples me," Fayyad has said. "I exist. I have power. I can project it. And we can do something about it." To those who would say it is impossible to build a state under occupation, Fayyad had a different view: "No one can stop us from building the state. Sovereignty is another issue. But no one can stop us from building it. Let's just go out and do it, and use the existential power of its existence to make it sovereign in some way. That's the way you transform the world."[8] Fayyad's reasoning was sound and rather compelling, but it was not how things ended up. Whereas Fayyad himself emphasized Palestinian self-reliance, agency, and initiative, "Fayyadism" ultimately became a substitute for Palestinian politics and a way to avoid dealing with the more structural problems of Israel's occupation. Fayyadism, in other words, was the latest incarnation of the "Oslo trade-off," but which had never actually worked. In the end, neither the success of Fayyad's internal reforms nor the improvement in security for Israelis produced any movement toward Palestinian statehood or ending the occupation.

During his six years as prime minister, Fayyad worked to enhance security coordination with Israel and improve local policing, which had helped to restore basic law and order and reestablish a measure of public confidence in Palestinian institutions. Fayyad's efforts to increase financial transparency within the PA also helped to scale back corruption, while sparking a modest, if brief, economic recovery in the West Bank. From a domestic political standpoint, however, Fayyad's tough fiscal and security policies, the areas for which he earned the most praise internationally, involved high costs and relatively low rewards for Palestinians. Pay cuts for government employees and increases in fuel prices alienated large segments of Palestinian society, while the PA's often harsh security measures against Palestinian militants brought activists from Hamas and Fatah into rare agreement in their opposition to Fayyad. The fact that, as George Washington University's Nathan Brown put it, the "entire program is based not simply on de-emphasizing or postponing democracy and human rights but on actively denying them for the present" further undercut the credibility of Fayyad's reform efforts.[9]

And how credible were they? The successes of Fayyadism had to be assessed within the context in which Fayyadism operated. The fact that nearly 30 percent of the PA's budget went toward security, as compared with the roughly 10 percent and 19 percent spent on health and education, respectively, raised questions about the nature and priorities of Palestinian governance in the West Bank.[10] The inordinate investment in security did produce tangible results—but mostly for Israelis. From 2009 until 2013, no Israelis were killed by Palestinians in Israel, and there were just thirty Israeli fatalities in the West Bank, including ten soldiers. By contrast, during the same five-year period, well over 600 Palestinians, at least half of them civilians, were killed by Israeli security forces or extremist settlers—not including the 170 killed during the eight-day Gaza war in late 2012.[11] Once again, improved security for Israelis did not lead to political progress or make their leaders more willing to compromise. Instead, the unprecedented calm along with the steady flow of donor funds to the PA became what many Palestinians sarcastically referred to as a "five-star occupation," in which the PA worked to ensure Israeli security while the international community picked up the tab.

Meanwhile, despite a brief economic recovery from 2009 to 2011, the West Bank remained worse off economically than it had been at the beginning of the Oslo process.[12] Once again, the biggest impediment to Palestinian economic growth in the West Bank remained Israel's system of internal closures, which carved up West Bank territory and prohibited Palestinians from developing 60 percent of the West Bank, including the resource-rich Jordan Valley.[13]

The fact that all of this occurred in a context of internal political stagnation and fragmentation raised even more questions. How far could institution building go in the absence of a functioning legislature and with few, if any, checks on the president's powers? What value was there in building institutions that could not reach the 40 percent of the population who lived in Gaza or the 300,000 Palestinians in East Jerusalem? As Nathan Brown, an American scholar specializing in Palestinian politics, observed, "For all his admirable qualities, what Fayyad has managed to do is to maintain many of the institutions built earlier and make a few of them more efficient. But he has done so in an authoritarian context that robs the results of domestic legitimacy."[14]

In other words, it wasn't a lack of credible Palestinian institutions that hampered the peace process but the other way around: the lack of a credible peace process, along with the paralysis of Palestinian institutional politics, crippled the development of Palestinian institutions. Even a highly skilled administrator such as Fayyad could not overcome the structural limitations imposed by the absence of sovereignty and the debilitating split between Hamas and the PA.[15] "As long as they're operating under an occupation," explained Howard Sumka, the former USAID mission director for the West Bank and Gaza, "there is very little incentive to have real competitive politics in an environment that's [not] really running things, and where you're so dependent on international donors for your livelihood and support."[16] Many Palestinians respected Fayyad, but some saw his program as an attempt to turn the PA "into an NGO-like body, a well-oiled administrative machine to facilitate the implementation of micro-projects funded by donor aid."[17]

Much as Bush's vision in 2002 had called on Palestinians to build a democracy without freedom, Fayyadism—or at least as it was perceived by many outsiders—seemed to bank on the hope that Palestinians could build a state without politics. For all its many successes, Fayyadism could not be a substitute for domestic politics and genuine political progress toward Palestinian statehood. For all of its many successes, Fayyadism had failed to deliver on its central promise. Not only had the PA's improved security performance and institutional reforms not brought about a state, but the Obama administration had actively worked to defeat even a symbolic recognition of Palestinian statehood while Congress had imposed new restrictions on the PA.

SHIFTING GOALPOSTS: THE KERRY NEGOTIATIONS

Fayyad's departure came just as the Obama administration was gearing up for another attempt at Israeli-Palestinian peacemaking. Despite Obama's pivot toward Asia and away from the broader Middle East, the administration singled out the goals of Israeli-Palestinian peace and curbing Iran's nuclear program as its top two priorities in the region. Obama's new secretary of state, Senator John Kerry, had a personal passion for the goal of Middle East peace as well as a strong grasp of the issues. Imbued with a sense of urgency, Kerry warned Congress that the window for a two-state solution was rapidly closing and that "we have some period of time, in one to one and a half to two years, or it is over."[18]

By July 2013, Kerry had convinced the parties to relaunch negotiations. Apart from Kerry's personal determination, however, very little had changed since the last round of negotiations, and the process collapsed after nine months. Despite an official presidential visit to Israel and the West Bank in spring 2013, the issue was not a top priority for Obama. Still feeling burned by his first foray into Israeli-Palestinian peace talks and preoccupied with upcoming midterm elections, Iran nuclear talks, and other priorities, Obama granted Kerry wide latitude but was not prepared to invest significant political capital of his own in the pursuit of a peace deal. Despite the best efforts of Kerry and his new special envoy for Middle East peace, Martin Indyk, the process remained detached from realities on the ground, including Israel's ever-expanding settlement enterprise and the growing power imbalance between the two sides. Netanyahu's center-right coalition felt little pressure to make major concessions while Abbas's leadership was too weak and divided to offer any of his own. Moreover, the addition of new Israeli demands and the nature of Kerry's "framework" proposal effectively shifted the goalposts, raising the stakes for Abbas while simultaneously lowering the expected return.

According to administration officials, the terms of the talks had been worked out between American and Israeli officials beforehand, leaving aside the Palestinians' main demands for a settlement freeze, a commitment to negotiate on the basis of the 1967 borders, and the release of hundreds of Palestinian political prisoners. Instead, Netanyahu promised Kerry a "slowdown" in settlement construction and agreed to release 104 pre-Oslo Palestinian prisoners in four phases. Given the sensitivities in Israel concerning the release of Palestinian prisoners, many of whom had blood on their hands, Netanyahu informed Kerry that he would have to approve some new settlement units to keep his coalition intact.[19] In return, the Palestinians would refrain from joining additional UN agencies for the duration of the talks. As a further incentive, Kerry promised to put together a substantial economic assistance package whose purpose would be "to fundamentally transform the Palestinian economy"; administration of the economic package would be overseen by the Quartet representative, Tony Blair.[20] The ambitious plan included some $600 million in aid to the PA from Arab Gulf states and another $4 billion in investments. (In the end the aid package remained largely unimplemented following the collapse of negotiations.)

Back in Ramallah, Kerry's proposal was met with intense skepticism within the Palestinian leadership.[21] Virtually everyone, including Abbas, doubted Netanyahu's commitment to a two-state solution. And although many liked Kerry personally, few within Abbas's inner circle believed that he would be able to "deliver" the Israeli leader. Despite strong opposition from the PLO Executive Committee and the Fatah Central Council, Abbas decided to move ahead with Kerry's negotiations but set a nine-month time limit on the talks. In the event the talks failed, Abbas would at least avoid being blamed, while pocketing some tactical benefits. Events in neighboring Egypt further reduced the potential costs of failure from Abbas's standpoint. The Egyptian military's overthrow, on July 3, 2013, of President Mohammed Morsi of the Muslim Brotherhood had put Hamas on the defensive and tilted the internal balance of power back in Abbas's favor.

With a few exceptions, the overall dynamics inside and outside the negotiating room were similar to those in previous negotiations. As the talks proceeded, Israeli authorities pushed through approvals for 13,000 settlement housing units.[22] Believing they had secured an Israeli commitment to show restraint during the negotiations, American officials were surprised by the scale of the new settlement plans. Moreover, according to Indyk, the fact that each batch of prisoner releases was accompanied by new settlement activity "undermined the whole exercise."[23] One of the two Palestinian negotiators tapped by Abbas to lead the talks with Israel, Mohammed Shtayyeh, publicly resigned in protest of the new settlement announcements. By late 2013 it was clear the talks had reached an impasse. Recognizing that reaching a comprehensive peace deal by the April 29, 2014, deadline was unlikely, U.S. officials shifted their focus to the more modest objective of laying out a "framework" outlining basic principles on each of the core issues of the conflict to serve as a basis for negotiating a final status agreement at a later stage.[24] The American framework would then be put to the two sides, who were expected to accept the document, each with their own unspecified reservations. The aim was to bring the two leaders into the "zone of possible agreement" and then work on bridging the differences. The exact shape of the "zone" or what constituted an "agreement" was not defined. The two-tiered approach drew comparisons to Oslo, although the administration insisted that it was not pursuing another interim accord. Nevertheless, Kerry's approach rested on the same type of incrementalism and "constructive ambiguity" that had long been hallmarks of the Oslo process.

Already believing that Abbas was willing to make far-reaching compromises, U.S. officials focused on getting Netanyahu into the "zone." By early 2014 Netanyahu had reportedly agreed to negotiate borders between Israel and Palestine on the basis of the 1967 lines and was prepared to accept vague language referring to Palestinian aspirations regarding Jerusalem, which Abbas angrily rejected. The Palestinian leader also had problems with two additional issues. The first was security. Not only had Netanyahu not moved from his insistence that Israel remain in the Jordan Valley, an area making up nearly one-fourth of the West Bank, for thirty to forty years, presumably as a bulwark against assorted "threats from the east," but in addition he later expanded the demand to include other parts of the West Bank.[25] Under an American proposal, the Israeli army would have been allowed to remain in the Jordan Valley for twelve to fifteen years after concluding a peace agreement. The Palestinians had indicated a willingness to accept a robust third-party presence in the Jordan Valley but considered the continued presence of Israeli forces on Palestinian soil unacceptable.

Equally problematic for Abbas was the question of what was innocuously termed "mutual recognition": Israel's insistence on being recognized "as a Jewish state." Netanyahu claimed that Palestinian refusal to accept Israel as the homeland of the Jewish people was "the root of the conflict," although the question of defining Israel as an exclusively Jewish state remained highly controversial even within Israeli Jewish society.[26] The demand, which had not been part of the Oslo Accord or either of Israel's treaties with Egypt (1979) or Jordan (1994), had first been raised by Israel at the 2007 Annapolis peace conference but was successfully kept off the agenda by the Palestinians.[27] But, whereas the Bush administration had decided not to press the matter, the Obama administration adopted the highly contentious demand more or less effortlessly.

Recognizing Israel's Jewish character may have seemed self-evident to Kerry and other administration officials, but it was an exceptionally difficult demand to make of Palestinians given their own history and its relation to the events that led to Israel's creation. Abbas "rejected that completely," recalled Indyk. "The harder we pushed on it, the harder he dug in against it."[28] The Palestinians argued the demand was superfluous since the PLO had already officially recognized Israel as a condition for opening a dialogue with the United States in 1988 and then again as part of the 1993 Oslo Declaration of Principles. More important, they claimed that recognizing Israel "as a Jewish state" would undermine the rights of Palestinian refugees while negating their own national and historical narratives.[29] "If Israel is the homeland of the Jewish people," explains the Palestinian British scholar Ahmad Khalidi, "then the Arab presence there becomes historically aberrant and contingent; the Palestinians effectively become historic interlopers and trespassers—a transient presence on someone else's national soil."[30] In effect, U.S. officials wanted the Palestinians to endorse a central component of the Zionist-Israeli national narrative without making any comparable demand on Israel to recognize Palestinian narratives or historical claims.

The "Jewish state" demand would be all the more difficult in light of the power dynamics between the two sides. Had it been part of a broader process of mutual reconciliation or if Israel had, in exchange, made a parallel offer by accepting responsibility for the Nakba, for example, the Palestinians might have reacted differently. However, for U.S. officials to ask Palestinian leaders to bestow moral legitimacy on Israel, even as it continued its occupation and the refugee issue remained unresolved, and without any reciprocal gestures or actions in return, would likely be seen by most Palestinians as something akin to official capitulation.

The American framework did make some gestures toward the Palestinians. In March, the U.S. team put together a new draft of the framework that more clearly stipulated a Palestinian capital in Jerusalem and which seemed to go further than Netanyahu was prepared to accept. According to published accounts of the talks, the document stated that "the permanent status agreement will have to provide for both Israel and Palestine to have their internationally recognized capitals in Jerusalem, with East Jerusalem serving as the Palestinian capital," but put off the status of the Old City, religious sites, and Jewish settlements in Jerusalem to be taken up in later negotiations. Kerry pressed Abbas for a response, but by this time, according to Indyk, the Palestinian leader had already "checked out" of the process as a result of the spike in settlement activity and the danger of agreeing to a framework agreement that would have required additional Palestinian concessions.[31] To avoid rejecting the American document outright, Abbas chose to remain silent. When pressed by Obama during their March 2014 meeting in Washington, Abbas continued to deflect. It was at that point that Obama reportedly lost his cool. "Don't quibble with this detail or that detail," Obama said. "The occupation will end. You will get a Palestinian state. You will never have an administration as committed to that as this one."[32] By saying yes, the president argued, the Palestinians would be putting the ball in Netanyahu's court, at which point the administration would be in a better position to pressure the Israeli leader. That the president of the most powerful nation on earth was asking the weakest actor in the entire arrangement to provide *him* with the political cover to apply pressure on a close but otherwise dependent U.S. ally seemed to sum up the distorted—and distortive—dynamics of the peace process.

The talks officially collapsed a few weeks later after Israel declined to carry out the fourth and final prisoner release, at which point Abbas shifted back to his two other tracks: signing letters of accession by the Palestinian state to fifteen international treaties and initialing a new reconciliation pact with Hamas on April 23. The administration expressed "disappointment" at the Palestinian reconciliation pact but said it would be willing to "work with" and continue funding the new Palestinian consensus government. It was the first meaningful shift in U.S. Gaza policy in seven years, for which it received considerable flak from Congress.[33] The Obama administration stopped short of officially blaming either side for the collapse, but Kerry hinted at Israel's responsibility for failing to live up to its commitment to release the last tranche of prisoners.[34] Kerry also suggested that Israel had the most to lose, warning that Israel would soon have to choose between its democratic and Jewish characters and that without a two-state solution, it risked becoming "an apartheid state." After getting heat for his remarks, the State Department clarified that Kerry was merely echoing warnings made by various Israeli leaders in recent years.[35]

This was not the first time American officials had presented what they considered to be a far-reaching proposal, only to be met with a non-response from the Palestinians. What explains Abbas's silence? Internal weakness was clearly one factor. Abbas's domestic standing was nothing like Arafat's at the time of Camp David in 2000 and was arguably worse than where he was during the Annapolis talks in 2007–08. Moreover, going into the Kerry negotiations, Abbas had the backing of neither the PLO leadership nor his own Fatah party, much less of the Palestinian public or political opponents such as Hamas. According to Indyk, Abbas "had so little legitimacy he was not willing to take that kind of risk."[36] Moreover, said Indyk, given the administration's inability to influence Israel's settlement policies and the reneged-on prisoner release, Abbas had reason to doubt Obama's ability to bring Netanyahu on board for the more difficult issues later on. "It was that combination of our inability to deliver on any of these things which led him to really doubt [us]—if you can't deliver on these small things, how can I rely on you to deliver on big concessions from Netanyahu?"[37] One of Obama's closest foreign policy advisers, Ben Rhodes, was even more blunt—albeit well after both he and his boss had left the White House. "They were never sincere in their commitment to peace," Rhodes said in June 2018 of Netanyahu's government. "They used us as cover, to make it look like they were in a peace process. They were running a play, killing time, waiting out the administration."[38] Rhodes's thirteenth-hour revelation seemed to vindicate Abbas's silence in response to Kerry's framework; if even American officials felt they were being played by Netanyahu, why should the Palestinians gamble everything on their ability to get concessions out of the Israeli leader?

The fact that the United States had allowed Israel to introduce new issues that had not been part of previous negotiations, particularly the "Jewish state" demand, only added to Abbas's reluctance to engage. Accepting Kerry's principles as a basis for future negotiations not only negated the Palestinians' own national narrative but also risked undermining the traditional ground rules, or "terms of reference," of the peace process, Resolution 242 and the land-for-peace formula—all in return for a vague promise of an Israeli withdrawal at an unspecified point in the future. Nathan Thrall of the International Crisis Group summarized Abbas's dilemma as follows: "Palestinians and Israelis would be trading fundamentally unlike assets, one tangible, the other intangible. Palestinians would give up intangible moral claims, acquiescing in the denial of their right to return and bestowing legitimacy on their dispossessors by recognizing the vast majority of the Palestinian homeland as a Jewish state. Israelis, by contrast, would be committing to a physical withdrawal from land under their full control."[39] In the meantime, given the huge power imbalance between the parties, any ambiguities were likely to be interpreted in Israel's favor or simply dictated by realities on the ground.

NEITHER PEACE NOR PROCESS

Following the collapse of the Kerry talks, President Obama declared "a holding period" in the peace process. By this time, however, there was very little left that could still reasonably be called a peace process. The two most visible components of the process, Fayyad's state-building project and American-sponsored peace negotiations, had been exhausted. The few conflict mitigation mechanisms that had existed under Oslo and the roadmap had long since ceased to function or had been abandoned, and the Obama administration showed little inclination to revive them or establish new ones. Tony Blair's decision in May 2015 to step down from his post as Quartet representative removed the last remaining vestige of the institution-building project. In practical terms, what remained of the Oslo process had neither the capacity to resolve the conflict nor the means to manage it—as the bloody

events during the second half of 2014 demonstrated. The outbreak of a
new Gaza war in June 2014, along with the recurring violence in East
Jerusalem later that year, once again underscored the dangers of continuing to exclude these areas from the peace process.

The match that ignited the war was actually struck in the West
Bank. Following the June 2014 kidnapping and presumed murder of
three Israeli teenagers in the West Bank, the Israeli army launched a
massive crackdown across the West Bank, mainly targeting Hamas activists. Hamas responded with a barrage of rocket fire at Israel from
Gaza, which soon ignited a full-scale war. Kerry's attempts to broker a
truce were stymied by Israel and the Sisi regime in Egypt, both of which
hoped to further squeeze Hamas and perhaps derail the reconciliation
deal with Fatah. By the time a cease fire agreement was signed ending the
fifty-one-day Israeli offensive, around 2,200 Palestinians, including
more than 500 children, had been killed and another 11,000 injured,
along with 18,000 homes destroyed and another 500,000 people internally displaced.[40] The war also proved costly for Israel, which suffered
its heaviest losses since the 2006 Lebanon war, including 66 soldiers
and 6 civilians, and further battered its image, with growing numbers of Americans viewing Israel as the aggressor in the conflict.[41]

In purely political terms, the heaviest price for the war was paid by
Abbas and the PA. The PA's apparent siding with the United States and
Israel in blaming Hamas for the violence provoked a popular backlash
against Abbas and exposed rifts within his own leadership. As the bombs
fell on Gaza, young Palestinians in the West Bank began to call for a
mass march on Abbas's headquarters, the Muqataa. "I was panicked. We
were [considered] traitors!" recalled Yasser Abed Rabbo, a senior PLO
figure who fell out with the Palestinian president after criticizing his
handling of the crisis. A PLO statement drafted by Abed Rabbo in
which he criticized the "terrorist assault" on Gaza and vowed to prosecute Israeli leaders for alleged war crimes helped to diffuse some of the
anger on the street but also ran afoul of the Palestinian president.[42]

As the August 26 cease fire began to take hold in Gaza, attention
shifted to Jerusalem, where a series of provocations by Jewish settlers
and restrictions on Muslim worship at the Al-Aqsa Mosque in September

2014 sparked a new round of violent protests and a rash of "lone wolf" attacks by Palestinians on Israelis. The fact that the two areas that seemed to witness the most persistent violence were also beyond the reach of both the PA and the peace process was not coincidental. The suffocating blockade on Gaza had produced three major wars in five years while the lack of clean water, fuel, and adequate health and education services, according to one UN study, threatened to make Gaza "uninhabitable" by 2020.[43] Meanwhile, since Oslo, East Jerusalem and its 300,000 Palestinian residents had lived in a kind of social and political limbo, segregated from Israel socially and economically while remaining physically and politically cut off from the West Bank and the Palestinian Authority. Palestinians made up some 38 percent of the city's population, but received just 12 percent of the municipal budget.[44] Israel's separate and unequal treatment of the city's Palestinian population in areas of taxation, housing, education, water, health services, and residency rights has been well documented by local and international rights groups.[45] Israel's crackdown on Palestinian Jerusalemites intensified after the failure of the Camp David summit and the outbreak of the Intifada.[46] For example, over half of Israel's more than 14,000 revocations of Palestinian Jerusalemites' residency rights since 1967 occurred since 2001.[47] As of 2014, more than 80 percent of Jerusalem's Palestinians lived below the poverty line.[48] At the same time, Israeli prohibitions on Palestinian civic, cultural, and political institutions and activities had rendered Palestinian Jerusalemites "political orphans and totally leaderless."[49]

Against the backdrop of violence in Jerusalem, and with his domestic standing at an all-time low, Abbas resumed his internationalization campaign, announcing plans for a new Security Council resolution calling for a Palestinian state along the 1967 border and an Israeli withdrawal from the West Bank, Gaza, and East Jerusalem within three years; he threatened to join the International Criminal Court if the Security Council vote failed. Meanwhile, as renewed American efforts to relaunch negotiations proved fruitless, the United States found itself increasingly isolated in its opposition to Abbas's internationalization efforts. On October 30, 2014, Sweden became the first EU member to

recognize the Palestinian state, followed by parliamentary endorse-
ments in Britain, Spain, and France. When the PLO-backed resolution
in the Security Council was defeated on December 30, Abbas retaliated
by signing the Rome Statute, the international treaty that established
the International Criminal Court. Abbas had been hesitant to join the
ICC, which had long been considered a red line for Israel and Congress,
often referred to as the "nuclear option." However, with broad segments
of Palestinian civil society and most political factions, including Hamas
and Islamic Jihad—both of which were themselves accused of war
crimes—demanding that he join the International Criminal Court,
Abbas could no longer afford to put the matter off.[50]

The more Abbas attempted to pull away from the peace process,
however, the more pro-Israel forces in Congress sought to tie the Palestinians' hands in the international arena. Along with the usual Israeli
and American sanctions, including the suspension of Palestinian tax
transfers by Israel to the PA and a congressional threat to halt $400 mil-
lion in aid to the PA, Congress adopted new legislation conditioning
the ability of the PLO to operate in the United States on the president's
certification that the Palestinians had not taken "any action" against
Israel at the International Criminal Court—the same law invoked by
President Trump to close down the PLO mission in Washington in
2018.[51] Tellingly, the new law explicitly tied the future of the PLO office in Washington to a presidential determination that the Palestinians were engaged in "serious peace talks" with Israel. The passage of
the law marked a new phase in the U.S.-led peace process, which was no
longer about resolving the conflict or ending Israel's occupation but had
morphed into a means for limiting Palestinian decision making and diplomatic options.

By early 2015, American peacemaking and the Palestinian leadership were both in freefall. Following Netanyahu's election to a third
consecutive term in March 2015, the Israeli prime minister assembled a
new ruling coalition, which he described as "more committed to settlements than any in Israel's history."[52] More than half of Israel's new
cabinet openly opposed a Palestinian state. Conceding that prospects
for a two-state solution looked "very dim," Obama said the U.S. would

"reassess" its approach to the Israeli-Palestinian peace process while focusing on identifying steps that could be taken to preserve the possibility of two states at some later stage.[53] Among other things, the president hinted at the possibility of not shielding Israel at the United Nations.[54] Once again, however, Obama disengaged from the Palestinian question and turned his attention to Iran. In July 2015, Obama scored a major political and diplomatic victory by pushing through a multilateral agreement designed to curtail Iran's ability to develop nuclear weapons. The Iran nuclear deal, which put constraints on Iran's nuclear program in exchange for an easing of international sanctions against Tehran, further strained Obama's troubled relationship with Netanyahu. However, it also demonstrated the president's willingness to defy the pro-Israel lobby and congressional Republicans when a clear, identifiable strategic interest was at stake.

Meanwhile, despite Abbas's getting a temporary boost from his ICC bid, his leadership continued to flounder. Despite a softening in the American and Israeli positions toward the new Palestinian consensus government since the 2014 war, the PA was still not operating in Gaza nearly a full year later. The ongoing stalemate between Fatah and Hamas helped further delay the reconstruction process. A weakened Hamas had shown a willingness to give up governing Gaza, but was not yet ready to relinquish its weapons or security role there. Abbas was equally reluctant to assume responsibility for Gaza's myriad social, economic, and security problems, for which he had few solutions. The growing prominence of jihadist groups operating in Gaza and across the border in the Sinai only increased the pressure on Hamas and added to Abbas's aversion to returning to Gaza.[55] Having practically exhausted his three tracks, an increasingly authoritarian and insecure Abbas began lashing out at would-be rivals and challengers real and imagined, while working to consolidate his grip on power. Along with the exiled former Gaza security chief, Muhammed Dahlan, and former premier Salam Fayyad, Abbas now added Yasser Abed Rabbo to his growing list of internal enemies, accusing the three men of a host of financial crimes and of conspiring to overthrow him. Meanwhile, public speculation over who might succeed the eighty-year-old Palestinian leader became a national preoccupation, as Abbas's popularity continued to sink. A poll released in September 2015 found that nearly two-thirds of Palestinians wanted Abbas to resign.[56]

With his domestic standing and political options dwindling, Abbas attempted one final bit of theatrics: he promised to deliver a "bombshell" during his upcoming speech before the UN General Assembly. The speech took place against the backdrop of heightened tensions and violent flare-ups in the West Bank following the July 31, 2015 firebombing of two Palestinian homes in the village of Duma by an extremist Israeli settler that killed an eighteen-month-old infant and other members of his family. After excoriating Israel over its settlement policies and failure to live up to signed commitments, the Palestinian president took a swipe at one of the centerpieces of the Oslo process itself. The PA "cannot continue to be bound by these agreements," Abbas declared, adding that "Israel must assume all of its responsibilities as an occupying power, because the status quo cannot continue." Abbas's carefully crafted words were just enough to remind U.S. and Israeli leaders that he still had some leverage but stopped short of renouncing the PA's security cooperation with Israel—an obligation he had previously characterized as "sacred."[57]

Abbas may not have anticipated how soon his words would be put to the test. Within a few days of his UN speech, Jerusalem was rocked by another wave of violence which soon spread to the West Bank. The unrest was provoked by Jewish extremists attempting to gain access to the Al-Aqsa Mosque compound, known to Jews as the Temple Mount, fueling fears that the extremists were seeking to alter a longstanding arrangement, known as the Status Quo, that had governed access the holy site since 1967 or to harm the Al-Aqsa Mosque. The perceived threat to the holy site set off a rash of stabbings, shootings, and car-ramming attacks by mostly young Palestinians that lasted throughout late 2015 and into early 2016. Israel's responses to these incidents and to the more typical clashes between Palestinian youths and Israeli forces often involved deadly force. During the first six months of the unrest, some 230 Palestinians, many of whom were not involved in violent attacks, and 30 Israelis were killed.[58]

As official Palestinian media praised the "Jerusalem intifada," PA forces continued to work quietly with Israel to quell the violence, highlighting a central dilemma for Abbas: the PA's security cooperation with Israel remained intensely unpopular with ordinary Palestinians and was also a major sticking point in the stalled reconciliation process with Hamas, but it was critical to the PA's continued international, and especially American, support and hence to its continued survival. Apart from the roughly 140,000 government jobs (including some 58,000 men serving in the various PA security services), which helped to sustain about one-third of Palestinian households in the West Bank, security coordination was perhaps the only other relatively successful aspect of the Oslo process. The future of both security cooperation and the PA itself was looking increasingly precarious, however, in light of the mounting popular frustration with the PA and the precipitous drop in international aid. Total foreign aid to the PA, which made up more than a third of its budget, had declined from around $1.2 billion in 2012 to $750 million in 2015.[59] Despite growing concern in Washington and in Israel over the possible collapse of the PA, administration officials conceded that they were "out of ideas" on how to move the process forward.[60]

THE OBAMA PARADOX

Obama's presidency ended much as it began: with seemingly contradictory gestures. In September 2016, the Obama administration concluded a new ten-year agreement providing a total of $38 billion in military aid to Israel, which the White House described as the "the largest single pledge of military assistance in U.S. history."[61] As the president and other U.S. officials were keen to point out, no American administration had provided more military aid to Israel than that of Barack Obama. Three months later, the administration took the unusual step of abstaining from a Security Council resolution condemning Israeli settlements as both illegal and a threat to Israeli-Palestinian peace. The resolution condemned Israeli settlements as a "flagrant violation" of international law and demanded an end to "all Israeli settlement activities" as "essential for salvaging the two-state solution." In addition to reiterating the international consensus on the illegality of Israeli settlements, the resolution also addressed incitement and terrorism by Palestinians. The administration's abstention produced a torrent of denunciations from the Israeli government, key Republican figures, and even members of the president's own party. A furious Netanyahu denounced the vote as "shameful" and "hostile to the State of Israel,"[62] while Speaker of the House Paul Ryan called it "a blow to peace that sets a dangerous precedent for further diplomatic efforts to isolate and demonize Israel."[63] President-elect Donald Trump labeled the resolution "extremely unfair" and pledged that under his administration "things will be different."[64]

The administration defended its stance at the UN as necessary to salvage what remained of a two-state solution. Secretary of State Kerry laid out the administration's thinking in unusually clear terms, explaining that the United States "could not in good conscience protect the most extreme elements of the settler movement as it tries to destroy the two-state solution." Moreover, Kerry insisted, Israel now faced a stark choice: "Israel can either be Jewish or democratic—it cannot be both." The alternative to an independent Palestinian state would mean "millions of Palestinians permanently living in segregated enclaves in the middle of the West Bank, with no real political rights, separate legal, education, and transportation systems, vast income disparities, under a permanent military occupation that deprives them of the most basic freedoms. Separate and unequal is what you would have. And nobody can explain how that works. Would an Israeli accept living that way? Would an American accept living that way? Will the world accept it?"[65]

Obama's decision to abstain at the Security Council alongside the unprecedented levels of military and political support his administration provided for Israel highlighted a central paradox of his presidency. Despite being widely viewed as more sympathetic to Palestinian grievances and less sentimental toward Israel, Obama was less willing than most of his predecessors to apply pressure on Israel or to bolster Palestinian leaders to advance the peace process. U.S. officials decried the status quo as "unsustainable" but actively worked to prevent attempts by the Palestinians to challenge that status quo, even when they were compatible with a two-state solution. In contrast to its treatment of Israeli settlements, the Obama administration devoted considerable time and resources to defeating Abbas's largely symbolic bids to gain recognition of a Palestinian state at the United Nations in 2011 and 2012. Notwithstanding the drama and controversy surrounding the December 2016 abstention, Obama did more to shield Israel at the United Nations than any other American president since 1967. In contrast to the one Security Council resolution critical of Israel that was allowed to pass under Obama, twenty-one were adopted under Reagan, nine under George H. W. Bush, three under Clinton, and six under George W. Bush.[66] Obama spent much of his presidency distancing himself from Bush's policies, but the more salient contrast was perhaps with another Democratic president, Bill Clinton. Both presidents had notoriously tense relationships with right-wing Israeli governments, in both cases led by Benjamin Netanyahu. Yet unlike Clinton, Obama did not attempt to leverage the U.S.-Israel relationship either to bolster the Palestinian leadership or to expand American peacemaking into previously uncharted territory.

In fact, Obama was arguably the first U.S. president in more than four decades who did not break any new ground politically or diplomatically between Israelis and Palestinians or otherwise leave his imprint on the peace process.[67]

- The Nixon/Ford administration was the first to pursue a clandestine dialogue with the PLO through the CIA in 1973–74, a grudging recognition that Palestinians would eventually have to play a role in the peace process.
- Jimmy Carter took this a step further by calling for the creation of a Palestinian "homeland" while attempting, albeit unsuccessfully, to bring the PLO into the Geneva peace process.
- Ronald Reagan was the first to initiate an official dialogue with the PLO in 1988, which, while short-lived, affirmed that the group could not be ignored.

- George H. W. Bush and his secretary of state, James Baker, made history by bringing Palestinians directly into the peace process for the first time at the 1991 Madrid peace conference.
- Bill Clinton outdid all of his predecessors, becoming the first U.S. president to receive a Palestinian leader at the White House following the signing of the 1993 Oslo Accord and the first to express support, albeit unofficially, for a Palestinian state.
- Even George W. Bush managed to break new ground. In addition to officially endorsing Palestinian statehood, Bush and his secretary of state, Colin Powell, pushed through the road-map peace plan, the first (albeit theoretical) corrective to the Oslo process. Bush's second secretary of state, Condi Rice also distinguished herself from her predecessors in earning the admiration of Palestinian officials.

This is not to say that Obama's policies toward the Israeli-Palestinian conflict were worse than those of his predecessors—far from it. Nor is it to suggest that the contributions of past presidents were on the whole positive in terms of advancing the cause of peace; they clearly were not. Yet what Nixon, Ford, Carter, Reagan, Bush the elder, Clinton, and Bush the son all had in common was that each of them took steps, however halting or grudgingly, that were necessary to move the process forward, which, given the exceedingly slow pace of change in U.S. policy, was not insignificant.

In fairness, Obama did make some important departures from his predecessors. The decision by the administration to drop its active opposition to internal Palestinian reconciliation was a crucial one in terms of allowing for the PA's eventual return to Gaza and a reconstruction process to begin. More important, Obama attempted to restore the basic principles undergirding the peace process, particularly when it came to the sanctity of the 1967 lines and the illegitimacy of Israeli settlements, both of which had been severely eroded by Israeli facts on the ground and the acquiescence of successive U.S. administrations.

Unfortunately, the situation required not just holding the line but actually moving the ball down the field. Obama was clearly not inclined to take bold steps such as recognizing a Palestinian state or calling for a Palestinian capital in East Jerusalem, both of which would have likely triggered a major backlash from pro-Israel political forces, including within his own party. But there were other less radical things the Obama administration could have done had it been more invested in an Israeli-Palestinian peace settlement.

- The administration could have translated its tough rhetoric on Israeli settlements into concrete actions, for example by targeting American charities that funded Israeli settlements or by stipulating that any future land swaps should be on a one-to-one basis. Neither of these measures would have required congressional approval.

- The administration could have devoted less time in getting the parties back to the negotiating table and more on trying to foster an environment where those negotiations could succeed. Given the recurring violence in places like Gaza and East Jerusalem, in particular, U.S. officials could have done more to impose constraints or some measure of accountability on the parties, for example, through official international inquiries or perhaps even putting forward new mechanisms and initiatives to replace the largely defunct Quartet and roadmap.

- Instead of waging an all-out diplomatic war against Abbas's mostly symbolic UN bids, Obama could have used these bids to boost the beleaguered Palestinian leader while nudging Netanyahu in a different direction, the way Clinton did with his visits to Gaza and Bethlehem in 1998.

- The administration might have moved the needle politically by making a bold statement on the future status of Jerusalem—as Senator Mitchell had advised Obama to do in 2011. Kerry's valedictory speech of December 2016 did state that an agreed resolution should provide "for Jerusalem as the internationally recognized capital of the two states," but it did not carry the same weight as a statement from the president would have done, and in any case Kerry's statement came too late in the game. One cannot help but wonder, whether such a statement on

Jerusalem might have preempted or mitigated in some way the actions taken by Trump.

These were not radical ideas but would have been fairly modest interventions, most of which had been done in one form or another by previous administrations, but which were still seen as politically unachievable. That said, there were reasons why Obama had adopted such a minimalist approach. It is entirely possible that the peace process Obama inherited was already broken beyond repair by the time he got to it. Moreover, given the hand he was dealt, and the political constraints he faced from Congress and Israel, Obama saw little value in investing heavily in the issue. As Robert Malley, who served in the Obama White House from March 2015 until January 2017, explains: "I believe President Obama felt that, if the parties were not going to move, and if he could not take the kinds of decisions that would make them move, it was better to do nothing than to perpetuate the illusion that the peace process would lead to peace. A process for the sake of process, he sensed, was simply a way to enable and prolong a damaging status quo."[68] Obama promised more and achieved less than most of his predecessors, but it must be said that he was more politically constrained than they were. As Israeli governments have drifted ever rightward and as the tone of Israeli politics has become increasingly triumphalist and maximalist, so too have pro-Israel forces in Washington, particularly among congressional Republicans. Whatever the reasons for Obama's inaction, it had consequences, particularly in light of who came after him.

Epilogue

If Jerusalem is off the table, then America is off the table as well.

—Nabil Abu Rudeineh, spokesman for Palestinian President Mahmoud Abbas, January 2018

Few had expected Donald J. Trump to be a conventional president. But even the celebrity billionaire and onetime reality TV host managed to raise eyebrows during his White House press conference with Prime Minister Benjamin Netanyahu on February 15, 2017, his first official meeting with a foreign leader after being sworn in as the forty-fifth president of the United States less than a month earlier.[1] "So I'm looking at two-state and one-state, and I like the one that both parties like," Trump told journalists assembled in the Oval Office after the two leaders' meeting. The president continued: "I'm very happy with the one that both parties like. I can live with either one. I thought for a while the two-state looked like it may be the easier of the two. But honestly, if Bibi and if the Palestinians—if Israel and the Palestinians are happy—I'm happy with the one they like the best."[2] The president's words took many in the room by surprise, including Netanyahu, who let out an audible chuckle.

THE TRUMP ERA: FROM AMBIVALENCE TO INDIFFERENCE

The president's remarks were more than a mere slip of the tongue or a sign of the steep learning curve that lay ahead for him on the decades-old Israeli-Palestinian conflict. Even as Trump continued to express a desire to broker what he called the "deal of the century," the Trump era signaled a notable shift in U.S. policy from ambivalence toward Palestinian leaders and Palestinian statehood to total indifference. Trump's leanings had been fairly clear from the outset. As a candidate, Trump pledged to move the U.S. embassy in Israel to Jerusalem, a longstanding demand of Evangelicals and other conservative elements of Trump's electoral base. Trump had cultivated a close relationship with the billionaire casino mogul Sheldon Adelson, a fan and funder of far-right Israeli causes who has also funneled tens of millions into Trump's and other Republican campaigns and has maintained a direct line to the president.[3]

Once Trump was in office, his administration adopted a decidedly more lax attitude toward Israeli settlements than its predecessors. Despite urging Israel to "hold back" on settlement construction, the White House also said, "We don't believe the existence of settlements is an impediment to peace."[4] Meanwhile, all three members of Trump's Middle East peace team—the president's son-in-law and senior adviser, Jared Kushner; his chief negotiator, Jason Greenblatt; and the newly appointed U.S. ambassador to Israel, David Friedman—were associated with the Israeli right and were reported to have substantial ties to the Israeli settler movement.[5] This was especially true of Friedman, whose references to Israel's "alleged occupation" of the West Bank and frequent advocacy on behalf of Israeli settlers and settlements alarmed Palestinians and much of the international community.[6] For the first twenty months of his presidency Trump declined to explicitly back Palestinian statehood before finally offering a halfhearted endorsement in September 2018: "I like [a] two-state solution. That's what I think works best. That's my feeling. Now you may have a different feeling. I don't think so. But I think [a] two-state solution works best."[7]

Despite serious misgivings about Trump, Abbas initially sought to ingratiate himself with the new president and present himself as a responsible peace partner. For the first ten months of the administration, Abbas and others within his circle heaped praise on Trump and welcomed the president's desire to broker the "ultimate deal" as a "historic opportunity" for peace.[8] Only after the PLO mission in Washington was notified by the State Department on November 17, 2017, that it was in violation of U.S. law and could soon be forced to close did the Palestinians begin to reconsider. The move apparently was triggered by comments made by Abbas several weeks earlier before the UN General Assembly in which he urged the International Criminal Court to investigate Israel and thus ran afoul of the 2015 law requiring the president to close down the PLO office unless the Palestinians rescinded their actions and entered into direct negotiations with Israel. By this time Palestinian officials were girding themselves for much worse news.

The decisive moment came on December 6, 2017. After weeks of speculation, Trump announced that the United States officially recognized Jerusalem as Israel's capital and would soon move its embassy there as well, thus fulfilling a major campaign pledge. This would take the issue of Jerusalem "off the table," Trump tweeted on January 18.[9] Not since Harry Truman defied the State Department and his intelligence community by recognizing Israel in May 1948 had a U.S. president decided such a weighty and consequential foreign policy matter almost entirely on the basis of domestic political considerations. In addition to overturning seventy years of official U.S. policy and international consensus, Trump's Jerusalem declaration marked a new low in American-Palestinian relations and called into question the United States' future role in the peace process. As one of the thorniest issues of the conflict and a powerful religious and cultural symbol for the three monotheistic faiths, the status of Jerusalem had long been seen as key to an Israeli-Palestinian settlement. The timing of the announcement was all the more puzzling coming after several months of intensive U.S. diplomacy between Israeli and Palestinian leaders in preparation for putting forward a major peace initiative.

Netanyahu and other Israeli officials hailed Trump's announcement as a victory for the Jewish people, while Palestinian leaders expressed shock and outrage. A furious Abbas announced that the United States had disqualified itself from serving as a peace broker and severed official ties with the administration. Abbas's boycott of Washington did not extend to Palestinian security and intelligence officials, however, who continued to meet with their American counterparts.[10] Despite Abbas's boycott, the administration said it would press ahead with its peace initiative. The Palestinians would be given a "cooling-off period" while key Arab allies such as Egypt and Saudi Arabia were expected to apply pressure on Abbas to return to the negotiating table. If push came to shove, the administration believed, Arab states could be counted on to move forward without the Palestinians—the so-called "outside in" approach long favored by Israel. The Palestinian leader showed no signs of softening his stance, however, which only grew angrier and more belligerent over time. Trump retaliated by cutting U.S. assistance to UNRWA (United Nations Relief Works Agency for Palestine Refugees in the Near East), the UN agency responsible for providing services to some five million Palestinian refugees, by nearly 80 percent and promised further aid cuts if the Palestinians persisted in boycotting the United States. Up until then, the United States had been the largest single donor to UNRWA, in part out of a sense of moral responsibility for the creation of the refugee problem in 1948.

Meanwhile, the embassy move was accompanied by violence, further hardening positions on both sides. Administration officials chose to inaugurate the new U.S. embassy in Jerusalem on May 14, the seventieth anniversary of Israel's independence and the day Palestinians commemorate the Nakba. That same day at least sixty Palestinian protesters demonstrating at the Gaza border fence were killed by Israeli forces, making it the deadliest day in the Israeli-Palestinian conflict since the 2014 Gaza war. The specter of U.S. officials, including Jared Kushner and Ivanka Trump, celebrating in Jerusalem as dozens of Palestinians were being killed less than sixty miles away seemed to illustrate how far removed the administration was from the realities of the conflict. As Israel faced a torrent of international criticism for its use of deadly force against largely unarmed protesters, the White House declined even to make the customary call on the Israelis to exercise restraint. "The responsibility for these tragic deaths rests squarely with Hamas," declared Press Secretary Raj Shah. Echoing the Israeli government line, Shah added, "Hamas is intentionally and cynically provoking this response. And as the Secretary of State said, Israel has the right to defend itself."[11]

Things went downhill from there. In late August, the White House announced it was cutting all $200 million in economic aid projects for the West Bank and Gaza, while leaving intact $60 million in U.S. assistance for Palestinian security coordination with Israel. According to a State Department spokesperson, Heather Nauert, continued funding for the Palestinians, which amounted to roughly one-tenth of the amount provided to Israel, was "not in the best interests of the U.S. national interest" and "does not provide value to the U.S. taxpayer."[12] Several days later the administration announced it was eliminating all remaining assistance to UNRWA as well as other humanitarian projects for the Palestinians. In response to the sudden aid cuts, the PLO's former ambassador in Washington, Husam Zomlot, accused the Trump administration of "weaponizing humanitarian and developmental aid as political blackmail" and of "dismantling decades of US vision and engagement in Palestine." The administration said the aid cuts were intended to force the Palestinians back to the negotiating table. However, the decision to defund UNRWA appears to be part of a broader effort by the administration and various congressional Republicans to "disrupt UNRWA" with the aim of eliminating the refugee status of millions of Palestinians in order to take the refugee issue "off the table."[13]

SQUARING THE CIRCLE

Trump's radical policy reversals on Jerusalem and refugees were not so much a "new approach" to resolving the conflict, as his administration has claimed, as they were the culmination of the old approach. The original laws requiring the relocation of the U.S. embassy to Jerusalem and the closure of the PLO office were enacted in 1995 and 1994, respectively, at the height of the Oslo process. These laws were themselves descendants of an earlier generation of anti-PLO laws dating back to the mid-1980s and ultimately to Henry Kissinger's 1975 Memorandum of Agreement with Israel. Moreover, Trump likely could not have taken such drastic leaps had his predecessors not already paved the way for him. Long before Trump arrived in the White House, George W. Bush, Bill Clinton, and other presidents going back to Lyndon Johnson had already been working to sideline the issue of Palestinian refugee rights. Likewise, years of steadily chipping away at UN Security Council Resolution 242 and the "land-for-peace" formula by lending tacit approval to Israeli settlement construction in East Jerusalem and other areas beyond Israel's 1967 borders were bound to take a toll. Indeed, there was historical precedent for pursuing a peace process while ignoring the basic ground rules of that peace process. A similar process occurred between 1948 and 1967 with regard to the Palestinian refugee problem and Resolution 194, both of which were seen as central to an Arab-Israeli peace settlement but were deferred at Israel's behest before eventually being denied altogether. Successive U.S. administrations have upheld Resolution 242 and the primacy of the 1967 lines as pillars of the peace process even as they simultaneously poked holes in them on Israel's behalf. Both Clinton and Bush decried Israeli settlements as obstacles to peace, only to carve out major exemptions that allowed Israel to continue building in East Jerusalem, the large settlement blocs, and other sensitive areas of the West Bank. Both Democratic and Republican administrations have called for an Israeli withdrawal and the creation of an independent Palestinian state but have consistently avoided challenging Israel's occupation.

If past U.S. presidents have spent most of the last quarter century trying to square a circle, Trump seems content to simply call the square a circle. Trump's peace team has kept a close hold on the contents of its much-touted peace plan, which has already been delayed several times since the Jerusalem announcement. (As of this writing, the plan is scheduled to be released in March 2019.) Regardless of when—or if— the plan is released, it is clearly not going to be based on the old rules of the peace process. Despite the president's back-handed support for a two-state solution, the Trump administration has avoided referring to Security Council Resolution 242 or calling for ending Israel's occupation. In addition, leaked details of the plan suggest something much less than a sovereign Palestinian state. The plan reportedly hinges on the creation of a Palestinian entity made up of noncontiguous patches of West Bank territory in return for massive international aid and economic assistance.[14] Meanwhile, the decision by the State Department to drop references to the West Bank and Gaza Strip as "occupied territories" from its annual human rights reports suggested that occupation denial, once the purview of the fringes of the Israeli and American right, is steadily becoming normalized at the official level.[15]

Even though the prospects of an American-brokered peace deal were already slim before Trump's arrival, his policies may have finally convinced Palestinian leaders that they have more to lose from remaining in an American-sponsored peace process than from walking away from it. To go along with a peace process in which neither Jerusalem, refugees, nor genuine sovereignty are on the table would likely eliminate what little remained of Abbas's credibility among Palestinians. On the other hand, continuing to boycott the United States effectively pulls the plug on the PLO's diplomatic strategy for more than three decades while potentially inviting even more punitive action from a volatile American president. Even if American officials manage to convince, or coerce, Abbas back to the negotiating table—which seems doubtful absent a major reversal in U.S. policy—it is unlikely he would be in a position domestically to sign a peace agreement, much less implement one.

Abbas's dilemma highlights the basic flaws of the U.S.-led peace process over the last quarter century. Through its ever-expanding arsenal of sticks and the gradual erosion of the diplomatic ground rules, Washington steadily increased the costs of Palestinian participation in the peace process while simultaneously diminishing its value. Persistent threats, pressure, and attempts to reorganize Palestinian political and institutional life succeeded in making Palestinian leaders more pliant but left them too weak to serve as effective negotiating partners. It was perhaps inevitable that Palestinians, as the weakest party in the negotiations, would bear the brunt of the chronic failures of the peace process, but the results have been equally destructive for the goal of a two-state solution. Instead of building a sound basis for a Palestinian state, the peace process has helped to reinforce Palestinian political fragmentation and weaken Palestinian governing institutions, with the notable exception of the PA's security apparatus in the West Bank. In those areas where the PA does not operate, and which were also exempted from the peace process—namely East Jerusalem and Gaza—instability and violence became the norm.

At the same time, the seemingly endless supply of carrots did not make Israeli leaders more amenable to compromise or encourage them to take risks for peace, but instead provided means to defray the political, economic, and even military costs of the occupation. In the absence of American or international pressure and any meaningful forms of accountability, Israeli leaders had no incentive to undertake the difficult and politically unpopular decisions that a two-state solution required, such as evacuating Jewish settlements, transferring territory to Palestinian sovereignty, and dividing Jerusalem. Although U.S. policymakers often lose sight of the fact, the relationship between Israelis and Palestinians is not just one of conflict; it is also a military occupation. Although one cannot completely level the playing field, effective mediation requires leverage with and accountability for *both* parties, not just the weaker one. By focusing on reassuring Israelis and reforming the Palestinians, rather than on challenging the dynamics that sustained the conflict—particularly Israel's ongoing occupation—U.S. mediation helped to reinforce, and even institutionalize, the vast power imbalance between the two sides and to preserve the status quo of the Israeli occupation. The questions of Palestinian political reforms, institution building, and economic development are worthy and necessary for Palestinians and even international donors to engage in. But they are not the primary drivers of the conflict or the reasons for Israel's lingering occupation in the way that Israel's ongoing denial of Palestinian human, civil, and political rights have been.

As a superpower and Israel's closest ally, the United States was uniquely positioned to broker peace between Israel and the Palestinians.

As a peace process veteran, Aaron David Miller, put it, "We, the United States, may not be an honest broker, but we can be an effective broker."[16] This assumed, however, that American presidents would be willing to set aside the "special relationship" with Israel and domestic political pressures, if only momentarily, on those issues that mattered most. This was rarely the case even before Trump took office. "The problem in resolving the Palestinian conflict is not between Israelis and Palestinians; it's inside of Washington," observed Bruce Riedel, a former CIA analyst who also served in the Clinton White House. "The real problem is the American deeply held position [of] Israel right or wrong."[17] In that sense, it would seem that American domestic politics have been at least as much an impediment to the success of the peace process as the "political cultures" of Israelis or Palestinians.

The persistence of Washington's blind spot regarding both Palestinian politics and Israeli power throughout its management of the peace process led to several costly mistakes and missed opportunities: Bill Clinton's decision to pin blame for the failure at Camp David summit and the spiraling violence of the Al-Aqsa Intifada solely on Arafat and the Palestinians; George W. Bush's passive response to the destruction of Palestinian political and governing institutions at the hands of Ariel Sharon and the IDF; the abandonment of the roadmap and its emphasis on parallel implementation on mutual accountability; the failure to capitalize on the election of President Mahmoud Abbas and the dramatic decline in violence in 2005; Barack Obama's unwillingness to challenge Israeli settlement expansion, the destabilizing Gaza blockade, and other negative trends that threatened the two-state solution.

To be sure, the Palestinians also carry blame for the impasse. Arafat's leadership cynically used violence and calculated chaos during the Intifada to convince the world of his relevance, although it generally achieved the opposite. Likewise, the willingness of Hamas and other armed factions to engage in violence against Israeli civilians eroded international sympathy for the Palestinian cause and played directly to Israel's strengths, namely its vaunted military prowess. Perhaps most damaging of all has been the internecine schism between Fatah and Hamas, which has paralyzed internal Palestinian politics and fostered violence and instability and also has been easily exploited by the Israelis to delay political progress. So long as Palestinian political actors, whether secular or Islamist, continue to prioritize their own partisan and parochial priorities over the interests of the wider Palestinian public, it is difficult to imagine any meaningful change in the condition of Palestinians on the ground.

Moreover, the fact that American policymakers still viewed the Palestinian cause almost exclusively through the lens of Israel and the peace process was not purely a function of Washington's blind spot; it was also a matter of official PLO strategy. Trump's attempts to rewrite the rules of the peace process have exposed the limits of the PLO's three-decades-old "American" strategy and forced many within Palestinian officialdom to rethink that strategy. In a June 2018 address at a West Bank university, the PLO's former representative to Washington, Husam Zomlot, described the decision to accept American mediation without first insisting on normalizing U.S.-Palestinian ties, including reversing the group's official terrorist designation, as a "historic mistake" on the part of the PLO. "It makes no sense for [the United States] to be a mediator between a 'strategic ally' and a 'terrorist.' This means you are not a mediator."[18] Indeed, the PLO leadership's overreliance on American deliverance seems to have come at the expense of Palestinian agency and initiative. "There's nothing bilateral about our relationship with the United States," says the former Palestinian premier Salam Fayyad. "We are incidental really. It was because of their interest in Israel. We sort of got in the way, and so they had to deal with us."[19]

But power dynamics are not everything, insists Fayyad. In his view, it is more important "to matter to Americans ideologically and morally. Only then could you become significant, regardless of having much less influence or power." For Fayyad, this means "encroaching on the domain of 'shared values' that Israel has virtually monopolized and projecting Palestinian aspirations, needs, and interests in ways that resonate with the narrative and worldview of ordinary Americans, appealing to the sense of fairness that Americans pride themselves on, rejection of inequality, support for the underdog, in addition to the way we govern ourselves and the idea of government by the people, for the people, and of the people." He continues, "If it's a matter of religion or 'Judeo-Christian heritage,' we really cannot compete. But the idea of living as a free people with dignity in a state of their own, that is something most Americans can relate to."[20] There are signs that such appeals are already beginning to resonate among segments of the American public.

A CHANGING AMERICAN POLITICAL LANDSCAPE

The Trump administration's inability to clearly endorse Palestinian statehood or acknowledge Israel's occupation points to deeper changes both inside the Republican Party and the American political landscape as a whole and a widening partisan divide over Israel and Palestine. Reflecting its steady shift to the right in recent years, the Republican Party formally expunged references to a two-state solution from its 2016 platform while noting that the party "reject[s] the false notion that Israel is an occupier."[21] A growing segment of the Republican base, particularly the large and influential constituency of Evangelical Christians for whom Israel and Zionism are closely tied to American identity and its presumed "Judeo-Christian" heritage, have also come to view Israel as a civilizational bulwark against Islamic radicalism.

Meanwhile, the sense of triumphalism that has pervaded much of Israeli politics is also evident on the American right. For example, the so-called Congressional Israel Victory Caucus, launched in April 2016 by a group of Republican Congress members, promotes the theory that, as the Jewish American historian Daniel Pipes puts it, "Palestinians will have to pass through the bitter crucible of defeat, with all its deprivation, destruction and despair, before the Israeli-Palestinian conflict will be resolved."[22] Such sentiment was reminiscent of the view of the New York congressman Walter Marion Chandler, who insisted almost a century earlier that Palestinian Arabs must "consent to Jewish government and domination" lest they "be driven from Palestine by force."[23]

A parallel, if less dramatic, shift also appears to be under way among Democrats, but in the opposite direction. Although support for Israel within the Democratic Party remains strong, the protracted nature of

the conflict and the brutality of Israel's occupation have led growing
numbers of the party's rank and file—younger, progressive, female vot-
ers, people of color, and liberal Jews—to question U.S. policies they
see as facilitating Israeli violations of Palestinian rights and as incompatible with American values. These changes have begun to percolate
from the grassroots up through the party establishment. Issues that
have long been uncontested, such as calling for the recognition of
Jerusalem as Israel's capital and avoiding mention of the Israeli occupation, are now being openly debated by party delegates for the first
time, as occurred during the 2012 and 2016 Democratic National
Committee platform debates.[24]

By 2016, the trend had made its way into presidential politics in the
form of Bernie Sanders's presidential campaign. As both Hillary Clinton
and the Republican pool of candidates offered up the usual platitudes
and often hyperbolic praise for Israel, Sanders put forth a considerably
more nuanced perspective that emphasized not only the need to safeguard Israeli security but also Palestinian rights. The United States
"cannot continue to be one-sided. There are two sides to the issue," observed Sanders in the fifth Clinton-Sanders debate, adding that "in the
long run if we are ever going to bring peace to that region which has
seen so much hatred and so much war, we are going to have to treat the
Palestinian people with respect and dignity."[25] The fact that Sanders
made these remarks during a nationally televised Democratic debate
with Clinton before an audience in Brooklyn, New York, seemed to
defy the conventional wisdom about what could or could not be said in
relation to Israel and Palestine in the context of American politics. The
relative overall success of the Sanders campaign and his continued
outspokenness on Israel and Palestine suggested that there now existed
a political constituency that was willing to reward candidates for taking up the issue of Palestinian rights, instead of punishing them.

Peter Beinart, a leading voice of the American Jewish left, credits
Sanders with fundamentally transforming Washington's political culture on Israel-Palestine by taking criticism of Israel into the political
mainstream. In June 2018 Beinart wrote: "While Obama, Kerry and
Clinton did sometimes criticize Israeli policy, they generally did so in

the language of Israeli self-interest, not of Palestinian human rights. Israeli settlement policy was bad for Israel, they argued, because it threatened Israel's future as a democratic Jewish state." By contrast, Beinart continued, "Sanders is betting that the political ground has shifted. In a sense, he's doing in the Democratic Party what Trump has done inside the GOP. For years, polls showed that ordinary Republicans were moving away from their party's elite on trade and immigration. But until Trump, no Republican presidential frontrunner had been sufficiently unconventional and sufficiently unafraid to put that proposition to the test. That's what Sanders is doing on Israel."[26]

There are signs that this trend may also be making inroads in Congress, long considered the epicenter of pro-Israel sentiment in American politics. Today, organizations on the right and center-right such as the American Israel Public Affairs Committee (AIPAC) and the Zionist Organization of America have competition from left-liberal Zionist groups such as J Street, the New Israel Fund, and the Israel Policy Forum. Growing numbers of congressional progressives are prepared to ignore the pro-Israel lobby entirely, including Congresswoman Betty McCollum of Minnesota, who along with twenty of her fellow Democrats sponsored a bill aimed at ending Israeli military detentions of Palestinian children. Although the bill stood little chance of becoming law, it was notable for being the first bill dealing with Palestinian human rights ever introduced in Congress.[27] In October 2018, 112 members of the U.S. House of Representatives and 34 U.S. Senators signed a letter to Secretary of State Mike Pompeo urging the administration to rescind its recent aid cuts to UNRWA, Jerusalem hospitals, and other Palestinian institutions.[28] Much as Edward Bliss Reed urged Congress to oppose the Balfour Declaration as being incompatible with American support for self-determination in 1922, growing numbers of Democratic politicians and activists are framing the current debate on Israel and Palestine in terms of American values. A senior congressional aide told me in August 2018, "In 2016, the Democratic [Party] debate was over the word 'occupation.' In 2020, the debate will be over the word 'apartheid.'" While such sentiment may seem dramatic, the growing partisan divide on Israel and Palestine has undoubtedly opened up the space for debate within U.S. politics.

NEITHER TWO STATES NOR ONE

The days of an exclusively American-dominated peace process are probably behind us. The questions now are whether a two-state solution and the Palestinian Authority can survive in the absence of a U.S.-led peace process, and what, if anything, might replace them, and the United States as an honest broker. Since announcing his boycott of the United States, Abbas has pledged to put the Palestinian file in the hands of the United Nations and has also appealed to other major powers such as the EU, France, Russia, and China to step up to the plate as mediators. Although these actors all have the potential to play an enhanced role in Arab-Israeli peacemaking, none currently has the necessary clout with both sides to serve as a credible alternative to American mediation. Meanwhile, in the international community achieving a two-state solution in Palestine has taken a backseat to other priorities such as international terrorism, the global refugee crisis, Iran, the Syrian civil war, and the humanitarian catastrophe in Yemen. And for many of the Palestinians' traditional Arab allies, such as Saudi Arabia and Jordan, the Palestinian issue no longer seems to be a priority or an impediment to establishing security and economic ties with Israel.

In the meantime, Abbas has pledged to forge ahead with his internationalization campaign by joining various treaties and international bodies. These may provide the embattled Palestinian leader with some momentary relief domestically, although there are already signs that such tactics are losing steam with his domestic constituency. Moreover, such measures are unlikely to produce any tangible changes on the ground over the longer term, particularly in light of continuing Palestinian disunity and the absence of a broader political strategy for all Palestinians, including the refugees and others of the diaspora.

Meanwhile, the future of the Palestinian Authority grows more precarious by the day. Abbas and other Palestinian leaders have often threatened to "hand over the keys" to Israel by voluntarily dissolving the

PA, in an attempt to force Israel to either change its behavior in the occupied territories or assume its responsibilities for governing them directly. Although this seems unlikely, any number of internal and external factors could lead to the PA's eventual collapse, including a precipitous drop in international donor aid, which now stands at nearly half of what it was in 2013.[29] The Trump administration's aid cuts could accelerate the PA's demise. At the same time, uncertainty over who (or what) might succeed the aging President Abbas raises the specter of a protracted power struggle within Fatah and perhaps even renewed Hamas-Fatah fighting. An ever-worsening humanitarian crisis in Gaza, exacerbated by the stalled internal reconciliation process and new sanctions on Gaza's population imposed by Abbas's leadership in Ramallah, adds yet another layer of instability. Since Abbas's decision in March 2017 to slash the salaries of PA employees and halt fuel payments to Israel that supply Gaza with electricity, Gaza has teetered on the edge of war. A new war between Israel and Hamas would not only be catastrophic for Gaza's civilian population but also could prove highly destabilizing for the already unpopular Abbas. This is in addition to the episodic violence in the West Bank and East Jerusalem. Although a sustained popular mobilization seems unlikely, given the fractured state of Palestinian politics, if and when conditions allow for a "third Intifada," it may be directed as much at Palestinian leaders as at the Israeli occupation. The broader question of whether the PA's continued existence was facilitating the goal of independence or the status quo is one that will ultimately be decided by the Palestinians themselves. The answer to that question will depend in large part on the ability of current or future Palestinian leaders to articulate an alternative vision, which does not yet exist.

However it may come about, the collapse of the PA would represent the most tangible—and most likely fatal—blow yet to the goal of two states. As we have seen, the precarious political consensuses within Israeli, Palestinian, and even American politics that have kept the two-state solution afloat since the 1990s are already crumbling. In Israel, a majority of Prime Minister Benjamin Netanyahu's ruling coalition openly opposes the creation of a sovereign Palestinian state in the West

Bank and Gaza Strip, while Israel's parliament, the Knesset, seems to be inching toward a policy of annexing the occupied territories.[30] Although polls still show a plurality of Israelis support the goal of two states, the Israeli public is more concerned with economic matters and external threats from Iran than with a resolution of the Palestinian issue.[31]

Support for a two-state solution is also waning among Palestinians in the occupied territories, traditionally the constituency that has been the most supportive of a two-state solution. Growing numbers of Palestinians, particularly those who came of age during the Oslo years, are abandoning the goal of Palestinian statehood in favor of a struggle for equal rights in a single state.[32] Among those who have lost faith in the "Oslo generation" is Tareq Abbas, the son of the Palestinian president. "If you don't want to give me independence, at least give me civil rights," the younger Abbas told the *New York Times*. "That's an easier way, peaceful way. I don't want to throw anything, I don't want to hate anybody, I don't want to shoot anybody. I want to be under the law."[33] Such sentiments, while increasingly pervasive, have not yet been translated into a concrete political program.

Despite the growing appeal of "one person, one vote" among Palestinians, there is currently no organized political movement or actor pushing in that direction on the Palestinian scene. This may have to do with the fragmented nature of Palestinian politics writ large, and thus could change with time. Even Hamas, which has a long history of violent opposition to the Oslo process and which rejects any recognition of Israel, has steadily come to terms with a Palestinian state in the West Bank, East Jerusalem, and Gaza Strip.[34] The fact that the vast majority of Israeli Jews remain opposed to the idea would suggest that a single, binational state is not yet politically viable. Any future resolution, whether based on a partition of the land or on some form of binationalism—or any of the possible options in between, such as confederation—should allow both Israeli Jews and Palestinian Arabs the basic right of self-determination. Conversely, any proposal or initiative that allows for the continued domination or subjugation of one group by the other is bound to fail and is likely to prolong the conflict. In the meantime, the ambiguous status quo, which allows for neither two states nor one state, is likely to continue indefinitely, perhaps until a major crisis forces a reshuffling of the political and diplomatic cards, as happened after the 1948 and 1967 wars.

For many, particularly those on the Israeli and American right, the status quo may seem like a tolerable, or perhaps even preferable, outcome. Given the century-long history of the conflict, however, there is little reason to expect things to remain as they are permanently. Nor would the demise of a two-state solution be entirely cost-free for the United States. Periodic outbursts of violence in Gaza and East Jerusalem may become less manageable and more costly for Israel, particularly if the void left by receding Palestinian politics and national institutions is filled by jihadists and other nihilist groups. The increasing prominence of nonviolent forms of mobilization by Palestinians and their supporters poses an entirely different set of challenges for which the Israeli military historically has been ill-equipped. The growing profile of the boycott, divestment, and sanctions (BDS) movement is particularly worrisome to Israel's leaders, as evidenced by the proliferation of legislative initiatives aimed at outlawing or otherwise prohibiting boycott efforts that target Israel or Israeli settlements.[35] The emergence of the BDS movement, founded in 2005 in response to a call by Palestinian civil society groups, was in many ways itself an outgrowth of the twin failings of the peace process—the failure of Palestinian leaders to effectively challenge the occupation and the absence of any meaningful constraints or accountability for Israel.

The prospect of Israel's maintaining indefinite control over millions of stateless Palestinians while denying them citizenship and other basic social and political rights raises difficult questions for American politicians as well. In his valedictory speech, former Secretary of State John Kerry, himself a committed supporter of Israel, summed up the dilemma facing the two countries: "How does Israel reconcile a permanent occupation with its democratic ideals? How does the U.S. continue to defend that and still live up to our own democratic ideals? Nobody has ever provided good answers to those questions because there aren't any."

Peace between Israelis and Palestinians seems more distant than ever, and the rising generation on both sides of the conflict has grown increasingly skeptical of negotiations. The end of the Oslo process and the decline of Palestinian politics have left an uneasy political and diplomatic vacuum that may not be filled anytime soon. On the other hand, the demise of what had been an outdated and highly ineffective peace process offers an opportunity to rethink old assumptions, formulas, and possible solutions. However, if the United States is ever to resume its preeminent role as a peace broker between Israelis and Palestinians, American policymakers will need to grapple with the basic realities of the conflict, including the corrosive and destabilizing effects of Israel's continued occupation and the need for a credible and cohesive Palestinian political leadership. Unless and until the United States can overcome its blind spot to Israeli power and Palestinian politics, its policies will be doomed to failure.

Notes

Introduction

1. Bernard Avishai, "A Plan for Peace That Still Could Be," *New York Times Magazine*, February 7, 2011 (https://www.nytimes.com/2011/02/13/magazine/13Israel-t.html).

2. William B. Quandt, *Camp David: Peacemaking and Politics* (Brookings Institution Press, 2016), p. 30.

Chapter 1

1. Glazebrook quoted in Frank E. Manuel, *The Realities of American-Palestine Relations* (Washington: PublicAffairs Press, 1949), p. 257.

2. *Establishment of a National Home in Palestine: Hearings Before the Committee on Foreign Affairs, on H. Con. Res. 52, Expressing Satisfaction at the Re-Creation of Palestine as the National Home of the Jewish Race, April 18, 19, 20, and 21*, 67th Cong., 2nd Sess. (1922), p. 161 (transcript: https://catalog.hathitrust.org/Record/100363603).

3. Ibid., p. 168.

4. Ibid., p. 170.

5. For more on British imperial interests in relation to Balfour, see Jonathan Schneer, *The Balfour Declaration: The Origins of the Arab-Israeli Conflict* (New York: Random House, 2010), p. 366. See also Bernhard Zand, "Century of Violence: What World War I Did to the Middle East," Spiegel Online International, January 31, 2014;

Ian Black, *Enemies and Neighbors: Arabs and Jews in Palestine and Israel, 1917–2017* (New York: Atlantic Monthly Press, 2017), p. 14; Charles D. Smith, *Palestine and the Arab-Israeli Conflict* (New York: St. Martin's Press, 1992), p. 55.

6. Kathleen Christison, *Perceptions of Palestine: Their Influence on U.S. Middle East Policy* (University of California Press, 1999), p. 19. See also Lawrence Davidson, "Historical Ignorance and Popular Perception: The Case of U.S. Perceptions of Palestine, 1917," *Middle East Policy* 3, no. 2 (1994): 126.

7. Davidson, "Historical Ignorance and Popular Perception," p. 126. See also Schneer, *Balfour Declaration*, p. 339.

8. See, for example, "No. 1 The Palestine Arab Delegation to the Secretary of State for the Colonies," February 21, 1922, in *Palestine: Correspondence with the Palestine Arab Delegation and the Zionist Organisation* (London: H.M. Stationery Office, June 1922); available at https://unispal.un.org/DPA/DPR/unispal.nsf/0/48A7E5584EE140348525 6CD8006C3FBE.

9. See Doreen Ingrams, *The Palestine Papers, 1917–1922: Seeds of Conflict* (London: Eland Books, 1972), p. 96.

10. Issa Khalaf, *Politics in Palestine: Arab Factionalism and Social Disintegration, 1939–1948* (State University of New York Press, 1991), p. 35.

11. Davidson, "Historical Ignorance and Popular Perception," p. 142.

12. Ibid. See also Karl E. Meyer, "Editorial Notebook; Woodrow Wilson's Dynamite," *New York Times*, August 14, 1991.

13. Quoted in Isaiah Friedman, *Palestine, a Twice-Promised Land: The British, the Arabs & Zionism: 1915–1920* (New Brunswick, N.J.: Transaction Publishers, 2000), p. 251.

14. Hisham H. Ahmed, "From the Balfour Declaration to World War II: The U.S. Stand on Palestinian Self-determination," *Arab Studies Quarterly* 12, nos. 1–2 (Winter–Spring 1990): 9–41.

15. See Andrew Patrick, *America's Forgotten Middle East Initiative: The King-Crane Commission of 1919* (New York: I. B. Tauris, 2015). For the complete report, see Henry C. King and Charles R. Crane, *The King-Crane Commission Report, August 28, 1919: Report of American Section of Inter-Allied Commission of Mandates in Turkey: An Official United States Government Report by the Inter-Allied Commission on Mandates in Turkey, American Section*, 1922 (https://wwi.lib.byu.edu/index.php/The_King-Crane _Report). For materials related to the commission's work, including meeting notes, correspondence, photos, maps, and an interactive map, see "King-Crane Commission Digital Collection" (http://www.oberlin.edu/library/digital/king-crane/search .html).

16. Quoted in Meyer, "Editorial Notebook; Woodrow Wilson's Dynamite." See also Lawrence Davidson, "Historical Ignorance and Popular Perception: The Case of U.S. Perceptions of Palestine, 1917," *Middle East Policy* 3, no. 2 (1994): 142.

17. Ahmed, "From the Balfour Declaration to World War II," p. 18. Quoted in Rafael Medoff, *Zionism and the Arabs: An American Jewish Dilemma, 1898–1948* (Westport, Conn.: Praeger, 1997), p. 26.

18. See, for example, *Establishment of a National Home in Palestine*, testimony of Rabbi David Philipson.

19. Christison, *Perceptions of Palestine*, p. 42.

20. See Zionist Organization of America, *The American War Congress and Zionism: Statements by Members of the American War Congress on the Jewish National Movement* (New York: Zionist Organization of America, 1919).

21. See "National Home for the Jewish People," *Congressional Record*, daily ed., June 30, 1922, H9, pp. 799–820.

22. See Lawrence Davidson, "Zionism, Socialism, and United States Support for Jewish Colonization of Palestine in the 1920s," *Arab Studies Quarterly* 18, no. 3 (Summer 1996): 8. See also Robert L. MacDonald, "A Land without a People for a People without a Land: Civilizing Mission and American Support for Zionism, 1880s–1929," Ph.D. thesis, Bowling Green State University, Graduate College, December 2012; Douglas Little, *American Orientalism: The United States and the Middle East since 1945* (University of North Carolina Press, 2008).

23. *Establishment of a National Home in Palestine*, pp. 2, 20, 125.

24. Ibid., pp. 35, 83, 133.

25. "National Home for the Jewish People" (Chandler statement).

26. For example, a petition submitted by the Palestine Arab Women's Congress to the League of Nations' Mandates Commission in 1932 "claimed self-government in order to obtain the abrogation of the Balfour Declaration, the abolition of the Mandate and the establishment of a national government with a view to attaining complete independence within an Arab Federation." See Nathan Feinberg, *Some Problems of the Palestine Mandate* (Tel Aviv, Palestine: Shoshani's Printing Co., 1936), p. 73. See also Gail J. Boling, "The U.S.-Proposed 'Trusteeship Agreement' for Palestine: The UN-Styled Plan That Could Have Avoided Forcible Displacement of the Palestinian Refugees in 1948," *Refuge* (February 2003), p. 6.

27. Rashid Khalidi, *The Iron Cage: The Story of the Palestinian Struggle for Statehood* (Boston: Beacon Press, 2007), p. 42. See also Abdul-Wahhab Said Kayyali, *Palestine: A Modern History* (Kent, UK: Croom Helm, 1978), p. 42.

28. See Covenant of the League of Nations, Article 22, Yale Law School, Lillian Goldman Law Library, Avalon Project (http://avalon.law.yale.edu/20th_century /leagcov.asp#art1).

29. Khalidi, *Iron Cage*, p. 19.

30. David Ben Gurion, "British Contributions to Arming the Hagana," in *From Haven to Conquest*, edited by Walid Khalidi (Beirut: Institute for Palestine Studies, 1987), pp. 371–74; Khalidi, *Iron Cage*, p. 109; Philip Mattar, *The Mufti of Jerusalem: Al-Hajj Amin Al-Husayni and the Palestinian National Movement* (Columbia University Press, 1988), p. 100; Winston S. Churchill, *The Second World War*, vol. 2, *Their Finest Hour* (New York: Bantam Books, 1962), pp. 148–49.

31. See Enrico Molinaro, *The Holy Places of Jerusalem in Middle East Peace Agreements: The Conflict between Global and State Identities* (Brighton, UK: Sussex Academic Press, 2009), p. 64; Khalidi, *Iron Cage*, p. 36.

32. Ibid., p. 78.

33. Philip Palin, E. H. Wildblood, and C. Vaughan Edwards, "The Palin Commission Report," Australian National University, 1922 (http://users.cecs.anu.edu.au /~bdm/yabber/yabber_palin.html).

34. See Walter Shaw and others, *Report of the Commission on the Palestine Disturbances of August, 1929, presented by the secretary of state for the colonies to Parliament by command of His Majesty* (London: H.M. Stationery Office, 1930 [henceforth cited as Shaw Commission report]; John Hope Simpson and others, *Palestine: Report on Immigration, Land Settlement and Development, by Sir John Hope Simpson, C.I.E., 1930* (London: H.M. Stationery Office, 1930). See also Eliel Löfgren and others, *Report of the Commission appointed by His Majesty's Government in the United Kingdom of Great Britain and Northern Ireland, with the approval of the Council of the League of Nations, to determine the rights and claims of Moslems and Jews in connection with the Western or Wailing Wall at Jerusalem*, report of the International Commission for the Wailing Wall (London: H.M. Stationery Office, December 1930).

35. Lauren Elise Apter, "Disorderly Decolonization: The White Paper of 1939 and the End of British Rule in Palestine," Ph.D. thesis, University of Texas, Austin, Department of History, 2008, p. 33.

36. For example, a search of the Foreign Relations of the United States turns up no mention of the early disturbances in Palestine or the various inquiries commissioned by the British. (Foreign Relations of the United States [henceforth cited as FRUS] is a book series published by the Office of the Historian, within the Department of State. For a list of all volumes and to find specific documents cited, see https://history.state .gov/historicaldocuments.) Nor was there any reference to the Palestine Arab Congress or any of its sessions held between 1919 and 1928, the appointment of al-Husseini, or the creation of the Supreme Muslim Council. The first reference to "Grand Mufti" is in "The Consul General at Jerusalem (Knabenshue) to the Secretary of State," September 1, 1929, FRUS, 1929, vol. 3, doc. 36, and to "Arab Executive" is in "The Consul General at Jerusalem (Knabenshue) to the Secretary of State," September 25, 1929, FRUS, 1929, vol. 3, doc. 44, p. 59; see also Shaw Commission report. Al-Husseini is not mentioned again until 1936, when he is mentioned by name in "The Consul General at Jerusalem (Morris) to the Secretary of State," April 25, 1936, FRUS, 1936, vol. 3, doc. 512, p. 435. The sole reference to any Palestinian political leadership prior to 1929 is contained in a single piece of correspondence from the U.S. ambassador in London, dated July 18, 1922, in connection with a visit by the Palestine-Arab Delegation to London to register its opposition to the Mandate and the Jewish national home. See United States Department of State, "The Ambassador in Great Britain (Harvey) to the Secretary of State, July 18, 1922," *Papers Relating to the Foreign Relations of the United States, 1922, Vol. II* (https://history.state.gov/historicaldocuments/frus1922v02/d235).

37. See Lawrence Davidson, "Competing Responses to the 1929 Arab Uprising in Palestine: The Zionist Press versus the State Department," *Middle East Policy* 5, no. 2 (May 1997): 102. Knabenshue's assessment of Arab grievances was consistent with the findings of the British Shaw Commission.

38. Quoted in Davidson, "Competing Responses to the 1929 Arab Uprising in Palestine," pp. 98–99.

39. For example, see "Arabs Here Assail Jewish Riot Views; Call Reports on Palestine Situation Unfair at Meeting—Blame Balfour Declaration," *New York Times*, August 29, 1929. See also Hani J. Bawardi, *The Making of Arab Americans: From Syrian Nationalism to U.S. Citizenship* (University of Texas Press, 2014), pp. 172–73.

40. See, for example, "The Consul General at Jerusalem (Morris) to Secretary of State," April 25, 1936, FRUS, 1936, vol. 3, doc. 512, which among other things discusses the al-Husseini–Nashashibi rivalry. On the other hand, the Higher Arab Committee, which was formed that same month, is not mentioned until September 4 of that year; see "The Ambassador of the United Kingdom (Bingham) to the Secretary of State," September 4, 1936, FRUS, 1936, vol. 3, doc. 526.

41. Khalidi, *Iron Cage*, pp. 12–13.

42. See Anglo-American Committee of Inquiry on Jewish Problems in Palestine and Europe, *A Survey of Palestine* (Beirut: Institute for Palestine Studies, 1946), p. 185.

43. Khalidi, *Iron Cage*, p. 42. See also Abdul-Wahhab Said Kayyali, *Palestine: A Modern History* (Kent, UK: Croom Helm, 1978), p. 12.

44. See Michael E. Jansen, *The United States and the Palestinian People* (Beirut: Institute for Palestine Studies, 1970), p. 31.

45. The first mention of the Haganah (also Hagana) in State Department cables appears in April 1936, some fifteen years after its formation (FRUS, 1936, vol. 3, p. 440). The Irgun is first referenced in December 1938, seven years after its founding (FRUS, 1938, vol. 2, p. 1000). The Stern Gang (also called Lehi), founded in 1939, was first mentioned in April 1944 (FRUS, 1944, vol. 5, p. 602). The founder of Revisionist Zionism, Ze'ev (Vladimir) Jabotinsky, first appears in State Department cables in March 1938 (FRUS, 1948, vol. 2, p. 651).

46. "The Consul General at Jerusalem (Wadsworth) to the Secretary of State," August 16, 1937, FRUS, 1937, vol. 2, doc. 701, p. 905.

47. *Report of the Palestine Royal Commission* (Geneva: League of Nations, 1937; also known as the Peel Commission).

48. See Benny Morris, *1948: A History of the First Arab-Israeli War* (Yale University Press, 2009), p. 19.

49. See Khalidi, *Iron Cage*, pp. 114–16.

50. Jansen, *The United States and the Palestinian People*, p. 27. See Chaim Simons, *A Historical Survey of Proposals to Transfer Arabs from Palestine 1895–1947* (1988; http://chaimsimons.net/transfer.html), pp. 278–83; Nur Masalha, *Expulsion of the Palestinians: The Concept of "Transfer" in Zionist Political Thought, 1882–1948* (Beirut: Institute for Palestine Studies, 1992); Judah L. Magnes, "Toward Peace in Palestine," *Foreign Affairs*, January 1943.

51. See "The Director of Near Eastern and African Affairs (Henderson) to the Acting Secretary of State," July 30, 1945, FRUS, 1945, vol. 2, doc. 1345, p. 1405.

52. See, for example, "Memorandum of Conversation, by the Chief of the Division of Near Eastern Affairs (Murray)," February 6, 1940, FRUS, 1940, vol. 3, doc. 768, p. 840. See also Morris, *1948*, p. 18; For more on American Zionists' support for transfer, see John B. Judis, *Genesis: Truman, American Jews, and the Origins of the Arab/Israeli Conflict* (New York: Farrar, Straus & Giroux, 2014), pp. 153–56, 160–63.

53. Christopher O'Sullivan, *FDR and the End of Empire: The Origins of American Power in the Middle East* (London: Palgrave Macmillan, 2012), p. 106.

54. Ibid., p. 114.

55. See O'Sullivan, *FDR and the End of Empire*, p. 115.

56. Kathleen Christison, *Perceptions of Palestine: Their Influence on U.S. Middle East Policy* (University of California Press, 1999), p. 49. See also Peter Grose, *Israel in the Mind of America* (New York: Knopf, 1983), pp. 138–39; Dan Tschirgi, *The Politics of Indecision* (New York: Praeger, 1983), pp. 90–91; Richard Breitman and Allan J. Lichtman, *FDR and the Jews* (Harvard University Press/Belknap Press, 2013), pp. 117–18; Monty Noam Penkower, *Decision on Palestine Deferred: America, Britain and Wartime Diplomacy, 1939–1945* (New York: Routledge, 2002), pp. 17–18.

57. "Memorandum," British Embassy to FDR, December 20, 1938, FDR Presidential Library & Museum, FDR's President's Secretary's File (PSF), 1933–1945, Box 16 (www.fdrlibrary.marist.edu/_resources/images/psf/psfa0437.pdf, p. 10).

58. "Hoover Urges Plan to Move Arabs from Palestine," *Pittsburgh Press*, November 19, 1945. See also Nur Masalha, *Imperial Israel and the Palestinians: The Politics of Expansion* (London: Pluto Press, 2000), p. 61; Jansen, *The United States and the Palestinian People*, p. 30.

59. Figures based on table reproduced in Khalidi, *From Haven to Conquest*, pp. 850–52. See also Walter Lehn, "The Jewish National Fund," *Journal of Palestine Studies* 3, no. 4 (Summer 1974): 87n; Robert Silverberg, *If I Forget Thee O Jerusalem: American Jews and the State of Israel* (New York: William Morrow, 1970), pp. 232–33; Samuel Halperin, *The Political World of American Zionism* (Wayne State University Press, 1961), pp. 270–78.

60. Ricky-Dale Calhoun, "Arming David: The Haganah's Illegal Arms Procurement Network in the United States, 1945–49," *Journal of Palestine Studies* 36, no. 4 (Summer 2007): 24. See also Walid Khalidi, *Before Their Diaspora: A Photographic History of the Palestinians, 1876–1948* (Washington: Institute for Palestine Studies, 1984), p. 308.

61. "Memorandum by President Roosevelt to the Secretary of State," May 17, 1939, FRUS, 1939, vol. 4, doc. 812, p. 757.

62. "Memorandum by the Assistant Chief of the Division of Near Eastern Affairs (Merriam)," October 15, 1943, FRUS, 1943, vol. 4, doc. 854, p. 816.

63. See "Memorandum by the Adviser on Political Relations (Murray)," October 15, 1943, FRUS, 1943, vol. 4, doc. 853 and "Memorandum by the Under Secretary of State (Stettinius) to the Secretary of State," November 26, 1943, FRUS, 1943, vol. 4, doc. 858. See also Evan M. Wilson, "The Palestine Papers, 1943–1947," *Journal of Palestine Studies* 2, no. 4 (Summer 1973): 33–54.

64. "The Secretary of State to the Minister in Egypt (Kirk)," May 26, 1943, FRUS, 1943, vol. 4, doc. 819, p. 787.

65. Michael J. Cohen, *Truman and Israel* (University of California Press, 1990), p. 48.

66. Richard Stevens, *American Zionism and U.S. Foreign Policy: 1942–1947* (New York: Pageant Press, 1962), p. 80.

67. John Snetsinger, *Truman, the Jewish Vote and the Creation of Israel* (Stanford: Hoover Institute Press, 1974), p. 20.

68. "President Roosevelt to Senator Robert F. Wagner," October 15, 1944, FRUS, 1944, vol. 5, doc. 671, pp. 615–16.

69. "The Acting Secretary of State to the Charge in Iraq (Moreland)," March 24, 1945, FRUS, 1945, vol. 8, doc. 679, pp. 697–704.

70. See "Memorandum by the Director of the Office of Near Eastern and African Affairs (Henderson) to the Secretary of State," August 24, 1945, FRUS, 1945, vol. 8, doc. 711, p. 728.

71. "Memorandum by the Acting Secretary of State to President Truman," May 14, 1945, FRUS, 1945, vol. 8, doc. 688; "Memorandum by the Chief of the Division of Near Eastern Affairs (Merriam) to the Director of the Office of Near Eastern and African Affairs," September 26, 1945, FRUS, 1945, vol. 8, doc. 724, p. 747. See also Stevens, *American Zionism and U. S. Foreign Policy*, p. 134. For angry reactions of Arab leaders, see "The Charge in Iraq (Moreland) to the Secretary of State," September 28, 1945, FRUS, 1945, vol. 8, doc. 726, p. 749.

72. Judis, *Genesis*, pp. 202–06.

73. Robert J. Donovan, *Conflict and Crisis: The Presidency of Harry S. Truman, 1945–1948* (University of Missouri Press, 1977), p. 322.

74. Government of the United Kingdom, "Political History of Palestine under British Administration," memo to the UN General Assembly, October 2, 1947.

75. Judis, *Genesis*, pp. 290–91.

76. See, for example, "Memorandum by the Deputy Director of the Office of Near Eastern and African Affairs (Villar) to the Under Secretary of State for Economic Affairs," September 27, 1946, FRUS, 1946, vol. 7, doc. 545.

77. Judis, *Genesis*, p. 193.

78. "The British Prime Minister (Attlee) to President Truman," October 4, 1946, FRUS, 1946, vol. 7, doc. 551, p. 705.

79. Judis, *Genesis*, pp. 290–91. See "Memorandum by the Ambassador to Iraq (Wadsworth) to the Director of the Office of Near Eastern and African Affairs (Henderson)," February 4, 1948, FRUS, 1948, vol. 5, part 2, doc. 24, p. 593.

80. Jansen, *United States and the Palestinian People*, p. 17.

81. Judis, *Genesis*, pp. 290–91, 224, 274, 276, 318, 331.

82. "Memorandum by the Director of the Office of Near Eastern and African Affairs (Murray) to the Acting Secretary of State," November 8, 1944, FRUS, 1944, vol. 5, doc. 688, p. 634. For more on the role of Yitzhak Shamir in the assassination of Lord Moyne, see Joanna Saidel, "Yitzhak Shamir: Why We killed Lord Moyne," *Times of Israel*, July 5, 2012.

83. For labeling of Irgun as a terrorist organization, see "The Consul at Jerusalem (Hooper) to the Secretary of State," November 3, 1945, FRUS, 1945, vol. 8, doc. 782, p. 809, and "The Ambassador in Poland (Biddle) to the Secretary of State," December 28, 1938, FRUS, 1938, vol. 2, doc. 821. For more on Irgun activities in the United States, see Judith Tydor Baumel, *The "Bergson Boys" and the Origins of Contemporary Zionist Militancy* (Syracuse University Press, 2005). See also Ben Hecht and Stuart Schoffman, "A Stone for His Slingshot," *Jewish Review of Books*, Spring 2014.

84. "Memorandum Prepared in the Department of State," September 9, 1947, FRUS, 1947, vol. 5, doc. 392, pp. 498–99.

85. Khalidi, *Before Their Diaspora*, p. 306.

86. Joseph Nevo, "The Arabs of Palestine 1947–48: Military and Political Activity," *Middle Eastern Studies* 23, no. 1 (January 1987): 6.

87. See "The Minister in Egypt (Tuck) to the Secretary of State," June 21, 1946, FRUS, 1946, vol. 7, doc. 491, p. 635. See also Zvi Elpelg, "Why Was Independent Palestine Never Created in 1948?" *Jerusalem Quarterly* 50 (Spring 1989): 6.

88. "The Consul General at Jerusalem (Wadsworth) to the Secretary of State," January 8, 1940, FRUS, 1940, vol. 3, p. 831.

89. See Khalidi, *Iron Cage*, pp. 115–16. See also Mattar, *The Mufti of Jerusalem*, pp. 100–103.

90. Amin al-Husseini, *Mudhakkirat al-Hajj Muhammed Amin al-Husayni* [Memoirs of Amin al-Husseini] (Damascus: 1999), p. 164. See also "Memorandum by the Adviser on Political Relations (Murray) to the Secretary of State," June 2, 1942, FRUS, 1942, vol. 4, doc. 648. See Khalidi, *Iron Cage*, pp. 115–16. See also Mattar, *The Mufti of Jerusalem*, pp. 100–103.

91. See "The Director of the Office of Near Eastern and African Affairs (Henderson) to the Secretary of State," September 22, 1947, FRUS, 1947, vol. 5, doc. 804, pp. 1154–59; "Memorandum Prepared in the Department of State," September 30, 1947, FRUS, 1947, vol. 5, doc. 810, pp. 1166–70; see also "Editorial Note," October 13, 1947, FRUS, 1947, vol. 5, doc. 819, pp. 1181–82.

92. United Nations, Department of Public Information, Press and Publications Bureau, "Final Meeting of the Special Committee on Palestine," press release PAL/93, August 31, 1947," United Nations Information System on the Question of Palestine; "Statement by the Secretary of State," September 17, 1947, FRUS, 1947, vol. 5, doc. 802; "Memorandum by the Director of the Office of Near Eastern and African Affairs (Henderson) to the Under Secretary of State (Lovett)," September 18, 1947, FRUS, 1947, vol. 5, doc. 803, p. 1152; "Memorandum Prepared in the Department of State," September 30, 1947, FRUS, 1947, vol. 5, doc. 810, p. 1167.

93. According to UN figures, the proposed Jewish state would have included 498,000 Jews and 497,000 Arabs, as compared with 10,000 Jews and 725,000 Arabs in the state proposed for the Arabs. Other estimates gave the Arabs a slight Arab majority in the proposed Jewish state, numbering 509,780 as compared with 499,020 Jews. See United Nations Conciliation Commission for Palestine, "Historical Survey of Efforts of the United Nations Conciliation Commission for Palestine to Secure the

Implementation of Paragraph 11 of General Assembly Resolution 194 (III)," October 2, 1961; Gail J. Boling, "The U.S.-Proposed 'Trusteeship Agreement' for Palestine: The UN-Styled Plan That Could Have Avoided Forcible Displacement of the Palestinian Refugees in 1948," *Refuge* 21, no. 2 (2003): 74.

94. Walid Khalidi, "A Palestinian Perspective on the Arab-Israeli Conflict," *Journal of Palestine Studies* 17, no. 4 (Summer 1985): 40.

95. "The Arab Higher Committee to the Consul General at Jerusalem (Macatee)," October 3, 1947, FRUS, 1947, vol. 5, doc. 811, p. 1170.

96. Judis, *Genesis*, pp. 274–75.

97. Cohen, *Truman and Israel*, p. 161.

98. Ibid., pp. 167–68. See, for example, CIA, "Consequences of Partition of Palestine," CIA report, November 28, 1947.

99. Cohen, *Truman and Israel*, p. 164.

100. Judis, *Genesis*, p. 280n90. See also Khalidi, *From Haven to Conquest*, pp. 727–29.

101. See Jansen, *The United States and the Palestinian People*, p. 19.

102. Judis, *Genesis*, p. 274.

Chapter 2

1. "Memorandum by Mr. Samuel K. C. Kopper of the Office of Near Eastern and African Affairs," January 27, 1948, FRUS, 1948, vol. 5 part 2, doc. 15, pp. 564–65. See also "Memorandum by the Director of the Policy Planning Staff (Kennan) to the Secretary of State," January 20, 1948, FRUS, 1948, vol. 5 part 2, doc. 10, p. 554n1; "Report by the Central Intelligence Agency," February 28, 1948, FRUS, 1948, vol. 5 part 2, doc. 69, pp. 666–76.

2. "Report by the Policy Planning Staff on Position of the United States with Respect to Palestine," January 19, 1948, FRUS, 1948, vol. 5 part 2, doc. 10, p. 549.

3. "Memorandum by the Director of the Policy Planning Staff (Kennan) to the Under Secretary of State (Lovett)," January 29, 1948, FRUS, 1948, vol. 5 part 2, doc. 18, p. 573; "Memorandum by the Director of the Policy Planning Staff (Kennan) to the Secretary of State," January 20, 1948, FRUS, vol. 5 part 2, doc. 10, pp. 546–54; "Memorandum by Mr. Samuel K. C. Kopper of the Office of Near Eastern and African Affairs," January 27, 1948, FRUS, 1948, vol. 5 part 2, doc. 15, p. 564.

4. "Memorandum Prepared in the Department of State," April 2, 1948, FRUS, 1948, vol. 5 part 2, doc. 133, pp. 778–796; "Draft Diary Entry for April 4, 1948, by the Secretary of Defense (Forrestal)," April 4, 1948, FRUS, 1948, vol. 5 part 2, doc. 134, pp. 797–98.

5. "A Decade of American Foreign Policy 1941–1949; United States Position on the Palestine Problem; Statement by Ambassador Warren R. Austin, United States Representative in the Security Council, March 19, 1948 (Excerpts)" (http://avalon.law .yale.edu/20th_century/decad166.asp); see also "The United States and the Recognition of Israel: A Chronology," Harry S. Truman Presidential Library and Museum (www .trumanlibrary.org/israel/palestin.htm), March 19, 1948, entry.

6. See also "Kastel Falls to Arabs; 400 Slain in Week: Key Hilltop Fort to Jerusalem Road Has Changed Hands Often in Fighting," *Washington Post*, April 12, 1948, p. 1; Irene L. Gendzier, *Dying to Forget: Oil, Power, Palestine, and the Foundations of U.S. Policy in the Middle East* (Columbia University Press, 2015), pp. 137, 140, 143.

7. Harry S. Truman, "The President's News Conference," March 25, 1948.

8. Gail J. Boling, "The U.S.-Proposed 'Trusteeship Agreement' for Palestine: The UN-Styled Plan That Could Have Avoided Forcible Displacement of the Palestinian Refugees in 1948," *Refuge*, February 2003.

9. "Memorandum of Conversation, by Secretary of State" May 12, 1948, FRUS, 1948, vol. 5 part 2, doc. 252, p. 975.

10. Raymond H. Geselbracht, "The United States and the Recognition of Israel: A Chronology," in Michael T. Benson, *Harry S. Truman and the Founding of Israel* (Westport, Conn.: Praeger, 1997).

11. Benny Morris, *The Birth of the Palestinian Refugee Problem Revisited* (Cambridge University Press, 2004), pp. 163–64, 262. See also Walid Khalidi, "Plan Dalet: Master Plan for the Conquest of Palestine," *Journal of Palestine Studies* 18, no. 1 (1988): 4-33; Sam Pope Brewer, "British Denounce Zionist Leaders, War on Terror; Palestine Government Tells Jewish Agency Condoning of Outrages May End Rights," *New York Times*, March 2, 1948, p. 1.

12. Estimates range between 200,000 and 350,000. See Yezid Sayigh, *Armed Struggle and the Search for State: The Palestinian National Movement, 1949–1993* (Oxford University Press, 1997), p. 3; Rashid Khalidi, *The Iron Cage: The Story of the Palestinian Struggle for Statehood* (Boston: Beacon Press, 2007), p. 131; Morris, *Birth of the Palestinian Refugee Problem Revisited*, p. 262.

13. Benny Morris, *1948: A History of the First Arab-Israeli War* (Yale University Press, 2008), p. 195. See also Khalidi, *Iron Cage*, p. 132.

14. Estimates range from under 15,000 to well over 20,000. See Walid Khalidi, *From Haven to Conquest* (Washington: Institute for Palestine Studies, 1987), p. 867. See also Simha Flapan, *The Birth of Israel: Myths and Realities* (New York: Pantheon Books, 1987), pp. 196–97.

15. Khalidi, *Iron Cage*, p. 131; Yoav Gelber, *Palestine 1948: War, Escape and the Emergence of the Palestinian Refugee Problem* (Eastbourne, UK: Sussex Academic Press, 2006), p. 12.

16. Yezid Sayigh, *Armed Struggle and the Search for State* (Oxford University Press, 1997), p. 14. See also Morris, *1948*, p. 195; Khalidi, *Iron Cage*, p. 132.

17. The Hashemite dynasties that ruled Jordan and Iraq were founded by the Sharif of Mecca, Hussein ibn Ali, who claimed direct descendancy from the Prophet Muhammad. In 1921, the British installed Hussein's third son, Feisal, as king of Iraq, where his descendants ruled until the 1958 Baathist military coup. Feisal's elder brother, Abdullah, became the king of Transjordan (later renamed Jordan), where his grandson, Abdullah II, remains king today.

18. Estimates of the total number of Palestinians displaced between 1947 and 1949 vary from 700,000 to 950,000. The UN put the figure at 800,000 to 900,000 as of Janu-

ary 1949. See United Nations Conciliation Commission for Palestine, "Historical Survey of Efforts of the United Nations Conciliation Commission for Palestine to Secure the Implementation of Paragraph 11 of General Assembly, Resolution 194," October 2, 1961.

19. See United Nations, "194 (III). Palestine—Progress Report of the United Nations Mediator," December 11, 1949.

20. "The Consul at Jerusalem (Wasson) to the Secretary of State," April 13, 1948, FRUS, 1948, vol. 5 part 2, doc. 145, p. 817.

21. "Editorial Note," April 26, 1948, FRUS, 1948, vol. 5 part 2, doc. 166, p. 838; "The Consul at Jerusalem (Wasson) to the Secretary of State," May 3, 1948, FRUS, 1948, vol. 5 part 2, doc. 206, pp. 889, 891; See also "Draft Memorandum by the Director of the Office of United Nations Affairs (Rusk) to the Under Secretary of State (Lovett)," May 4, 1948, FRUS, 1948, vol. 5 part 2, doc. 210, p. 894.

22. "The Consul at Jerusalem (Burdett) to the Secretary of State," February 28, 1949, FRUS, 1949, vol. 6, doc. 494, p. 778.

23. "Policy Paper Prepared in the Department of State," March 15, 1949, FRUS, 1949, vol. 6, doc. 533, p. 828.

24. "Policy Paper Prepared in the Department of State," March 15, 1949, FRUS, 1949, vol. 6, doc. 533, p. 837; "The Consul at Jerusalem (Burdett) to the Secretary of State," January 29, 1949, FRUS, 1949, vol. 6, doc. 435, pp. 711–12; "The Consul at Jerusalem (Burdett) to the Secretary of State," February 28, 1949, FRUS, 1949, vol. 6, doc. 494, p. 778; "The Consul at Jerusalem (Burdett) to the Secretary of State," July 6, 1949, FRUS, 1949, vol. 6, doc. 813, p. 1204; "The Ambassador in the United Kingdom (Douglas) to the Secretary of State," August 6, 1948, FRUS, 1948, vol. 5 part 2, doc. 517, p. 1295; Larry Collins and Dominique Lapierre, *O Jerusalem!* (New York: Simon & Schuster, 1972), p. 588.

25. "The Ambassador in France (Bruce) to the Secretary of State," June 12, 1949, FRUS, 1949, vol. 6, doc. 753, p. 1124.

26. FRUS, 1948, vol. 5, p. 1479.

27. "The Consul at Jerusalem (Burdett) to the Secretary of State," February 28, 1949, FRUS, 1949, vol. 6, doc. 494, p. 778.

28. "The Minister in Switzerland (Vincent) to the Secretary of State," May 16, 1949, FRUS, 1949, vol. 6, doc. 660, p. 1013.

29. See, for example, Benny Morris, *The Birth of the Palestinian Refugee Problem, 1947–1949* (Cambridge University Press, 1989), as compared with Ilan Pappé, *The Ethnic Cleansing of Palestine* (London: Oneworld Publications, 2006); Ahron Bregman, *Israel's Wars: A History since 1947* (New York: Routledge, 2000), p. 13. See also Simha Flapan, *The Birth of Israel: Myths and Realities* (New York: Pantheon, 1988), pp. 92–93; Martin Gilbert, *Israel: A History* (New York: HarperPerennial, 2008), p. 156; Nur Masalha, *Expulsion of the Palestinians: The Concept of "Transfer" in Zionist Political Thought, 1882–1948* (Beirut: Institute of Palestine Studies, 1992), pp. 176–77.

30. James G. McDonald, *My Mission in Israel. 1948–1951* (New York: Simon & Schuster, 1951), p. 176

31. "The Secretary of State to the Special Representative of the United States in Israel (McDonald)," September 1, 1948, FRUS, 1948, vol. 5 part 2, doc. 573, pp. 1366–69.

32. Malcolm Kerr, *America's Middle East Policy: Kissinger, Carter and the Future* (Beirut: Institute for Palestine Studies, 1980), p. 9n1.

33. See Morris, *1948*, p. 192. See also Avi Shlaim, *Collusion across the Jordan: King Abdullah, the Zionist Movement, and the Partition of Palestine* (Columbia University Press, 1988), pp. 110–21, 205–10.

34. William Roger Louis, *Ends of British Imperialism: The Scramble for Empire, Suez, and Decolonization* (New York: I. B. Tauris, 2006), p. 444. See also Morris, *1948*, pp. 42, 270, 311.

35. See "The British Embassy to the Department of State," January 5, 1948, FRUS, 1948, vol. 5 part 2, doc. 1, p. 535; "Memorandum of Conversation, by Secretary of State," May 12, 1948, FRUS, 1948, vol. 5 part 2, doc. 252, p. 973; "The Secretary of State to the Special Representative of the United States in Israel (McDonald)," September 1, 1948, FRUS, 1948, vol. 5 part 2, doc. 573, pp. 1366–69; "Memorandum by Mr. Robert M. McClintock to the Director of the Office of United Nations Affairs (Rusk)," September 3, 1948, FRUS, 1948, vol. 5 part 2, doc. 577, pp. 1371–72; Donald Neff, *Fallen Pillars: U.S. Policy towards Palestine and Israel since 1945* (Beirut: Institute for Palestine Studies, 2002), p. 88.

36. "The Secretary of State to the Acting Secretary of State," November 15, 1948, FRUS, 1948, vol. 5 part 2, doc. 765, p. 1596.

37. "Memorandum by Mr. John E. Horner," May 4, 1948, FRUS, 1948, vol. 5 part 2, doc. 213, p. 899.

38. See Zvi Elpeleg, "Why Was Independent Palestine Never Created in 1948?" *Jerusalem Quarterly* 50 (Spring 1989): 9.

39. See Ahmed Hilmi Pasha, "Palestine Progress Report of the United Nations Mediator on Palestine: Cablegram Dated 28 September 1948 from the Premier and Acting Foreign Secretary of All-Palestine Government to the Secretary-General Concerning Constitution of All-Palestine Government," October 14, 1948, UN doc. no. A/C.1/330.

40. See Philip Mattar, *The Mufti of Jerusalem: Al-Hajj Amin al-Husayni and the Palestinian National Movement* (Columbia University Press, 1988), pp. 119–21, 131–32.

41. Elpeleg, "Why Was Independent Palestine Never Created in 1948?," p. 20. See also Avi Shlaim, "The Rise and Fall of the All-Palestine Government in Gaza," *Journal of Palestine Studies* 20, no. 1 (Autumn 1990): 40, 49.

42. "The Acting Secretary of State to Certain Diplomatic Offices," October 2, 1948, FRUS, 1948, vol. 5 part 2, doc. 640, pp. 1447–48. Note that many communications cited are cables, hence the telegrammic writing style.

43. "Mr. Wells Stabler to the Acting Secretary of State," December 6, 1948, FRUS, 1948, vol. 5 part 2, doc. 810, p. 1647. See also Gendzier, *Dying to Forget*, pp. 189–90.

44. See, for example, "The Acting Secretary of State to Mr. Mark F. Ethridge," January 19, 1949, FRUS, 1949, vol. 6, doc. 408, p. 682.

45. "Memorandum of Telephone Conversation, by the Acting Secretary of State," September 29, 1948, FRUS, 1948, vol. 5 part 2, doc. 627, p. 1430. See also Neff, *Fallen Pillars*, pp. 89–90.

46. See "Letter from the Agent of the Provisional Government of Israel to the President of the United States, May 15, 1948"; Flapan, *Birth of Israel*, p. 13.

47. "The Acting Secretary of State to the Secretary of State, at London," October 31, 1948, FRUS, 1948, vol. 5 part 2, doc. 721, p. 1535. See also John B. Judis, *Genesis: Truman, American Jews, and the Origins of the Arab/Israeli Conflict* (New York: Farrar, Straus & Giroux, 2014), p. 334; Michael Joseph Cohen, *Truman and Israel* (University of California Press, 1990), pp. 254–56.

48. Cohen, *Truman and Israel* (1990), p. 256.

49. See Ghada Hashem Talhami, *Palestinian Refugees: Pawns to Political Actors* (Hauppage, N.Y.: Nova Science, 2003), p. 54; "Mr. Stuart W. Rockwell to the Secretary of State," August 16, 1949, FRUS, 1949, vol. 6, doc. 912, p. 1319; "Memorandum of Conversation, by the Secretary of State," April 26, 1949, FRUS, 1949, vol. 6, doc. 610, p. 945.

50. "The Acting United States Representative at the United Nations (Jessup) to the Secretary of State," July 27, 1948, FRUS, 1948, vol. 5 part 2, doc. 487, p. 1248; Morris, *Birth of the Palestinian Refugee Problem Revisited*, pp. 318–19.

51. "The Ambassador in France (Bruce) to the Secretary of State," June 12, 1949, FRUS, 1949, vol. 6, doc. 753, pp. 1124–25.

52. "Mr. Mark F. Ethridge to the Secretary of State," April 13, 1949, FRUS, 1949, vol. 6, doc. 592, p. 914.

53. Gendzier, *Dying to Forget*, pp. 239, 301, 307.

54. Ibid., p. 239.

55. "The President to Mr. Mark F. Ethridge, at Jerusalem," April 29, 1949, FRUS, 1949, vol. 6, doc. 617, p. 957.

56. "The Acting Secretary of State to the Embassy in Israel," May 28, 1949, FRUS, 1949, vol. 6, doc. 705, pp. 1072-74.

57. See Neff, *Fallen Pillars*, p. 76.

58. Quoted in ibid., pp. 76–77.

59. "The Minister in Lebanon (Pinkerton) to the Secretary of State," March 28, 1949, FRUS, 1949, vol. 6, doc. 563, pp. 876–78. See "Oral History Interview with Mark F. Ethridge," June 4, 1974 (www.trumanlibrary.org/oralhist/ethridge .htm).

60. "The Consul at Jerusalem (Burdett) to the Secretary of State," July 6, 1949, FRUS, 1949, vol. 6, doc. 813, p. 1205.

61. "Memorandum by Mrs. Dorothy H. Morgret in the Office of the Secretary of State," March 10, 1949, FRUS, 1949, vol. 6, doc. 519, p. 831.

62. "Mr. Stuart W. Rockwell to the Secretary of State," August 15, 1949, FRUS, 1949, vol. 6, doc. 908, p. 1313.

63. See UN General Assembly, Resolution 302 (IV), Assistance to Palestine Refugees, A/RES/302 (IV) (December 8, 1949).

64. Talhami, *Palestinian Refugees*, p. 72.

65. Deborah J. Gerner, "Missed Opportunities and Roads Not Taken: The Eisenhower Administration and the Palestinians," *Arab Studies Quarterly* 12, no. 1/2 (Winter–Spring 1990): 73.

66. Quoted in "Report on the Near East; Address by Secretary Dulles," *Department of State Bulletin*, June 15, 1953, pp. 831–35.

67. "United States Objectives and Policies with Respect to the Near East," NSC 155/1, July 14, 1953; "Statement of Policy by the National Security Council," July 14, 1953, FRUS, vol. 9 part 1, doc. 145, pp. 399–406.

68. "Report on the Near East; Address by Secretary Dulles."

69. "Policy Paper Prepared in the Department of State," March 15, 1949, FRUS, 1949, vol. 6, doc. 533, p. 837. See also "The Chargé in Jordan (Fritzlan) to the Department of State," April 3, 1952, FRUS, 1952–1954, vol. 9 part 1, doc. 418.

70. "Memorandum by the Deputy Assistant Secretary of State for Near Eastern, South Asian, and African Affairs (Jernegan) to the Secretary of State," August 10, 1953, FRUS, 1952–1954, vol. 9 part 1, doc. 648; Kathleen Christison, *Perceptions of Palestine: Their Influence on U.S. Middle East Policy* (University of California Press, 1999), pp. 99–100. See also Gerner, "Missed Opportunities and Roads Not Taken," p. 75.

71. "Memorandum of a Conversation, Department of State, Washington, December 5, 1957," December 5, 1957, FRUS, 1955–1957, vol. 7, doc. 419, p. 843.

72. Ibid., p. 844.

73. Ibid., p. 843n8.

74. United Nations Conciliation Commission for Palestine, "United Nations Economic Survey Mission for the Middle East—Final Report," December 28, 1949, UN doc. no. A/AC.25/6.

75. Talhami, *Palestinian Refugee*, p. 65; "Memorandum by the Acting Regional Planning Adviser, Bureau of Near Eastern, South Asian, and African Affairs (Hoskins), to the Assistant Secretary of State for Near Eastern, South Asian, and African Affairs (Byroade)," July 25, 1952, FRUS, 1952–1954, vol. 9 part 1, doc. 81, p. 261.

76. For more on the link between transfer and resettlement schemes, see Talhami, *Palestinian Refugees*, p. 53; Nur Masalha, *Imperial Israel and the Palestinians: The Politics of Expansion* (London: Pluto Press, 2000), p. 62. On "by preference," see Gerner, "Missed Opportunities and Roads Not Taken," p. 83.

77. See Talhami, *Palestinian Refugees*, p. 58; Association for Diplomatic Studies and Training, Foreign Affairs Oral History Project, "Eugene H. Bird," 1994. See also, "At 90, a Former Foreign Service Officer Looks at Gaza Then, and Now," *Los Angeles Times*, August 8, 2014.

78. "The Chargé in Jordan (Seelye) to the Department of State," October 13, 1953, FRUS, 1952–1954, vol. 9 part 1, doc. 687, p. 1353-55.

79. "Notes on Conference Between the Secretary of State and Delegation of Refugee Leaders, Edited by the Attaché in Jordan (Cassin)," May 15, 1953, FRUS, 1952–1954, vol. 9 part 1, doc. 20, pp. 51–54.

80. Yezid Sayigh, *Armed Struggle and the Search for State* (Oxford University Press, 1997), p. 59. See also Benny Morris, *Israel's Border Wars, 1949–1956: Arab Infiltration, Israeli Retaliation, and the Countdown to the Suez War* (Oxford University Press, 1993), p. 145; Jacob Tovy, *Israel and the Palestinian Refugee Issue: The Formulation of a Policy, 1948–1956* (New York: Routledge, 2014), pp. 59–60.

81. "The Qibya (Israel-Jordan) Incident: United Nations Security Council Resolution, November 24, 1953" (http://avalon.law.yale.edu/20th_century/mid009.asp), citing an untitled article in the *Department of State Bulletin*, October 26, 1953, p. 552; Isaac Alteras, *Eisenhower and Israel: U.S.-Israeli Relations, 1953–1960* (University Press of Florida, 1993), p. 87.

82. Bregman, *Israel's Wars*, pp. 50–51.

83. Yezid Sayigh, *Armed Struggle and the Search for State* (Oxford University Press, 1997), p. 88.

84. Quoted in Moshe Shemesh, "The Founding of the PLO 1964," *Middle Eastern Studies* 20, no. 4 (October 1984): 105. See also Moshe Shemesh, *The Palestinian Entity 1959–1974: Arab Politics and the PLO* (London: Frank Cass, 1996), p. 1.

85. Sayigh, *Armed Struggle and the Search for State*, p. 68. See "Telegram from the Embassy in Jordan to the Department of State," December 11, 1966, FRUS, 1964–1968, vol. 18, doc. 362, pp. 707–11.

86. CIA, Central Intelligence Bulletin, February 15, 1958 (www.foia.cia.gov/sites/default/files/document_conversions/5829/CIA-RDP79T00975A003500130001-8.pdf); See also "Telegram from the Embassy in Jordan to the Department of State," August 12, 1957, FRUS, 1955–1957, vol. 13, doc. 104; "Letter from the Under Secretary of State (Herter) to the Ambassador in Lebanon (McClintock)," February 13, 1958, FRUS, 1958–1960, vol. 13, doc. 7; "Telegram from the Embassy in Jordan to the Department of State," January 5, 1956, FRUS, 1955–1957, vol. 13, doc. 11; CIA, Central Intelligence Bulletin, August 12, 1951.

87. CIA, Central Intelligence Bulletin, March 14, 1958 (www.foia.cia.gov/sites/default/files/document_conversions/5829/CIA-RDP79T00975A003600120001-8.pdf).

88. "Memorandum from the Assistant Secretary for Near Eastern and South Asian Affairs (Talbot) to Secretary of State Rusk," May 1, 1961, FRUS, 1961–1963, vol. 17, doc. 39.

89. "Circular Telegram from the Department of state to Certain Near Eastern and North African Posts," April 15, 1961, FRUS, 1961–1963, vol. 17, doc. 34.

90. "Memorandum From Secretary of State Rusk to President Kennedy," November 26, 1961, FRUS, 1961–1963, vol. 17, doc. 145.

91. See, for example, "Memorandum of Conversation," November 30, 1961, FRUS, 1961–1963, vol. 17, doc. 146; "Memorandum from Secretary of State Rusk to President Kennedy," November 26, 1961, FRUS, 1961–1963, vol. 17, doc. 145; "Circular Telegram from the Department of State to Certain Posts," September 26, 1963, FRUS, 1962–1963, vol. 18, doc. 330.

92. "The Ambassador in Egypt (Caffery) to the Department of State," December 11, 1954, FRUS, 1952–1954, vol. 9 part 1, doc. 931, p. 1716.

93. The first State Department document to mention Fatah is dated May 28, 1965. Among declassified CIA materials, the first reference to Fatah is dated September 7, 1965. "Circular Telegram from the Department of State to Certain Posts," May 28, 1965, FRUS, 1964–1968, vol. 18, doc. 220; CIA, Central Intelligence Bulletin, September 7, 1965 (www.cia.gov/library/readingroom/docs/CIA-RDP79T00975A0085 00050001-2.pdf).

94. "Intelligence Memorandum," December 2, 1966, FRUS, 1964–1968, vol. 18, doc. 356; CIA, Central Intelligence Bulletin, January 20, 1967 (www.foia.cia.gov/sites /default/files/document_conversions/5829/CIA-RDP79T00975A009600030001-2 .pdf).

95. "Research Memorandum from the Deputy Director of the Bureau of Intelligence and Research (Denney) to Acting Secretary of State Ball," May 11, 1964, FRUS, 1964–1968, vol. 18, doc. 54.

96. "Circular Telegram from the Department of State to Certain Posts," November 17, 1964, FRUS, 1964–1968, vol. 18, doc. 106, pp. 237–38; See also "Special Report Prepared by the Central Intelligence Agency," December 3, 1965, FRUS, 1964–1968, vol. 18, doc. 255.

97. "Circular Airgram from the Department of State to Certain Posts," March 30, 1965, FRUS, 1964–1968, vol. 18, doc. 199.

98. "Memorandum of Conversation," April 8, 1965, FRUS, 1964–1968, vol. 18, doc. 204; "Telegram from the Department of State to the Mission to the United Nations," October 5, 1965, FRUS, 1964–1968, vol. 18, doc. 239.

99. "Memorandum of Conversation," April 8, 1965, FRUS, 1964–1968, vol. 18, doc. 204.

100. "Special Report Prepared in the Central Intelligence Agency," November 27, 1964, FRUS, 1964–1967, vol. 33, doc. 314; "Circular Telegram from the Department of State to Certain Posts," November 17, 1964, FRUS, 1964–1968, vol. 18, doc. 106, pp. 237–38.

101. "Special Report Prepared by the Central Intelligence Agency," December 3, 1965, FRUS, 1964–1968, vol. 18, doc. 255.

102. "Intelligence Memorandum," December 2, 1966, FRUS, 1964–1968, vol. 18, doc. 356.

103. Christison, *Perceptions of Palestine*, p. 105.

104. Ibid., p. 106.

105. "Telegram from the Department of State to the Embassy in the United Arab Republic," May 11, 1961, FRUS, 1961–1963, vol. 17, doc. 47.

106. "Memorandum of Conversation," June 7, 1962, FRUS, 1961–1963, vol. 17, doc. 289. See also, "Memorandum of Conversation," November 14, 1961, FRUS, 1961–1963, vol. 17, doc. 139; "Paper Prepared in the Bureau of Near Eastern and South Asian Affairs," June 30, 1962, FRUS, 1961–1963, vol. 17, doc. 314.

107. Zaha Bustami, "The Kennedy/Johnson Administrations and the Palestinians," *Arab Studies Quarterly* 12, no. 1/2 (Winter–Spring 1990): 101–20, p. 109.

108. See Abraham Ben-Zvi, *John F. Kennedy and the Politics of Arms Sales to Israel* (New York: Frank Cass Publishers, 2005), pp. 65–120; Dennis Ross, *Doomed to Succeed: The U.S.-Israel Relationship from Truman to Obama* (New York: Farrar, Straus & Giroux, 2015), pp. 66–67; Christison, *Perceptions of Palestine*, p. 107; Neff, *Fallen Pillars*, p. 171.

109. Michael B. Oren, *Six Days of War: June 1967 and the Making of the Modern Middle East* (New York: Presidio Press, 2003), p. 26.

110. "Memorandum from U.S. Consulate in Jerusalem to State Department (Declassified)," March 30, 1964. Obtained via Freedom of Information Act request.

111. "Telegram from the Department of State to the Embassy in Israel," December 9, 1965, FRUS, 1964–1968, vol. 18, doc. 256, pp. 524–25; "Circular Telegram from the Department of State to Certain Posts," November 17, 1964, FRUS, 1964–1968, vol. 18, doc. 106, pp. 237–38.

112. "Telegram from the Consulate General in Jerusalem to the Department of State," April 18, 1962, FRUS, 1961–1963, vol. 17, doc. 253; "Telegram from the Embassy in Italy to the Department of State," May 15, 1962, FRUS, 1961–1963, vol. 17, doc. 272; "Memorandum of Conversation," March 14, 1962, FRUS, 1961–1963, vol. 17, doc. 213.

113. "Memorandum of Conversation," June 1, 1964, FRUS, 1964–1968, vol. 18, doc. 65.

114. "Telegram from the Department of State to the Embassy of Israel," July 28, 1966, FRUS, 1964–1968, vol. 18, doc. 310.

115. Lyndon Baines Johnson, *The Vantage Point: Perspectives of the Presidency, 1963–1969* (New York: Holt, Rinehart & Winston, 1971), pp. 303–04.

116. Walid Khalidi, "A Palestinian Perspective on the Arab-Israeli Conflict," *Journal of Palestine Studies* 17, no. 4 (Summer 1985): 36.

Chapter 3

1. Epigraph: "Memorandum of Conversation," August 7, 1976, FRUS, 1969–1976, vol. 26, doc. 292.

2. Quoted in Kai Bird, *The Good Spy* (New York: Broadway Books 2014), p. 100.

3. Quoted in Donald Neff, *Fallen Pillars: U.S. Policy Towards Palestine and Israel Since 1945* (Beirut: Institute of Palestine Studies, 2002), p. 113.

4. Sheila Ryan, "Israel's Invasion of Lebanon: Background to the Crisis," *Journal of Palestine Studies*, special issue, 11, no. 4, and 12, no. 1 (Summer–Autumn 1982): 24.

5. Unlike the English text, the French version of the resolution included the definite article, "*les* territoires," thus implying a withdrawal from all the Arab territories occupied by Israel.

6. "Association for Diplomatic Studies and Training, Foreign Affairs Oral History Project (henceforth cited as ADST), "Ambassador Alfred L. Atherton, Jr." 1990.

7. Ibid.; "Johnson Warns Israel against 'Unilateral' Annexation of Old City of Jerusalem," Jewish Telegraphic Agency, June 29, 1967; "Circular Telegram From the Department of State to All Posts," July 5, 1967, FRUS, 1964–1968, vol. 19, doc. 344;

"Telegram From the Department of State to the Embassy in Israel," August 12, 1967, FRUS, 1964-1968, vol. 19, doc. 416.

8. See, for example, "Telegram From the Department of State to the Embassy in Jordan," April 11, 1968, FRUS, 1964–1968, vol. 20, doc. 143.

9. Malcolm H. Kerr, "America's Middle East Policy: Kissinger, Carter and the Future," IPS Papers no. 14 (Washington: Institute for Palestine Studies, 1980), p. 15.

10. Henry Kissinger, *White House Years* (New York: Simon & Schuster, 1979), p. 369; Paul Thomas Chamberlin, *The Global Offensive: The United States, the Palestine Liberation Organization, and the Making of the Post–Cold War Order* (Oxford University Press, 2012), p. 85.

11. Kissinger, *White House Years*, p. 369.

12. Yezid Sayigh, *Armed Struggle and the Search for State* (Oxford University Press, 1997), p. 147.

13. Chamberlin, *Global Offensive*, p. 46.

14. Rex Brynen, *Sanctuary and Survival: The PLO in Lebanon* (Boulder: Westview Press, 1990), p. 39.

15. Ibid., pp. 42–43.

16. Sayigh, *Armed Struggle and the Search for State*, p. 252.

17. Rashid Khalidi, "The United States and Palestine," *Cairo Review of Global Affairs*, Spring 2015. See also W. A. Terrill, "The Political Mythology of the Battle of Karameh," *Middle East Journal* 55, no. 1 (2001): 91–111.

18. See, for example, Arthur J. Goldberg, "Fifth Emergency Special Session, General Assembly," 1554th Plenary Meeting, July 14, 1967, UN doc. no. A/PV.1554 (https://unispal.un.org/DPA/DPR/unispal.nsf/0/66E65FB1AA7CFD3085257345004 FFE4F).

19. ADST, "Atherton."

20. "Memorandum From Harold H. Saunders of the National Security Council Staff to the President's Special Assistant (Rostow)," December 4, 1967, FRUS, 1964–1968, vol. 20, doc. 7; "Fedayeen—'Men of Sacrifice,'" CIA Intelligence Report, December 1970 (www.foia.cia.gov/sites/default/files/document_conversions/14/esau-47 .pdf).

21. Chamberlin, *Global Offensive*, p. 42.

22. Ibid., p. 83.

23. For example, see "Memorandum From the Assistant Secretary of State for Near Eastern and South Asian Affairs (Sisco) to Secretary of State Rogers," January 6, 1970, FRUS, 1969–1976, vol. 24, doc. 18.

24. For example, see CIA Intelligence Bulletins, October 16, 1968 (www.foia.cia.gov /sites/default/files/document_conversions/5829/CIA-RDP79T00975A012300090001-5 .pdf), and December 12, 1968 (www.foia.cia.gov/sites/default/files/document_conversions /5829/CIA-RDP79T00975A012700100001-9.pdf).

25. For example, see "Minutes of a National Security Council Meeting," February 1, 1969, FRUS, 1969–1976, vol. 24, doc. 3. See also "Memorandum From the Chairman of the Interdepartmental Group for Near East and South Asia (Sisco) to the

Chairman of the Review Group (Kissinger)," November 21, 1969, FRUS, 1969–1976, vol. 24, doc. 133.

26. See "Memorandum From the Assistant Secretary of State for Near Eastern and South Asian Affairs (Sisco) to Secretary of State Rogers," January 6, 1970, FRUS, 1969–1976, vol. 24, doc. 18; "Paper Prepared by the National Security Council Staff," June 4, 1970, FRUS, 1969–1976, vo. 24, doc. 82; "Memorandum of Conversation," January 13, 1971, FRUS, 1969–1976, vol. 24, doc. 93; "Memorandum From Peter Rodman of the National Security Council Staff to the President's Assistant for National Security Affairs (Kissinger)," December 31, 1969, FRUS, 1969–1976, vol. 24, doc. 76; "Airgram From the Department of State to the Embassies in Turkey, Pakistan, the United Kingdom, and Iran," December 28, 1972, FRUS, 1969–1976, vol. 24, doc. 36; "Paper Prepared by Harold Saunders of the National Security Council Staff," July 11, 1972, FRUS, 1969–1976, vol. 24, doc. 118; "Airgram From the Department of State to the Embassies in Turkey, Pakistan, the United Kingdom, and Iran," December 28, 1972, FRUS, 1969–1976, vol. 24, doc. 36.

27. William B. Quandt, "Skewed Perceptions: Yasir Arafat in the Eyes of American Officials, 1969–2004," in *Scripting Middle East Leaders: The Impact of Leadership Perceptions on US and UK Foreign Policy*, edited by Lawrence Freeman and Jeffry H. Michaels (London: Bloomsbury, 2013), p. 102.

28. Tad Szulc, *The Illusion of Peace: Foreign Policy in the Nixon Years* (New York: Viking Press, 1978), p. 312.

29. Sayigh, *Armed Struggle and the Search for State*, p. 151.

30. "Paper Prepared by the National Security Council Staff," November 13, 1970, FRUS, 1969–1976, vol. 23, doc. 182.

31. Richard M. Nixon, "The Arab-Israeli Conflict," *Richard M. Nixon: 1971—Containing the Public Messages, Speeches, and Statements of the President* (Ann Arbor: University of Michigan Library, 1971), p. 289.

32. Ryan, "Israel's Invasion of Lebanon, p. 25.

33. Henry Kissinger, *Years of Upheaval* (Boston: Little, Brown, and Company, 1982), pp. 503, 625, 628, 1139. See, for example, "Paper Prepared by Harold Saunders of the National Security Council Staff," July 11, 1972, FRUS, 1969–1976, vol. 24, doc. 118. See also Kissinger, *Years of Upheaval*, pp. 503, 1139.

34. Kissinger, *Years of Upheaval*, p. 628. See also ADST, "Under Secretary Joseph J. Sisco," 1990.

35. Kissinger, *Years of Upheaval*, pp. 625, 503, 624–29.

36. Ibid., p. 1038.

37. Bird, *Good Spy*, pp. 353–54.

38. Arafat may have been inspired by the opening of back-channel U.S.-Egyptian talks between Kissinger and Sadat's national security adviser, Hafez Ismail, during the first half of 1973. See White House, "Memorandum of Conversation," May 20, 1973 (www2.gwu.edu/~nsarchiv/NSAEBB/NSAEBB98/octwar-02a.pdf); "Memorandum: Meeting with Hafiz Ismail," June 2, 1973 (www2.gwu.edu/~nsarchiv/NSAEBB/NSAEBB98/octwar-02b.pdf).

39. See, for example, "Intelligence Memorandum, Washington, June 1973," June 1973, FRUS, 1969–1976, vol. E-6, doc. 217.

40. "Memorandum of Conversation," August 3, 1973, FRUS, 1969–1976, vol. 25, doc. 81, note 2.

41. Kissinger, *Years of Upheaval*, p. 626.

42. "Memorandum of Conversation," August 3, 1973.

43. Kissinger, *Years of Upheaval*, p. 758.

44. "Memorandum of Conversation," December 17, 1975 (www2.gwu.edu /~nsarchiv/NSAEBB/NSAEBB193/HAK-12-17-75.pdf).

45. Kissinger, *Years of Upheaval*, p. 625.

46. Ibid., p. 1053.

47. Ibid., p. 628.

48. "Backchannel Message from the Deputy Director of Central Intelligence (Walters) to Secretary of State Kissinger," November 4, 1973, FRUS, 1969–1976, vol. 25, doc. 318.

49. Ibid. See also Kissinger, *Years of Upheaval*, p. 629.

50. "Backchannel Message from the Deputy Director of Central Intelligence (Walters) to Secretary of State Kissinger," November 4, 1973, n3.

51. "Backchannel Message from the Deputy Director of Central Intelligence (Walters) to the President's Assistant for National Security Affairs (Kissinger)," November 4, 1973.

52. "Memorandum of Conversation," June 22, 1976, FRUS, 1969–1976, vol. 26, doc. 290.

53. Goldberg, *Jewish Power*, p. 247.

54. CIA, Central Intelligence Bulletin, December 14, 1973.

55. Ibid.

56. Anders Persso, *The EU and the Israeli–Palestinian Conflict 1971–2013: In Pursuit of a Just Peace* (Lanham, Md.: Lexington Books, 2015), p. 75.

57. CIA, Central Intelligence Bulletin, March 6, 1974 (www.foia.cia.gov/sites /default/files/document_conversions/5829/CIA-RDP79T00975A026200120001-7.pdf).

58. See Sayigh, *Armed Struggle and the Search for State*, p. 322. "Backchannel Message From the Deputy Director of Central Intelligence (Walters) to the President's Assistant for National Security Affairs (Kissinger)," March 8, 1974, FRUS, 1969–1976, vol. 26, doc. 30, n7. See also Kissinger, *Years of Upheaval*, p. 1036.

59. See, for example, CIA, Central Intelligence Bulletin, February 25, 1974 (www.foia .cia.gov/sites/default/files/document_conversions/5829/CIA-RDP79T00975A 026200040001-6.pdf); U.S. State Department telegram from American embassy, Beirut, to secretary of state re: "Arafat's Latest Efforts to Out-Maneuver Fedayeen Diehards," May 2, 1974 (http://aad.archives.gov/aad/createpdf?rid=98875&dt=2474&dl=1345).

60. Chamberlin, *Global Offensive*, p. 239.

61. Ibid.

62. Ibid., p. 240.

63. Kissinger, *Years of Upheaval*, p. 629.

64. "Memorandum of Conversation," February 8, 1974, FRUS, 1969–1976, vol. 26, doc. 23; "Memorandum of Conversation," March 8, 1974, FRUS, 1969–1976, vol. 26, doc. 31.

65. "PLO Sole Legitimate Representative of the Palestinian People—LAS Rabat Summit; Resolution on Palestine, Seventh Arab League Summit Conference, October 28, 1974," available at United Nations: The Question of Palestine (website) (www .un.org/unispal/document/plo-sole-legitimate-representative-of-the-palestinian -people-las-rabat-summit-resolution/).

66. Kissinger, *Years of Upheaval*, p. 787.

67. UN General Assembly, Resolution 3237, "Observer Status for the Palestine Liberation Organization," A/RES/3237(XXIX), November 22, 1974 (www.un.org/en/ga /search/view_doc.asp?symbol=A/RES/3237(XXIX)); UN General Assembly, Resolution 3236, "Question of Palestine," A/RES/3236(XXIX), November 22, 1974 (www .un.org/en/ga/search/view_doc.asp?symbol=A/RES/3236(XXIX)); U.S. Department of State, telegram from Joseph Sisco to Henry Kissinger re Palestinian Resolution at UN General Assembly, November 20, 1974 (http://aad.archives.gov/aad/createpdf?rid =246419&dt=2474&dl=1345).

68. See United Nations General Assembly, "President: Mr. Abdelaziz Bouteflika (Algeria), Agenda Item 108, Question of Palestine (continued)," November 21, 1974.

69. Nabeel Shaath, author interview, Ramallah, August 22, 2013.

70. See Judith Cummings, "Aide Beaten at Palestinian Office Here," *New York Times*, October 30, 1974.

71. See Bird, *Good Spy*, p. 174.

72. See U.S. Department of State, "Contacts with PLO Representatives," November 26, 1974 (http://aad.archives.gov/aad/createpdf?rid=256045&dt=2474&dl=1345).

73. See "Visa Ineligibility: Palestine Liberation Organization," December 22, 1974 (http://aad.archives.gov/aad/createpdf?rid=272586&dt=2474&dl=1345); See also "Visas and Status of PLO UN Observers," April 15, 1975 (http://aad.archives.gov/aad /createpdf?rid=28906&dt=2476&dl=1345); "PLO Plans for New York Observer Office," March 5, 1975 (http://aad.archives.gov/aad/createpdf?rid=212692&dt=2476&dl =1345); "Visa Ineligibility: Palestine Liberation Organization," January 16, 1975 (http:// aad.archives.gov/aad/createpdf?rid=126377&dt=2476&dl=1345).

74. Brookings Institution Middle East Study Group, *Toward Peace in the Middle East*, report (Brookings Institution, December 1975).

75. See House of Representatives, "The Palestine Issue in the Middle East Peace Efforts" Hearings, Committee on International Relations, 94th Congress (http://babel .hathitrust.org/cgi/pt?id=purl.32754077071516;page=root;seq=3;view=image;size =100;orient=0), p. 203.

76. J. William Fulbright, "The Clear and Present Danger," speech, November 2, 1974 (www.speeches-usa.com/Transcripts/jw_fulbright.html); for statements by Senators George McGovern and Charles Percy, see "Israel in the US Senate," *Journal of Palestine Studies* 4, no. 4 (Summer 1975): 167–69.

77. See James G. Abourezk, *Advise and Dissent: Memoirs of South Dakota and the U.S. Senate* (Chicago: Lawrence Hill Books, 1989), p. 240; Frank Starr, "The Words That Arafat Won't Say," *Chicago Tribune*, June 30, 1975, section 2, p. 2.

78. See Harold H. Saunders, "Statement of Harold H. Saunders, Deputy Assistant Secretary for Near Eastern and South Asian Affairs, Department of State," Hearings, House Committee on International Relations, 94th Congress, pp. 176, 178 (https://babel.hathitrust.org/cgi/pt?view=image;size=125;id=purl.32754077071516;page=root;seq=3).

79. See Bernard Gwertzman, "U.S. Seeks Talks on P.L.O., Denies a Change in Policy," *New York Times*, December 31, 1976.

80. Ahron Bregman, *Cursed Victory: A History of Israel and the Occupied Territories* (New York: Pegasus, 2014), pp. 94–95.

81. Goldberg, *Jewish Power*, p. 239.

82. See "Memorandum of Agreement between the Governments of Israel and the United States," September 1, 1975 (http://history.state.gov/historicaldocuments/frus1969-76v26/d227).

83. See, for example, Statement of Farouk Khaddoumi, UN Security Council, "Thirty-First Year, 1879th Meeting," January 26, 1979, UN doc. no. S/PV.1879 (https://unispal.un.org/DPA/DPR/unispal.nsf/0/D0242E9E210D937585256C6E0054DF8A).

84. UN General Assembly, Resolution 3375, "Invitation to the Palestine Liberation Organization to participate in the efforts for peace in the Middle East," November 10, 1975, UN doc. no. A/RES/3375 (XXX) (https://unispal.un.org/DPA/DPR/unispal.nsf/0/7E0524B7EAD4A9E4852560DE004EFDC7); U.S. Department of State, telegram from American embassy, Tel Aviv, to secretary of state, Washington, re "Meeting with Prime Minister Rabin," December 23, 1975 (http://aad.archives.gov/aad/createpdf?rid=62586&dt=2476&dl=1345).

85. See U.S. State Department telegrams: from American embassy, Beirut, to secretary of state, re "Possible Silver Lining in Connection with Current Lebanese Situation," July 14, 1976 (https://aad.archives.gov/aad/createpdf?rid=158013&dt=2082&dl=1345); re "Proposal for US Support of PLO-led Palestinian State," July 24, 1976 (https://aad.archives.gov/aad/createpdf?rid=149882&dt=2082&dl=1345); re "Suggestion US Advocate Palestinian State on West Bank," August 4, 1976 (https://aad.archives.gov/aad/createpdf?rid=50472&dt=2082&dl=1345); re "U.S. Views on a Possible Palestinian State," August 5, 1976 (http://aad.archives.gov/aad/createpdf?rid=45916&dt=2082&dl=1345).

86. Osamah Khalil, "Oslo's Roots: Kissinger, the PLO, and the Peace Process," Al-Shabaka Policy Brief, September 4, 2013 (http://al-shabaka.org/briefs/oslos-roots-kissinger-plo-and-peace-process/).

87. "PLO Trial Balloon," *Washington Post*, March 2, 1976.

88. "Memorandum of Conversation," August 7, 1976, FRUS, 1969–1976, vol. 26, doc. 292.

89. ADST, "Ambassador Robert B. Oakley," 1992. See also "Memorandum from William Quandt of the National Security Council Staff to the President's Assistant

for National Security Affairs (Brzezinski)," September 19, 1977, FRUS, 1977–1980, vol. 8, doc. 103; Sameer Abraham, "The PLO at the Crossroads: Moderation, Encirclement, Future Prospects," *Middle East Report* 80 (September–October 1979): pp. 54–65 (www .merip.org/mer/mer80/plo-crossroads \l _8_); "U.S. Rebuffs Washington PLO Office," *Palestine* 2, no. 1 (February 1977): 1, 4–6, 16.

90. Bernard Gwertzman, "U.S. Orders P.L.O. Representative to Leave Country," *New York Times*, November 24, 1976.

91. See Bird, *Good Spy*, p. 176. See also Gordon Thomas, *Gideon's Spies: The Secret History of the Mossad* (New York: Thomas Dunne Books, 2000), pp. 281–82.

92. See White House, "Question and Answer Session with the President," press release, June 20, 1976; James M. Markham, "Peace Force in Beirut; Syrian and Libyan Troops of Arab Peace Force Arrive in Beirut," *New York Times*, June 22, 1976, p. 73; Bird, *Good Spy*, pp. 176–77.

93. Khalil, "Oslo's Roots."

94. See "Memorandum of Conversation," June 22, 1976, FRUS, 1969–1976, vol. 26, doc. 290. See also Kissinger, *Years of Renewal*, p. 1053.

95. "U.S. Rebuffs Washington PLO Office."

96. CIA, "Internal Politics of the Palestine Liberation Organization," report, February 6, 1975 (www.foia.cia.gov/document/cia-rdp80r01731r002300100002-8).

97. Jimmy Carter, *Keeping Faith: Memoirs of a President* (New York: Bantam Books, 1982), p. 277.

98. E. H. Knoche, "Interest of PLO Chairman Arafat in Establishing a Dialogue with the United States Government," memo to National Security Advisor Zbigniew Brzezinski, February 8, 1977 (www.foia.cia.gov/sites/default/files/document_conversions /1821105/1977-02-08.pdf).

99. See ADST, "Ambassador Nicholas A. Veliotes," 1992; ADST, "Arthur R. Day," 1990.

100. George E. Gruen, "The United States, Israel, and the Middle East," *American Jewish Yearbook, Volume 79 (1979)* (www.ajcarchives.org/main.php?GroupingId =10113), p. 125.

101. See ADST, "Oakley"; ADST, "Veliotes."

102. James Carter, "Toledo, Ohio Remarks and a Question-and-Answer Session at a Town Meeting," October 25, 1980, American Presidency Project (website) (www .presidency.ucsb.edu/ws/?pid=45376); ADST, "Oakley"; ADST, "Veliotes"; Jimmy Carter, *White House Diary* (New York: Macmillan, 2010), p. 352.

103. William Quandt, author interview (telephone), February 27, 2015.

104. "Telegram From the Department of State to the Embassy in Lebanon," August 17, 1977, FRUS, 1977-1980, vol. 8, doc. 93.

105. Sayigh, *Armed Struggle and the Search for State*, p. 422.

106. "Telegram From the Department of State to the Embassy in Lebanon," August 17, 1977, FRUS, 1977–1980, vol. 8, doc. 93. See also "Memorandum from William Quandt of the National Security Council Staff to the President's Assistant for National Security Affairs (Brzezinski)," September 19, 1977, FRUS, 1977–1980, vol. 8, doc. 103.

107. Seth Tillman, *The United States in the Middle East: Interests and Obstacles* (Indiana University Press, 1982), p. 228.

108. "Telegram From the Embassy in Lebanon to the Department of State," August 23, 1977, FRUS, 1977–1980, vol. 8, doc. 98.

109. For a U.S. Government analysis of the internal debate within the PLO, see "Central Intelligence Agency Intelligence Information Cable," August 20, 1977, FRUS, 1977–1980, vol. 8, doc. 97.

110. Yasir Arafat and Zahid Mahmood: "Interview 2. Yasir Arafat: The U.S., the PLO and the Three Formulas," *Journal of Palestine Studies* 15, no. 4 (Summer 1986): 19.

111. Tillman, *United States in the Middle East*, pp. 226–27.

112. See, for example, "National Intelligence Daily Cable for Tuesday, 28 February 1978" (www.foia.cia.gov/sites/default/files/document_conversions/5829/CIA-RDP79T00975A030500010094-9.pdf).

113. See "Israeli Settlements in Gaza and the West Bank (Including Jerusalem), Their Nature and Purpose," July 1, 1984, United Nations Information System on the Question of Palestine (https://unispal.un.org/DPA/DPR/unispal.nsf/0/B658E2F2D24BC43885256C780054B750). See also Marvin Howe, "Lebanon Says Israel Occupies 6 Key Hills," *New York Times*, September 22, 1977.

114. See "Brzezinski Denies Harshness: American Jews Angered by U.S. Stand," *Los Angeles Times*, October 3, 1977, p. B12; "The United States, the Soviet Union and a Middle East Peace," October 1977, and "Memorandum to Hamilton Jordan," Office of the Chief of Staff Files, Hamilton Jordan's Confidential Files, Middle East, October 1977, Container 35 (https://www.jimmycarterlibrary.gov/digital_library/cos/142099/35/cos_142099_35_18-Middle_East_1977_1.pdf).

115. See "Memorandum of Conversation," October 5, 1977, FRUS, 1977–1980, vol. 8, doc. 124, attachment.

116. Sayigh, *Armed Struggle and the Search for State*, p. 424.

117. Gruen, "The United States, Israel, and the Middle East," p. 150.

118. "Brzezinski Sees Role for Moderate Palestinians in Resolving Mideast Conflict; Role for PLO Left Open," Jewish Telegraphic Agency, January 9, 1978 (www.jta.org/1978/01/09/archive/brzezinski-sees-role-for-moderate-palestinians-in-resolving-mideast-conflict-role-for-plo-left-open).

119. Yasser Arafat, "The PLO Position," *Journal of Palestine Studies* 7, no. 3 (Spring 1978): 172. See also "Statement by the Central Committee of Fateh, issued by 'WAFA,' Beirut, May 3, 1978," in "Documents and Source Material: Arab Documents on Palestine and the Arab-Israeli Conflict," *Journal of Palestine Studies* 7, no. 4 (Summer 1978): 197.

120. Carter, *White House Diary*, pp. 178–79. See also Dennis Ross, *Doomed to Succeed* (New York: Farrar, Straus and Giroux, 2015), p. 163; Nathan Thrall, *The Only Language They Understand: Forcing Compromise in Israel and Palestine* (New York: Metropolitan Books, 2017), p. 29.

121. Quandt, February 27, 2015, interview.

122. Tillman, *The United States in the Middle East*, p. 59.

123. William B. Quandt, *Camp David: Peacemaking and Politics* (Brookings Institution Press, 1986), p. 322.

124. Ibid., p. 323.

125. Cyrus Vance, *Hard Choices: Critical Years in America's Foreign Policy* (New York: Simon & Schuster, 1983), p. 180.

126. William Quandt, author interview (telephone), June 13, 2013. See also Jimmy Carter, *Keeping Faith: Memoirs of a President* (New York: Bantam Books, 1982), pp. 347–48.

127. See CIA Memo re "Yasir Arafat's Preference to Deal Directly with the United States Government Rather Than to Discuss a Middle East Peace with Egyptian President Anwar al-Sadat," October 14, 1978 (www.foia.cia.gov/sites/default/files/document _conversions/1821105/1978-10-14a.pdf).

128. See David Barsamian, "Edward Said: The Israel/PLO Accord," *Z Magazine*, December 1993, p. 52 (http://desip.igc.org/ArafatRejectsCarter.html).

129. Bruce Riedel of the Brookings Institution, quoted in Bird, *Good Spy*, p. 208.

Chapter 4

1. George Shultz, "Working for Peace and Freedom," address to the American Israel Public Affairs Committee, May 17, 1987 (https://archive.org/stream/departmen tofstat87212421291987unit%20/1%20page/n21/mode/2up).

2. See Ze'ev Schiff and Ehud Yaari, *Israel's Lebanon War* (New York: Simon & Schuster, 1986), pp. 97–99. See also Caspar Weinberger, *Fighting for Peace: Seven Critical Years in the Pentagon* (New York: Grand Central, 1990), pp. 141–43; Association for Diplomatic Studies and Training, Foreign Affairs Oral History Project (henceforth cited as ADST), "Ambassador Robert S. Dillon," p. 104.

3. Yezid Sayigh, *Armed Struggle and the Search for State: The Palestinian National Movement, 1949–1993* (Oxford University Press, 1997), p. 522.

4. Rex Brynen, *Sanctuary and Survival: The PLO in Lebanon* (Boulder: Westview Press, 1990), p. 169.

5. Schiff and Yaari, *Israel's Lebanon War*, p. 211.

6. Ahron Bregman, *Israel's Wars, 1947–93* (New York: Routledge, 2000), p. 102.

7. ADST, "Morris Draper," pp. 82–83.

8. Sheila Ryan, "Israel's Invasion of Lebanon: Background to the Crisis," *Journal of Palestine Studies*, special issue, 11, no. 4, and 12, no. 1 (Summer–Autumn 1982): 34.

9. John Boykin, *Cursed Is the Peacemaker: The American Diplomat Versus the Israeli General, Beirut 1982* (Belmont, Calif.: Applegate Press, 2002), p. 55.

10. Yossi Melman and Dan Ravi, *Friends in Deed: Inside the U.S.-Israel Alliance, 1948–1994* (New York: Levant Books, 1994), p. 219; Alexander M. Haig Jr., *Caveat: Realism, Reagan and Foreign Policy* (London: Weidenfeld & Nicolson, 1984), p. 317.

11. ADST, "Dillon," pp. 117–18.

12. See, for example, Ann M. Lesch, "U.S. Policy toward the Palestinians in the 1980s," *Arab Studies Quarterly* 12, nos. 1–2 (1990): 167–89.

13. Quoted in Mattia Toaldo, *The Origins of the US War on Terror: Lebanon, Libya and American Intervention in the Middle East* (New York: Routledge, 2013), p. 74.

14. John L. Helgerson, *Getting to Know the President: CIA Briefings of Presidential Candidates 1952–1992* (Washington: Center for the Study of Intelligence, 2001), chapter 6, "Reagan and Bush: A Study in Contrasts," p. 121.

15. Boykin, *Cursed Is the Peacemaker*, p. 54.

16. Dennis Ross, *Doomed to Succeed* (New York: Farrar, Straus & Giroux, 2015), p. 193. George P. Shultz, *Turmoil and Triumph: My Years as Secretary of State* (New York: Charles Scribner's Sons, 1993), p. 48. See also Harvey Sicherman, *Palestinian Autonomy, Self-Government, and Peace* (Boulder: Westview Press, 1993), p. 65.

17. ADST, "Wat Cluverius," pp. 39–40.

18. ADST, "Ambassador Nicholas A. Veliotes," 1990.

19. Ibid., p. 127.

20. Bernard Gwertzman, "Reagan Administration Held 9-Month Talks with P.L.O.," *New York Times*, February 19, 1984.

21. ADST, "Veliotes," p. 127; Yasir Arafat and Zahid Mahmood, "Interview 2: Yasir Arafat: The U.S., the PLO and the Three Formulas," *Journal of Palestine Studies* 15, no. 4 (Summer 1986): 22.

22. Sayigh, *Armed Struggle and the Search for State*, p. 531.

23. Daniel Trotta, "Reagan Diaries Reveal President's Private Musings," Reuters, May 1, 2007.

24. UN Security Council, "Union of Soviet Socialist Republics: Revised Draft Resolution," August 6, 1982, UN doc. no. S/15347/Rev.1 (http://www.un.org/en/ga/search/view_doc.asp?symbol=S/15347/Rev.1); Ralph Mandel, "Israel in 1982: The War in Lebanon," in *American Jewish Year Book 1984*, vol. 84, edited by Milton Himmelfarb and David Singer (New York: Jewish Publication Society of America, 1983), p. 15.

25. Boykin, *Cursed Is the Peacemaker*, p. 98.

26. Thomas L. Friedman, *From Beirut to Jerusalem* (New York: Picador, 1989), p. 161.

27. Sayigh, *Armed Struggle and the Search for State*, p. 551.

28. See Boykin, *Cursed Is the Peacemaker*, p. 268. See also Seth Anziska, "A Preventable Massacre," *New York Times*, September 16, 2012.

29. See Friedman, *From Beirut to Jerusalem*, p. 159. See also Ihsan A. Hijazi "Israeli Looted Archives of P.L.O. Officials Say," *New York Times*, October 1, 1982.

30. Boykin, *Cursed Is the Peacemaker*, p. 268.

31. Shultz, *Turmoil and Triumph*, p. 105.

32. "Casualties of Mideast Wars," *Los Angeles Times*, March 8, 1991.

33. Sayigh, *Armed Struggle*, p. 541; "Casualties of Mideast Wars."

34. Boykin, *Cursed Is the Peacemaker*, p. 311.

35. Ibid., p. 77. See also Schiff and Yaari, *Israel's Lebanon War*.

36. See, for example, Human Rights Watch, "Ariel Sharon's Troubling Legacy: Evaded Prosecution over Sabra and Shatilla Massacres," January 11, 2014.

37. ADST, "Under Secretary Philip C. Habib," 1984, p. 66.

38. There is also evidence that Osama bin Laden may have received shelter and training in Lebanon in 1993. See Kai Bird, *The Good Spy* (New York: Broadway Books, 2015), pp. 321, 355.

39. Jeremy M. Sharp, "U.S. Foreign Aid to Israel," Congressional Research Service, September 16, 2010.

40. Shultz, *Turmoil and Triumph*, pp. 49–50, 97.

41. ADST, "Veliotes," p. 139.

42. CIA, "US-Israeli Differences over the Camp David Peace Process," August 24, 1982.

43. Daniel Kurtzer, interview by author, Washington, March 25, 2015.

44. Kathleen Christison, "The Arab-Israeli Policy of George Shultz," *Journal of Palestine Studies* 18, no. 2 (1989): 41.

45. See, for example, Ellie Rekhes, "The West Bank and the Gaza Strip," in *Middle East Contemporary Survey*, edited by Itamar Rabinovich (Boulder: Westview Press, 1988), pp. 261–62. See also Souad Dajani, *Eyes without Country: Searching for a Palestinian Strategy of Liberation* (Temple University Press, 1995), p. 117.

46. See "Israel Deports Two West Bank Mayors to Lebanon," Washington, Pa., *Observer Reporter*, December 6, 1980 (https://news.google.com/newspapers?nid =6w2ZCmoKEM0C&dat=19801206&printsec=frontpage&hl=en).

47. See Foundation for Middle East Peace, "Comprehensive Settlement Population 1972–2011" (https://fmep.org/resource/comprehensive-settlement-population -1972-2010/).

48. See Salim Tamari, "In League with Zion: Israel's Search for a Native Pillar," *Journal of Palestine Studies* 12, no. 4 (1983): 42.

49. ADST, "Ambassador Brandon H. Grove, Jr.," 1994, p. 160.

50. CIA, National Intelligence Estimate, "Outlook for Palestinians," August 15, 1984.

51. ADST, "Grove," p. 160

52. Daniel Kurtzer, interview by author, Washington, March 25, 2015.

53. Richard Murphy, interview by author (telephone), October 5, 2015.

54. Shultz, *Turmoil and Triumph*, p. 1020. See also George Shultz, "News Conference of December 6," December 6, 1985 (https://archive.org/stream/departmentofstata 1986unit/departmentofstata1986unit_djvu.txt).

55. See, for example, Ronald Reagan, "Remarks and a Question-and-Answer Session at a Working Luncheon with Out-of-Town Editors," October 16, 1981; Ronald Reagan, "Interview with Reporters on Domestic and Foreign Policy Issues," December 23, 1983; "54 Lawmakers Urge Olympic Committee to Reject Any Application by the PLO to Participate in 1984 Olym," Jewish Telegraphic Agency, April 11, 1984; *Ability of Civil and Criminal Actions against Yassir Arafat's Palestine Liberation Organization (PLO)*, Hearing before the Subcommittee on Security and Terrorism of the Committee on the Judiciary, United States Senate, 99th Cong., 2nd sess., April 23, 1986, pp. 1–2.

56. See, for example, CIA, Special National Intelligence Estimate, "The Middle East Peace Process," January 1985; Ronald Reagan, "Written Responses to Questions Submitted by the Kuwaiti Newspaper *Al-Qabas*," May 12, 1987.

57. Dennis Ross, "Acting with Caution: Middle East Policy Planning for the Second Reagan Administration," WINEP Policy Papers no. 1 (Washington: Washington Institute, 1985), pp. 43–44.

58. ADST, "Veliotes," p. 127; Ward Sinclair and Lou Cannon, "Reagan Unaware of Contacts with PLO, Aides Say," *Washington Post*, February 20, 1984. See also Kathleen Christison, *Perceptions of Palestine* (University of California Press, 2001), p. 205.

59. Nabil Shaath, interview by author, Ramallah, August 22, 2013.

60. *Cases of United States Visas Granted to Officials of the PLO During the Reagan Administration (Ability of Civil And Criminal Actions Against Yassir Arafat's Palestine Liberation Organization (PLO)*, Hearing before the Subcommittee on Security and Terrorism of the Committee on the Judiciary, United States Senate, 99th Cong., 2nd sess., April 23, 1986.

61. Charles Hill, interview by author (telephone), October 8, 2015.

62. Lesch, "U.S. Policy toward the Palestinians in the 1980s," p. 176.

63. See, for instance, "AIPAC Policy Statement," *Near East Report*, April 27, 1984, p. 70.

64. See "The PLO's Valuable Ally: The United Nations," United Nations Assessment Project Study, Heritage Foundation Backgrounder, December 17, 1985.

65. Rajai M. Abu-Khadra, "The Closure of the PLO Offices," *Journal of Palestine Studies* 17, no. 3 (Spring 1988): 54.

66. B'Tselem—The Israeli Information Center for Human Rights in the Occupied Territories, "Fatalities in the First Intifada" (www.btselem.org/statistics/first_intifada_tables).

67. See "Khalil al-Wazir Death: Israel Admits to Assassination of Abu Jihad, Arafat Deputy in 1988," Associated Press, November 1, 2012.

68. Bruce Riedel, interview by author, Washington, September 18, 2013.

69. Murphy interview, October 5, 2015.

70. See Anthony Wanis–St. John, *Back Channel Negotiation: Secrecy in the Middle East Peace Process* (Syracuse University Press, 2011), p. 46.

71. Daniel Kurtzer, interview by author, Washington, March 25, 2015.

72. Ibid.

73. ADST, "Ambassador William Andreas Brown," p. 413.

74. Shultz, *Turmoil and Triumph*, p. 1043.

75. Naseer Aruri, "The United States and Palestine: Reagan's Legacy to Bush," *Journal of Palestine Studies* 18, no. 3 (1989): 16.

76. James A. Baker III, *The Politics of Diplomacy* (New York: Putnam, 1995), p. 118.

77. Public Law 101-246: 104. Stat. 71, Feb. 16, 1990 (http://uscode.house.gov/statutes/pl/101/246.pdf).

78. Robert Pelletreau, interview by author, Woods Hole, Mass., April 13, 2016.

79. Ibid.

80. Barry Rubin, "The United States and the Middle East," in *Middle East Contemporary Survey: 1990*, vol. 14, edited by Ami Ayalon (Boulder: Westview Press, 1990), p. 21.

81. Baker, *Politics of Diplomacy*, p. 118.

82. Pelletreau interview, April 13, 2016.

83. Ibid.

84. Yasser Abed-Rabbo, interview by author, Washington, November 20, 2013. See also Hanan Ashrawi, *This Side of Peace* (New York: Simon & Schuster, 1994), p. 58.

85. ADST, "Ambassador Edmund James Hull," 2005, p. 79.

86. Salah Khalaf (Abu Iyad), "Lowering the Sword," *Foreign Policy* no. 78 (Spring 1990): 94.

87. William B. Quandt, personal communication, June 17, 2017.

88. Baker, *Politics of Diplomacy*, p. 130. See Ashrawi, *This Side of Peace*, p. 67.

89. Sayigh, *Armed Struggle and the Search for State*, p. 641.

90. Judith Miller, "After the War: The P.L.O.; Arafat Sees No Damage to P.L.O. in War Stand," *New York Times*, March 15, 1991.

91. Kurtzer interview, March 25, 2015.

92. Baker, *Politics of Diplomacy*, p. 415.

93. Ibid., p. 423. Hanan Ashrawi, interview by author, Ramallah, February 14, 2016.

94. Hanan Ashrawi, interview by author, Ramallah, November 15, 2012.

95. Hanan Ashrawi, interview by author, Ramallah, August 13, 2013.

96. For the complete anecdote, see Ashrawi, *This Side of Peace*, pp. 86–87.

97. Baker, *Politics of Diplomacy*, p. 492.

98. Sayigh, *Armed Struggle and the Search for the State*, p. 660.

99. Sari Nusseibeh, interview by author, Jerusalem, November 7, 2012; Ashrawi interview, February 14, 2016; Akram Baker, interview by author (telephone), September 17, 2013.

100. ADST, "Edward Abington," 2012, unpublished (transcript in author's collection).

101. Quoted in "The Madrid Peace Conference," *Journal of Palestine Studies* 21, no. 2 (Winter 1992): 118.

102. Baker, *Politics of Diplomacy*, p. 117.

103. Ashrawi, *This Side of Peace*, p. 120.

Chapter 5

1. Yezid Sayigh, *Armed Struggle and the Search for State: The Palestinian National Movement, 1949–1993* (Oxford University Press, 1998), p. 655–56. See also Ghassan Khatib, *Palestinian Politics and the Middle East Peace Process: Consensus and politics in the Palestinian negotiating team* (New York: Routledge, 2009), pp. 85–91.

2. Khatib, *Palestinian Politics and the Middle East Peace Process*, p. 79.

3. Dennis Ross, *The Missing Peace: The Inside Story of the Fight for Middle East Peace* (New York: Farrar, Straus & Giroux, 2004), pp. 102–03.

4. "Draft Minutes, Meeting with the Americans," June 23, 1993, Papers of the Palestinian Delegation (www.palestine-studies.org/sites/default/files/uploads/files /Minutes%20Kurtzer%2C%20Miller%20meeting%2023%20June%2093.pdf). See also Rashid Khalidi, *Brokers of Deceit: How the U.S. Has Undermined Peace in the Middle East* (Boston: Beacon Press, 2013), p. 55.

5. Ross, *Missing Peace*, p. 119.

6. Khalidi, *Brokers of Deceit*, pp. 55–56.

7. Sayigh, *Armed Struggle and the Search for State*, p. 660.

8. Khaled Hroub, *Hamas: Political Thought and Practice* (Washington: Institute for Palestine Studies, 2000), p. 102.

9. Khatib, *Palestinian Politics and the Middle East Peace Process*, p. 88.

10. See, for instance, Avi Shlaim, "The Oslo Accord," *Journal of Palestine Studies* 23, no. 3 (1993–1994): 32 (www.palestine-studies.org/jps/fulltext/39986). See also Sayigh, *Armed Struggle and the Search for State*, p. 659.

11. B'tselem—The Israeli Information Center for Human Rights in the Occupied Territories (henceforth cited as B'Tselem), "Fatalities in the First Intifada" (www .btselem.org/statistics/first_intifada_tables).

12. As of May 1999, 18 percent of the West Bank was under full Palestinian Authority control ("Area A"); another 21 percent was under joint Palestinian-Israeli control ("Area B"); most of the Gaza Strip was under Palestinian-Israeli control.

13. Shlaim, "Oslo Accord," p. 38.

14. "Knesset Opposition and Settlers Up in Arms over Peace Agreement," Jewish Telegraphic Agency, August 31, 1993.

15. Edward Said, *Peace and Its Discontents: Essays on Palestine in the Middle East Peace Process* (London: Trafalgar Square, 1995), pp. 4, 7–8.

16. Jamil Hilal, "PLO Institutions: The Challenge Ahead," *Journal of Palestine Studies* 23, no. 1 (Autumn 1993): 58.

17. Sayigh, *Armed Struggle and the Search for State*, p. 658.

18. Khaled Hroub, *Hamas: A Beginner's Guide*, 2nd ed. (New York: Pluto Press, 2010), p. 53.

19. See Dan Ephron and Terry Gross, "Revisiting Rabin's Assassination, and the Peace That Might Have Been," *Fresh Air*, NPR, October 13, 2015; Noam Sheizaf, "Rabin's Assassination Marked the End of the Two-State Solution," Al Jazeera, November 4, 2015; Rebecca Collard, "Why the Murder of the Israeli Prime Minister Doomed Peace Negotiations," *Time*, November 4, 2015.

20. Hilal, "PLO Institutions," p. 46.

21. See, for example, Yezid Sayigh and Khalil Shikaki, *Strengthening Palestinian Public Institutions*, Independent Task Force Report (New York: Council on Foreign Relations, 1999).

22. Hilal, "PLO Institutions," p. 51. For more on local Palestinians' fears of PLO authoritarianism early on in the Oslo process, see Youssef Ibrahim, "Some Gazans Fearful Arafat Could Choke Off Democracy," *New York Times*, August 7, 1994; Nathan J. Brown, "Palestinian Civil Society in Theory and in Practice," Paper prepared

for the annual meeting of the International Political Science Association, Structure of Government section, Washington (May 2003); Khalil Shikaki, "The Peace Process, National Reconstruction, and the Transition to Democracy in Palestine," *Journal of Palestine Studies* 25, no. 2 (Winter 1996): 5–20.

23. See, for example, Madeline Albright, *Madame Secretary: A Memoir* (New York: Miramax Books, 2003), pp. 289, 296.

24. Brynjar Lia, *Building Arafat's Police: The Politics of International Police Assistance in the Palestinian Territories after the Oslo Agreement* (London: Ithaca Press, 2007), p. 289; Elaine Sciolino, "Violence Thwarts C.I.A. Director's Unusual Diplomatic Role in Middle East Peacemaking," *New York Times*, November 13, 2000; Aaron David Miller, *The Much Too Promised Land* (New York: Bantam Books, 2008), p. 272.

25. Ross, *Missing Peace*, p. 189n.

26. Chris Wake, "An Unaided Peace? The (Unintended) Consequences of International Aid on the Oslo Peace Process," *Conflict, Security & Development* 8, no. 1 (2008): 109; Scott Lasensky and Robert Grace, "Dollars and Diplomacy: Foreign Aid and the Palestinian Question," United States Institute of Peace, August 10, 2006.

27. See Clyde Mark, "Palestinians and Middle East Peace: Issues for the United States," CRS Issue Brief for Congress, March 16, 2005 (https://fas.org/sgp/crs/mideast /IB92052.pdf); see also "S. 1487 (103rd): Middle East Peace Facilitation Act of 1993" (www.govtrack.us/congress/bills/103/s1487/text); Sec. 7040 of P.L. 114-113): "Consolidated Appropriations Act, 2016," December 18, 2015 (www.congress.gov/114/plaws /publ113/PLAW-114publ113.pdf).

28. Wake, "An Unaided Peace?," p. 111.

29. Ibid., pp. 114–15. See also Scott Lasensky, "Underwriting Peace in the Middle East: US Foreign Policy and the Limits of Economic Inducements," *Middle East Review of International Affairs* 6, no. 1 (March 2002): 94–95; Nigel Roberts, "Hard Lessons from Oslo: Foreign Aid and the Mistakes of the 1990s," in *Aid, Diplomacy and Facts on the Ground: The Case of Palestine*, edited by Michael Keating, Anne Le More, and Robert Lowe (London: Chatham House, 2006), p. 19.

30. Wake, "An Unaided Peace?," p. 113.

31. Deborah Sontag, "Quest for Mideast Peace: How and Why It Failed," *New York Times*, July 26, 2001; World Bank, "World Development Indicators," World DataBank (http://databank.worldbank.org/data/reports.aspx?source=2&country=PSE).

32. See Secretariat of the Ad Hoc Liaison Committee (Japan and the World Bank), "Aid Effectiveness in the West Bank and Gaza," June 2000 (http://prrn.mcgill.ca /research/documents/WB_AEreport2000/WorldBank_AidEffectiveness_3.pdf), p. 12. See also Lasensky, "Underwriting Peace in the Middle East," p. 95.

33. Sarah Roy, "De-development Revisited: Palestinian Economy and Society since Oslo," *Journal of Palestine Studies* 28, 3 (Spring 1999): 79.

34. Lasensky, "Underwriting Peace in the Middle East," p. 96.

35. See Manal Jamal, "Democracy Promotion, Civil Society Building, and the Primacy of Politics," *Comparative Political Studies* 45 (January 2012): 3–31.

36. Roberts, "Hard Lessons from Oslo," p. 19.

37. Wake, "An Unaided Peace?," p. 124.

38. Gore quoted in "America and the Middle East," *Proceedings of the Washington Institute on Near East Policy's Soref Symposium*, April 4–5, 1996, p. 13; See also Human Rights Watch, *Human Rights Watch World Report 1997: Events of 1996*, p. 296. See also Human Rights Watch, *Palestinian Self-Rule Areas—Human Rights under the Palestinian Authority*, September 1, 1997, vol. 9, no. 10 (www.refworld.org/docid/3ae6a7d50.html); Melissa Boyle Mahle, "A Political-Security Analysis of the Failed Oslo Process," Middle East Policy Council.

39. Bruce Riedel, interview by author, Washington, September 18, 2013.

40. Miller, *The Much Too Promised Land*, p. 123.

41. "Interview with Dennis Ross," William J. Clinton Presidential History Project, January 12, 2006 (https://millercenter.org/the-presidency/presidential-oral-histories /dennis-ross-oral-history-middle-east-envoy). See also Lamis Andoni, "US Envoy to Try to Salvage Mideast Talks but Both the Palestinians and Israelis Find Fault in US Intervention," *Christian Science Monitor*, July 7, 1993; Elaine Sciolino, "U.S. Plan Focuses on Some Self Rule for Palestinians," *New York Times*, July 1, 1993.

42. See Gad Yaacobi, *Breakthrough: Israel in a Changing World*, p. 57.

43. Edward P. Djerejian, assistant secretary for Near Eastern and South Asian Affairs, *Developments in the Middle East, March 1993*, testimony, Hearing before the Subcommittee on Europe and the Middle East of the Committee on Foreign Affairs, House of Representatives, 103rd Cong., 1st sess., March 9, 1993.

44. Robert H. Pelletreau, assistant secretary of state for Near Eastern Affairs, *Developments in the Middle East, March 1994*, Hearing and Markup of H. Con. Res. 124, testimony before the Subcommittee on Europe and the Middle East of the Committee on Foreign Affairs, House of Representatives, 103rd Cong., 2nd sess., March 1, 1994.

45. J. J. Goldberg, *Jewish Power: Inside the American Jewish Establishment* (Reading, Mass.: Addison-Wesley, 1996), pp. 54–56, 263.

46. Daniel Kurtzer, Scott Lasensky, William Quandt, Steven Spiegel, and Shibley Telhami, *The Peace Puzzle: America's Quest for Arab-Israeli Peace 1989–2011* (Cornell University Press: 2013), p. 116.

47. Clyde R. Mark, "Israel: U.S. Foreign Assistance," CRS Issue Brief for Congress (Washington: Congressional Research Service, April 26, 2005).

48. Miller, *The Much Too Promised Land*, pp. 252, 263.

49. Figures derived from Foundation for Middle East Peace, "Comprehensive Settlement Population, 1972–2011," January 13, 2012 (http://fmep.org/resource/compre hensive-settlement-population-1972-2010/).

50. Ross, *Missing Peace*, p. 329. See also Dennis Ross, *Doomed to Succeed: The U.S.-Israel Relationship from Truman to Obama* (New York: Farrar, Straus & Giroux, 2015), pp. 280–81.

51. See Ross, *Missing Peace*, pp. 332, 335, 337–40; Steve Lee Myers, "Welcoming Arafat, Clinton Rebukes Israel," *New York Times*, March 4, 1997; Paul Lewis, "U.S. Again Vetoes a Move by U.N. Condemning Israel," *New York Times*, March 22, 1997.

52. Ross, *Missing Peace*, pp. 262, 338.

53. Joseph Saba, interview by author, Washington, May 13, 2016.

54. Wake, "An Unaided Peace?," p. 123.

55. Ross, *Missing Peace*, p. 119.

56. William Quandt, interview by author (Skype), June 13, 2013.

57. "Chronology, February–May 1998," *Journal of Palestine Studies* 27, no. 4 (Summer 1998): 181.

58. Albright, *Madam Secretary*, p. 302.

59. Ross, *Missing Peace*, p. 480.

60. Ahmed Qurie, *Beyond Oslo, the Struggle for Palestine: Inside the Middle East Peace Process from Rabin's Death to Camp David* (New York: I. B. Tauris, 2008), p. 72.

61. Qurie, *Beyond Oslo*, p. 72.

62. William J. Clinton, "Remarks to the Palestine National Council and Other Palestinian Organizations in Gaza City," *Public Papers of the Presidents of the United States: William J. Clinton, 1998*, p. 2176. See also Ross, *Missing Peace*, pp. 437–38, 485; Miller, *The Much Too Promised Land*, p. 310; see also Qurie, *Beyond Oslo*, pp. 74–75.

63. Kurtzer and others, *Peace Puzzle*, p. 119.

64. Ibid., pp. 108, 132. See also William Quandt, "Skewed Perceptions: Yasir Arafat in the Eyes of American Officials, 1969–2004," in *Scripting Middle East Leaders: The Impact of Leadership Perceptions on U.S. and UK Foreign Policy*, edited by Sir Lawrence Freedman and Jeffrey Michaels (New York: Bloomsbury Academic, 2013), p. 110; Miller, *The Much Too Promised Land*, pp. 294, 307; Robert Malley and Hussein Agha, "Camp David: The Tragedy of Errors," *New York Review of Books*, August 9, 2001; David Hirst, "Don't Blame Arafat," *The Guardian*, July 16, 2004.

65. See Jeremy Pressman, "Visions in Collision: What Happened at Camp David and Taba?" *International Security* 28, no. 2 (Fall 2003): 5–43; Martin S. Indyk, "Are Yasser Arafat and the Palestinian Authority Credible Partners for Peace?," testimony before the U.S. House Armed Services Committee, Special Oversight Panel on Terrorism, 107th Cong., 2nd sess., June 6, 2002, pp. 14–15.

66. Deborah Sontag, "And Yet So Far: A Special Report; Quest for Mideast Peace: How and Why It Failed," *New York Times*, July 26, 2001, was one of the first detailed accounts of the Camp David summit to be published. See also Robert Malley and Hussein Agha, "Camp David: The Tragedy of Errors," *New York Review of Books*, August 9, 2001; Robert Malley and Hussein Agha, "Camp David and After: An Exchange (2. A Reply to Ehud Barak)," *New York Review of Books*, June 13, 2002; Charles Enderlin, *Shattered Dreams: The Failure of the Peace Process in the Middle East, 1995–2002* (New York: Other Press, 2003); Clayton E. Swisher, *The Truth about Camp David: The Untold Story about the Collapse of the Middle East Peace Process* (New York: Nation Books, 2004); Miller, *The Much Too Promised Land*, pp. 288–89. See also Pressman, "Visions in Collision," p. 28.

67. Kurtzer and others, *Peace Puzzle*, p. 108.

68. Ibid., p. 133.

69. Robert Malley and Hussein Agha, "Camp David: The Tragedy of Errors," *New York Review of Books*, August 9, 2001.

70. Miller, *The Much Too Promised Land*, pp. 304, 243–04.

71. Swisher, *The Truth about Camp David*, p. 295.

72. See Kurtzer and others, *Peace Puzzle*, p. 137; Riedel interview, September 18, 2013.

73. See, for example, Palestinian Center for Policy and Survey Research, "Palestinian Public Opinion Poll No (1): Camp David Summit, Chances for Reconciliation and Lasting Peace, Violence and Confrontations, Hierarchies of Priorities, and Domestic Politics," July 27–29, 2000 (www.pcpsr.org/en/node/254).

74. "Deadlock and Danger: Camp David's Failure Will Be Exploited," *The Guardian*, July 25, 2000; See also "URGENT—Hamas Calls on Palestinian Delegation to Pull Out from Summit," Agence France Presse, July 27, 2000; "Hundreds of Islamic Militants Demonstrate in West Bank against Camp David," Agence France Presse, July 21, 2000; David Zev Harris, "Hamas: Militant Israeli Generals Must Be Threatened," *Jerusalem Post*, July 27, 2000; "Hamas Supports Arafat in Rare Official Television Interview," Agence France Presse, July 26, 2000.

75. Pressman, "Visions in Collision," p. 27.

76. See U.S. Department of State, "Sharm El-Sheikh Fact-Finding Committee Report," April 30, 2001 (https://2001-2009.state.gov/p/nea/rls/rpt/3060.htm).

77. See Amnesty International, *Broken Lives—A Year of Intifada* (London: Amnesty International Publications, 2001), p. 14. See also B'Tselem, "Illusions of Restraint: Human Rights Violations during the Events in the Occupied Territories, 29 September–2 December 2000," December 2000; Jeremy Pressman, "The Second Intifada: Background and Causes of the Israeli-Palestinian Conflict," *Journal of Conflict Studies* 23, no. 2 (Fall 2003): 114–41.

78. Cited in "Documents and Source Material," *Journal of Palestine Studies* 30, no. 2 (2001): 158. See also U.S. Department of State, "Secretary of State Madeleine K. Albright, Interview on CNN's Late Edition, 10/8/2000 (transcript)"; Jane Perlez, "After Gaza Rocket Attack, State Dept. Gives Israel Stern Warning," *New York Times*, November 21, 2000.

79. White House, "Press Briefing by Jake Siewert," January 3, 2001. See also "Transcript of Clinton's Remarks to the Israel Policy Forum Gala," January 8, 2001 (http://edition.cnn.com/2001/WORLD/meast/01/08/clinton.transcript/).

80. Martin Indyk, *Innocent Abroad: An Intimate Account of American Peace Diplomacy in the Middle East* (New York: Simon & Schuster, 2009), p. 370.

81. Pressman, "Visions in Collision," p. 15.

82. Presidential Oral Histories, Bill Clinton Presidency, "Samuel R. Berger Oral History, Deputy Assistant to the President for National Security Affairs; National Security Advisor," March 24–25, 2005; see also Ross, *Doomed to Succeed*, p. 689.

83. Of the 43 Israelis killed, 19 were Israeli soldiers or police forces, while roughly half of the nearly 300 Palestinians killed had had no part in the violence. See B'Tselem, "Fatalities before Operation 'Cast Lead.'"

84. Senior PLO official, interview by author, Ramallah, August 23, 2013.

85. Malley and Agha, "Camp David."

86. Senior Palestinian official, interview by author (name, location, and date withheld to protect source).

87. Indyk, *Innocent Abroad*, pp. 376, 296; Albright, *Madame Secretary*, pp. 482, 483, 494; Presidential Oral Histories, Bill Clinton Presidency, "Samuel R. Berger Oral History"; see also Ross, *Missing Peace*, pp. 40, 265, 338.

88. Riedel interview, September 18, 2013.

89. Presidential Oral Histories, Bill Clinton Presidency, "Samuel R. Berger Oral History"; see also Albright, *Madame Secretary*, p. 483.

90. Quoted in Indyk, *Innocent Abroad*, p. 14.

Chapter 6

1. Elliott Abrams, *Tested by Zion* (Cambridge: Cambridge University Press, 2013), p. 35.

2. See United Nations, *Report of the Secretary-General Prepared Pursuant to General Assembly Resolution ES-10/10 (Report on Jenin)(A/ES-10/186)*, August 1, 2002; Brian Whitaker, "UN Report Details West Bank Wreckage," *The Guardian*, August 2, 2002; Human Rights Watch, *Jenin: IDF Military Operations*, report, May 2002.

3. George W. Bush, *Decision Points* (New York: Crown, 2010), p. 399.

4. Daniel C. Kurtzer, Scott B. Lasensky, William B. Quandt, Steven L. Spiegel, Shibley Z. Telhami, *The Peace Puzzle: America's Quest for Arab-Israeli Peace, 1989–2011* (Cornell University Press, 2013), p. 155.

5. Condoleezza Rice, *No Higher Honor: A Memoir of My Years in Washington* (New York: Crown, 2011), p. 55.

6. Daniel E. Zoughbie, *Indecision Points: George W. Bush and the Israeli-Palestinian Conflict* (2014), pp. 144–47.

7. See B'Tselem—The Israeli Information Center for Human Rights in the Occupied Territories (henceforth cited as B'Tselem), "Fatalities before Operation 'Cast Lead'" (www.btselem.org/statistics/fatalities/before-cast-lead/by-date-of-event).

8. Bob Woodward, *State of Denial: Bush at War, Part III* (New York: Simon & Schuster, 2007), p. 76.

9. Ibid.

10. Brian Whitaker, "Sharon Likens Arafat to Bin Laden," *The Guardian*, September 14, 2001; Zoughbie, *Indecision Points*, p. 12.

11. "U.S. President Bush's Speech to United Nations," November 10, 200; see also Woodward, *State of Denial*, p. 76; Zoughbie, *Indecision Points*, p. 23.

12. Abrams, *Tested by Zion*, p. 16. See also Dennis Ross, *Doomed to Succeed: The U.S.-Israel Relationship from Truman to Obama* (New York: Farrar, Straus & Giroux, 2015), p. 306.

13. Stephen Hadley, interview by author, Washington, July 2010.

14. See "State Dept. Blasts Israel on Orient House," Jewish Telegraphic Agency, August 14, 2001.

15. Cheryl A. Rubenberg, *The Palestinians: In Search of a Just Peace* (Boulder, Colo.: Lynne Rienner, 2003), pp. 350–53; Palestinian NGO Emergency Initiative in Jerusa-

lem, *Report on the Destruction to Palestinian Governmental Institutions in Ramallah Caused by IDF Forces Between March 29 and April 21, 2002 (updated Report April 22)*; see also Uri Avnery, "The Real Aim," *Gush Shalom*, April 27, 2002 (http://zope.gush-shalom .org/home/en/channels/avnery/archives_article192); Amira Hass, "Operation Destroy the Data," *Haaretz*, April 24, 2002.

16. Justin Huggler, "Israeli Siege of Arafat 'Is Killing Peace Hope,'" *The Independent*, September 28, 2002.

17. White House, "President to Send Secretary Powell to Middle East," press release, April 4, 2002.

18. Abrams, *Tested by Zion*, p. 33.

19. Rice, *No Higher Honor*, p. 141.

20. Bush, *Decision Points*, p. 400.

21. Rice, *No Higher Honor*, p. 137.

22. "Terrorism and Nationalism," *Washington Post*, editorial, April 24, 2002.

23. White House, "President Bush Calls for New Palestinian Leadership," press release, June 24, 2002.

24. Zoughbie, *Indecision Points*, p. 28.

25. Abrams, *Tested by Zion*, p. 151.

26. See James Bennet, "Sharon Is Sorry Israel Didn't Kill Arafat in the 80's," *New York Times*, February 1, 2002. See also Rice, *No Higher Honor*, p. 142.

27. U.S. Department of State, "U.S. Criticizes Israeli Actions in Ramallah," September 23, 2002 (https://2001-2009.state.gov/p/nea/rls/rm/13629.htm).

28. Flynt Leverett, quoted in Kurtzer and others, *Peace Puzzle*, p. 306n107. See also Ross, *Doomed to Succeed*, p. 315; "U.S. Criticizes Israeli Actions in Ramallah" (https://2001-2009.state.gov/p/nea/rls/rm/13629.htm).

29. Senior Palestinian official, interview by author (name, location, and date withheld to protect source).

30. Abrams, *Tested by Zion*, pp. 318, 42, 15, 16, 60.

31. See preamble of official text, United Nations, "A Performance-Based Road Map to a Permanent Two-State Solution to the Israeli-Palestinian Conflict."

32. See, for example, Chris McGreal, "Sharon Derides EU Peace Efforts," *The Guardian*, January 20, 2003; "Sharon Gets Tough as Elections Near," Associated Press, January 20, 2003.

33. Steven R. Weisman, "U.S. Joins Partners on Plan for Mideast, but Not Timing," *New York Times*, December 21, 2002.

34. Abrams, *Tested by Zion*, p. 84.

35. See Israel Ministry of Foreign Affairs, "Letter from Dov Weissglass, Chief of the PM's Bureau, to National Security Adviser, Dr. Condoleezza Rice," April 18, 2004 (www.mfa.gov.il/MFA/Peace+Process/Reference+Documents/Letter+Weissglas -Rice+18-Apr-2004.htm); Israel Ministry of Foreign Affairs, "Israel's Response to the Roadmap, As Published on the Knesset Website," May 25, 2003 (www.mfa.gov.il/MFA /Peace+Process/Reference+Documents/Israel+Response+to+the+Roadmap+25-May -2003.htm).

36. John Ward Anderson, "Palestinians Wary of Peace Plan Shift; Some Call New Approach One-Sided," *Washington Post*, July 24, 2003.

37. Daniel Kurtzer to Palestinian negotiators, Tel Aviv, April 29, 2004, and Elliot Abrams to Palestinian negotiators, Washington, September 29, 2004 (author's notes, in author's files).

38. See Yehezkel Lein and Alon Cohen-Lifshitz, "Under the Guise of Security: Routing the Separation Barrier to Enable the Expansion of Israeli Settlements in the West Bank," report (Jerusalem: B'Tselem, December 2005) (www.btselem.org /download/200512_under_the_guise_of_security_eng.pdf). See also United Nations, *The Impact of Israel's Separation Barrier on Affected West Bank Communities; Report of the Mission to the Humanitarian and Emergency Policy Group (HEPG) of the Local Aid Coordination Committee (LACC)*, May 2003, pp. ii–iii (https://unispal.un.org/DPA/DPR /unispal.nsf/5ba47a5c6cef541b802563e000493b8c/084e7278b1a3491385256d1d0065b c42/$FILE/Wallreport.pdf).

39. See International Court of Justice, "Legal Consequences of the Construction of a Wall in the Occupied Palestinian Territory" (https://www.icj-cij.org/en/case/131).

40. See Israel Ministry of Foreign Affairs, "Address by PM Ariel Sharon, at the Fourth Herzliya Conference, Dec 18-2003" (www.mfa.gov.il/mfa/pressroom/2003 /pages/address%20by%20pm%20ariel%20sharon%20at%20the%20fourth%20 herzliya.aspx); Aluf Benn, "PM Says His 'Hands Are Clean' of Allegations He Took Bribes," *Haaretz*, April 6, 2004, quoted in Anne Le More "Killing with Kindness: Funding the Demise of a Palestinian State," *International Affairs* 81 (2005): 981–99.

41. Rice, *No Higher Honor*, p. 281.

42. White House, "Statement on the Israeli Cabinet Decision Approving the Prime Minister's Disengagement Plan," press release, June 6, 2004.

43. Amos Harel, "Shin Bet: Palestinian Truce Main Cause for Reduced Terror," *Haaretz*, January 2, 2006.

44. See Palestinian Center for Policy and Survey Research, "Palestinian Public Opinion Poll No (14)," December 1–5, 2004 (www.pcpsr.org/en/node/241); Palestinian Center for Policy and Survey Research, "Special Poll—Pre Elections—30 and 31 December 2004" (www.pcpsr.org/en/node/471).

45. World Bank, "Disengagement, the Palestinian Economy and the Settlements" (Washington: World Bank, June 23, 2004), pp. 2–3.

46. Mohammed Samhouri, "Gaza Economic Predicament One Year after Disengagement: What Went Wrong?" Middle East Brief (Brandeis University, Crown Center for Middle East Studies: November 2006).

47. See World Bank, "Stagnation or Revival? Israeli Disengagement and Palestinian Economic Prospects: Overview" (Washington: World Bank, December 1, 2004), p. 25; World Bank, "Disengagement, the Palestinian Economy and the Settlements."

48. Kurtzer and others, *Peace Puzzle*, p. 196.

49. Howard Sumka (former USAID mission director), interview by author, Washington, June 20, 2013.

50. Abrams, *Tested by Zion*, p. 124. See White House, "President Welcomes Palestinian President Abbas to the White House," press release, May 26, 2005.

51. Kurtzer and others, p. 195.

52. Sumka interview, June 20, 2013.

53. Samhouri, "Gaza Economic Predicament One Year after Disengagement"; See also World Bank, *West Bank and Gaza, Country Economic Memorandum: Growth in West Bank and Gaza: Opportunities and Constraints*, report no. 36320 WBG, vol. 1, Main Volume (Washington: World Bank, September 2006).

54. Bush, *Decision Points*, p. 406–07.

55. United Nations, "Quartet Statement, London, 30 January 2006."

56. Akiva Eldar, "Quartet to Hold Key Talks on fate of its Mideast Peacemaking Role," *Haaretz*, May 3, 2006.

57. Adel Zaanoun, "OPT: Senior Palestinian Official Urges Hamas to Follow Roadmap," Relief Web, January 31, 2006 (https://reliefweb.int/report/israel/opt-senior -palestinian-official-urges-hamas-follow-roadmap).

58. Nathan Thrall, *The Only Language They Understand: Forcing Compromise in Israel and Palestine* (New York: Metropolitan Books, 2017), p. 116.

59. International Monetary Fund and World Bank, "West Bank and Gaza Economic Developments in 2006—A First Assessment," March 2007 (link to download file: www.imf.org/external/np/wbg/2007/eng/032607ed.pdf); World Bank, "The Impending Palestinian Fiscal Crisis, Potential Remedies" (Washington: May 7, 2006).

60. Álvaro de Soto, "End of Mission Report," May 2007, p. 15 (http://image .guardian.co.uk/sys-files/Guardian/documents/2007/06/12/DeSotoReport.pdf).

61. David Rose, "Gaza Bombshell," *Vanity Fair*, April 2008.

62. See "Despite Hamas Win, Palestinians Want Peace with Israel," Agence France Presse, January 30, 2006.

63. Scott Wilson and Glenn Kessler, "U.S. Funds Enter Fray in Palestinian Elections," *Washington Post*, January 22, 2006.

64. For examples of "internal closures," see "OPT: Additional West Bank Internal Closures," October 18, 2005 (https://reliefweb.int/report/occupied-palestinian -territory/opt-additional-west-bank-internal-closures).

65. See Sherifa Zuhur, "Hamas and Israel: Conflicting Strategies of Group-Based Politics" (Strategic Studies Institute: December 2008); Khaled Hroub, "A 'New Hamas' through Its New Documents," *Journal of Palestine Studies* 35, no. 4 (Summer 2006): 6–27; Khaled Hroub, *Hamas: A Beginner's Guide*, 2nd ed. (New York: Pluto Press, 2010), pp. 29, 139–40, 142–43.

66. See, for instance, "Proposal for Creating Suitable Conditions for Ending the Conflict," *Palestine-Israel Journal* 13, no. 4 (2007).

67. de Soto, "End of Mission Report," p. 46.

68. Rose, "Gaza Bombshell."

69. Rice, *No Higher Honor*, pp. 551–52.

70. Rose, "Gaza Bombshell." See also International Crisis Group, "After Gaza," Report 68, August 2, 2007.

71. Rose, "Gaza Bombshell."

72. Sourani and Abrams quoted in Thrall, *Only Language They Understand*, p. 117.

73. Rice, *No Higher Honor*, p. 601.

74. See Le More, "Killing with Kindness, p. 995; Khaled Elgindy, "The Middle East Quartet: A Post-Mortem," Analysis Paper no. 25 (Brookings Institution, Saban Center for Middle East Policy at Brookings, February 2012).

75. Oxfam GB et al., "The Gaza Strip: A Humanitarian Implosion," research report, March 1, 2008 (the report was produced by a coalition of international aid organizations); World Food Programme, "80% of Palestinians Dependent on WFP Aid," January 9, 2009 (www.wfp.org/content/80-palestinians-dependent-wfp-aid); Rose, "Gaza Bombshell."

76. Sumka interview, June 20, 2013.

77. See Ian Black, "Palestinian PM Fayyad Says West Bank Settlement Must End for Peace," *The Guardian*, December 15, 2008 (www.theguardian.com/world/2008/dec /15/fayyad-west-bank-israel); Permanent Observer Mission of Palestine to the United Nations, "Statement by Mr. H.E. Mahmoud Abbas, President of the State of Palestine, Chairman of the Executive Committee of the Palestinian Liberation Organization, President of the Palestinian National Authority before the United Nations General Assembly Sixty-sixth Session," September 23, 2011.

78. Condoleezza Rice, speech at American Task Force on Palestine inaugural gala, October 11, 2006.

79. Omer Zenany, "The Annapolis Process (2007–2008): Negotiation and Its Discontents" (Tel Aviv University, Tami Steinmetz Center for Peace Research, Ramat Aviv and Molad, 2015).

80. Grant Rumley and Amir Tibon, *The Last Palestinian: The Rise and Reign of Mahmoud Abbas* (Amherst, N.Y.: Prometheus Books, 2017), p. 147.

81. Ahmed Qurei, *The Full Palestinian Story of Negotiations, From Oslo to Annapolis, (4) Annapolis Negotiations, 2007–2008* (in Arabic) (Beirut: Institute for Palestine Studies, 2014), p. 43.

82. Ahmed Qurei, interview by author, Abu Dis (West Bank), May 12, 2014.

83. Hanan Ashrawi, correspondence with author (email), August 24, 2018.

84. Hanan Ashrawi, interview by author, Ramallah, August 13, 2013.

85. John Darby and Roger MacGinty, *The Management of Peace Processes* (New York: St. Martin's Press, 2000), p. 254.

Chapter 7

1. United Nations Human Rights Council, "Human Rights in Palestine and other Occupied Arab Territories: Report of the United Nations Fact Finding Mission on the Gaza Conflict," United Nations and the Rule of Law (webpage), September 15, 2009.

2. "President Obama Delivers Remarks to State Department Employees," *Washington Post*, January 22, 2009.

3. On Har Homa, see *Wikipedia*, s.v. "Har Homa." For additional demographic information see Jerusalem Municipality and Jerusalem Institute for Israel Studies, *Sta-*

tistical Yearbook of Jerusalem for the years 2003 to 2010 (http://en.jerusaleminstitute.org
.il/?cmd=statistic.582), Table III/16, "Population of Jerusalem, by Age, Quarter, Sub-
Quarter, and Statistical Area"; on public versus private construction, see Table X/11,
"Dwellings Starts and Completed in Jerusalem, by Number of Dwellings, Area of
Building and Sub-Quarter."

4. Fred Attewill, "Bush Calls on Israel to End Occupation of Palestinian Land,"
The Guardian, January 10, 2008.

5. See "Obama Slams Bush, Former Pres. Clinton's Mideast Diplomacy," Reuters,
April 21, 2008.

6. For the full text of the letter, see Medea Benjamin, "Hamas Delivers Peace Letter to President Obama," Common Dreams, June 4, 2009.

7. U.S. Department of State, "Press Availability with Egyptian Foreign Minister
Ahmed Ali Aboul Gheit," May 27, 2009; see also Josh Ruebner, *Shattered Hopes* (London: Verso, 2013), pp. 64–65.

8. Dennis Ross, *Doomed to Succeed: The U.S.-Israel Relationship from Truman to
Obama* (New York: Farrar, Straus & Giroux, 2015), p. 372. U.S. Department of State,
"Remarks with Israeli Foreign Minister Avigdor Lieberman," June 17, 2009; Herb Kei-
non, "Released Clinton E-mail Reignites Question Whether Obama Reneged on
Bush Settlement Commitments," *Jerusalem Post*, July 7, 2015. See also Daniel Kurtzer,
"The Facts on Israel's Settlements," *Washington Post*, June 14, 2009.

9. White House, "Remarks by the President at the Opening Plenary Session of the
Nuclear Security Summit," April 13, 2010.

10. See, for example, General David H. Petraeus, testimony before the Senate
Armed Services Committee, on the Posture of U.S. Central Command, March 16, 2010
(www.c-span.org/video/?292551-1/central-command-special-operations-budget).

11. Scott Wilson, "Obama Searches for Middle East Peace," *Washington Post*,
July 14, 2012.

12. See George Mitchell, *Charlie Rose Show*, January 6, 2010.

13. Ruebner, *Shattered Hopes*, pp. 74–75.

14. Palestine Papers, "Meeting Minutes, Saeb Erekat and David Hale, September 17, 2009, 9:00am, NAD Jericho" (www.jewishvirtuallibrary.org/jsource/arabs
/PalPaper091709.pdf).

15. Wilson, "Obama Searches for Middle East Peace."

16. Palestine Papers, "Comments on US Non-Paper," January 14, 2010 (http://
transparency.aljazeera.net/files/5009.PDF); Palestine Papers, "Meeting Summary:
Dr. Saeb Erekat - Senator George Mitchell, State Department, October 1 2009" (http://
transparency.aljazeera.net/files/4842.PDF).

17. The full text of "Human Rights in Palestine and Other Occupied Territories; Report of the United Nations Fact Finding Mission on the Gaza Conflict," is
available at www2.ohchr.org/english/bodies/hrcouncil/docs/12session/A-HRC-12
-48.pdf.

18. "Goldstone Report: Israel and Palestinians Respond to UN," *BBC News*, January 29, 2010.

19. Amira Haas, "PA Move to Thwart Goldstone Gaza Report Shocks Palestinian Public," *Haaretz*, October 4, 2009.

20. "Goldstone Fall-out Plagues Abbas," *BBC News*, October 9, 2009.

21. "PA Blamed for Goldstone Vote Delay," *NewsGrid*, Al Jazeera, October 6, 2009.

22. Paul Richter, "Hillary Rodham Clinton's Harsh Words Stun Israel," *Los Angeles Times*, March 14, 2010; Laura Rozen, "What Biden Told Netanyahu behind Closed Doors: 'This Is Starting to Get Dangerous for Us,'" *Politico*, March 10, 2010.

23. Quoted in Tovah Lazaroff, "The Window for a Negotiated Peace Ends in September," *Jerusalem Post*, March 23, 2011.

24. See, for example, M.S., "Here Comes Your Non-violent Resistance," *The Economist*, May 17, 2011. See also Jesse Rosenfeld and Joseph Dana, "A Palestinian Revolt in the Making?" *The Nation*, May 26, 2011; Samuel Sockol and Joel Greenberg, "Israel Troops, Palestinians Clash at Golan Heights Frontier," *Washington Post*, June 5, 2011. For a Palestinian perspective on the implications of a "Palestinian Spring" for the PLO and the Palestinian national movement, see Jamil Hilal, "Palestinian Answers in the Arab Spring," Al-Shabaka Policy Brief, May 6, 2011 (http:\\al-shabaka.org\\policy-brief\\politics\\palestinian-answers-arab-spring). See also Adam Shatz, "Is Palestine Next?" *London Review of Books*, July 14, 2011, 8–14.

25. Senior Palestinian official, interview by author, Ramallah, December 19, 2010.

26. Saeb Erekat, "Change in the Arab World and Its Impact on the USA, the West, Palestine and Israel" (in Arabic), *Al-Dirasat*, 2012 (Qatar), p. 45.

27. See Joel Greenberg, "Fatah-Hamas Pact Called New Chance for Peace," *Washington Post*, May 9, 2011.

28. White House, "Remarks by the President on the Middle East and North Africa," press release, May 19, 2011.

29. U.S. Department of State, "Remarks at the Saban Center for Middle East Policy 2012 Saban Forum Opening Gala Dinner," November 30, 2012 (https://2009-2017.state.gov/secretary/20092013clinton/rm/2012/11/201343.htm).

30. U.S. Department of State, Victoria Nuland, "Daily Press Briefing," February 9, 2012.

31. Wilson, "Obama Searches for Middle East Peace."

32. Ruebner, *Shattered Hopes*, pp. 117–19. See also Ross, *Doomed to Succeed*, p. 382.

33. See White House, "President Welcomes Palestinian President Abbas to the White House," press release, May 26, 2005; Michael O'Brien, "Obama 'Disrespected' Israel, Threw It 'under the Bus,' Says Romney," *The Hill*, May 19, 2011.

34. See Palestinian Center for Policy and Survey Research, Palestinian Public Opinion Poll No (39), March 17–19, 2011; ibid., Palestinian Public Opinion Poll No (41), September 15–17, 2011.

35. See, for example, "West Bank Cheers Mahmoud Abbas after UN vote," *BBC News*, December 2, 2012; "West Bank Hails Return of Abbas after UN Vote," *NewsGrid*, Al Jazeera, December 3, 2012; Judith Sudilovsky, "Palestinians Celebrate UN Vote," CNEWA (Catholic Near East Welfare Association), December 5, 2012. See Jerusalem Media and Communication Centre, "Poll No. 78, Dec. 2012—Gaza, Resis-

tance and the UN Bid, December 20, 2012," December 20, 2012 (www.jmcc.org /Documentsandmaps.aspx?id=858).

36. Mahmoud Abbas, "The Long Overdue Palestinian State," *New York Times*, May 16, 2011, p. A27. On the rationale behind the Palestinian UN strategy, see Dan Ephron, "The Wrath of Abbas," interview, *Newsweek*, April 24, 2011. See also Khaled Elgindy, "Palestine Goes to the UN: Understanding the New Statehood Strategy," *Foreign Affairs*, September–October 2011, 102–13.

37. Paddy Smyth, "A 'Tsunami' That Would Change Little on Ground," *Irish Times*, September 3, 2011.

38. Ethan Bronner, "Israel's West Bank General Warns against Radicals," *New York Times*, October 11, 2011. See also David Makovsky, testimony, "Promoting Peace? Reexamining U.S. Aid to the Palestinian Authority, Part II," Hearing Before the Committee on Foreign Affairs, House of Representatives, 112th Cong., 1st Sess., September 14, 2011, pp. 32, 34 (www.gpo.gov/fdsys/pkg/CHRG-112hhrg68296/pdf /CHRG-112hhrg68296.pdf).

39. See "US to Oppose Palestinian Recognition at UN," *World Affairs*, Voice of America, July 25, 2011; Josh Rogin, "Wendy Sherman Promises U.S. Veto of Palestinian Statehood at U.N.," *Foreign Policy*, September 7, 2011.

40. Paolo Verzone, "Palestinian Leader Mahmoud Abbas's Frustration with Obama," *Newsweek*, April 24, 2011; Ruebner, *Shattered Hopes*, p. 113; See Lazar Berman, "Leaked Cables Show CIA Attempts to Contact Hamas," *Times of Israel*, February 24, 2015.

41. Josh Rogin, "Wendy Sherman Promises U.S. Veto of Palestinian Statehood at U.N.," *Foreign Policy*, September 7, 2011.

42. See "UNESCO Votes to Admit Palestine as Full Member," *UN News*, October 31, 2011; Barak Ravid, "Israel Drops Opposition to Renewal of U.S. Funding to UNESCO at Kerry's Behest," *Haaretz*, December 9, 2015.

43. United Nations, Human Rights Council, *Report of the United Nations High Commissioner for Human Rights on the Implementation of Human Rights Council Resolutions S-9/1 and S-12/1*, advance version, March 6, 2013, pp. 4, 12.

44. Robert M. Danin, "Ending Gaza's Isolation," Policy Innovation Memorandum No. 35 (New York: Council on Foreign Relations, July 16, 2013).

45. See Israel Ministry of Foreign Affairs, "Security Cabinet Declares Gaza Hostile Territory," September 19, 2007.

46. United Nations, Office for the Coordination of Humanitarian Affairs, "1967–2017: 50 Years of Occupation," *Monthly Humanitarian Bulletin*, May–June 2017 (special edition).

47. World Food Programme, "80% of Palestinians Dependent on WFP Aid," January 9, 2009 (www.wfp.org/content/80-palestinians-dependent-wfp-aid). According to a report by the UN's Office for the Coordination of Humanitarian Affairs, "More than 70% of Gaza's population receives some form of international aid, the bulk of which is food assistance," and 47 percent of households are moderately or severely food insecure. See United Nations, Office for the Coordination of Humani-

tarian Affairs, *The Gaza Strip: The Humanitarian Impact of the Blockade*, November 14, 2016, pp. 1–2.

Chapter 8

1. Epigraph: Palestinian official quoted in Matthew Kalman, "'Useless, Useless, Useless': The Palestinian Verdict on Tony Blair's Job," *The Independent*, December 16, 2012.

2. World Bank, "Building the Palestinian State: Sustaining Growth, Institutions, and Service Delivery," Economic Monitoring Report to the Ad Hoc Liaison Committee, April 13, 2011, p. 5.

3. "Palestinians Shutter Shops, Block Roads with Burning Tires to Protest Spiraling Prices," Associated Press, September 10, 2012.

4. For more on the problematic nature of the Paris Protocol and the challenges posed by the conditions in which it was implemented, see Mohammed Samhouri, "Revisiting the Paris Protocol: Israeli-Palestinian Economic Relations, 1994–2014," *Middle East Journal* 70, no. 4 (Autumn 2016): 579–607.

5. Thomas L. Friedman, "Green Shoots in Palestine," *New York Times*, August 4, 2009.

6. Akiva Eldar, "A Day in the Life of the Palestinian Ben-Gurion," *Haaretz*, February 11, 2010.

7. Palestinian National Authority, "Palestine: Ending the Occupation, Establishing the State, Program of the Thirteenth Government, August 2009," p. 8.

8. Salam Fayyad, interview by author, Ramallah, August 14, 2013.

9. Nathan J. Brown, "Are Palestinians Building a State?" (Washington: Carnegie Endowment for International Peace, June 2010), p. 2.

10. See Palestinian National Authority, Ministry of Finance, Monthly Reports for 2013—December Report, "Table 6-B: Expenditures by PA organizations (Commitment Basis), Jan–Dec 2013 (thousand NIS)," "Grand Total" and total expenditure for "Ministry of Interior and National Security," "Ministry of Health," "Ministry of Education," and "Ministry of Higher Education" (www.pmof.ps/documents/10180/268204/Dec.2013.Eng.updated.pdf/bd916f97-e54a-46eb-a35f-fd77a500e3bd).

11. United Nations, Office for the Coordination of Humanitarian Affairs, personal communication from OCHA researcher.

12. World Bank, "Fiscal Challenges and Long Term Economic Costs," Economic Monitoring Report to the Ad Hoc Liaison Committee (Washington: World Bank, March 19, 2013). See also Samhouri, "Revisiting the Paris Protocol; World Bank Group, *West Bank and Gaza Investment Climate: Fragmentation and Uncertainty*, report no. AUS2122 (Washington: April 2014).

13. World Bank, "Fiscal Challenges and Long Term Economic Costs."

14. Brown, "Are Palestinians Building a State?"

15. For more on the limitations of state building under occupation, see Raja Khalidi and Sobhi Samour, "Neoliberalism as Liberation: The Statehood Program and the Remaking of the Palestinian National Movement," *Journal of Palestine Studies* 40

(Winter 2011): 6–25. See also Yezid Sayegh, "Policing the People, Building the State: Authoritarian Transformation in the West Bank and Gaza," Carnegie Paper (Washington: Carnegie Endowment for International Peace, February 2011); Brown, "Are Palestinians Building a State?"

16. Howard Sumka (former USAID mission director), interview by author, Washington, June 20, 2013.

17. Ibrahim Shikaki and Joanna Springer, "Building a Failed State: Palestine's Governance and Economy Delinked," Al-Shabaka Policy Brief (New York: Al-Shabaka, Palestinian Policy Network, April 21, 2015).

18. *Securing U.S. Interests Abroad: The FY 2014 Foreign Affairs Budget*, Hearing before the Committee on Foreign Affairs, House of Representatives, 113th Cong., 1st sess., April 17, 2013 (Government Printing Office, 2013).

19. Ben Birnbaum and Amir Tibon, "The Explosive, Inside Story of How John Kerry Built an Israel-Palestine Peace Plan—and Watched It Crumble," *New Republic*, July 20, 2014.

20. U.S. Department of State, "Initiative for the Palestinian Economy," Remarks by Anne W. Patterson, Assistant Secretary for Near Eastern and North African Affairs, March 8, 2014.

21. See Khaled Abu Aker and Jodi Rudoren, "Palestinians Call Kerry's Formula for Talks Insufficient," *New York Times*, July 18, 2013.

22. Jodi Rudoren and Isabel Kershner, "Arc of a Failed Deal: How Nine Months of Mideast Talks Ended in Disarray," *New York Times*, April 28, 2014.

23. Martin Indyk, interview by author, Washington, August 26, 2016.

24. See Patrick Martin, "Leaked Details Show Modest Goals for Kerry's Mideast Peace Plan," *Globe and Mail*, February 12, 2014.

25. Aspen Institute, "In Conversation with US Special Envoy for Israeli-Palestinian Negotiations," Aspen Ideas Festival, July 2, 2014. See also Geoffrey Aronson, "Allen Security Plan Stuck in Start," *Al Monitor*, December 12, 2013; Michael Shmulovich, "Netanyahu Won't Back Down on Demand That IDF Stay in Jordan Valley," *Times of Israel*, February 8, 2014.

26. "Netanyahu: Root of Palestinian Conflict Is Not Territory," *Daily Monitor*, May 2, 2013. See also Jodi Rudoren, "Sticking Point in Peace Talks: Recognition of a Jewish State," *New York Times*, January 1, 2014; Tova Dvorin, "Peace Deal 'Moving Further Away,' Says Netanyahu," Israel National News, March 11, 2014. See "Israel's Jewish Nation-State Bill: A primer," *Haaretz*, November 25, 2014; Jonathan Lis, "Netanyahu Tells Knesset: I'm Determined to Pass Jewish Nation-State Bill," *Haaretz*, November 26, 2014; Stuart Winer, "'Jewish State' Bill Faces Harsh Criticism in and out of Coalition," *Times of Israel*, November 23, 2014. See also Joe Braunold, "What Is a Jewish State," *Haaretz*, March 1, 2012.

27. See Diana Buttu, "Behind Israel's Demand for Recognition as a Jewish State: Chronicles of a Death Foretold: The Kerry Negotiations," *Journal of Palestine Studies* 43, no. 3 (Spring 2014): n2.

28. Indyk, author interview. See also Rudoren, "Sticking Point in Peace Talks."

29. Ahmad S. Khalidi, "Why Palestinians Can't Recognize the Jewish State," in *On the Recognition of the "Jewish State,"* edited by Honaida Ghanim (Ramallah, Palestine: Madar-Palestinian Forum for Israeli Studies, 1987), p. 62 (www.academia.edu /19594809/On_the_Recognition_of_a_Jewish_State). See also Buttu, "Behind Israel's Demand for Recognition as a Jewish State."

30. Khalidi, "Why Palestinians Can't Recognize the Jewish State," p. 62.

31. Indyk, author interview; See also TOI staff, "Abbas 'Exploded with Rage' at Kerry over 'Insane' Framework Proposals," *Times of Israel*, February 27, 2014.

32. Birnbaum and Tibon, "Explosive, Inside Story of How John Kerry Built an Israel-Palestine Peace Plan—and Watched It Crumble."

33. See U.S. State Department, Jen Psaki, "Daily Press Briefing," April 23, 2014 (https://2009-2017.state.gov/r/pa/prs/dpb/2014/04/225092.htm); "Obama Administration to Work with Palestinian Unity Government," Reuters, June 2, 2014.

34. See John Kerry, "National Security and Foreign Policy Priorities in the FY 2015 International Affairs Budget," testimony before the U.S. Senate Committee on Foreign Relations, 113th Cong., 2nd sess., April 8, 2014, transcript (www.foreign.senate .gov/imo/media/doc/04 08 2014, International Affairs Budget1.pdf), p. 36.

35. See Josh Rogin, "Kerry Warns Israel Could Become 'An Apartheid State,'" *Daily Beast*, April 27, 2014.

36. Indyk, author interview.

37. Ibid.

38. Adam Entous, "Donald Trump's New World Order: How the President, Israel, and the Gulf States Plan to fight Iran—and Leave the Palestinians and the Obama Years Behind," *New Yorker*, June 18, 2018.

39. See also Nathan Thrall, "Obama and Palestine: The Last Chance," *New York Review of Books*, September 9, 2016.

40. United Nations, Human Rights Council, *Report of the Independent Commission of Inquiry Established Pursuant to Human Rights Council Resolution S-21/1*, June 24, 2015.

41. See Gallup, "Latest Gallup Poll Shows Young Americans Overwhelmingly Support Palestine," *Mint Press News*, August 4, 2014; Frank Newport, "Middle East Update: U.S. Support for Israel, Hamas Is Stable," Gallup.com, August 5, 2014. See also Pew Research Center, "Public Uncertain, Divided Over America's Place in the World," April 2016 (Washington, D.C.), p. 41.

42. Yasser Abed-Rabbo, interview by author, Ramallah, July 16, 2016. See also Yasser Abed Rabbo, *Statement Issued by the Palestinian Leadership* (in Arabic), video, Al-Fajer TV, July 22, 2014 (www.youtube.com/watch?v=tZzpAqVmmVE); Yasser Abed Rabo, *Abed Rabbo: Gaza is the Mother of all Palestinians* (in Arabic), video, Wattan News Agency, July 21, 2014 (www.youtube.com/watch?v=K9ZCk42t-JI); comments of Basam Naim and Yasser Abed Rabbo, *Middle East Air Strikes Reax*, video, AP Archive, December 27, 2008 (www.aparchive.com/metadata/youtube/701f9b5e9a2465ac0cfb7e26 02c4f1be).

43. Jack Linshi, "Gaza Could Become 'Uninhabitable' by 2020, U.N. Report Warns," *Time*, September 1, 2015.

44. Ir Amim, "Jerusalem Municipality Budget Analysis for 2013: Share of Investment in East Jerusalem," December 2014. Ir Amim is an Israeli nonprofit that describes its mission as working "for an equitable and stable Jerusalem with an agreed political future."

45. See, for example, Bill Van Esveld, *Separate and Unequal: Israel's Discriminatory Treatment of Palestinians in the Occupied Palestinian Territories* (New York: Human Rights Watch, December 2010) (www.hrw.org/sites/default/files/reports/iopt1210webwcover_0 .pdf); Amnesty International "Troubled Waters: Palestinians Denied Fair Access to Water—Israeli-Occupied Palestinian Territories," report, 2009 (www.amnestyusa.org /wp-content/uploads/2017/04/mde150272009en.pdf); B'Tselem—The Israeli Information Center for Human Rights in the Occupied Territories, *East Jerusalem*, report, November 11, 2017 (www.btselem.org/jerusalem); Amnesty International, "Israel and Occupied Palestinian Territories 2017/2018," report (www.amnesty.org/en/countries /middle-east-and-north-africa/israel-and-occupied-palestinian-territories/report-israel -and-occupied-palestinian-territories/).

46. See Zvi Benninga, "Beyond the Separation Wall: A Visit to Jerusalem's Forsaken Enclaves," *+972 Magazine*, August 23, 2012 (https://972mag.com/beyond-the -separation-wall-a-visit-to-jerusalems-forsaken-enclaves/54368/); Michael Schaeffer Omer-Man, "E. Jerusalem Palestinians Demand Running Water Be Restored," *+972 Magazine*, March 26, 2014. See UN Office for the Coordination of Humanitarian Affairs, Occupied Palestinian Territory, "2017 Humanitarian Response Plan," December 2016, p. 9. See also Mara Rudman and Brian Katulis, "A Practical Plan on the Israeli-Palestinian Front," security report (Washington: Center for American Progress, December 21, 2016); UN Office for the Coordination of Humanitarian Affairs, Occupied Palestinian Territory, "East Jerusalem: Key Humanitarian Concerns, Update August 2014," August 2014.

47. B'Tselem—The Israeli Information Center for Human Rights in the Occupied Territories, "Statistics on Revocation of Residency in East Jerusalem," January 11, 2011, updated May 27, 2015.

48. Nir Hasson, "Four Out of Five East Jerusalemites Live in Poverty, a Sharp Rise over Past Years," *Haaretz*, March 2006.

49. Daoud Kuttab, "The Leaderless Political Orphans of Jerusalem Revolt," *Huffington Post/The Blog*, October 30, 2014. See also State of Palestine, Negotiations Affairs Department, "Altering the Character of Jerusalem: The Forced Closure of Palestinian Institutions in Palestine's Capital," October 2, 2014.

50. Tovah Lazaroff, "Poll: Palestinians Prefer Suing Israel at the ICC Rather Than Starting Third Intifada," *Jerusalem Post*, June 10, 2014.

51. See "Consolidated Appropriations Act, 2016," PL 114–113, 114th Cong., December 18, 2015.

52. White House, "On-the-Record Press Call on the U.N. Security Council Resolution on Israeli Settlement Activity," press release, December 23, 2016; Prime Minister's Office, "PM Netanyahu's Remarks at the Start of the Weekly Cabinet Meeting," December 18, 2016.

53. Barak Ravid, "Obama Says 'Real Policy Difference' between Israel, U.S.," *Haaretz*, March 24, 2015.

54. Nicholas Casey and Carol E. Lee, "Israel's Netanyahu Reverses Position on Palestinian State Again," *Wall Street Journal*, March 19, 2014.

55. See Daoud Kuttab, "Radical Islamists Add to Hamas' Burden," *Al-Monitor*, June 8, 2015.

56. Palestinian Center for Policy and Survey Research, "Palestinian Public Opinion Poll No—57," September 17–19, 2015. See also Karin Laub and Mohammed Daraghmeh, "Abbas Out of Options, Out of Sync with Angry Palestinians," Associated Press, September 28, 2015.

57. Elhanan Miller, "Abbas Vows to Uphold 'Sacred' Security Coordination with Israel," *Times of Israel*, May 28, 2014.

58. See "Death in Numbers: A Year of Violence in the Occupied Palestinian Territory and Israel," Ma'an News Agency, October 4, 2016, updated January 5, 2017.

59. Adnan Abu Amer, "Why Donor Countries Are Giving Less to the Palestinians," *Al-Monitor*, February 24, 2015. World Bank, "US$40 Million Grant to the Palestinian Authority to Support Institutional Reforms," press release, February 11, 2016.

60. John Kerry, "Remarks at the Brookings Institution's 2015 Saban Forum," December 5, 2015; Barak Ravid, "Israeli Ministers Hold Marathon Meetings on Possibility of PA's Collapse," *Haaretz*, November 27, 2015 http://www.haaretz.com/israel-news/.premium-1.688680

61. White House, "Fact Sheet: Memorandum of Understanding Reached with Israel," press release, September 14, 2016.

62. See Prime Minister's Office, "PM Netanyahu's Remarks at the Start of the Weekly Cabinet Meeting," December 22 and December 25, 2016.

63. Rebecca Kheel, "Obama Faces Widespread Backlash After Abstaining from UN Israel Vote," *The Hill*, December 23, 2016.

64. See Donald Trump, "The Resolution Being Considered at the UN Security Council," Facebook post, December 22, 2016. The complete post reads: "The resolution being considered at the United Nations Security Council regarding Israel should be vetoed. As the United States has long maintained, peace between the Israelis and the Palestinians will only come through direct negotiations between the parties, and not through the imposition of terms by the United Nations. This puts Israel in a very poor negotiating position and is extremely unfair to all Israelis."

65. John Kerry, "Remarks on Middle East Peace," Dean Acheson Auditorium, Washington, December 28, 2016.

66. See Lara Friedman, "Israel's Unsung Protector: Obama," *New York Times*, April 10, 2016.

67. See Khaled Elgindy, "Obama's Record on Israeli-Palestinian Peace: The President's Disquieting Silence," *Foreign Affairs*, October 5, 2016.

68. Robert Malley, correspondence with author, September 20, 2018.

Epilogue

1. Epigraph: Rudeineh quoted in Jordan Fabian, "Trump Threatens to Cut More Aid to Palestinians," *The Hill*, January 25, 2018.

2. White House, "Remarks by President Trump and Prime Minister Netanyahu of Israel in Joint Press Conference," press conference, Washington, February 15, 2017.

3. Chris McGreal, "Sheldon Adelson: The Casino Mogul Driving Trump's Middle East Policy," *The Guardian*, June 8, 2018; see also Jeremy W. Peters, "Sheldon Adelson Sees a Lot to Like in Trump's Washington," *New York Times*, September 22, 2018.

4. White House, "Statement by the Press Secretary," February 2, 2017.

5. See, for example, Chris Riotta, "Jared Kushner Failed to Disclose He Led a Foundation Funding Illegal Israeli Settlements before UN Vote," *Newsweek*, December 3, 2017.

6. Gary Willig, "Ambassador Friedman: Stop Using the Word 'Occupation,'" *Times of Israel*, December 26, 2017.

7. David Brennan, "Trump to Netanyahu: 'I Like The Two-State Solution . . . I Don't Even Have to Speak to Anybody,'" *Newsweek*, September 26, 2018.

8. Amir Tibon, "Abbas Sees 'Historic Opportunity' for Peace under Trump, Says Palestinian Envoy," *Haaretz*, April 28, 2017.

9. The complete tweet: "We have taken Jerusalem, the toughest part of the negotiation, off the table, but Israel, for that, would have had to pay more. But with the Palestinians no longer willing to talk peace, why should we make any of these massive future payments to them?" (Donald Trump, @realDonaldTrump, Twitter, January 2, 2018).

10. See Jack Khoury and Amir Tibon, "Despite Diplomatic Boycott, Palestinian Intel Chief Held Rare Meeting with Mike Pompeo in Washington," *Haaretz*, May 28, 2018.

11. Jonathan Allen, "White House Backs Kushner, Blames Hamas for Palestinian Deaths," *NBC News*, May 14, 2018.

12. U.S. State Department, Heather Nauert, "Daily Press Briefing," August 28, 2018.

13. Colum Lynch and Robbie Gramer, "Trump and Allies Seek End to Refugee Status for Millions of Palestinians," *Foreign Policy*, August 3, 2018.

14. Anne Barnard, David M. Halbfinger, and Peter Baker, "Talk of a Peace Plan That Snubs Palestinians Roils Middle East," *New York Times*, December 3, 2017.

15. "Amir Tibon, "Under Trump, U.S. Human Rights Report No Longer Calls West Bank 'Occupied,'" *Haaretz*, April 21, 2018.

16. "Aaron David Miller: 'An Effective Broker,'" Al Jazeera, August 26, 2013.

17. Bruce Riedel, interview by author, Washington, September 18, 2013.

18. Husam Zomlot, speaking at The Policy and Conflict Resolution Studies Center, Arab-American University (in Arabic), Ramallah, West Bank, June 27, 2018 (posted on Facebook: www.facebook.com/PCRSC/videos/2044188792485930/).

19. Salam Fayyad, interview by author, August 14, 2013.

20. Salam Fayyad, correspondence with author, September 21, 2018.

21. Republican Party, "Republican Platform 2016" (https://prod-cdn-static.gop
.com/media/documents/DRAFT_12_FINAL%5b1%5d-ben_1468872234.pdf).

22. Daniel Pipes, "A New Strategy for Israeli Victory," *Commentary*, December 14,
2016. See also "The Congressional Israel Victory Caucus is Launched, with Plenty of
Fanfare," Middle East Forum, April 27, 2017 (www.meforum.org/articles/2017/the
-congressional-israel-victory-caucus-is-launche).

23. "National Home for the Jewish People," *Congressional Record*, daily ed., June 30,
1922, 799–820, statement of Rep. Walter Marion Chandler.

24. Naftali Bendavid and Jared Favole, "Platform Change on Status of Jerusalem
Sparks Debate," *Wall Street Journal*, September 5, 2012; Tal Kopan and Elise Labott,
"Hillary Clinton's Views on Israel Win Out in DNC Platform, for Now," CNN,
June 26, 2016. See also KC Johnson, "Why Democrats Are Abandoning Israel," *Washington Post*, August 18, 2017; John Cassidy, "The Democratic Debate: A Surprising Exchange on Israel," *New Yorker*, April 15, 2016; Molly O'Toole, "Inside the Democratic
Party's Showdown over Israel-Palestine," *Foreign Policy*, June 29, 2016.

25. Team Fix, "The Brooklyn Democratic Debate Transcript, Annotated," *Washington Post*, April 14, 2016.

26. Peter Beinart, "Bernie Sanders' Criticism of Israel Is Radical. And He's Taking It Mainstream," *The Forward*, June 11, 2018.

27. Defense for Children International—Palestine, "Year-in-Review: Worst Abuses
against Palestinian Children in 2017."

28. Cassandra Gomes-Hochberg, "Majority of Democratic Congress Members
Plea to Restore UNRWA Aid," *Jerusalem Post*, October 3, 2018.

29. Juha Kahkonen and Yan Sun, *West Bank and Gaza: Report to the Ad Hoc Liaison
Committee* (Washington: International Monetary Fund, March 9, 2018); see also Gregg
Carlstrom, "How Israel Won the War and Defeated the Palestinian Dream," *Newsweek*, August 29, 2017.

30. Luke Baker, "Netanyahu Non-committal on Palestinian Statehood as He Heads
to U.S.," Reuters, February 13, 2017; Jonathan Lis, "Netanyahu Blocks Settlement Annexation Bill from Coming to a Vote," *Haaretz*, February 12, 2018.

31. See, for example, Palestinian Center for Policy and Survey Research,
"Palestinian-Israeli Pulse," poll results, August 1, 2017 (www.pcpsr.org/en/node/696).

32. See, for example, Palestinian Center for Policy and Research, "Public Opinion
Poll No–67" (conducted March 17–18), press release, April 1, 2018 (www.pcpsr.org/en
/node/725).

33. Jodi Rudoren, "A Divide among Palestinians on a Two-State Solution," *New
York Times*, March 18, 2014.

34. See, for instance, "Hamas Accepts Palestinian State with 1967 Borders," Al
Jazeera, *NewsGrid*, May 2, 2017; Eyder Peralta, "Hamas Foreign Minister: We Accept
Two-State Solution with '67 Borders," *The Two-Way*, NPR, May 17, 2011.

35. For a summary of congressional and other anti-BDS initiatives, see Foundation for Middle East Peace, "The Stealth Campaign to Use U.S. Law to Support

Settlements: In Congress," July 2, 2018 (https://fmep.org/wp/wp-content/uploads /pending-BDS-Conflation-bills-in-Congress.pdf), and Lara Friedman, "The Stealth Campaign to Support Settlements/Gag Free Speech—in States," Foundation for Middle East Peace, July 9, 2018 (https://fmep.org/resource/stealth-campaign-use-u-s -law-support-settlements-taking-battle-states-updatedexpanded-table/). See also Brian Hauss, "The New Israel Anti-Boycott Act Is Still Unconstitutional," American Civil Liberties Union, March 7, 2018.

Index

Surnames starting with "al-" are alphabetized by remaining portion of name.